A
DICTIONARY AND GLOSSARY
OF
THE KOR-AN

WITH
COPIOUS GRAMMATICAL REFERENCES AND EXPLANATIONS OF
THE TEXT

A DICTIONARY AND GLOSSARY OF THE KOR-AN

WITH
COPIOUS GRAMMATICAL REFERENCES AND EXPLANATIONS OF THE TEXT

JOHN PENRICE

To save thee trouble, Choose the easiest path-ARAB PROVERB

GYAN

Published by

Gyan Publishing House
5, Ansari Road
Daryaganj, New Delhi-110002
Phone: 011-47034999, 9811692060
E-mail: books@gyanbooks.com

Distribution Network
gyanbooks.com
India, USA, Canada, UK, Australia, France

ISBN : 978-81-212-3321-7 (PB)
First Published, London, 1873

2nd Impression 2020

Printed at: Gyan Press, Delhi.

A
Dictionary and Glossary of the Kor-an
Author: John Penrice

سِلْكُ الْبَيَانِ فِي مَنَاقِبِ الْقُرْآنِ

PREFACE.

THAT a competent knowledge of the Ḳor-ân is indispensable as an introduction to the study of Arabic literature will be admitted by all who have advanced beyond the rudiments of the language. From the purity of its style and elegance of its diction it has come to be considered as the standard of Arabic even by those who have no belief in its pretensions to a divine origin, while so great is its authority among the followers of Moḥammad, that it would be difficult to name a work by any Mussulman writer which does not abound in allusions to its precepts or in quotations from its pages.

It is not to be expected that all the transcendant excellencies and miraculous beauties discovered in the Ḳor-ân by its commentators and others should immediately unveil themselves to our cold and unsympathizing gaze; beauties there are, many and great; ideas highly poetical are clothed in rich and appropriate language, which not unfrequently rises to a sublimity far beyond the reach of any translation; but it is unfortunately the case that many of those graces which present themselves to the admiration of the finished scholar are but so many stumbling-blocks in the way of the beginner; the marvellous conciseness which adds so greatly to the force and energy of its expressions cannot fail to perplex him, while the frequent use of the ellipse leaves in his mind a feeling of vagueness not altogether out of character in a work of its oracular and *soi-disant* prophetic nature.

It has been the privilege of the Ḳor-ân rather to impose its own laws upon grammar than to accept them from other sources; and as it was written originally without vowel points, it is not surprising that a good deal of difficulty has been experienced in framing rules to meet the various readings that have thence crept in.

The following pages have been compiled in the hope that they may prove of service to the beginner in mastering some of the difficulties to which I have referred; they will be found to contain much, which to the more advanced student may appear trivial or unnecessary, but which will not be without value if it lighten the labours of those for whose use the book is principally designed; it has no claim to originality, it merely presents to the reader in a succinct form that which the writer has culled for his benefit from the works of others.

The edition of the Ḳor-ân which I have chosen for my text is that by Fluegel, printed at Leipzig in 1834; the Concordance by the same author has been my sheet-anchor throughout. Each word will be found under its verbal root; where none exists it must be looked for in its alphabetical place; so also in the case of words which have seemed likely to puzzle the beginner; many of these have been separately arranged in their alphabetical order, but withdrawn a little within the marginal line; thus for example the word كَهَيْئَةِ may be looked for either under كَ or under its root هَاءَ. The vowel of the aorist has been given where it is known; I have generally added the *original* meaning, and where such meaning is not to be found in the Ḳor-ân the words are printed in Italics. I must here claim indulgence for the fault—if fault it be—of having given the English of the infinitive instead of the third person singular of the preterite, or grammatical root of the verb; it seems more convenient and less roundabout to say that ضَرَبَ means to strike, although no one would be likely to commence the study of the Ḳor-ân without being fully aware that the word should in strictness be rendered "He struck"; while upon this point I may observe that although there is no true infinitive in Arabic, the abstract noun or noun of action frequently supplies its place; the letters n.a. merely refer to the forms of the different nouns of action, not necessarily to their meaning; this also applies to the participles, written part. act. and pass.; these names have been retained for convenience sake, and mark the *form only* of the verbal adjectives, which, being constantly employed as substantives, are generally so rendered.

It is hardly necessary that I should offer any apology to my readers for the frequent references I have made to De Sacy's Grammaire Arabe; the study of the French language is now so universal, as almost to render a translation superfluous; the letters D. S. Gr. etc. refer to the second edition.

I have not, as a rule, thought it necessary to notice the various readings of disputed passages, nor the numerous interpretations of the same passage which abound in the Commentaries; those who may wish to extend their researches in this direction will find an ample field in the works of the two great authorities El Beiḍâwëe and Ez-Zamakhsharëe; the Commentary of the former, as being the more grammatical, is the one I have generally consulted. Free use has been made of the Dictionaries of Freytag and Johnson, principally the former; to them, as well as to Sale's well-known translation, my acknowledgments are especially due.

From the many careful revisions the work has undergone, both previously, and also in passing through the press, I have good grounds for hoping that but few typographical errors have escaped detection; entire freedom from such is hardly to be expected, but the short table of errata will, I feel confident, comprise the greater part; for all other shortcomings I must seek the indulgence of my readers, trusting that my humble efforts may have provided for them in the words of my title "A clue of elucidation to the intricate passages of the Ḳor-ân."

J. PENRICE.

BRAMERTON LODGE, NORWICH,
3rd February, 1873.

A

DICTIONARY

OF

THE KOR-ÂN.

أ A prefixed particle answering to the Latin *num* or *an*, Whether? Is it? When the first of two consecutive propositions begins with أ, and the second with أَمْ, both may frequently be taken in a dubitative sense; as ءَأَنْذَرْتَهُمْ أَمْ لَمْ تُنْذِرْهُمْ 2 v. 5, "Whether thou warn them, or whether thou warn them not;" أ is often found prefixed to other particles, as, أَئِنَّكَ "Art thou verily?" أَفَبِنِعْمَةِ ٱللّٰهِ يَجْحَدُونَ 16 v. 73, "Do they then deny the beneficence of God?" When this particle is followed by another أ one of them is generally omitted; as أَنْتَ for ءَأَنْتَ; so likewise when followed by Wesla, in which case the alif of union is suppressed, as أَللّٰهُ for ءَآللّٰهُ, etc. D. S. Gr. T. 1, pp. 71 and 99.

أَبَّ aor. i. and o. *To move.* أَبٌّ acc. أَبًّا That which the earth produces as food.

آبَآءُ plur. of أَبٌ for أَبَوٌ q. v.

أَبَارِيقُ (2nd declension) pl. of إِبْرِيقٌ (*Pers.*), Goblets.

أَبَتِ for أَبِي, see أَبٌ for أَبَوٌ.

أَبْتَرُ see بَتَرَ.

إِبْتِغَآءُ n.a. viii. f. of بَغَى q.v.

أَبَدَ aor. i. and o. *To be wild* (*an animal*); aor. i. *To remain in a place.* أَبَدًا Eternally, ever, for ever.

إِبْرٰهِيمُ Abraham; a noun of the second declension, of Hebrew origin, D. S. Gr. T. 1, p. 404.

أُبَرِّئُ and أُبْرِئُ 1 pers. sing. aor. iv. and ii. forms of بَرَأَ q.v.

أَبَقَ aor. a. and i. To flee (with إِلَى), properly, *as a slave.*

أَبَلَ *To be or have many camels.* إِبِلٌ and إِبْلٌ Camels; a generic noun like *sheep.* إِبَّالَةٌ plur. أَبَابِيلُ (2nd declension) Flocks (of birds).

إِبْلِيسُ Iblees, Satan, see بَلَسَ.

إِبْنٌ for بَنَوٌ from بَنَى q.v.

أَبٌ for أَبَوٌ A father; when in connexion with a complement, nom. أَبُو, gen. أَبِي, acc. أَبَا; يَا أَبَتِ for يَا أَبِي O! my Father; D. S. Gr. T. 2, p. 91; Dual أَبَوَانِ Parents, and in connexion أَبَوَا, oblique أَبَوَيْ, as أَبَوَاهُ and أَبَوَيْهِ His two parents; Plur. آبَآءٌ Fathers, ancestors, for أَأْبَاوٌ like أَفْعَالٌ, the final و being changed into hamza after ا quiescent; D. S. Gr. T. 1, pp. 97 and 113.

أَبْوَابٌ plur. of بَابٌ q.v.

أَبَى aor. a. and i. To dislike, disdain, refuse, to be averse from (with أَنْ, and also with إِلَّا), as فَأَبَى ٱلظَّالِمُونَ إِلَّا كُفُورًا 17 v. 101, "But the wicked have rejected (the truth) or only (receive it) with ingratitude."

إِتَّسَقَ viii. f. of وَسَقَ q.v.

أَتْقَنَ see تِقْنٌ.

إِتَّقَى viii. f. of وَقَى q.v.

أَتَوَكَّأُ 1 pers. sing. aor. v. f. of وَكَأَ q.v.

أَتَى aor. i. To come, come to (with acc. or with لِ); to bring to (with بِ of thing and acc. of pers.); to pass, come to pass, come upon (with عَلَى); to do, commit (an act, with acc. or with بِ). آتِ for آتِي, fem. آتِيَةٌ part. act. One who comes to, as إِنَّهُمْ آتِيهِمْ عَذَابٌ 11 v. 78, "Verily there is coming upon them a punishment." مَأْتِيٌّ part. pass. with an active signification, That which is come to pass; at 19 v. 62 it has a future signification, thus, كَانَ وَعْدُهُ مَأْتِيًّا "His promise will come to pass."— آتَى IV. To cause to come, bring, produce, give (with double accus.). إِيتَاءٌ n. a. The bestowing of gifts. مُؤْتٍ plur. مُؤْتُونَ part. act. One who gives. Pass. أُؤْتِيَ, or with the omission of the second hamza, أُوتِيَ D. S. Gr. T. 1, p. 97; Ex. ٱلَّذِينَ أُوتُوا ٱلْكِتَابَ; A phrase which is exactly rendered in colloquial English by "Those who have been given the Scripture;" D. S. Gr. T. 2, p. 125.

أَثَّ aor. a. i. and o. *To be luxuriant.* أَثَاثٌ Household stuff, anything which constitutes wealth.

أَثَامٌ see أَثِمَ.

أَثَرَ aor. o. and i. To relate; to excite, raise (dust, with acc. and بِ). أَثَرٌ A trace, footstep; Plur. آثَارٌ Traces, monuments of antiquity. أَثَارَةٌ A relic.— آثَرَ IV. To choose, prefer (with acc. and عَلَى).

أَثَلَ aor. i. *To be firmly rooted.* أَثْلٌ (generic noun) Tamarisks.

أَثَمَ aor. o. and a. *To pronounce guilty*, and أَثِمَ aor. a. *To sin.* إِثْمٌ n. a. A sin, guilt, iniquity. أَثَامٌ Punishment of wickedness. آثِمٌ part. act. One who sins, an evil-doer. أَثِيمٌ A wicked person. — تَأْثِيمٌ n.a. II. f. Accusation of crime.

أَجَّ aor. o. *To burn.* أُجَاجٌ Bitter, salt (water).

إِجْتَبَى viii. f. of جَبَا q.v.

أُجْتُثَّ pass. viii. f. of جَثَّ q.v.

أَجْدَاثٌ plur. of جَدَثٌ A sepulchre.

أَجَرَ aor. o. and i. *To pay wages*, serve for hire. أَجْرٌ n.a. A reward; Plur. أُجُورٌ Wages, dowers. — إِسْتَأْجَرَ X. To hire.

أَجَلَ *To fix a term.* أَجْلٌ A cause, the sake, as مِنْ أَجْلِ ذَلِكَ "on that account." أَجَلٌ A fixed term, predetermined period. — أَجَّلَ II. To appoint a fixed term (with acc. and لِ). مُؤَجَّلٌ part. pass. with act. signification, as كِتَابًا مُؤَجَّلًا 3 v. 139, "According to the Book which fixes the appointed term of all things." For this adverbial use of the accusative see D. S. Gr. T. 2, p. 67, *et seq.*

أَجِنَّةٌ plur. of جَنِينٌ fr. جَنَّ q.v.

أَجْنِحَةٌ plur. of جَنَاحٌ from جَنَحَ q.v.

أُجُورٌ Wages, Plur. of أَجْرٌ.

أَحَادِيثُ plur. of حَدِيثٌ, Tales.

أَحَاطَ iv. f. of حَاطَ q.v.

أَحِبَّاءُ plur. of حَبِيبٌ see حَبَّ.

أَحَدٌ One, any one; Fem. إِحْدَى, see وَحِدَ.

أَحْلَامٌ plur. of حُلْمٌ and حِلْمٌ see حَلَمَ.

أَحْوَى see حَوَى.

أَخْبَتَ iv. f. of خَبَتَ q.v.

أَخْدَانٌ plur. of خِدْنٌ q.v.

أُخْدُودٌ A pit, from خَدَّ q.v.

أَخَذَ aor. o. To take, receive (with acc. and also with بِ); to accept, take away, punish, afflict (with acc. of pers. and بِ, فِى, or عَلَى); to make a compact (with عَلَى of pers. or with acc.); to seize upon, seize (with acc. or with بِ of thing); to take in hand and arrange, as قَدْ أَخَذْنَا أَمْرَنَا مِنْ قَبْلُ 9 v. 50, "We had ordered our affairs beforehand." أَخْذٌ n.a. The act of taking, punishment. أَخْذَةٌ noun of unity, A punishment. آخِذٌ part. act. One who takes. — آخَذَ or أَاخَذَ aor. يُؤَاخِذُ III. To punish (with acc. of pers. and بِ of the crime).—إِتَّخَذَ for إِئْتَخَذَ D. S. Gr. T. 1, p. 236, VIII. To take, take to one's-self; with وَلَدًا it means to beget, as إِتَّخَذَ ٱللّٰهُ وَلَدًا 2 v. 110, "God hath begotten issue;" to receive, make, make for one's-self, as كَمَثَلِ ٱلْعَنْكَبُوتِ ٱتَّخَذَتْ بَيْتًا 29 v. 40, "Like the spider (who) maketh for herself a house;" at 38 v. 63 أَتَّخَذْنَاهُمْ is for أَاتَّخَذْنَاهُمْ, the alif of union being suppressed after the interrogative particle أَ, D. S. Gr. T. 1, p. 71; to hold or reckon, as يَتَّخِذُ مَا يُنْفِقُ قُرُبَاتٍ عِنْدَ ٱللّٰهِ 9 v. 100, "He considers what he expends as a means of bringing him nigh unto God;" to act, behave (with kindness), as at 18 v. 85 (with فِى of person). اِتِّخَاذٌ n.a. Act of taking to one's-self. مُتَّخِذٌ part. act. One who takes.

أَخِرَ No verbal root, the verb not being used in the first form; *Latter, The last.* آخَرُ for أَأْخَرُ (2nd declension) Another, other, the last; Fem. أُخْرَى D. S. Gr. T. 1, p. 351; Plur. آخَرُونَ; Fem. أُخَرُ for أُخَرٌ, the more usual form, D. S. Gr. T. 1, pp. 359 and 407; فِى أُخْرَاكُمْ 3 v. 147, "In your rear." آخِرٌ, Fem. آخِرَةٌ Last, the last, the end, latter end; ٱلْآخِرُونَ The last, the latest posterity; ٱلْآخِرَةُ The next (life) as opposed to ٱلدُّنْيَا.—أَخَّرَ II. aor. يُؤَخِّرُ To do a thing after another, do anything last, defer, leave undone, put off (with acc. and عَنْ), as وَلَئِنْ أَخَّرْنَا عَنْهُمُ ٱلْعَذَابَ 11 v. 11, "And verily if we put off their punishment;" to give a respite to any one (with acc. and إِلَى).—تَأَخَّرَ V. To remain behind, come after another.—إِسْتَأْخَرَ X. To stay behind, delay, wish to delay. مُسْتَأْخِرٌ part. act. One who tarries behind.

أَخْزَيْتَ 2 pers. sing. pret. iv. f. of خَزِىَ q.v.

أَخْفَى iv. f. of خَفِىَ q.v.

أَخِلَّآءُ (2nd declension) plur. of خَلِيلٌ, rt. خَلَّ q.v.

أَخُنْهُ aor. cond. 1 pers. sing. with هُ affixed, from خَانَ q.v.

أَخٌ for أَخَوٌ; when in connexion with a complement nom. أَخُو, gen. أَخِى, acc. أَخَا A brother; Dual, أَخَوَانِ, oblique أَخَوَيْنِ, and in construction أَخَوَا and أَخَوَىْ; Plur. إِخْوَةٌ and إِخْوَانٌ; the latter generally means companions or friends. أُخْتٌ for أَخَوَةٌ A sister; Plur. أَخَوَاتٌ; Dual أُخْتَانِ, oblique أُخْتَيْنِ, see D. S. Gr. T. 1, p. 358.

أَدَّ aor. a. i. and o. *To fall on, oppress.* إِدٌّ Stupendous, grievous.

إِدَّارَأْتُمْ for تَدَارَأْتُمْ 2 pers. plur. vi. f. of دَرَأَ q.v.

إِدَّارَكَ vi. f. of دَرَكَ q.v.

أَدُّوا Cause to come; Imperat. ii. f. of أَدَّى q.v.

أَدَآءٌ see أَدَّى.

أَدْبَارٌ see دَبَرَ.

آدْرَؤُا Imperative plural of دَرَأَ q.v.

أَدْعِيَآءُ plur. of دَعِىٌّ An adopted son, rt. دَعَا q.v.

أَدْلَى iv. f. of دَلَا q.v.

أَدِمَ aor. a. *To be tawny.* آدَمُ (2nd declension), Adam; D. S. Gr. T. 1, p. 404.

أَدْنَى More vile, etc. fr. دَنَا q.v.

أَدْهَى More grievous, fr. دَهَى q.v.

أَدَى aor. i. *To become thick (milk).* أَدَآءٌ for أَدَايٌ Payment; the final ي being converted into hamza after ا quiescent; D.S.Gr. T. 1, p.113.— أَدَّى II. To cause to come, to pay back, restore (with acc. and إِلَى); aor. يُؤَدِّى as فَلْيُؤَدِّ "Then let him restore (it)."

إِذْ and إِذَا Behold, if, when, then, at that time. إِذًا Then, in that case; These words are regarded by the Arab grammarians as indeclinable nouns; They enter into composition with other words, as حِينَئِذٍ and يَوْمَئِذٍ Then, at that time, on that day when; so also إِذَا after the interrogative particle أ as أَئِذَا Is it then? etc. For the various effects produced by these particles upon the tenses of verbs the reader is referred to D. S. Gr. T. 1, p. 171, *et seq.*, and also p. 522: إِذْ and إِذَا are constantly employed in the Korân to commence a sentence without any antecedent; the words اُذْكُرْ مَا كَانَ "Remember what occurred," being then understood.

أَذْقَانٌ plur. of ذَقْنٌ A chin, see ذَقَنَ.

أَذَقْنَا 1 pers. plur. pret. iv. f. of ذَاقَ q.v. See also D. S. Gr. T. 1, p. 246.

أَذِلَّةٌ plur. of ذَلِيلٌ, rt. ذَلَّ q.v.

أَذَنَ *To give ear;* and أَذِنَ aor. a. To suffer, grant permission, permit (with لِ of pers. and بِ of thing, also with أَنْ of the verb); to hearken to (with لِ). *Note.* When the Imperative of this verb is preceded by فَ it is written فَأْذَنْ as at 2 v. 279; see D. S. Gr. T. 1, p. 232, *note.*

إِذْنٌ n. a. Permission. أُذُنٌ Fem. An ear; Plur. آذَانٌ. أَذَانٌ A declaration.— أَذَّنَ II. To cry aloud, make a proclamation (with أَنْ or with بِ of thing). مُؤَذِّنٌ part. act. A public crier, a *Muezzin.*— آذَنَ IV. To make known to, proclaim to (with acc. of pers.); to assure. — تَأَذَّنَ V. To cause a proclamation to be made, cause to be declared. — إِسْتَأْذَنَ X. To ask permission (with أَنْ or with acc. of pers. and لِ of thing); at 9 vv. 44 and 45 it means to ask leave to be excused, to ask a dispensation; see D. S. Gr. T. 2, p. 467, where this ellipse is explained.

أَذِىَ aor. a. *To be hurt.* أَذًى for أَذَىٌ D. S. Gr. T. 1, p. 111; n.a. injury, ill-treatment, offence, annoyance, anything noxious, such as illness or pollution.— آذَى IV. To injure, vex, annoy, offend, afflict; aor. يُؤْذِى; فَآذُوهُمَا 4 v. 20, "Then punish them both;" *properly,* "do them both some injury"; Commentators differ as to what this injury should be; Pass. أُوذِىَ 29 v. 9, for أُؤْذِىَ for أُأْذِىَ, see 3 v.194; see also D. S. Gr. T. 1, p. 95, § 187.

أَرَكَ see أَرَائِكُ.

أَرَبَ aor. i. *To tie (a knot) tight,* and أَرِبَ aor. a. *To want.* إِرْبَةٌ n.a. want, a necessity, as غَيْرِ أُولِى ٱلْإِرْبَةِ 24 v. 31, "Who have no need (of women)." مَآرِبُ (2nd declension) plur. of مَأْرَبَةٌ Necessities, necessary uses.

أَرْبَابٌ plur. of رَبٌّ q.v.

أَرْبَى iv. f. of رَبَا q.v.

إِرْتَابَ viii. f. of رَابَ for رَيَبَ q.v.

أَرْجَآءٌ plur. of رَجًا A side, rt. رَجَا q.v.

أَرْجِهْ Put him off! See رَجَا.

أَرْدَى iv. f. of رَدَى q.v.

أَرْبَا for أَرْبَى iv. f. of رَبَا q.v.

أَرْضٌ fem. The Earth, earth, land, a country.

أَرَكَ aor. i. and o. *To feed on the tree* أَرَاكٌ (*a camel*). أَرَائِكُ (2nd declension) plur. of أَرِيكَةٌ Thrones, couches.

أَرَمَ aor. i. *To bite.* إِرَمُ (2nd declension) Irem, the city of the tribe of 'Àd.

أَرَى 1 pers. sing. aor. of رَأَى q.v.

أَزَّ aor. o. and i. *To make a loud crash,* incite; تَؤُزُّهُمْ 19 v. 86, "That they may incite them;" 3 pers. fem. sing. aor. after the broken plural اَلشَّيَاطِينُ; for the use of the aorist indicative when in dependance on another verb, see D. S. Gr. T. 1, p. 201. أَزٌّ n.a. An instigation.

إِزْدَادُوا see زَادَ for زَيَدَ.

أَزَرَ *To be strong.* أَزْرٌ n.a. Back, loins.—آزَرَ IV. To make strong. آزَرُ Àzer (2nd declension), The name given to Abraham's father Terah; derived from the Chaldean name of the planet Mars.

أَزِفَ aor. a. To draw near. آزِفَةٌ The day of judgment.

أَزْكَى see زَكَى.

أَزْوَاجٌ plur. of زَوْجٌ, rt. زَاجَ q.v.

أَسَّ *To cry Is! Is! in driving sheep.*—أَسَّسَ II. To found, lay foundations (with acc. and عَلَى); the logical root being أُسٌّ *A foundation.*

أَسَاطِيرُ (2nd declension) plur. *probably* of أَسْطَارٌ from سَطَرَ q.v.

أَسَاوِرُ (2nd declension) plur. of سِوَارٌ A bracelet, fr. سَارَ q.v.

أَسْبَابٌ plur. of سَبَبٌ, rt. سَبَّ q.v.

أَسْبَاطٌ plur. of سِبْطٌ A tribe, rt. سَبَطَ q.v.

إِسْتَبْرَقٌ Silk of a thick texture, brocade; possibly derived from بَرَقَ to glitter.

إِسْتَجَابَ x. f. of جَابَ for جَوَبَ q.v.

إِسْتَحَقَّ x. f. of حَقَّ q.v.

إِسْتَحْوَذَ x. f. of حَاذَ q.v.

إِسْتَزَلَّ x. f. of زَلَّ q.v.

إِسْتَطَاعَ x. f. of طَاعَ q.v.

إِسْتَعِذْ imperat. x. f. of عَاذَ q.v.

إِسْتَغْنَى x. f. of غَنِيَ q.v.

إِسْتَفْزِزْ imperat. x. f. of فَزَّ q.v.

إِسْتَكَانَ x. f. of كَانَ q.v.

أُسْتُهْزِئَ pass. x. f. of هَزِئَ q.v.

إِسْتَهْوَتْ fem. 3 pers. sing. x. f. of هَوَى q.v.

إِسْتَوْقَدَ x. f. of وَقَدَ q.v.

إِسْتَوَى viii. f. of سَوَى q.v.

إِسْتَيْأَسَ x. f. of يَئِسَ q.v.

إِسْتَيْقَنَ x. f. of يَقِنَ q.v.

أَسْحَارٌ plur. of سَحَرٌ The morning, rt. سَحَرَ q.v.

أَسْرِ Journey by night! Imperat. iv. f. of سَرَى q v.

أَسَرَ aor. i. To bind, make prisoner. أَسْرٌ n.a. A ligament, a joint. أَسِيرٌ A prisoner, captive; Plur. أَسْرَى and أُسَارَى (2nd declension); the latter of these forms is restricted by De Sacy to words of the form فَعْلَانُ; see his Grammar, T. 1, p. 369, § 863.

إِسْرَائِيلُ (2nd declension) Israel; a Hebrew word, meaning *Prince of God.* See Genesis xxxii. 28.

أَسْرَى iv. f. of سَرَى q.v., see also أَسَرَ.

أَسِفَ aor. a. *To be grieved.* أَسَفٌ grief, as يَا أَسَفَى for أَسَفِي 12 v. 84, "Oh my grief!" or, "How great is my grief!" D. S. Gr. T. 2, p. 90, *note.* أَسِفٌ Indignant, or affected at the same time with grief and indignation.—آسَفَ IV. To provoke to anger.

إِسْمٌ and أَسْمَاءٌ, see سَمَا.

أَطَّلَعَ for أَأَطْتَلَعَ , أَ interrogative, and viii. f. of طَلَعَ q.v.

إِطْمَأَنَّ iv. f. of طَمْأَنَ quadriliteral, rt. طَمَنَ q.v.

أَطْوَارًا Of different kinds; plur. of طَوْرٌ, rt. طَارَ q.v.

أَعْتَدَ iv. f. of عَتَدَ q.v.

إِعْتَدَى viii. f. of عَدَا q.v.

إِعْتَرَى viii. f. of عَرَا for عَرَوَ q.v.

أَعِدُّوا see عَدَّ.

أَعْدَآءٌ plur. of عَدُوٌّ , rt. عَدَا q.v.

أَعِزَّةٌ plur. of عَزِيزٌ , rt. عَزَّ q.v.

إِعْصَارٌ A whirlwind, rt. عَصَرَ q.v.

أُعِيذُ 1 pers. sing. aor. iv. f. of عَاذَ q.v.

أَغْرَيْنَا 1 pers. plur. pret. iv. f. of غَرَا q.v.

أَغْلَالٌ plur. of غُلٌّ A collar, rt. غَلَّ q.v.

أَغْنَى iv. f. of غَنِيَ q.v.

أَغْوَى iv. f. of غَوَى q.v.

أَفَّ *To say* أُفٍّ Fy! as أُفٍّ لَكُمَا Fy on you both! According to the author of the Kamoos there are forty different ways of spelling this word.

أَفَآءَ iv. f. of فَآءَ for فَيَءَ q.v.

أَفَاضَ iv. f. of فَاضَ for فَيَضَ q.v.

أَفَبِالْبَاطِلِ "Do they then (believe) in that which is vain?" 16 v. 74 and 29 v. 67; composed of the interrogative particle أَ, the conjunction فَ, the preposition بِ, the article أَل, and the word بَاطِل Vanity, or anything vain.

إِفْتَدَى viii. f. of فَدَى q.v.

إِفْتَرَى viii. f. of فَرَى q.v.

أَفْضَى iv. f. of فَضَا q.v.

أَفَعَيِينَا "Were we then exhausted?" composed of the interrogative particle أَ, the conjunction فَ, and the first pers. plur. pret. of عَيِيَ, rt. عَيَّ q.v.

أَفَقَ aor. i. *To dress leather.* أُفُقٌ The horizon; وَهُوَ بِٱلْأُفُقِ ٱلْأَعْلَى 53, v. 7, "And he (appeared) in the highest point of the horizon," viz., the

إِسْمَعِيلُ (2nd declension) Ishmael, meaning in the Hebrew *God shall hear.*

أَسَنَ aor. i. and o. *To be putrid and stinking (water).* آسِنٌ Corrupt, putrid: مِنْ مَآءٍ غَيْرِ آسِنٍ 47 v. 16, "Of incorruptible water."

أَسَا aor. o. *To be healed.* أُسْوَةٌ A pattern, example worthy of imitation.

أَسِيَ aor. a. To be sad, solicitous about (with عَلَى).

أَشْتَاتًا Separately; acc. plur. of شَتٌّ, rt. شَتَّ q.v.

أَشْيَعَةٌ plur. of شَحِيحٌ, rt. شَحَّ q.v.

أَشِدَّآءُ (2nd declension) plur. of شَدِيدٌ, see شَدَّ.

أَشَرَ aor. o. *To cut, saw;* and أَشِرَ aor. a. *To exult.* أَشِرٌ Insolent, an insolent person.

أَشْقَى Most wretched; comp. form of شَقَا q.v.

أَشْكُوا I make my complaint; 1 pers. sing. aor. of شَكَا q.v.

إِشْمَأَزَّتْ see شَمَزَ.

أَشْيَاعٌ plur. of شِيعَةٌ, see شَاعَ.

آصَالٌ plur. of أَصِيلٌ, rt. أَصَلَ q.v.

أَصْبُ 1 pers. sing. aor. cond. of صَبَا q.v.

أَصَدَ *To cover over (a pot).*—مُؤْصَدَةٌ fem. part. pass. iv. f. Covered over, vaulted over.

أَصَرَ aor. i. *To bind.* إِصْرٌ A covenant, burthen.

أَصَرَّ iv. f. of صَرَّ q.v.

إِصْطَفَى viii. f. of صَفَا q.v.

إِصْطَنَعْتُ 1 pers. sing. pret. viii. f. of صَنَعَ q.v.

أَصْفَى iv. f. of صَفَا q.v.

أَصْلٌ plur. أُصُولٌ The lowest part, bottom, root. أَصِيلٌ The evening; Plur. أُصُلٌ; Plur. of Plur. آصَالٌ.

أَصْلَابٌ plur. of صُلْبٌ dorsal vertebræ, rt. صَلَبَ q.v.

أَضَآءَ iv. f. of ضَآءَ for ضَوَأَ q.v.

أَضْطَرُّ 1 pers. sing. aor. viii. f. of ضَرَّ q.v.

أَطَاعَ iv. f. of طَاعَ q.v.

Angel Gabriel. آفَاقٌ plur. of أُفُقٌ Tracts or regions of the earth; سَنُرِيهِمْ آيَاتِنَا فِى ٱلْآفَاقِ 41 v. 53, "We will show them our signs in the regions of the earth"; to wit, The conquests of the true believers.

أَفَكَ aor. i. *To lie*, cause to tell lies, or put on a false appearance, as at 7 v. 114; to turn aside (with عَنْ); to frustrate, render silly. إِفْكٌ A falsehood, lying invention, lying, false; as تُرِيدُونَ . . . . أَئِفْكًا آلِهَةً 37 v. 84, "Do ye choose a falsehood (viz.) gods, etc.?" أَئِفْكًا is here put for أَإِفْكًا. أَفَّاكٌ A great liar.—مُؤْتَفِكٌ part. act. viii. f. which has a passive signification, That which is overthrown or turned upside down; أَلْمُؤْتَفِكَاتُ The cities which were overthrown, viz. Sodom and Gomorrah.

أَفَلَ aor. i. and o. To set (the sun). آفِلٌ part. act. That which sets.

أَفْنَانٌ plur. of فَنَنٌ, rt. فَنَّ q.v.

أَفْوَاهٌ plur. of فَمٌ A month, see فَاهَ for فَوَهَ.

أُفَوِّضُ 1 pers. sing. aor. of فَوَّضَ q.v.

أَفْئِدَةٌ plur. of فُؤَادٌ, rt. فَأَدَ q.v.

أَقَاوِيلُ (2nd declension) plur. of أَقْوَالٌ plur. of قَوْلٌ A saying, discourse, see قَالَ for قَوَلَ.

أَقَّتَ A definite time, for وَقَّتَ; rt. وَقَتَ q.v.—أُقِّتَتْ II. (no 1st form) To fix a certain time. De Sacy, quoting El Beiḍâwee, says in his Grammar, T. 1, p. 103, *note*, that the word أُقِّتَتْ which occurs at 77 v. 11 is for وُقِّتَتْ.

إِقْتَدِهْ see قَدَا.

أُقْنُتِى fem. imperat. of قَنَتَ q.v.

أَقْنَى see قَنَى.

أَقْوَاتٌ plur. of قُوتٌ Food, rt. قَاتَ q.v.

أَكَادُ 1 pers. sing. aor. of كَادَ for كَوِدَ q.v.

أَكْدَى iv. f. of كَدَا q.v.

إِكْرَاهٌ n.a. iv. f. of كَرِهَ q.v.

أَكْسُوهُمْ Clothe them; Imperat. of كَسَا q.v.

أَكَلَ aor. o. To eat, devour, consume (with acc. or with مِنْ, بِ, or فِى); to make use of, enjoy, as at 4 v. 3; Imperat. كُلْ, fem. كُلِى. أَكْلٌ n.a. The act of eating, a devouring; أَكْلًا In a greedy, devouring manner. أُكُلٌ Food, as fruit, or whatever is eaten; وَٱلزَّرْعَ مُخْتَلِفًا أُكُلُهُ 6 v. 142, "And corn, the food from which (is) various in kind;" For the construction of this and similar sentences see D. S. Gr. T. 2, pp. 79 and 270. آكِلٌ part. act. One who eats. أَكَّالٌ Greedy, a great eater. مَأْكُولٌ part. pass. Eaten.

أَكْمَامٌ plur. of كِمٌّ A bud, rt. كَمَّ q.v.

أَكِنَّةٌ and أَكْنَانٌ plurs. of كِنٌّ, rt. كَنَّ q.v.

أَلْ The definite article, The; when not at the beginning of a sentence, it is always written with a وَصْلٌ thus ٱلْ; the ا then loses all sound and becomes mute. D. S. Gr. T. 1, p. 64.

أَلَّ aor. o. and i. *To be shaken*. إِلًّا acc. of إِلٌّ Consanguinity, relationship. Freitag gives أَلَّ as the root of this word.

أَلَا from أَ interrogative and لَا not; Is it not? Are there not? etc.

آلَ for أَوَلَ, rt. آلَ for أَوَلَ q.v.

آلَآءٌ plur. of أَلًى, rt. أَلَا for أَلَوَ q.v.

أَلَّا for أَنْ لَا That not; as, that (I do) not, etc. It governs the aorist in the subjunctive mood.

إِلَّا for إِنْ لَا Unless, except, if not; It commonly governs the accusative. For the rules of syntax connected with إِلَّا see D. S. Gr. T. 2, p. 403, *et seq*.

أَللَّآئِى A fem. form of أَلَّذِى q.v.

أَلْبَابٌ plur. of لُبٌّ, see لَبَّ.

أَلَتَ aor. i. To diminish, defraud (with acc. of pers. and مِنْ of thing), as وَمَا أَلَتْنَاهُمْ مِنْ عَمَلِهِمْ مِنْ شَيْءٍ 52 v. 21, "And we will not defraud them of any of their works."

إِلْتَفَّ viii. f. of لَفَّ q.v.

إِلْحَادٌ n.a. iv. f. of لَحَدَ q.v.

إِلْحَافٌ n.a. iv. f. of لَحَفَ q.v.

أَلْحِقْنِي Join me; Imperat. iv. f. of لَحِقَ q.v.

أَلَذُّ (2nd declension) comparat. adjective fr. لَذَّ q.v.

أَلَّذِي (He, the man) who, (him) whom, (the thing) which; Fem. أَلَّتِي; Dual أَلَّذَانِ; Plur. أَلَّذِينَ; fem. plur. أَللَّاتِي and أَللَّائِي; De Sacy instead of the last form gives أَللَّاءِ and أَللَّايِ; see his Grammar, T. 1, p. 446; According to the rule given at § 232, p. 113 of the same volume, أَللَّاءِ would seem to be the most correct way of spelling it; see also his observations on these pronouns, or, as he calls them, conjunctive adjectives, vol. 1, p. 443, *et seq.*, and vol. 2, p. 343, *et seq.* The antecedent is frequently omitted; see an instance at 28 v. 14.

الر Letters placed at the commencement of the 10th, 11th, 12th, 14th, and 15th chapters; see الم.

أَلْسِنَةٌ plur. of لِسَانٌ, rt. لَسَنَ q.v.

أَلِفَ aor. a. *To be accustomed (to a place), to join together.* أَلْفٌ A thousand; considered by some as the root; Dual أَلْفَانِ, oblique أَلْفَيْنِ; Plur. آلَافٌ and أُلُوفٌ.— أَلَّفَ II. To unite, join together, reconcile (with بَيْنَ); aor. يُؤَلِّفُ. مُؤَلَّفَةٌ fem. part. pass. Reconciled, as وَالْمُؤَلَّفَةِ قُلُوبُهُمْ 9 v. 60, "And those whose hearts are reconciled:" For the construction of this sentence see D. S. Gr. T. 2, p. 277.— إِيلَافٌ n.a. iv. f. A compact, uniting together.

أَلْفَافٌ see لَفَّ.

أَلْقَى iv. f. of لَقَا q.v.

أَلْقَابٌ plur. of لَقَبٌ A nickname.

أَلْقَى iv. f. of لَقِيَ q.v.

أَلَمْ Am I not? Is it not? etc. from أَ interrogative and لَمْ not; used also in conjunction with other particles, as أَوَلَمْ, أَوَلَمَّا, أَفَلَمْ, etc.

الم Letters found at the commencement of the second and several other chapters of the Ḳorân. Concerning the meaning of these and other letters found at the commencement of various chapters, differences of opinion have always existed among commentators; but it is held by many of the ablest of the Mussulman Doctors that the true meaning has never been communicated to any mortal, Moḥammad alone excepted. See Sale's Ḳorân, introductory remarks, section iii. *Note.* These and similar letters are to be pronounced at full length, *alif, lâm, meem*, etc.

أَلِمَ aor. a. To suffer (pain). أَلِيمٌ painful.

المر Letters at the commencement of the thirteenth chapter, see الم.

المص Letters at the commencement of the seventh chapter, see الم.

أَلَهَ *To adore.* إِلٰهٌ; Dual oblique إِلٰهَيْنِ; Plur. آلِهَةٌ A Deity, God. أَللّٰهُ God, The God, The only God; A word which embraces all the names by which the Mussulmans designate the Deity. وَاللّٰهِ and تَاللّٰهِ By God! لِلّٰهِ To God, belonging to God, as إِنَّا لِلّٰهِ 2 v. 151, "Verily we are God's." أَللّٰهُمَّ A form of invocation, O God! The م being added to compensate the omission of the particle يَا; it is said to stand for يَا أَللّٰهُ أُمَّنَا بِخَيْرٍ "O God! instruct us in righteousness!"

أَلْهَاكُمْ It has occupied you ; iv. f. of لَهَا q.v. and كُمْ.
أَلْهَمَ iv. f. of لَهِمَ q.v.

أَلَا aor. o. *To be wanting in duty*, to fail (with acc. of pers. and thing), as لَا يَأْلُونَكُمْ خَبَالًا 3 v. 114, "They will not fail to corrupt you." آلَاءٌ plur. of إِلًى for أَلْيٌ, Benefits.—آلَى IV. for أَأْلَى (possibly derived from an obsolete root أَلِيَ) To swear, vow abstinence from (with مِنْ), as يُؤْلُونَ 3 pers. plur. aor. at 2 v. 226.— إِيْتَلَى VIII. To swear, as لَا يَأْتَلِ . . . أَنْ يُؤْتُوا 24 v. 22, "Let not (the wealthy) swear that they will *not* give." *Note.* The ellipse of the negative is usual after an oath ; the oath itself implying a negation, unless there appear some precise indication to the contrary; D. S. Gr. T. 2, p. 474.

أَلْوَانٌ plur. of لَوْنٌ A species, q.v.

إِلَى To, towards, as far as (but not including); For the difference between حَتَّى and إِلَى see حَتَّى; in, on, or at, as لَيَجْمَعَنَّكُمْ إِلَى يَوْمِ ٱلْقِيَامَةِ 4 v. 89, "Verily he will gather you together on the day of resurrection;" with, or in addition to, as, لَا تَأْكُلُوا أَمْوَالَهُمْ إِلَى أَمْوَالِكُمْ 4 v. 2, "Do not devour their substance in addition to your own;" in this and similar instances there appears to be an ellipse of the word تَضُمُّونَهَا "*by adding it*," or of some similar word; إِلَى أَنْ Until. As a general rule إِلَى indicates the term or limit beyond which an action does not extend.

إِلْيَاسُ (2nd declension) Elias. إِلْيَاسِينَ 37 v. 130 Ilyâseen; this word is supposed by some to be the plur. of إِلْيَاسُ and to mean Elias and his followers, but it is probable that the termination ين is only added for the sake of the rhyme, and that both words designate the same person; as سَيْنَاءُ and سِينِينَ are both names of Mount Sinai.

أَمْ Or; a conjunction generally used in the second of two alternative propositions, the first of which is preceded by أَ; both may frequently be rendered "whether;" see أَ.

أَمَّ aor. o. *To seek, intend, propose.* آمِّينَ oblique plur. part. act. Those who seek, or are intending (to visit). أُمٌّ A mother, Plur. أُمَّهَاتٌ; *origin, principle*, a capital, place of abode, foundation, as أُمُّ ٱلْكِتَابِ 3 v. 5, "The foundation (or fundamental part) of the Book." *Note.* The contents of the Ḳorân are classed by Moḥammad under two heads; the first, which is called أُمُّ ٱلْكِتَابِ or the fundamental part, contains those passages whose meaning is plain and obvious; the other portions are metaphorical; the words أُمُّ ٱلْكِتَابِ at 13 v. 39 and 43 v. 3 mean "The original of the Book," and refer to the table on which God's decrees are recorded; it is also a name sometimes given to the opening chapter: أُمُّ ٱلْقُرَى The metropolis, Mecca: ٱبْنَ أُمَّ 7 v. 149 for ٱبْنَ أُمِّي Son of my mother, D. S. Gr. T. 2, p. 91, *note*; in some manuscripts the words يَا ٱبْنَ أُمِّي at 20 v. 95 are written in one word يَبْنَؤُمَّ, D. S. Gr. T. 1, p. 99. أُمَّةٌ Plur. أُمَمٌ A people, nation, race, a party (especially of the same religion), a fixed and definite term, a certain time, a religion, as عَلَى أُمَّةٍ 43 vv. 21 and 22, "In the practice of a religion;" an Imâm, or model of religion. أَمَامٌ Before; أَمَامَهُ 75 v. 5, "(For that which is) before him," *i.e.* "for the future." إِمَامٌ sing. and plur.; the Plur. of which is أَئِمَّةٌ A leader in religion, a model, example, rule, pattern, or book for guidance or instruction. أُمِّيٌّ One who can neither read nor write, illiterate, an epithet of Mohammad, ignorant, Pagan, one who is ignorant of the Scriptures. أَمَّا As for; occasionally put for أَمْ مَا Or that which, or what. إِمَّا Either, or whether, in which sense it requires to be repeated before each of the alternative propositions of a sentence; D. S. Gr. T. 1, p. 573; instances however occur where instead of إِمَّا being repeated, أَوْ is substituted, thus, إِمَّا يَبْلُغَنَّ عِنْدَكَ ٱلْكِبَرَ أَحَدُهُمَا أَوْ كِلَاهُمَا 17 v. 24, "Whether one of them attain old age with thee or both of them:" when standing for إِنْ مَا If (the مَا being expletive), no repetition is necessary, thus فَإِمَّا يَأْتِيَنَّكُمْ مِنِّي هُدًى 2 v. 36, "And if a direction shall come to you from me."

إِمَاءٌ plur. of أَمَةٌ A maid-servant, see أَمَا for أَمَوَ.

أَمَانَةٌ A deposit, rt. أَمِنَ q.v.

أَمَانِيُّ plur. of أُمْنِيَّةٌ Desires, rt. مَنَى q.v.

أَمَتَ aor. i. *To determine, to be curved.* أَمْتٌ A curve, anything which shows ups and downs.

أَمَةٌ A maid-servant, rt. أَمَا for أَمَوَ q.v.

إِمْتَازَ viii. f. of مَازَ q.v.

إِمْتَحَنَ viii. f. of مَحَنَ q.v.

أَمَدَ *To be finished*, and أَمِدَ *To be angry.* أَمَدٌ *Anger*, the term of existence, a space, term, terminus.

أَمَرَ aor. o. To command, order, enjoin (with أَنْ or لِ or with acc. of pers. and بِ of thing); تَأْمُرُونِّي "Ye order me," 39 v. 64, is for تَأْمُرُونَنِي; Imperat. مُرْ, when preceded by the conjunction وَ it is written وَأْمُرْ, D. S. Gr. T. 1, p. 232. أَمْرٌ n.a. A command, decree, matter, thing, business; Plur. أُمُورٌ; عَنْ أَمْرِي Of my own will. إِمْرٌ A serious matter, a strange thing. آمِرٌ part. act. One who commands. أَمَّارٌ Prone. إِيتَمَرَ— VIII. To take counsel together, deliberate about (with بِ); Imperat. إِيتَمِرْ, and with وَ, وَأْتَمِرْ.

إِمْرُؤٌ gen. إِمْرِئٍ A man, rt. مَرَأَ q.v.

أَمْسِ Yesterday, (no verbal root).

أَمْعَاءٌ plur. of مِعًى An intestine.

أَمَلَ aor. o. *To hope.* أَمَلٌ n.a. Hope.

أَمْلَى iv. f. of مَلَا q.v.

أَمِنَ aor. a. To be secure, trust (with acc. of pers. and بِ of thing), put trust in (with acc. of pers. and عَلَى), to be secure from (with acc.), as فَلَا يَأْمَنُ مَكْرَ ٱللّٰهِ 7 v. 97, "For (no one) is secure from the stratagem of God." أَمْنٌ n.a. Security; at 2 v. 119 it means a place of security. آمِنٌ part. act. One or that which is secure, safe, secure. أَمِينٌ Faithful, trustworthy, secure. أَمَنَةٌ Security. أَمَانَةٌ A pledge, covenant, faith, a trust. مَأْمُونٌ part. pass. Secured. مَأْمَنٌ A place of security.—آمَنَ IV. To make sure or secure (with acc. of pers.); to have faith in, believe (with بِ). إِيمَانٌ for إِأْمَانٌ D. S. Gr. T. 1, p. 95, § 185 and 187 n.a. A believing, faith, heartfelt belief, see إِسْلَامٌ. مُؤْمِنٌ part. act. One who believes.—إِيتَمَنَ Pass. أُوتُمِنَ VIII. To be entrusted with the custody of anything.

أُمْنِيَّةٌ Anything wished for, rt. مَنَى q.v.

أَمَا aor. o. *To mew like a cat, to become a maid-servant.* أَمَةٌ for أَمَوَةٌ D. S. Gr. T. 1, p. 358, A maid-servant; Plur. إِمَاءٌ.

أَنْ That, in order that, lest, that not; when followed by a verb in the aorist, such verb is generally put in the subjunctive; when put before a noun or pronoun it governs it in the accusative, and is then written with the teshdeed أَنَّ. This conjunction is frequently used after قَالَ or some similar verb, with an ellipse of the word "*saying*," thus, وَإِذْ نَادَى رَبُّكَ مُوسَى أَنِ ٱئْتِ ٱلْقَوْمَ ٱلظَّالِمِينَ 26 v. 9, "And (remember) when thy Lord called unto Moses (saying) go unto the wicked people;" when used in the sense of lest, for fear that, or in order that (it may) not, it is generally necessary *as a rule* that the preceding proposition should contain some word which carries with it the idea of prohibition, hindrance, or obstacle, as إِنَّا جَعَلْنَا عَلَى قُلُوبِهِمْ أَكِنَّةً أَنْ يَفْقَهُوهُ 18 v. 55, "Verily we put veils over their hearts that they should not understand it (the Korân)." The above rule however is by no means without exceptions, several of which occur in the Korân; thus at 7 v. 171 أَنْ تَقُولُوا must be rendered "lest ye should say," where there is an entire ellipse of the negative; a similar ellipse is common in case of an oath, see إِئْتَلَى, rt. أَلَا. بِأَنْ and لِأَنْ That. كَأَنْ As though. أَلَّا That not, for أَنْ لَا.

أَنَّ is used with every kind of prefix and affix, and may be rendered that, since, because; when followed by the affixed pronouns as أَنَّهُ etc. it loses its influence over the following noun; D. S. Gr. T. 1, p. 567.

إِنْ If, differs from لَوْ inasmuch as the former is simply conditional, as if (إِنْ) you are wise; while the latter supposes what is not the case, as if (لَوْ) you were wise; this is made clear by the following example: إِنْ تَدْعُوهُمْ لَا يَسْمَعُوا دُعَآءَكُمْ وَلَوْ سَمِعُوا مَا ٱسْتَجَابُوا لَكُمْ 35 v. 15, "If you call upon them they will not hear your prayer, and if they heard they would not answer you." إِنْ gives a future signification to verbs in the preterite, unless where كَانَ is interposed, D. S. Gr. T. 1, p. 181, *et seq.*; it has sometimes a negative meaning, as إِنْ أَجْرِيَ إِلَّا عَلَى ٱلَّذِى فَطَرَنِى 11 v. 53, "My reward is not (due) except from him who created me." أَئِنْ and لَئِنْ for أَإِنْ and لَإِنْ.

إِنَّ like أَنَّ is used with almost every kind of prefix and affix; when without an affixed pronoun it governs nouns in the accusative: it has an affirmative meaning, and may generally be rendered verily, or indeed; it is sometimes written without the teshdeed, and must not then be confounded with the conjunction إِنْ if.

إِنَّمَا called by the Arabs حَرْفُ ٱلْحَصْرِ, or particle of restriction, may frequently be rendered only; the مَا is occasionally a simple expletive, and the word has then the force of إِنَّ, but it no longer governs the accusative. De Sacy gives the rules for all these particles in his usual admirable manner, and to his Grammar I refer the reader for the fullest information on the subject.

أَنَا I; personal pronoun.

آنَآءٌ plur. of أَنًى for أَنْىٌ Hours, rt. أَنَى q.v.

إِنَاثًا acc. plur. of أُنْثَى, rt. أَنُثَ q.v.

أَنَاسِىُّ plur. of إِنْسِىٌّ, rt. أَنِسَ q.v.

أَنَامٌ (collective noun) Creatures; no verbal root.

أَنَامِلُ (2nd declension) plur. of أَنْمُلَةٌ Finger-ends. rt. نَمَلَ q.v.

أَنْبَآءٌ plur. of نَبَأٌ, rt. نَبَأَ q.v.

أَنْبَتَ iv. f. of نَبَتَ q.v.

إِنْبَجَسَ vii. f. of بَجَسَ q.v.

أَنْبِيَآءُ (2nd declension) plur. of نَبِيٌّ or نَبِيءُ A prophet, rt. نَبَأَ q.v.

أَنْتَ Thou; personal pronoun masc.; Plur. أَنْتُمْ; Dual أَنْتُمَا.

إِنْتَبَذَ viii. f. of نَبَذَ q.v.

إِنْتَثَرَ viii. f. of نَثَرَ q.v.

إِنْتَشَرَ viii. f. of نَشَرَ q.v.

إِنْتَصَرَ viii. f. of نَصَرَ q.v.

إِنْتَقَمَ viii. f. of نَقَمَ q.v.

إِنْتَهُوا 3 pers. plur. viii. f. of نَهَى q.v.

أَنُثَ *To be soft* (iron). أُنْثَى Plur. إِنَاثٌ A female; Oblique dual أُنْثَيَيْنِ.

أَنْدَادٌ plur. of نِدٌّ An idol, rt. نَدَّ q.v.

أَنِسَ aor. a. *To be familiar.* إِنْسٌ (collective noun) Mankind, human beings, man. إِنْسَانٌ common gender, Man; Plur. أُنَاسٌ (*commonly contracted into* نَاسٌ). إِنْسِيٌّ A man; Plur. أَنَاسِيُّ (2nd declension); D. S. Gr. T. 1, p. 402.—آنَسَ IV. *To render familiar,* perceive (with acc. and مِنْ).—إِسْتَأْنَسَ X. *To be familiar,* to ask permission, beg pardon. مُسْتَأْنِسٌ part. act. One who is familiar.

أَنْسَابٌ plur. of نَسَبٌ, rt. نَسَبَ q.v.

أَنْشَأَ iv. f. of نَشَأَ q.v.

أَنْصَتَ iv. f. of نَصَتَ q.v.

أَنِفَ aor. a. *To turn up the nose at, to go before.* آنِفًا Just now, lately: the logical root is أَنْفٌ A nose.

أَنْفَالٌ plur. of نَفَلٌ, rt. نَفَلَ q.v.

أَنْفُسٌ plur. of نَفْسٌ A soul, rt. نَفَسَ q.v.

إِنْفَضَّ vii. f. of فَضَّ q.v.

أَنْكَالٌ plur. of نِكْلٌ A fetter, rt. نَكَلَ q.v.

أَنُلْزِمُكُمُوهَا see لَزِمَ.

إِنْهَ imperative of نَهَى q.v.

أَنَى aor. i. To arrive (the time, with لِ); *to be boiling hot.* إِنَى for إِنًى A fitting time, convenient opportunity, as غَيْرَ نَاظِرِينَ إِنَاهُ 33 v. 53, "Without looking to his convenience." آنٍ for آنِيٌ part. act. Boiling hot (water); Fem. آنِيَةٌ. آنَآءٌ plur. of أَنَى for أَنًى D. S. Gr. T. 1, p. 111, A fitting time, a part of time; آنَآءَ ٱللَّيْلِ 20 v. 130, "The hours of the night." آنَآءٌ Time. آنِيَةٌ plur. of إِنَآءٌ A vessel.

أَنَّى How, in what way, in what way soever, Where, whence, from whence; D. S. Gr. T. 1, pp. 185 and 205.

إِهْتَزَّ viii. f. of هَزَّ q.v.

أَهْلٌ People, a family or household; أَهْلُ ٱلْكِتَابِ The people of the Book, *i.e.* Jews and Christians, also called أَهْلُ ٱلذِّكْرِ or, Those who have charge of the oracles of God; أَهْلُ ٱلْإِنْجِيلِ Christians, the people of the Gospel; أَهْلُ ٱلنَّارِ The inhabitants of Hell-fire; worthy of (with genitive).

أَهِلَّةٌ plur. of هِلَالٌ, New moons, rt. هَلَّ q.v.

أَهْوَآءٌ plur. of هَوًى A desire, rt. هَوَى q.v.

أَوْ Or, either, whether, unless; D. S. Gr. T. 1, p. 571, and T. 2, p. 28.

أَوَّهٌ see آهٌ for أَوْهُ.

آبَ for أَوَبَ aor. o. *To return.* إِيَابٌ n.a. The act of returning. أَوَّابٌ A sincere penitent, one who frequently returns, one who turns seriously to God. مَآبٌ A place of return.—أَوَّبَ II. To sing the praises of God by saying سُبْحَانَ ٱللّٰهِ; أَوِّبِي fem. imperative.

أَوْبَارٌ plur. of وَبَرٌ, rt. وَبَرَ q.v.

أَوْتَادٌ plur. of وَتِدٌ, rt. وَتَدَ q.v.

أُوتُمِنَ pass. viii. f. of أَمِنَ q.v.

أَوْثَانٌ plur. of وَثَنٌ An idol.

أَوْحَى iv. f. of وَحَى q.v.

آدَ for أَوَدَ, aor. يَؤُدُ for يَؤُودُ D. S. Gr. T. 1, p. 104, *To bend*, oppress by its gravity.

أَوْدِيَةٌ plur. of وَادٍ A valley, rt. وَدَى q.v.

أُوذِيَ pass. iv. f. of أَذِيَ q.v.

أَوْزَارٌ plur. of وِزْرٌ, rt. وَزَرَ q.v.

أَوْسَطُ see وَسَطَ.

أَوْعَى iv. f. of وَعَى q.v.

أَوْفَى comparative and iv. f. of وَفَى q.v.

أَوْقَدَ iv. f. of وَقَدَ q.v.

آلَ for أَوَلَ aor. o. *To return, to be before.* آلٌ A people, race, family. أَوَّلٌ, Fem. أُولَى First, former, prior, the first beginning; ٱلْأَوَّلُونَ The ancients, those of former days.—أَوَّلَ II. *To bring back, explain.* تَأْوِيلٌ n.a. Interpretation, explanation, determination (of a dispnte).

أُولَآءِ These; plur. of ذَا This; D. S. Gr. T. 1, p. 439.

أُولَٰٓئِكَ Those; plur. of ذَٰلِكَ or ذَاكَ That; D.S. Gr. T. 1, p. 440; أُولَٰٓئِكُمْ Those of your's.

أُولُوا Obliqne أُولِي; Fem. أُولَاتُ; a plural adjective wanting the sing., unless, according to some, it is to be considered as a plural of ذُو Possessed of, endued with, as أُولُوا ٱلْأَلْبَابِ Those gifted with (nnderstanding) hearts; أُولُوا ٱلْأَمْرِ Those in anthority; أُولَاتُ حَمْلٍ Women with child. *Note.* The ا at the end of أُولُوا is what is called أَلِفُ ٱلْوِقَايَةِ or alif of precaution, to prevent the final و being taken for the conjunction *and.*

أَوْلَى comp. form of adj. fr. وَلِيَ q.v.

أَوْلِيَآءُ see وَلِيَ.

آنَ for أَوَنَ aor. o. *To be tranquil.* آنٌ A time, moment; ٱلْآنَ adv. Now, at this present time.

آهٍ *Ah! alas!* أَوَّاهٌ A compassionate person, one who shows pity hy frequently sighing, and saying ah! or alas!

أَوَى aor. يَأْوِي (a verh hamzated and donhly imperfect), To betake one's-self for rest or shelter, have recourse to (with إِلَى); سَآوِي 1 pers. sing. aor. with the prefix سَ; فَأْوُوا "Then fly!" 2 pers. plur. imperat. D. S. Gr. T. 1, p. 232 *note.* آيَةٌ Plur. آيٌ and آيَاتٌ A sign, miracle, a name given to the verses of the Korân, each of which is held to he a miracle. مَأْوًى A place of abode, mansion.—آوَى IV. To care for, or receive as a guest, provide a refuge or abode for (with acc. and إِلَى); Aor. يُؤْوِي.

إِي Yea, verily; used only in affirming hy oath.

أَيٌّ pronoun of comm. gend. Whosoever, whichever, Who? which? What? أَيُّمَا Whichever.

إِيَّا a particle prefixed to prononns in the accus. when "isolated" or not affixed; it is employed in cases where a verb governs two or more pronouns in the accus. one of which cannot he conveniently affixed; D. S. Gr. T. 2, p. 378; also where it is desired to place the pronoun before the verb, as إِيَّاكَ نَعْبُدُ in the opening chapter; occasionally it is nsed in addition to the affixed pronoun, as وَإِيَّايَ فَٱتَّقُونِي, 2 v. 38, "And I, (or as for me), fear me;" D. S. Gr. T. 1, p. 461.

إِيَابٌ n.a. of. آبَ for أَوَبَ q.v.

أَيَامَى plur. of أَيِّمٌ, rt. آمَ for أَيَمَ q.v.

أَيَّانَ When?

إِيتَآءٌ n.a. iv. f. of أَتَى q.v.

آدَ for أَيَدَ aor. i. *To be firm.* أَيْدٌ n.a. Strength.—أَيَّدَ II. To strengthen (with acc. and عَلَى or بِ); aor. يُؤَيِّدُ.

أَيْدِيهِمْ Their hands; oblique plur. of يَدٌ, rt. يَدَى q.v.

أَيْكٌ and أَيْكَةٌ (noun of unity) A wood; أَصْحَابُ ٱلْأَيْكَةِ The inhabitants of a wood near Midian, to whom the prophet Sho'aib was sent.

إِيلَافٌ n.a. iv. f. of أَلِفَ q.v.

أَامَ for أَيَمَ aor. i. *To be unmarried.* أَيَامَى (2nd declension) plur. of أَيِّمٌ An unmarried man or woman, whether single or widowed.

إِيمَانٌ n.a. iv. f. of أَمِنَ q.v. أَيْمَانٌ plur. of يَمِينٌ, see يَمَنَ.

أَئِمَّةٌ plur. of إِمَامٌ, rt. أَمَّ q.v.

أَيْنَ Where? whither? أَيْنَمَا Wherever, whithersoever; D. S. Gr. T. 1, pp. 185, 194, and 205.

أَإِنَّكَ Art thou verily? from أَ interrogative, إِنَّ and كَ the affixed personal pronoun.

أَيَّةُ or أَيُّهَا, Fem. أَيَّتُهَا an Interjection, O thou! O ye! etc.; it is followed by the substantive with the definite article آل, as أَيُّهَ ٱلْمُؤْمِنِينَ "O true believers!" 12 v. 70, "O أَيَّتُهَا ٱلْعِيرُ ye of the Caravan!"

أَيُّوبُ (2nd declension) Job.

ب

بِ an inseparable preposition, prefixed to the word it governs, which when a noun is put in the genitive; it has divers significations, as In, by, at, with, to, into, upon, for, or by reason of; from, as مَا غَرَّكَ بِرَبِّكَ 82 v. 6, "What hath seduced thee from thy Lord?" It is used with أَتَى, جَآءَ, رَاحَ and many other verbs to render them transitive, or join them to an indirect complement, thus أَتَى بِهِ "He brought it"; *literally*, "he came with it." بِ is frequently an expletive, when put before the complement of a negative proposition, as مَا ٱللّٰهُ بِغَافِلٍ 2 v. 69, "God is not negligent"; it is also an expletive in some other cases, as كَفَى بِٱللّٰهِ شَهِيدًا 13 v. 43, "God is an all sufficient witness." For the various usages of بِ see D. S. Gr. T. 1, p. 469, *et seq.*

بَابِلُ Babel (2nd declension, D.S.Gr.T.1, p.404).

بَادٍ see بَدَا for بَدَوَ.

بَارِئٌ see بَرَأَ.

بَاغٍ see بَغَى.

بَأَرَ aor. a. *To dig a well.* بِئْرٌ fem. A well.

بَئِسَ aor. a. for بَأُسَ *To be wretched, miserable;* بِئْسَ for بَئِسَ To be bad, miserable; the latter is one of those anomalous verbs, named by the Arabs أَفْعَالُ ٱلْمَدْحِ وَٱلذَّمِّ or "verbs of praise and blame," which are not conjugated, the only inflexion taken by بِئْسَ being the feminine بِئْسَتْ "She was miserable;" the vowel of the first radical letter is suppressed, and that of the second is put in its place, see D. S. Gr. T. 1, p. 263, and T. 2, p. 221. بَأْسٌ Severity, vengeance, valour, force. بَئِيسٌ Grievous. بَائِسٌ part. act. Needy. بَأْسَآءُ (Bodily) misfortune.—إِبْتَأَسَ VIII. To be grieved (with بِ); لَا تَبْتَئِسْ "Be not grieved," 11 v. 38.

بَتَرَ aor. o. *To cut off the tail.* أَبْتَرُ (2nd declension) Childless.

بَتَكَ aor. i. and o. *To cut, cut off.*—بَتَّكَ II. To cut off, with the idea of repetition; فَلَيُبَتِّكُنَّ 4 v. 118, "Verily they shall cut off."

بَتَلَ aor. o. *To cut off, separate.*—تَبْتِيلٌ n.a. II form,

A life of complete separation from the world and devotion to God.—تَبَتَّلَ V. To devote one's-self wholly to God's service (with إِلَى), as at 73 v. 8.

بَثَّ aor. i. and o. To disperse, disseminate (with acc. and فِى). بَثٌّ Sorrow. مَبْثُوثٌ Scattered, spread abroad.—مُنْبَثٌّ part. pass. VII. f. Scattered abroad.

بَجَسَ aor. i. and o. *To let water flow.*—إِنْبَجَسَ VII. To burst forth (water), see إِنْفَجَرَ.

بَحَثَ aor. a. To scratch the ground like a hen (with فِى).

بَحَرَ *To slit a camel's ears.* بَحْرٌ Plur. بِحَارٌ and أَبْحُرٌ The sea, a large body of water; بَحْرَانِ dual, The two bodies of water, viz., salt and fresh. بَحِيرَةٌ Baheera, the name given among the Pagan Arabs to a camel which they turned loose to feed, after slitting its ears.

بَخَسَ aor. a. To diminish, withhold what is due (with acc. of thing and مِنْ of pers. or with double acc.). بَخْسٌ A deficiency, small, trifling.

بَخَعَ *To slaughter (a sheep) by cutting its throat, to kill one's-self with grief.* بَاخِعٌ part. act. One who frets himself to death (with acc. of pers. and عَلَى or أَنْ).

بَخِلَ aor. a. To be covetous, avaricious, covetous of (with بِ). بُخْلٌ Avarice.

بَدَأَ aor. a. To begin, create (with acc. and also with بِ); وَهُمْ بَدَؤُكُمْ "And they began (with) you (to assault you)," 9 v. 13.—أَبْدَأَ IV. To create, make anew; Aorist يُبْدِئُ.

بَدَرَ aor. o. *To make haste.* بَدْرٌ Bedr, name of a place near Mecca; *The moon when full;* Plur. بُدُورٌ. بِدَارًا Hastily.

بَدَعَ aor. a. *To produce something new.* بِدْعٌ New, new-fangled. بَدِيعٌ The Creator, as maker of a new creation.—إِبْتَدَعَ VIII. To bring forward a novelty.

بَدَلَ *To change.* بَدَلًا For a change.—بَدَّلَ II. To substitute, change one thing for another (with acc. or with double acc. and بِ). تَبْدِيلٌ n.a. An exchange. مُبَدِّلٌ part. act. One who changes.—أَبْدَلَ IV. To substitute, give in exchange (with double acc.)—تَبَدَّلَ V. To exchange (with acc. and بِ).—إِسْتَبْدَلَ X. To wish to exchange (with acc. and بِ); to put in the place of another (with acc. and غَيْرٌ). إِسْتِبْدَالٌ An exchange.

بَدَنَ aor. o. *To be corpulent.* بَدَنٌ A body. بُدْنٌ plur. of بَدَنَةٌ 22 v. 37, Camels sacrificed at Mecca.

بَدَا aor. o. To begin, to be manifest, to appear (with لِ or مِنْ); to enter the mind; ثُمَّ بَدَا لَهُمْ 12 v. 35, "Then it occurred to them." بَدْوٌ A desert. بَادٍ for بَادِئٌ part. act., see D. S. Gr. T. 1, p. 111; Plur. بَادُونَ A dweller in the country; بَادِىَ ٱلرَّأْيِ "At first thought," 11 v. 29.—أَبْدَى IV. To make to appear, show, manifest (with بِ or with acc. and لِ). مُبْدٍ for مُبْدِئٌ part. act. One who makes manifest.

بَذَرَ aor. a. *To sow.*—بَذَّرَ II. To dissipate, squander. تَبْذِيرًا Profusely. مُبَذِّرٌ part. act. A spendthrift.

بَرَّ aor. a. To be pious, just, act justly towards (with accus. of pers.) بَرٌّ Plur. أَبْرَارٌ Beneficent, liberal, just, kind; Dry land as opposed to sea. بِرٌّ Piety, kindness, that which is just and proper. بَرَرَةٌ plur. of بَارٌّ part. act. Innocent, pious.

بَرَأَ aor. a. To create. بَرِئٌ Plur. بَرِيئُونَ and بُرَآءُ Sound, free, innocent; with مِنْ, Clear, guiltless of; Ex. إِنِّي بَرِئٌ مِمَّا تُشْرِكُونَ 6 v. 78, "Verily I am innocent of that which ye associate (with God)." بَرَآءَةٌ same as بَرِئَ. بَرَآءٌ Immunity. بَرِيَّةٌ A creature. بَارِئٌ part. act. The Maker, Creator, God.—بَرَّأَ II. To absolve, acquit; Ex. مَا أُبَرِّئُ نَفْسِي 12 v. 53, "I do not absolve myself," (also with acc. and مِنْ). مُبَرَّءٌ part. pass. Absolved.—أَبْرَأَ IV. To cure, heal.—تَبَرَّأَ V. To free one's-self, clear one's-self (with مِنْ); تَبَرَّأْنَا إِلَيْكَ 28 v. 63, "We are free (from them and turn) to thee."

بَرَجَ *To eat and drink in large quantities.* بُرُوجٌ plur. of بُرْجٌ A tower, sign of the Zodiac.—تَبَرَّجَ V. To deck one's-self. تَبَرُّجٌ n.a. The ornamenting one's-self in an ostentatious manner; Ex. لَا تَبَرَّجْنَ تَبَرُّجَ ٱلْجَاهِلِيَّةِ 33 v. 33, "Deck not yourselves with the ostentation of (the time of) ignorance." مُتَبَرِّجٌ part. act. Decking one's-self out.

بَرَحَ *To turn to the left, as a deer, which was thought unlucky;* and بَرِحَ aor. a. To cease, leave off, quit.

بَرَدَ aor. o. *To be cold.* بَرْدٌ n.a. Cold, cool, coolness. بَرَدٌ Hail. بَارِدٌ part. act. That which cools, refreshes.

بَرَزَ To go forth, as out upon a plain (with لِ, إِلَى, or مِنْ); to be manifest (with لِ). بَارِزٌ part. act. One who goes forth; بَارِزَةً 18 v. 45, In an extended form, like a plain.—بَرَّزَ II. To make manifest (with لِ).

بَرْزَخٌ A partition or interstice, a bar; the abode of departed spirits, Hades; No verbal root.

بَرِصَ aor. a. *To be leprous.* أَبْرَصُ (2nd declension) Leprous.

بَرَقَ aor. o. *To shine,* and بَرِقَ To be smitten with astonishment, to be dazzled. بَرْقٌ n.a. of بَرَقَ Lightning, thunderbolt. إِسْتَبْرَقٌ Brocade, see p. 5.

بَرَكَ aor. o. *To kneel down like a camel, stand firm.* بَرَكَةٌ Plur. بَرَكَاتٌ Blessings.—بَارَكَ III. To bless (with acc. and with فِي or عَلَى); Pass. بُورِكَ. مُبَارَكٌ part. pass. Blessed.—تَبَارَكَ VI. To be blessed; تَبَارَكَ ٱللّٰهُ *Literally,* "God was blessed," or "Blessed be God;" the Preterite being used for the Aorist in an optative sense in the same way as تَعَالَى q.v. For this use of the Preterite see D. S. Gr. T. 1, p. 169.

بَرَمَ *To twist.*—أَبْرَمَ IV. *To twist together and make firm,* to fix, settle (a plan). مُبْرِمٌ part. act. One who fixes upon a plan, 43 v. 79.

بَرْهَنَ *To demonstrate, convince.* بُرْهَانٌ An evident proof.

بَزَغَ *To insert a lancet, rise (as the sun).* بَازِغٌ part. act. Rising.

بَسَّ aor. o. *To drive gently,* to crumble to dust. بَسٌّ n.a. A crumbling to dust; بُسَّتِ ٱلْجِبَالُ بَسًّا 56 v. 5, "The mountains shall be crumbled into dust."

بَسَرَ *To do anything out of season,* to be of an austere countenance. بَاسِرٌ part. act. Austere and dismal-looking.

بَسَطَ aor. o. To expand, extend, enlarge, stretch, stretch forth (with acc. and لِ, إِلَى, or فِي). بَسْطٌ n.a. Extension, expansion. بَسْطَةٌ Excellence, increase of stature. بِسَاطٌ A carpet. بَاسِطٌ part. act. One who stretches out; بَاسِطُوا أَيْدِيهِمْ 6 v. 93, "Stretching forth their hands;" *Literally,* "Stretchers forth of their hands;" بَاسِطُوا is here put for بَاسِطُونَ which loses its ن as being antecedent to أَيْدِيهِمْ; the Alif is added as an Alif of precaution or matter for contemplation.—بَصَّرَ II. To make to see, shew, make manifest.—أَبْصَرَ IV. To see, consider, cause to see (with acc. or with بِ of pers.): For two different interpretations of أَبْصِرْ at 18 v. 25, and 19 v. 39 see أَسْمِعْ iv. f. of سَمِعَ. مُبْصِرٌ part. act. One who sees, that which renders evident, or enables one to see, visible, manifest.—مُسْتَبْصِرٌ part. act. X. f. A clever and far-seeing person.

بَصَلٌ An onion, and when used in a collective or generic sense, Onions.

بَضَعَ *To cut off a part.* بِضْعٌ A part, a small number (from 3 to 9 or to 5, or from 1 to 4, or from 4 to 9), also seven; بِضْعَ سِنِينَ 12 v. 42, "A few years;" بِضْعَ is here put in the accus. as indicating the circumstance of time, see D. S. Gr. T. 2, p. 69. بِضَاعَةٌ A portion of goods, sum of money, merchandize.

بَطُؤَ *To be slow.*—بَطَّأَ II. To retard; وَإِنَّ مِنكُمْ لَمَن لَّيُبَطِّئَنَّ 4 v. 74, "And verily there is (a portion) of you who tarry (or cause to tarry) behind." *Note.* In cases where the 2nd form of a verb has a neuter signification, the Ellipse of a complement may frequently be inferred; D. S. Gr. T. 1, p. 133.

بَطَرَ aor. o. *To split;* بَطِرَ aor. a. To be insolent. بَطَرٌ Carelessness, insolence.

بَطَشَ aor. i. and o. To lay hold, take or seize by force, make an onslaught upon (with بِ). بَطْشٌ n.a. Force, violence, vengeance. بَطْشَةٌ Force, power, severity.

بَطَلَ aor. o. To be in vain, perish. بَاطِلٌ part. act. That which is vain, false, falsehood, vanity; ٱلْبَاطِلُ is the opposite to ٱلْحَقُّ, see 13 v. 18.—أَبْطَلَ IV. To cause to be in vain, frustrate,

أَلِفُ ٱلْوِقَايَةِ, the object of which is to prevent the final و from being taken for the conjunction وَ *and;* for the construction see D. S. Gr. T. 2, p. 183. مَبْسُوطَتَانِ 5 v. 69, part. pass. fem. dual "(His two hands are) stretched out."

بَسَقَ *To spit, to be tall.* بَاسِقٌ Tall (as a Palm-tree).

بَسَلَ *To look fierce.*—أَبْسَلَ IV. To deliver over to perdition.

بَسَمَ aor. i. *To smile.*—تَبَسَّمَ V. Same as بَسَمَ.

بَشَرَ *To peel off the bark.* بَشْرٌ and بُشْرٌ A bringer of good tidings. بَشَرٌ A man, men, human beings; masc. and fem. sing. and plur. بُشْرَى Good news; بُشْرَاكُمْ 57 v. 12, "Good news to you;" ي is replaced by ا before the affixed pronoun, see D. S. Gr. T. 1, p. 118. بَشِيرٌ A bearer of good tidings.—بَشَّرَ II. (used with accus. of person and بِ of the thing, or with أَنَّ), To announce good news; sometimes used ironically; Ex. فَبَشِّرْهُمْ بِعَذَابٍ أَلِيمٍ 3 v. 20, "Then announce to them a painful punishment." مُبَشِّرٌ part. act. One who announces joyful news.—بَاشَرَ III. To go in unto (a wife).— أَبْشَرَ IV. To receive pleasure from good news (with بِ of thing).—إِسْتَبْشَرَ X. To rejoice, especially in good news (with بِ). مُسْتَبْشِرَةٌ part. act. fem. One who rejoices.

بَصَرَ To see, look at (with بِ); to understand. بَصَرٌ Plur. أَبْصَارٌ Sight, eye-sight, sense of seeing; كَلَمْحِ ٱلْبَصَرِ 16 v. 79, "Like the twinkling of an eye;" In the plur. it generally means "Eyes." بَصِيرٌ Seeing, a Seer, or Beholder, One who sees or understands. بَصِيرَةٌ Plur. بَصَائِرُ An evidence, evident argument or demonstration; عَلَى بَصِيرَةٍ 12 v. 108, "By a manifest demonstration." تَبْصِرَةٌ A make ineffectual. مُبْطِلٌ part. act. One who deals in vanities.

بَطَنَ aor. o. *To enter into the inmost parts of anything*, to lie hid. بَطْنٌ n.a. Plur. بُطُونٌ Belly, interior part. بَاطِنٌ part. act. That which is hidden, inner part, inside, interior. بِطَانَةٌ An inner vest; *metaphorically*, An intimate friend, 3 v. 114; Plur. بَطَآئِنُ (2nd declension) Inner linings, 55 v. 54.

بَعَثَ aor. a. To send (with acc. and لِ, بِ, and فِى, also with عَلَى); to make manifest, raise up, raise from sleep or from the dead (with acc. of pers.). بَعْثٌ n.a. The resurrection. مَبْعُوثٌ part. pass. *Sent*, raised from the dead.—إِنْبَعَثَ VII. To be sent. إِنْبِعَاثٌ n.a. The being sent.

بَعْثَرَ To scatter abroad, turn upside down, tear forth.

بَعُدَ To be far off, go a long way off, perish; بَعُدَتْ عَلَيْهِمُ ٱلشُّقَّةُ 9 v. 42, "The way seemed far to them." بَعْدُ when used as an adverb is indeclinable, Afterwards, again; when employed as a preposition it is used in the Accusative بَعْدَ, or in the genitive if preceded by مِنْ, as مِنْ بَعْدِ After, see D. S. Gr. T. 1, p. 508, and T. 2, p. 152. بُعْدٌ A distance; بُعْدًا Away with; أَلَا بُعْدًا لِعَادٍ 11 v. 63, "Was it not (said), Away with 'Ād!" بَعِيدٌ Distant, far off, remote, as رَجْعٌ بَعِيدٌ 50 v. 3, "A return remote from the imagination, or from possibility."—بَاعَدَ III. To cause a distance to intervene (with بَيْنَ) as at 34 v. 18.—مُبْعَدٌ part. pass. IV. f. Far removed.

بَعِرَ *To become full grown (a camel)*. بَعِيرٌ comm. gend. A full-grown camel.

بَعْضٌ A portion of anything, some; one another; Ex. آهْبِطُوا بَعْضُكُمْ لِبَعْضٍ عَدُوٌّ 2 v. 34, "Get ye down, an enemy one to another;" used for both masc. and fem. and for all numbers. بَعُوضَةٌ A gnat; verbal root بَعِضَ *To be stung by gnats*.

بَعَلَ aor. a. *To be in a married state*. بَعْلٌ Baal, a husband; Plur. بُعُولَةٌ.

بَغَتَ aor. a. *To come upon suddenly*. بَغْتَةً On a sudden, suddenly.

بَغَضَ aor. o. *To hate*. بَغْضَآءُ (2nd declension) Violent hatred.

بَغْلٌ *A mule;* Plur. بِغَالٌ Mules.

بَغَى aor. i. To transgress, pass beyond bounds; to seek, desire (with double acc. or with acc. and فِى, عَنْ, or عَلَى); to act unjustly or insolently towards (with عَلَى of pers. or فِى of thing). بَغْىٌ n.a. Injustice, injury, oppression, iniquity; بَغْيًا In an insolent manner. بَغِىٌّ A harlot. بِغَآءٌ Fornication. بَاغٍ part. act. for بَاغِىٌ, see D. S. Gr. T. 1, p. 111, Desiring, lusting.—إِنْبَغَى VII. To be fit and proper, becoming, easy, desirable, suitable, expedient (with لِ and أَنْ).—إِبْتَغَى VIII. To desire, covet, seek, seek for (with acc. and إِلَى, فِى, عِنْدَ, مِنْ, or بِ). إِبْتِغَآءٌ n.a. A seeking, desire of.

بَقَرَ aor. a. *To slit open*. بَقَرٌ collective noun, Oxen. بَقَرَةٌ comm. gend. *An ox*, a cow.

بَقَعَ *To go away into any country*. بُقْعَةٌ A corner of ground.

بَقَلَ aor. o. *To appear, push forth*. بَقْلٌ generic noun, Herbs, pot-herbs.

بَقِىَ aor. a. To remain. بَاقٍ part. act. for بَاقِىٌ D. S. Gr. T. 1, p. 111, Remaining, that which remains, or survives, permanent, constant, the rest; أَلْبَاقِيَاتُ ٱلصَّالِحَاتُ 18 v. 44, and 19 v.

79, "Pious works or words, whicb are permanent." بَقِيَّةٌ A relic, that which is left; Ex. بَقِيَّتُ ٱللّٰهِ 11 v. 87, "That which is left you by God." *Note.* The letter ت is occasionally snbstitnted for the ة, see D. S. Gr. T. 1, p. 276, *note;* أُولُوا بَقِيَّةٍ 11 v. 118, "Endued with prudence or virtne." أَبْقَى (2nd declension) comp. form, More or most lasting, enduring, permanent.—أَبْقَى IV. To leave remaining, leave alive, suffer to remain. —سَبَقَ see إِسْتَبَقُوا.

بَكَّةُ (2nd declension) Becca, a name of Mecca; see D. S. Gr. T. 1, p. 404.

بَكَرَ aor. o. *To be early in the morning.* بِكْرٌ A virgin, a young heifer; Plnr. أَبْكَارٌ Virgins. بُكْرَةً In tbe morning, early in the morning.—إِبْكَارٌ n.a. IV. f. The morning.

بَكِمَ *To be dumb.* أَبْكَمُ (2nd declension), Plur. بُكْمٌ Dumb.

بَكَى aor. i. To weep, weep for (with acc. or with عَلَى). بُكِيٌّ Weeping.—أَبْكَى IV. To cause to weep.

بَلْ A particle whicb affirms that wbich follows it, but contradicts or corrects that which went before; thus it may be translated Bnt, not so but, on the contrary, or rather, nay ratber, still more, &c. according to the context; for the difference between بَلْ and لٰكِنْ see D. S. Gr. T. 1, p. 565.

بَلَدَ *To stay or remain in a place.* بَلَدٌ Plnr. بِلَادٌ A region, country, territory. بَلْدَةٌ A country, territory.

بَلَسَ *A man of desperate character;* tbere is no verbal root of this word in the first form.—أَبْلَسَ IV. To be overcome witb grief, to be desperate, strnck dumb with despair. مُبْلِسٌ part. act. Seized with despair. إِبْلِيسُ (2nd declension) Iblees, Tbe Devil.

بَلِعَ aor. a. To swallow np.

بَلَغَ aor. o. To arrive at, reach, attain one's object, obtain (with acc.), as at 18 v. 75. بَالِغٌ part. act. Arriving at, bringing to a conclusion, attaining its end, excellent, consnmmate; Ex. حِكْمَةٌ بَالِغَةٌ 54 v. 5, "Consummate wisdom;" also, that which is paramount over, أَمْ لَكُمْ أَيْمَانٌ عَلَيْنَا بَالِغَةٌ 68 v. 39, "Have ye any oaths which shall be binding upon ns?" بَلَاغٌ A warning, preaching, that which is published, sent, or brougbt to any one. بَلِيغٌ Affecting, eloquent. مَبْلَغٌ A goal, perfection, bighest pitch.—بَلَّغَ II. To make to arrive, publish, bring (with donble acc.).—أَبْلَغَ IV. To cause to reach, bring, deliver a message (with double acc.).

بَلَا aor. o. To try, prove, experience (witb acc. and بِ or فِي), see note to تَلَا; بَلِيَ aor. a. To become worn with age, to be worn ont. بَلَآءٌ A trial.—أَبْلَى IV. To try by experiment.—إِبْتَلَى VIII. To prove by trial or examination, try either by prosperity or adversity (witb acc. and بِ), see 89 vv. 14 and 16, where it is used in both senses. مُبْتَلٍ for مُبْتَلِيٌ D. S. Gr. T. 1, p. 111, part act. One wbo proves.

بَلَى Yea, surely, verily, nay but verily, on the contrary; this particle is nsed after a negative proposition (interrogative or otherwise), and affirms the contrary of such proposition to be the truth; hence it differs from نَعَمْ which assents to the preceding proposition; see D. S. Gr. T. 1, p. 514.

بَنَانٌ collective noun, The tips of the fingers, see D. S. Gr. T. 1, p. 381; the verbal root is بَنَّ *To stand fast.*

بَنَى aor. i. To build, construct (with acc. and بِ, لِ or عَلَى). إِبْنٌ for بَنَوٌ A son; Plur. أَبْنَآءٌ, also بَنُونَ, obliquo بَنِينَ, and when in connexion with a complement بَنُو and بَنِى; Dual إِبْنَانِ and إِبْنَيْنِ, or in connexion إِبْنَا and إِبْنَى; بَنِىَّ My sons, D. S. Gr. T. 1, p. 459: بُنَىٌّ diminutive, A little son. إِبْنَتٌ A daughter, see بَنِيَّةٌ; Plur. بَنَاتٌ; إِبْنَتَىْ oblique dual, My two daughters, see بَنِىٌّ. *Note.* In all these words the prefixed إ, when it does not begin a sentence, is marked with a wesla; D.S.Gr.T.1, p. 66. بِنَآءٌ A ceiled roof. بَنَّآءٌ A builder, architect. بُنْيَانٌ A building. مَبْنِىٌّ for مَبْنُوىٌ part. pass. Built, D. S. Gr. T. 1, p. 108.

بَهَتَ aor. a. To confound. بُهْتَانٌ Slander, calumny; the root of this word is said to be بَهَا *To be accustomed.*

بَهَجَ aor. a. *To make joyful.* بَهْجَةٌ Beauty, delight. بَهِيجٌ Beautiful, delicious.

بَهَلَ aor. a. *To leave one at liberty.*—إِبْتَهَلَ VIII. To invoke, imprecate (the wrath of God).

بَهَمَ *To wean lambs, or kids;* the first form is wanting. بَهِيمَةٌ An animal; بَهِيمَةُ ٱلْأَنْعَامِ Brute beasts, cattle: the logical root is بَهْمٌ *Lambs or kids.*

بَآءَ aor. o. for بَوَءَ *To bring back,* bring down, take upon one's-self (with بِ); to draw upon one's-self; Ex. فَقَدْ بَآءَ بِغَضَبٍ مِنَ ٱللّٰهِ 8 v. 16, "He will draw down on himself the wrath of God;" the preterite being used with a future signification; D. S. Gr. T. 1, p. 158.—بَوَّءَ II. To prepare a dwelling for, locate any one (with double acc. also with لِ of pers. and acc. of place, or acc. of pers. and فِى). مُبَوَّأٌ A place for dwelling in.—تَبَوَّءَ V. To take possession of, occupy a dwelling, provide a dwelling for one's-self (with acc. of thing and لِ of pers.). *Note.* بَآءَ is one of those verbs which are at the same time concave and hamzated; for the rules for the suppression (or otherwise) of the hamza see D. S. Gr. T. 1, p. 62, *et seq.*; and also the rules for the permutation of infirm letters.

بَابٌ Plur. أَبْوَابٌ A door, gate.

بَارَ aor. o. To perish, to be in vain. بُورٌ One who is lost, wicked. بَوَارٌ Perdition.

بَالَ aor. o. *To make water.* بَالٌ Heart, mind, thought, intention, condition.

بَاتَ aor. i. and a. To pass the night. بَيْتٌ Plur. بُيُوتٌ A house, abode, family. بَيَاتٌ A night attack.—بَيَّتَ II. To meditate by night, attack by night.

بَادَ aor. i. *To go away (from one's friends),* perish.

بَاضَ aor. i. *To excel in whiteness.* بَيْضٌ collective noun, Eggs; D. S. Gr. T. 1, p. 381. أَبْيَضُ, Fem. بَيْضَآءُ; Plur. بِيضٌ for بُيْضٌ D. S. Gr. T. 1, p. 360, White, clear.—إِبْيَضَّ IX. To become white (with مِنْ).

بَاعَ aor. i. *To sell.* بَيْعٌ n.a. Interchange by sale, selling, merchandizing, barter. بِيَعٌ plur. of بِيعَةٌ Churches.—بَايَعَ III. To make a contract with, *properly,* by striking hands (with accus. of person or بِ of thing; also with acc. of pers. and عَلَى أَنْ).—تَبَايَعَ VI. To sell to one another.

بَانَ aor. i. *To be distinct and separate.* بَيْنَ Between, as بَيْنَ يَدَيْهِ "Between his two hands," *i.e.* before him, in his presence; This word, though commonly used as a preposition, is properly a noun in the accus. meaning an interval, and sometimes a connexion; when preceded by a preposition it is declined, see D. S. Gr. T. 1, p. 498. بَيِّنٌ Manifest, evident. بَيِّنَةٌ An evident testimony or demonstration, evidence, proof. تِبْيَانٌ An exposition, explanation.—بَيَّنَ II. To show, make manifest, make known, declare, explain, become manifest (with acc. and لِ or with لِ of pers. and أَنْ). مُبَيِّنٌ part. act. manifest.—أَبَانَ IV. *To make manifest*, to articulate distinctly, see 43 v. 52. بَيَانٌ n.a. An argument, clear demonstration, eloquence, faculty of clearly explaining, explanation. مُبِينٌ part. act. That which is manifest, open, perspicuous.—تَبَيَّنَ V. To be or become manifest, clear (with لِ or أَنْ or with لِ and أَنْ); to be distinct (with مِنْ); to be made known (with لِ); to perceive, as تَبَيَّنَتِ ٱلْجِنُّ أَنْ 34 v. 13, "The Genii perceived that;" also, to use discernment, or discrimination, vid. 4 v. 96, and 49 v. 6.—إِسْتَبَانَ X. To be manifest. مُسْتَبِينٌ part. act. same as مُبِينٌ.

ت

ت By; preposition prefixed as a form of oath to the word أَللّٰهِ, as تَٱللّٰهِ "By God."

تَابُوتٌ An ark.

تَأْثِيمٌ n.a. ii. f. of أَثِمَ q.v.

تَأَخَّرَ v. f. of أَخِرَ q.v.

تَأَذَّنَ v. f. of أَذِنَ q.v.

تَأْسَ 2 pers. sing. aor. cond. of أَسِيَ q.v.

تَأْوِيلٌ n.a. ii. f. of آلَ for أَوَلَ q.v.

تَبَّ *To cut off*, perish. تَبَابٌ Loss.—تَتْبِيبٌ n.a. II. f. A loss, detriment.

تَبَارٌ see تَبَرَ.

تَبْتَئِسْ 2 pers. sing. aor. cond. viii. f. of بَئِسَ q.v.

تَبَرَ aor. i. *To break, destroy.* تَبَارٌ Destruction.—تَبَّرَ II. To break in pieces. تَتْبِيرٌ n.a. Utter destruction. مُتَبَّرٌ part. pass. Destroyed, broken up.

تَبَرَّأَ v. f. of بَرَأَ q.v.

تَبَرَّجَ v. f. of بَرَجَ q.v.

تَبَوَّأَ v. f. of بَآءَ q.v.

تَبِعَ aor. a. To follow. تَبَعٌ and تَابِعٌ A follower, one who follows, or attends upon any one. تُبَّعٌ Name and title of the king of the Himyarites. تَبِيعٌ A helper, protector.—أَتْبَعَ IV. To follow, follow up, make to follow (with double acc.); to pursue, prosecute, continue; Ex. فَأَتْبَعَ سَبَبًا 18 v. 83, "Then he continued his way."—مُتَتَابِعٌ part. act. VI. f. Successive.—إِتَّبَعَ VIII. To follow, follow up. إِتِّبَاعٌ n.a. A following after. مُتَّبَعٌ part. pass. One who is pursued.

تَبَيَّنَ v. f. of بَانَ q.v.

تَتْبِيبٌ n.a. ii. f. of تَبَّ q.v.

تَتْرًا or تَتْرَى fem. One after another; said to be derived from وَتْرٌ q.v. see D. S. Gr. T. 1, p. 293.

تَثْبِيتٌ n.a. ii. f. of ثَبَتَ q.v.

تَجَافَى vi. f. of جَفَا q.v.

تَجَرَ aor. o. *To traffic.* تِجَارَةٌ Merchandize, traffic, bargain, merchandizing.

تَجَسَّسَ v. f. of جَسَّ q.v.

تَجَلَّى v. f. of جَلَا q.v.

تَحَاضَّ vi. f. of حَضَّ q.v.

تَحَاوُرٌ n.a. vi. f. of حَارَ q.v.

تَحْتَ *That which is below, the lower part;* This word, which is properly a substantive, is used (*though not in the Korán*) as an adverb, and is then indeclinable, as تَحْتُ *Down, below;* When employed as a preposition it is put in the accus. تَحْتَ Beneath, as مَا تَحْتَ ٱلثَّرَى 20 v. 5, "That which is beneath the earth;" If preceded by مِنْ it is put in the genitive, as مِنْ تَحْتِهَا "From beneath it," see D. S. Gr. T. 1, p. 509, and T. 2, p. 152.

تَحَرَّى v. f. of حَرَى q.v.

تَحْرِيرٌ n.a. ii. f. of حَرَّ q.v.

تَحَسَّسَ v. f. of حَسَّ q.v.

تَحِلَّةٌ see حَلَّ.

تَحْوِيلٌ n.a. ii. f. of حَالَ q.v.

تَحِيَّةٌ see حَىَّ.

تَخَافَتَ vi. f. of خَفَتَ q.v.

تَخَلَّى v. f. of خَلَا q.v.

تَخَوُّفٌ see خَافَ.

تَدَلَّى v. f. of دَلَا q.v.

تَذْلِيلٌ n.a. ii. f. of ذَلَّ q.v.

تُرَاثٌ From وَرِثَ q.v. See also D. S. Gr. T. 1, p. 293.

تَرَاقِىَ acc. plur. of تَرْقُوَةٌ A breast-bone: It seems doubtful whether this word ought not to be derived from رَقِىَ q.v.

تَرِبَ *To have much earth, to hold earth in the hand.* تُرَابٌ Earth, dust. أَتْرَابٌ plur. of تِرْبٌ Of the same age. تَرَآئِبُ (2nd declension) plur. of تَرِيبَةٌ A breast-bone. مَتْرَبَةٌ Poverty; مِسْكِينًا ذَا مَتْرَبَةٍ 90 v. 16, "A poor man intimately acquainted with his mother Earth."

تَرَدَّدَ v. f. of رَدَّ q.v.

تُرْزَقَانِ see رَزَقَ.

تَرِفَ *To enjoy the good things of this life.*—أَتْرَفَ IV. To bestow the good things of this life (with acc. of pers. and فِى). مُتْرَفٌ part. pass. Endowed with—and hence, enjoying—the good things of this life.

تَرَكَ aor. o. To leave, leave alone, abandon (with acc. and عِنْدَ ,فِى ,عَلَى ,مِنْ خَلْفِهِ or); أَحَسِبَ ٱلنَّاسُ أَنْ يُتْرَكُوا أَنْ يَقُولُوا 29 v. 1, "Do men think that they shall be left alone in saying?" *i.e.* "That it is enough for them to say;" وَتَرَكْنَا عَلَيْهِ etc. 37 v. 76, "And we left (these words, or this blessing) upon him;" with an ellipse of هَذَا ٱلْكَلَامَ or similar words. تَارِكٌ part. act. One who leaves, or leaves out; تَارِكِى for تَارِكِينَ 11 v. 56, as being antecedent to the word آلِهَتِنَا, "We will not leave our Gods," D. S. Gr. T. 2, p. 183.

تَزَاوَرُ for تَتَزَاوَرُ, see زَارَ.

تَزْدَرِى 2 pers. sing. aor. viii. f. of زَرَا q.v.

تَزَوَّدَ v. f. of زَادَ for زَوَدَ q.v.

تَزَيَّلَ v. f. of زَالَ for زَيَلَ q.v.

تَسُبُّوا see سَبَّ.

تَسْتَفْتِيَانِ see فَتَا.

تِسْعٌ The number nine: For observations on the numerals, see عَشَرَ. تِسْعُونَ Ninety.

تُسَمَّى 2 pers. sing. aor. pass. ii. f. of سَمَا q.v.

تَسْنِيمٌ Tasneem, name of a fountain in Paradise, said to be so called, because conveyed to the highest part of heaven; from سَنِمَ To be tall (a camel).

تَسَوَّرَ v. f. of سَارَ for سَوَرَ q.v.

تَسُؤْ 3 pers. fem. sing. aor. cond. of سَآءَ q.v.

تُشَاقُّونَ 2 pers. plur. aor. act. iii. f. of شَقَّ q.v. N.B. There is no difference between the active and passive.

تَشَاوُرٌ see شَارَ.

تَصْدِيَةٌ n.a. ii. f. of صَدَا q.v.

تَصْلِيَةٌ n.a. ii. f. of صَلَى q.v.
تَصْطَلُونَ see إِصْطَلَى viii. f. of صَلَى.
تُطِعْ 2 pers. sing. aor. cond. iv. f. of طَاعَ q.v.
تَطْمَئِنَّ 2 pers. sing. aor. iv. f. of طَمْأَنَ quadriliteral verb, rt. طَمَنَّ q.v.
تَطَوَّعَ v. f. of طَاعَ q.v.
تَطَيَّرَ v. f. of طَارَ for طَيَرَ q.v.
تَعْدُ 2 pers. sing. aor. cond. of عَدَا q.v.
تَعَسَ *To perish.* تَعْسٌ n.a. Destruction; تَعْسًا لَهُمْ 47 v. 9, "May perdition seize them."
تَعَاطَى vi. f. of عَطَا q.v.
تَعَفُّفٌ n.a. v. f. of عَفَّ q.v.
تَغَابُنٌ n.a. vi. f. of غَبَنَ q.v.
تَغُرَّنَّ 3 pers. fem. sing. aor. energ. of غَرَّ q.v.
تَغَيُّظٌ n.a. v. f. of غَاظَ q.v.
تَفَاخُرٌ n.a. vi. f. of فَخَرَ q.v.
تَفَاوُتٌ n.a. vi. f. of فَاتَ q.v.
تَفَثَ *To perform the sacred rites at Mecca; also, to cleanse.* تَفَثٌ Two interpretations are given of this word; according to one it means filth, and according to the other, the observance of certain rites and ceremonies imposed upon the Pilgrims at Mecca, among which were cleansing the person, shaving, etc. Thus the phrase لِيَقْضُوا تَفَثَهُمْ 22 v. 30 may mean, "Let them put an end to their want of cleanliness," or, "Let them complete the rites" above mentioned.
تَفَكَّهُونَ see فَكِهَ.
تَقِ see وَقَى.
تُقَاةٌ see وَقَى.
تَقْشَعِرُّ see قُشَعْرٌ.
تِقْنٌ *Nature, mud.*—أَتْقَنَ IV. To establish firmly. This verb is not found in the primitive form.
تَقَوَّلَ v. f. of قَالَ q.v.

تَقْوَى n.a. of وَقَى q.v.
تَقْوِيمٌ n.a. ii. f. of قَامَ q.v.
تَقَى aor. i. *To fear.* أَتْقَى (2nd declension) comp. form, Greatly fearing, most pious. تَقِيٌّ God-fearing, devout. These words seem to owe their derivation to the viii. f. of وَقَى q.v.
تَكُ for تَكُنْ. 2 pers. sing. aor. cond. of كَانَ q.v.
تَكْوِيرٌ n.a. ii. f. of كَارَ q.v.
تَلَّ To lay prostrate (with acc. of pers. and لِ).
تَلَاقٍ n.a. vi. f. of لَقِيَ q.v.
تَلَظَّى v. f. of لَظِيَ q.v.
تِلْقَآءَ n.a. of لَقِيَ q.v.
تَلَقَّى v. f. of لَقِيَ q.v.
تِلْكَ fem. of ذَلِكَ q.v.
تَلَهَّى see لَهَا.
تَلَا aor. o. To follow, rehearse, read, declare, meditate (with acc. of thing and عَلَى of pers., also with acc. and فِي). *Note.* The ا called أَلِفُ ٱلْوِقَايَةِ, or Alif of precaution, is sometimes found added to the words يَتْلُو and تَتْلُو, though properly only added to servile و to distinguish it from وَ *and*, D. S. Gr. T. 1, p. 109. أَلتَّالِيَاتُ fem. plur. of تَالٍ part. act. "Those who read." تِلَاوَةٌ n.a. A reading.
تَلْوُوا see لَوَى.
تَمَّ aor. i. To be entire, complete, perfect, fulfilled (with عَلَى of pers.).—أَتَمَّ IV. To complete (with acc. and إِلَى or بِ of thing, also with acc. and إِلَى, عَلَى, or لِ of pers.); to perfect, accomplish, fulfil, perform. تَمَامٌ n.a. Something complete, perfect; Ex. آتَيْنَا مُوسَى ٱلْكِتَابَ تَمَامًا 6 v. 155, "We gave Moses the Book, a perfect Law," etc. مُتِمٌّ part. act. One who makes perfect.

تَمَاثِيلُ plur. of تِمْثَالٌ, see مَثَلَ.

تَمَارَى vi. f. of مَرَى q.v.

تَمْتَرُونَ 2 pers. plur. aor. viii. f. of مَرَى q.v.

تَمَتَّعَ v. f. of مَتَعَ q.v.

تَمَطَّى v. f. of مَطَا q.v.

تَمَنَّى v. f. of مَنَى q.v.

تَمِيدَ see مَادَ.

تَمَيَّزُ for تَتَمَيَّزُ, see مَازَ.

تَنَابَزَ vi. f. of نَبَزَ q.v.

تَنَاجَى vi. f. of نَجَا q.v.

تَنَازَعَ vi. f. of نَزَعَ q.v.

تَنَاوُشٌ n.a. vi. f. of نَاشَ q.v.

تَنْزِيلٌ n.a. ii. f. of نَزَلَ q.v.

تَنَفَّسَ v. f. of نَفَسَ q.v.

تَنْكِيلٌ n.a. ii. f. of نَكَلَ q.v.

تَنُّورٌ An oven (*a word of foreign origin*); it also means a place whence waters gush forth.

تَنِيَا see وَنَى.

تَهِنُوا see وَهَنَ.

تَوَارَى vi. f. of وَرَى q.v.

تَوَاصَى vi. f. of وَصَى q.v.

تَابَ aor. o. To repent towards God (with إِلَى); to turn one's-self in a repentant manner; to relent towards men,—as God,—(with عَلَى). تَوْبٌ and تَوْبَةٌ Repentance. تَائِبٌ part. act. One who repents. تَوَّابٌ Very repentant, relenting. مَتَابٌ A penitent conversion; إِلَيْهِ مَتَابِ 13 v. 29, "Unto him must be my conversion;" مَتَابِ is here put for مَتَابِي, D. S. Gr. T. 1, p. 459.

تُؤْذُونَنِي see أَذِيَ.

تَارَ for دَارَ *To go round.* تَارَةٌ A time.

تَوْرَاةٌ The Pentateuch.

تُورُونَ see وَرَى.

تَوَفَّنِي see وَفَى.

تَوْفِيقٌ see وَفِقَ.

تَوْكِيدٌ n.a. ii. f. of وَكَدَ q.v.

تَوَكَّلَ v. f. of وَكَلَ q.v.

تَوَلَّى v. f. of وَلِيَ q.v.

تُؤْوِي see أَوَى.

تَيَمَّمَ v. f. of يَمَّ q.v.

تِينٌ A fig; no verbal root.

تَاهَ aor. i. To wander about distractedly (with فِي).

ث

ثَبَتَ To be firm, steadfast, constant. ثَابِتٌ part. act. Remaining firmly fixed, firm, steadfast. ثُبُوتٌ Steadfast, fixing.—ثَبَّتَ II. To confirm, set fast, establish (with acc. and بِ). تَثْبِيتٌ n.a. A confirmation, establishment.—أَثْبَتَ IV. To confirm; to keep in bonds, 8 v. 30.

ثُبَاتٌ see ثَبَى.

ثَبَرَ aor. o. *To keep back, lose, perish.* ثُبُورٌ Destruction. مَثْبُورٌ part. pass. One who is lost.

ثَبَطَ *To keep back, hinder.*—ثَبَّطَ II. To make slothful.

ثَبَى *To collect, congregate.* ثُبَاتٍ 4 v. 72, "In bodies;" accus. plur. of ثُبَةٌ the fem. of ثُبَى for ثُبَيٌ A company or body of men. *Note.* Many nouns in the fem. sing. lose their third Radical when it is ء, و, or ي; where they take the regular form of Plural this Radical is sometimes omitted, and sometimes retained; see D. S. Gr. T. 1, p. 358.

ثَجَّ aor. o. *To flow.* ثَجَّاجٌ Pouring forth abundantly.

ثَخُنَ *To be thick.*—أَثْخَنَ IV. *To do something great,* make a great slaughter (with فِى); slay in great numbers (with acc. of pers.).

ثَرَبَ aor. i. *To blame.*—تَثْرِيبٌ n.a. II. f. Blame.

ثَرِىَ *To be moist, as the earth after rain.* ثَرًى for ثَرَىٌ and ثَرَيٌ, and with the article اَلثَّرَى The Earth.

ثَعَبَ *To cause to flow.* ثُعْبَانٌ A serpent.

ثَقَبَ aor. o. *To perforate, penetrate, shine.* ثَاقِبٌ part. act. Shining; اَلنَّجْمُ ٱلثَّاقِبُ 86 v. 3, "The star of piercing brightness," by some supposed to be Saturn, which is called اَلثَّاقِبُ.

ثَقِفَ aor. a. To find, catch, take, gain the mastery over (with accus. of pers.).

ثَقُلَ To be heavy, grievous; to be a grievous matter (with فِى). اَلثَّقَلَانِ generally interpreted to mean "men and genii," as at 55 v. 31, dual of ثَقَلٌ *Baggage.* أَثْقَالٌ plur. of ثِقْلٌ A burden. ثَقِيلٌ Heavy; Plur. ثِقَالٌ. مِثْقَالٌ A weight.—أَثْقَلَ IV. To grow heavy, oppress, weigh down. مُثْقَلٌ Fem. مُثْقَلَةٌ part. pass. Burdened; إِنْ تَدْعُ مُثْقَلَةٌ 35 v. 19, "If a burdened (soul) cry out;" the word نَفْسٌ being understood.—إِثَّاقَلَ for تَثَاقَلَ VI. To be borne down heavily, incline heavily downwards (with إِلَى); For the employment of those forms which take teschdeed on the first Radical, see D. S. Gr. T. 1, p. 220.

ثَلَّ *To perish.* ثُلَّةٌ A crowd, a number of people.

ثَلَثَ aor. o. *To take a third part of anything.* ثَلَٰثٌ and ثَلَٰثَةٌ Three (see عَشَرَ). ثَلَٰثُونَ Thirty. ثُلُثٌ One third part; Dual ثُلُثَانِ and in conjunction ثُلُثَا and ثُلُثَىِ Two-thirds, D. S. Gr. T. 1, p. 415. ثَالِثٌ Fem. ثَالِثَةٌ Third. ثُلَٰثَ Three by three, in threes, or three pairs; Ex. أُولِى أَجْنِحَةٍ مَّثْنَى وَثُلَٰثَ وَرُبَٰعَ 35 v. 1, "Having two and three and four pairs of wings;" At 4 v. 3 ثُلَٰثَ may be rendered "By threes;" This word is of the second declension, it answers to the Latin *Ternus;* D. S. Gr. T. 1, p. 426.

ثَمَّ aor. o. *To tread.* ثَمَّ There, in that direction. ثُمَّ Then (after an interval).

ثَمُودُ Thamood, name of an ancient tribe of Pagan Arabians, destroyed for their impiety. This word in the Korân is always of the 2nd declension; see D. S. Gr. T. 1, p. 405.

ثَمَرَ *To bear fruit.* ثَمَرٌ Fruit, wealth, possessions. ثَمَرَةٌ A fruit; noun of unity or individuality; see D. S. Gr. T. 1, p. 300.—أَثْمَرَ IV. To bear fruit.

ثَمَنَ aor. o. *To take the eighth part.* ثَمَنٌ A price. ثُمُنٌ One part out of eight. ثَامِنٌ The eighth. ثَمَانٍ (for ثَمَانِىٌ) fem. and ثَمَانِيَةٌ masc. Eight; see عَشَرَ, see also مَثَانٍ, rt. ثنى. ثَمَانُونَ Eighty.

ثَنَى aor. a. and i. *To bend,* fold, double. ثَانٍ for ثَانِىٌ The second; also part. act. Turning, as ثَانِىَ عِطْفِهِ 22 v. 9, "One who turns his side," or "A turner of his side," *i.e.* Proud. إِثْنَانِ masc. and إِثْنَتَانِ fem., and in the oblique cases إِثْنَيْنِ and إِثْنَتَيْنِ Two. إِثْنَا عَشَرَ masc. and إِثْنَتَا عَشْرَةَ fem., and in the oblique cases إِثْنَىْ عَشَرَ and إِثْنَتَىْ عَشْرَةَ Twelve; These forms which admit only the above inflexions are considered as adverbial expressions; D. S. Gr. T. 1, p. 420. مَثْنَى By twos, in pairs, two and two; another form of this numeral (but not found in the Ḳorân) is ثُنَآءَ; These forms are equivalent to the Latin *Binus;* see ثُلَاثُ. مَثَانٍ and with the article اَلْمَثَانِى A name given either to the whole Ḳorân, or to those passages which are frequently repeated; some interpret it to mean the first chapter, as at 15 v. 87, آتَيْنَاكَ سَبْعًا مِنَ ٱلْمَثَانِى "We have given thee seven (verses) of those which are to be frequently repeated;" others interpret it to mean the seven long chapters. مَثَانٍ for مَثَانِىُ without the nunnation (Sing. مَثْنَى), is one of those irregular plurals which are of the second declension, with this peculiarity, that in the nominative and genitive they preserve the tanween, as مَثَانٍ, but reject it in the accusative, as مَثَانِىَ; the latter word occurs at 39 v. 24, where it may be rendered "double or repeated portions;" see D. S. Gr. T. 1, pp. 410 and 111 § 226. The rule as given by the grammarian Moṭarrezëe is as follows: Speaking of those irregular plurals which are of the second declension he says, "If the second of the two letters which follow Alif quiescent happen to be a ي it is suppressed in the nom. and gen. and the tanween is affixed, but in the accus. يَ is retained without tanween." For an explanation of the passage at 39 v. 24 see مُتَشَابِهٌ, rt. شِبْهٌ. *Note.* Other singulars have also been assigned to مَثَانٍ, as مُثَنًّى, مَثْنَى, or مَثْنٍ.—إِسْتَثْنَى X. To make an exception, as وَلَا يَسْتَثْنُونَ 68 v. 18, "And they did not make an exception" (by saying إِنْ شَآءَ ٱللّٰهُ).

ثَابَ aor. o. *To return.* ثَوَابٌ A reward. ثِيَابٌ plur. of ثَوْبٌ Raiment. مَثَابَةٌ A place of resort. مَثُوبَةٌ A reward, recompense.—ثَوَّبَ II. To repay (with double acc.).—أَثَابَ IV. To reward with, give as a recompense (with double acc.).

ثَارَ aor. o. *To be stirred up* (*as dust*).—أَثَارَ IV. To plough, break up the earth, excite, raise (as dust, clouds, etc.).

ثَوَى aor. i. *To abide in a place.* ثَاوٍ for ثَاوِىٌ part. act. A dweller. مَثْوَى A dwelling, abode; أَكْرِمِى مَثْوَاهُ 12 v. 21, "Make his abode honourable;" see D. S. Gr. T. 1, p. 118.

ثَيَّبَ (no first form) *To have connexion, as a husband and wife.* ثَيِّبٌ A woman who has left her husband after the first interview.

ج

جَأَرَ aor. a. *To low,* supplicate God with groaning (with إِلَى of pers.).

جَالُوتُ (2nd declension) Goliath.

جَبَّ *To cut off.* جُبٌّ A well, cistern.

جِبْتٌ Jibt, An idol, false deity.

جَبَرَ *To bind, make fast.* جَبَّارٌ Strong, powerful, gigantic, having absolute power, proud, perverse. اَلْجَبَّارُ The Mighty One, a name of the Deity.

جِبْرِيلُ The Angel Gabriel.

جَبَلَ aor. i. and o. *To form, create.* جَبَلٌ Plur. جِبَالٌ A mountain, and especially Mount Sinai. جِبِلٌّ and جِبِلَّةٌ A crowd, multitude; اَلْجِبِلَّةَ ٱلْأَوَّلِينَ 26 v. 184, "The former generations;" see D. S. Gr. T. 2, p. 268.

جَبُنَ *To be cowardly.* جَبِينٌ *Cowardly;* the temple, side of the forehead.

جَبَهَ aor. a. *To strike on the forehead.* جِبَاهٌ plur. of جَبْهَةٌ A forehead.

جَبَا for جَبَأَ aor. a. and i. To collect or gather tribute, or as tribute (with إِلَى of place). اَلْجَوَابِ Poet. licence for اَلْجَوَابِى plur. of جَابِيَةٌ A cistern, see جَوَارٍ, rt. جَرَى; see also إِجْتَبَى—.ثَنَى, rt. مَثَانِى VIII. To choose (with acc. and مِنْ or إِلَى).

جَثَّ *To cut off.*—إِجْتَثَّ VIII. To tear up, root up (with acc. and مِنْ فَوْقِ).

جَثَمَ aor. i. and o. *To lie with the breast on the ground.* جَاثِمٌ part. act. One lying on his breast.

جَثَا aor. i. and o. *To kneel.* جَاثٍ Fem. جَاثِيَةٌ part. act. Kneeling; The Plur. is جِثِىٌّ for جُثُوٌّ, D. S. Gr. T. 1, pp. 108 and 362.

جَحَدَ To deny, refuse, reject (with بِ).

جَحَمَ aor. a. *To light a fire.* جَحِيمٌ fem. Hell, hell-fire, any fiercely burning fire.

جَدَّ aor. i. *To be of great wealth or dignity.* جَدٌّ Majesty, glory. جَدِيدٌ New. جُدَدٌ plur. of جُدَّةٌ A track or way on a hill-side.

جَدَثٌ Plur. أَجْدَاثٌ A sepulchre; no verbal root.

جَدَرَ *To be covered with pustules,* to fence in. جِدَارٌ Plur. جُدُرٌ A wall. أَجْدَرُ More fitting or easier, compar. form (2nd declension), D. S. Gr. T. 1, p. 403.

جَدَلَ aor. i. and o. *To twist firmly.* جَدَلًا In a contentious manner; مَا ضَرَبُوهُ لَكَ إِلَّا جَدَلًا 45 v. 58, "They only propounded this to thee in the hope of a dispute." جِدَالٌ A dispute.—جَادَلَ III. To dispute (with بِ of means and فِى or عَنْ of subject); to dispute with (with acc. of pers.), as لِيُجَادِلُوكُمْ 6 v. 121, "That they should dispute with you;" أَتُجَادِلُونَنِى 7 v. 69, "Will ye dispute with me?" مُجَادِلَةٌ part. act. fem. One who disputes.

جَذَّ *To hasten.* جُذَاذٌ A broken piece; جُذَاذًا In fragments. مَجْذُوذٌ part. pass. Broken; غَيْرَ مَجْذُوذٍ Uninterrupted.

جَذَعَ *To keep without food, amputate.* جِذْعٌ Plur. جُذُوعٌ The trunk of a Palm-tree.

جَذَا aor. o. *To stand firm.* جَذْوَةٌ A burning coal or firebrand.

جَرَّ aor. o. To draw, drag (with acc. and إِلَى).

جَرَحَ *To wound,* gain, acquire for one's-self. جُرُوحٌ plur. of جُرْحٌ A wound. جَوَارِحُ (2nd declension) plur. of جَارِحَةٌ Beasts of prey.—إِجْتَرَحَ VIII. To endeavour to acquire; اَلَّذِينَ اجْتَرَحُوا السَّيِّآتِ 45 v. 20, "Those who seek to do evil."

جَرَدَ *To tear off.* جَرَادٌ comm. gend. noun of species, A locust.

جَرَزَ aor. o. *To cut off.* جُرُزٌ Dry (ground) bare of herbage.

جَرَعَ *To drink (water).*—تَجَرَّعَ V. To sip.

جَرَفَ aor. o. *To carry off the whole of anything.* جُرُفٌ A water-worn bank of earth.

جَرَمَ aor. i. *To commit a crime,* to drive one (into sin, with أَنْ of following verb). جُرْمٌ A sin; لَا جَرَمَ No doubt! An adverbial expression, D. S. Gr. T. 1, p. 521.—أَجْرَمَ IV. To be guilty of sin. إِجْرَامٌ n.a. Sin. مُجْرِمٌ part. act. A sinner.

جَرَى aor. i. To flow, run, happen (with لِ, also with فِى or إِلَى). جَارِيَةٌ part. act. fem. Running, a vessel; The Ark, 69 v. 11; Plur. جَوَارٍ, and with the article اَلْجَوَارِى, for which by Poetic licence is substituted ٱلْجَوَارِ both in the nominative and genitive cases, see note on مَثَانِى, rt. ثَنَى; see also D. S. Gr. T. 2, p. 497. مَجْرَى for مَجْرًى D. S. Gr. T. 1, p. 111, The course of a ship, as مَجْرَاهَا 11 v. 43, "During her course;" D. S. Gr. T. 1, p. 118.

جَزَأَ aor. a. *To take a part of anything.* جُزْءٌ A part, portion, individuality; At 43 v. 14 the word جُزْءًا is by some taken to mean "Daughters."

جَزَعَ *To pass over;* and جَزِعَ To be impatient. جَزُوعًا Impatiently.

جَزَا aor. o. *To subdue;* and جَزَى aor. i. To satisfy, recompense for good or evil, give as a reward (with double acc. or with acc. or بِ of thing for which reward, etc. is given); to give an equivalent, or make satisfaction for (with عَنْ or with double acc.). جَازٍ for جَازِىٌ part. act. One who makes satisfaction for another (with عَنْ). جَزَآءٌ Compensation, satisfaction, equivalent, retribution, reward. جِزْيَةٌ Tribute, especially that exacted from Jews and Christians.—جَازَى III. To reward.

جَسَّ aor. o. *To handle.*—تَجَسَّسَ V. To inquire curiously into (by handling, etc.).

جَسِدَ *To stick to the body (blood).* جَسَدٌ n.a. A body; عِجْلًا جَسَدًا 7 v. 146, "A calf in a bodily shape."

جَسُمَ *To have a large body.* جِسْمٌ A body, Plur. أَجْسَامٌ; أَجْسَامُهُمْ 63 v. 4, "Their Persons."

جَعَلَ aor. a. To place, put, impose, make, appoint, constitute, ordain, attribute (with لِ of pers. and acc. of thing or with double acc. also with acc. and فِى, عَلَى, or مِنْ); to hold, regard or esteem, as at 29 v. 9; Used with أَنْ of following verb at 56 v. 81. جَاعِلٌ part. act. He who places, etc.

جَفَأَ *To cast scum and foam upon the bank (a river).* جُفَآءٌ Froth, as يَذْهَبُ جُفَآءً 13 v. 18, "It passes off like froth."

جَفَنَ *To serve up camel's flesh in a large dish.* جِفَانٌ plur. of جَفْنَةٌ A large dish, trencher.

جَفَا aor. o. and i. *To treat harshly.*—تَجَافَى VI. To be removed from (with عَنْ).

جَلَّ aor. i. *To be glorious.* جَلَالٌ Majesty.

جَلَبَ aor. i. and o. *To drag, excite.*—أَجْلَبَ IV. To attack, assault (with عَلَى).

جَلْبَبَ *To put on a* جِلْبَابٌ. جَلَابِيبُ (2nd declension) plur. of جِلْبَابٌ A large outer covering worn by women.

جَلَدَ aor. i. *To wound the skin,* scourge. جَلْدَةٌ n.a. A flogging, blow with a rod. جِلْدٌ Plur. جُلُودٌ Skins, hides.

جَلَسَ *To sit in Eastern fashion,* in which respect it differs from قَعَدَ. مَجَالِسُ (2nd declension) plur. of مَجْلِسٌ A place of sitting or assembly.

جَلَا aor. o. *To be clear and manifest.* جَلَآءٌ Banishment.—جَلَّى II. To make manifest, reveal; وَٱلنَّهَارِ إِذَا جَلَّاهَا 91 v. 3, "By the day when it reveals her (the Sun) in all her splendour."—تَجَلَّى V. To appear in glory (with لِ).

جَمَّ aor. i. and o. *To abound.* جَمٌّ Much.

جَمَحَ aor. a. To be refractory.

جَمَدَ aor. o. *To congeal, to be firm.* جَامِدَةٌ part. act. That which is firmly fixed.

جَمَعَ aor. a. To collect, gather together, assemble, unite; to have connexion with, marry (with بَيْنَ), as وَأَنْ تَجْمَعُوا بَيْنَ ٱلْأُخْتَيْنِ 4 v. 27, "(It is forbidden you) to take two sisters to wife," or "intermarry;" to gather together—against, with acc. and لِ;—at, with acc. of pers. and

ل or إِلَى of time; it is also used with acc. and عَلَى as at 6 v. 35, and with بَيْنَ of persons assembled as at 34 v. 25. جَمْعٌ n.a. An assembly, multitude, a gathering together, crowd; أَكْثَرُ جَمْعًا 28 v. 78, "Who have amassed (wealth) more abundantly;" *Literally*, "more abundant in amassing (wealth);" يَوْمَ ٱلْتَقَى ٱلْجَمْعَانِ 3 v. 149, "The day of the meeting of the two hosts;" عَلَيْنَا جَمْعَهُ وَقُرْآنَهُ 75 v. 17, "Upon us devolves the collection (of its scattered sentences), and the proper method of reading it." جَامِعٌ part. act. One who gathers together, etc. جُمُعَةٌ A congregation, as يَوْمُ ٱلْجُمُعَةِ The day of the congregation, Friday. جَمِيعٌ Collected, assembled, all, an army; At 36 v. 32 جَمِيعٌ is used for مَجْمُوعٌ, see D. S. Gr. T. 1, p. 540, *note*: جَمِيعًا adverbially, Altogether, wholly. أَجْمَعُ Plur. أَجْمَعُونَ All, The whole. مَجْمَعٌ A place of meeting together. مَجْمُوعٌ part. pass. Assembled.— أَجْمَعَ IV. To agree together, concert a plan or design (with أَنْ of following verb); to agree upon (with acc.).— إِجْتَمَعَ VIII. To be gathered together (with لِ); conspire (with عَلَى). مُجْتَمِعٌ part. act. Gathered together.

جَمَلَ aor. o. *To collect*; and جَمُلَ *To be handsome*. جَمَلٌ A camel. جَمَالٌ Grace, elegance; لَكُمْ فِيهَا جَمَالٌ 16 v. 6, "They are a credit to you." جَمِيلٌ Becoming, decorous, honourable, gracious. جُمْلَةٌ An aggregate, something complete, as a sentence; جُمْلَةً وَاحِدَةً 25 v. 34, "As one complete and perfect whole." جِمَالَةٌ plur. of جَمَلٌ A camel.

جَنَّ aor. i. *To be covered*; aor. o. To cover (with عَلَى). جِنٌّ collective noun, Genii, demons, spirits, as opposed to men. جَنَّةٌ Plur. جَنَّاتٌ A garden, Paradise. جُنَّةٌ A covering, cloak. جِنَّةٌ Madness, frenzy; used also in a collective sense, or as plur. of جِنٌّ Genii; see D. S. Gr. T. 1, p. 382. أَجِنَّةٌ plur. of جَنِينٌ Anything covered, a fœtus. جَانٌّ A serpent, genius, demon; ٱلْجَانُّ 15 v. 27, for أَبُو ٱلْجِنِّ "The Father of Devils;" or the part for the whole, Jinn or Genii. مَجْنُونٌ part. pass. Mad, possessed of the Devil.

جَنَبَ aor. i. and o. To turn aside, cause to turn from or avoid (with acc. and أَنْ lest). جَنْبٌ Plur. جُنُوبٌ A side; ٱلصَّاحِبِ بِٱلْجَنْبِ 4 v. 40, "The familiar friend;" مَا فَرَّطْتُ فِى جَنْبِ ٱللّٰهِ 39 v. 57, "What I have neglected (of my duty) towards God." جُنُبٌ A stranger, coming from afar, One suffering from pollution; عَنْ جُنُبٍ 28 v. 10, "From afar off." جَانِبٌ A side, tract of country; نَأَى بِجَانِبِهِ 17 v. 85, "He drew aside."— جَنَّبَ II. To cause to turn aside, remove away from (with double acc.).— تَجَنَّبَ V. To turn away or withdraw one's-self from (with acc.).— إِجْتَنَبَ VIII. To turn aside from, avoid.

جَنَحَ aor. a. i. and o. To incline (with لِ). جَنَاحٌ comm. gend. Plur. أَجْنِحَةٌ A hand, wing, arm, arm-pit; وَٱخْفِضْ جَنَاحَكَ 15 v. 88, "And behave with humility;" *Literally*, "Lower thy wing." جُنَاحٌ A crime.

جُنْدٌ Plur. جُنُودٌ An army, troops, forces, a host, companions; no verbal root.

جَنَفَ aor. i. *To decline*; and جَنِفَ aor. a. *To deviate (from the truth)*. جَنَفٌ n.a. A swerving from the right way.— مُتَجَانِفٌ part. act. VI. f. Inclining to evil (with لِ).

جَنَى aor. i. *To gather (fruit).* جَنًى for جَنَى Fruit; as جَنَى ٱلْجَنَّتَيْنِ 55 v. 54, "The fruit of the two gardens," D. S. Gr. T. 1, p. 110. جَنِيٌّ Fresh (dates) ready gathered.

جَهَدَ aor. a. *To be diligent.* جَهْدٌ n.a. A striving with might and main; The words جَهْدَ أَيْمَانِهِمْ at 5 v. 58 and elsewhere may be translated "Their most binding oaths." جُهْدٌ Power, ability; لَا يَجِدُونَ إِلَّا جُهْدَهُمْ 9 v. 80, "They find nothing (to give) but the fruit of their labour."—جَاهَدَ III. To strive, contend with, fight—especially against the enemies of Islàm —(with acc. of pers. and عَلَى أَنْ, as at 31 v. 14, also with بِ, فِى, or لِ). جِهَادٌ n.a. A contending, striving, a going forth to fight (in the Holy War). مُجَاهِدٌ part. act. One who strives, one who goes forth to fight in the cause of Islàm.

جَهَرَ aor. a. To be manifest, publish abroad, speak aloud (with بِ of thing and لِ of pers.). جَهْرٌ That which is manifest, loud speaking, open and public speaking. جَهْرًا Openly, publicly. جَهْرَةً Openly, visibly, manifestly. —جِهَارًا n.a. III. f. In public, openly.

جَهَزَ aor. a. *To rush on a wounded man with intent to slay him.* جَهَازٌ Paraphernalia, things necessary for a journey.—جَهَّزَ II. To fit out with provisions or other necessaries (with acc. of pers. and بِ of thing).

جَهِلَ aor. a. To be ignorant. جَاهِلٌ part. act. One who is ignorant. جَهُولٌ Very ignorant and foolish. جَهَالَةٌ Ignorance. جَاهِلِيَّةٌ State of ignorance, condition of the Pagan Arabs before the time of Mohammad.

جَهَنَّمُ fem. Hell, Gehenna, from the Hebrew גֵּיא הִנֹּם The Valley of Hinnom, where human sacrifices were made by fire to Moloch: This word on account of its foreign origin and feminine gender is of the second declension; D. S. Gr. T. 1, p. 404.

جَوٌّ Air, The Firmament.

جَبَا see جَوَابِ.

جَرَى see جَوَارٍ.

جَرَحَ see جَوَارِحُ.

جَابَ aor. o. To split, cleave, cut out. جَوَابٌ An answer, see iv. f.—أَجَابَ IV. To return an answer, hence, to hearken to (with acc. of pers. or thing). مُجِيبٌ part. act. One who returns an answer, as فَلَنِعْمَ ٱلْمُجِيبُونَ 37 v. 73, "And verily we returned a gracious answer;" *Literally,* "And verily they who gave the answer were gracious."—إِسْتَجَابَ X. To respond (with لِ of pers. and أَنْ), to answer, hearken to (with لِ of pers. or بِ).

جَادَ aor. o. *To be good.* جِيَادٌ plur. of جَوَادٌ Swift coursers. جُودِىٌّ "El Judée," A name of Mount Ararat.

جَارَ aor. o. *To turn aside.* جَارٌ Near, one who is near, a neighbour. جَائِرٌ part. act. One who turns aside.—جَاوَرَ III. To be a neighbour, to dwell near (with acc. and فِى).—أَجَارَ IV. To protect, deliver—from punishment, etc.—(with acc. of pers. and مِنْ); وَلَا يُجَارُ عَلَيْهِ 23 v. 90, "Neither is he protected of any;" *Literally,* "Neither is it protected over him," or "is any protection (thrown) over him:" for the use of Passive Verbs in an impersonal manner see D. S. Gr. T. 2, p. 129; see also at جِىءٌ.—مُتَجَاوِرٌ part. act. VI. f. Near to one another.—إِسْتَجَارَ X. To ask for protection.

جَازَ aor. o. *To go.*—جَاوَزَ III. To pass on or over,

to cause to pass over (with بِ of pers. and acc. of thing).—تَجَاوَزَ VI. To pass by or over (with عَنْ).

جَاسَ aor. o. To search, explore.

جَاعَ aor. o. To hunger. جُوعٌ Hunger.

جَافَ aor. o. *To penetrate inwardly, to be hollow.* جَوْفٌ The belly, the interior.

جَآءَ aor. i. To come, come to, arrive at (with acc. or with لِ, إِلَى, مِنْ, or عَلَى); with بِ it means to come with, *i.e.* to bring; Like أَتَى it may sometimes be rendered to do or commit (an action), as at 18 v. 70; Pass. جِيءَ sometimes written جِىٓءَ for جِيءَ, as وَجِىٓءَ بِٱلنَّبِيِّينَ 39 v. 69, "And the prophets shall be brought." *Note.* In the above form of construction the verb is impersonal, like *Ventum est* in Latin; see D. S. Gr. T. 2, p. 129.—أَجَآءَ IV. To make to come; hence, to lead or drive (with acc. of pers. and إِلَى).

جَابَ aor. i. *To cut out a garment at the neck.* جَيْبٌ Plur. جُيُوبٌ The bosom of a shirt or vest.

جَادَ for جَيِدَ aor. a. D. S. Gr. T. 1, p. 243, *To have a long and beautiful neck.* جِيدٌ A neck.

ح

حَبَّ aor. i. *To love.* حَبٌّ Grain, corn. حَبَّةٌ noun of unity, One grain. حُبٌّ Love; عَلَى حُبِّهِ 2 v. 172, "Out of love for him," *i.e.* "for God." أَحَبُّ comparative adjective of the 2nd declension, D. S. Gr. T. 1, pp. 324 and 403, More beloved, more pleasing, preferable. أَحِبَّآءُ and with the affixed pronoun أَحِبَّآؤُهُ, the hamza being changed into و with damma in the middle of a word, D. S. Gr. T. 1, p. 118, plur. of حَبِيبٌ Beloved. مَحَبَّةٌ Love.—حَبَّبَ II. To render lovely (with acc. of thing and إِلَى of pers.).—أَحَبَّ IV. To love, will, desire, like (with acc. or with أَنْ of following verb).—إِسْتَحَبَّ X. To love, prefer (with acc. and عَلَى).

حَبَرَ aor. o. *To make beautiful,* delight, make joyful. أَحْبَارٌ plur. of حَبْرٌ or حِبْرٌ A (Jewish) Priest or Doctor.

حَبَسَ aor. i. To restrain, hinder, shut up.

حَبِطَ aor. a. To be vain, fruitless, to perish (with عَنْ or فِى).—أَحْبَطَ IV. To render vain; وَسَيُحْبِطُ 47 v. 34, aor. with وَ and سَ prefixed, "And he shall make (their works) of no avail."

حَبَكَ aor. i. and a. *To weave well (a garment).* حُبُكٌ plur. of حِبَاكٌ A way or track; *especially,* the paths of the Stars.

حَبَلَ *To take a wild beast with a snare or halter.* حَبْلٌ n.a. Plur. حِبَالٌ A rope, vein, compact, or covenant.

حَتَمَ aor. i. *To inspire.* حَتْمٌ n.a. A decree.

حَتَّى Even to, up to, down to, as far as, until, in order that; This particle is used in four different ways.

1st. It is used as a preposition to indicate a certain term, and when thus employed governs the genitive case, as حَتَّى مَطْلَعِ ٱلْفَجْرِ 97 v. 5, "Until the time of the rising of the dawn."

2ndly. As a conjunction or adverb, meaning "and even," or "up to an extreme point inclusive;" thus it differs from إِلَى, which signifies "Up to," or "As far as, but not including;" Ex. أَكَلْتُ ٱلسَّمَكَةَ حَتَّى رَأْسَهَا "I ate the fish, head and all;" if we say إِلَى رَأْسِهَا we mean "as far as the head, and no further:" No instance of this use of حَتَّى occurs in the Korân.

3rdly. As a conjnnction serving to connect a proposition with that which precedes it; it then means "until," and has grammatically no effect on the succeeding proposition; thns at 6 v. 149, كَذَٰلِكَ كَذَّبَ ٱلَّذِينَ مِنْ قَبْلِهِمْ حَتَّى ذَاقُوا بَأْسَنَا "In like manner did they who went before them accuse (the prophets) of falsehood, until they tasted onr severity." *Note.* In the Korân it is freqnently followed by إِذَا; D. S. Gr. T. 1, pp. 175 and 202, *note.*

Lastly. It governs a verb in the subjunctive mood, when that verb has a futnre signification; it then means "until," or "in order that;" Ex. فَلَنْ أَبْرَحَ ٱلْأَرْضَ حَتَّى يَأْذَنَ لِي أَبِي 12 v. 80, "I will on no account quit the conntry, until my Father give me permission;" It may sometimes bear either interpretation; thus at 49 v. 9, فَقَاتِلُوا ٱلَّتِي تَبْغِي حَتَّى تَفِيءَ إِلَى أَمْرِ ٱللَّهِ "Then fight against (that party) which is in the wrong, until (or so that) they return to obedience to God."

حَثَّ *To excite.* حَثِيثًا Qnickly.

حَجَّ *To contend with,* go on a pilgrimage to (with acc.). حَجٌّ n.a. The pilgrimage to Mecca. حِجٌّ same as حَجٌّ. حَاجٌّ part. act. One who performs the pilgrimage. حَجِيجٌ plnr. of حِجَّةٌ *A single pilgrimage,* a year. حُجَّةٌ A dispnting, cause of dispute, argument; as ٱلْحُجَّةُ ٱلْبَالِغَةُ 6 v. 150, "The conclnsive argument."—حَاجَّ III. To dispnte abont (with فِي); to dispute with (with acc. of pers. and فِي or عِنْدَ).—تَحَاجَّ VI. To dispnte with one another (with فِي).

حَجَبَ *To cover, shut out.* حِجَابٌ A veil, curtain. مَحْجُوبٌ part. pass. Shut ont (with عَنْ).

حَجَرَ aor. o. *To hinder* (with عَلَى). حِجْرٌ n.a. Anything forbidden, unlawful, a wall or dam, understanding; Plur. حُجُورٌ A bosom, guardianship; لِذِي ٱلْحِجْرِ 89 v. 4, "For one gifted with intelligence." ٱلْحِجْرُ The conntry inhabited by the trihe of Thamood; The words حِجْرًا مَحْجُورًا occur twice in the 25th chap.; in the 24th verse they appear to mean "Far be it from ns," like "Ne licitum sit;" In the 55th verse they mean "a wall which it is forbidden them (the two Seas) to pass." حَجَرٌ Plnr. حِجَارَةٌ A rock, stone. حُجْرَةٌ Plur. حُجُرَاتٌ A private chamber. مَحْجُورٌ part. pass. Forhidden.

حَجَزَ aor. o. *To make a camel lie down;* to restrain (with acc. and عَنْ). حَاجِزٌ part. act. One who hinders, a bar, dam to keep back water.

حَدَّ aor. o. *To sharpen, limit, define.* حُدُودٌ plur. of حَدٌّ A prescribed limit, ordinance. حَدِيدٌ Iron, Plur. حِدَادٌ Sharp.—حَادَّ III. To hinder, stand in the way of, oppose.

حَدِبَ *To be humpbacked.* حَدَبٌ An elevation of the ground: Instead of this word which occurs at 21 v. 96 some copies have جَدَثٍ signifying "A grave."

حَدَثَ *To be new, to happen.* حَدِيثٌ A novelty, event; something which has lately happened, a story, history, narrative, discourse; لَهْوَ ٱلْحَدِيثِ 31 v. 5, "The Indicrons tale." أَحَادِيثُ (2nd declension) plur. of حَدِيثٌ Tales, sayings; يُعَلِّمُكَ مِنْ تَأْوِيلِ ٱلْأَحَادِيثِ 12 v. 6, "He shall teach thee the interpretation of (dark) sayings;" جَعَلْنَاهُمْ أَحَادِيثَ 23

v. 46, "We have made them (idle) tales," or "like a tale that is told."—حَدَّثَ II. To declare, narrate, acquaint (with acc. of pers. and بِ of the thing).—أَحْدَثَ IV. To cause to happen, bring about, produce (with acc. and لِ of pers.). مُحْدَثٌ part. pass. That which is newly produced or revealed.

حَدَقَ aor. i. *To surround.* حَدَآئِقُ (2nd declension) plur. of حَدِيقَةٌ A garden planted with trees.

حَذِرَ aor. a. To beware, take heed of, fear (with acc. also with أَنْ of the verb). حِذْرٌ Precaution. حَذَرٌ n.a. Fear. حَاذِرٌ part. act. One who is cautious, provident. مَحْذُورٌ part. pass. That which is to be feared.—حَذَّرَ II. To caution against (with double acc.).

حَرَّ aor. a. i. and o. *To become free, to be hot.* حَرٌّ n.a. Heat. حُرٌّ A free-man. حَرُورٌ fem. A hot wind blowing by night. حَرِيرٌ Silk.—حَرَّرَ II. *To free from slavery, devote to the service of God.* تَحْرِيرٌ n.a. The giving freedom, as تَحْرِيرُ رَقَبَةٍ 5 v. 91, "The freeing of a neck (from the yoke of slavery)." مُحَرَّرًا part. pass. acc. "Dedicated to God's service," 3 v. 31.

حَرَبَ aor. o. *To spoil one's goods.* حَرْبٌ fem. n.a. War. مِحْرَابٌ Plur. مَحَارِيبُ (2nd declension) A private chamber; *a niche in the wall of a mosque marking the direction of Mecca.*—حَارَبَ III. To fight against (with acc. of pers.).

حَرَثَ aor. i. and o. *To till the ground,* sow seed. حَرْثٌ n.a. A field, cultivated ground, produce of the same, fruits of the earth, tillage.

حَرِجَ aor. a. *To be oppressed by closeness or difficulty.* حَرَجٌ n.a. Narrow, a restriction, difficulty, crime.

حَرَدَ aor. i. *To perforate, intend.* حَرْدٌ n.a. A purpose.

حَرَسَ *To guard.* حَرَسٌ collective noun, Guards.

حَرَصَ aor. i. To desire ardently (with عَلَى). حَرِيصٌ Greedy, eager (with عَلَى). أَحْرَصُ superlative form, Most greedy.

حَرَضَ *To milk dry, to corrupt one's-self.* حَرَضٌ At the last extremity from disease.—حَرَّضَ II. To instigate, excite (with acc. and عَلَى).

حَرَفَ aor. i. *To change.* حَرْفٌ A verge, margin, manner; عَلَى حَرْفٍ 22 v. 11, "After a way, or upon the verge—as it were—(of religion)."—حَرَّفَ II. To pervert (with acc. and عَنْ).—مُتَحَرِّفٌ part. act. V. f. One who turns aside (with لِ).

حَرَقَ aor. i. and o. *To gnash the teeth, to burn.* حَرِيقٌ Burning.—حَرَّقَ II. To burn.—إِحْتَرَقَ VIII. To be burnt.

حَرَكَ *To refuse what is due,* and حَرُكَ *To be moved.*—حَرَّكَ II. To move (with acc. and بِ).

حَرَمَ aor. i. *To prohibit.* حَرَمٌ A holy place, asylum. حُرُمٌ plur. of حَرَامٌ Prohibited, unlawful, sacred, sanctified, as believers during the Pilgrimage. أَلْحُرُمَاتُ The Sacred Ordinances of God. مَحْرُومٌ part. pass. Forbidden; At 51 v. 19 this word seems to mean "Prevented by shame, or a sense of decorum;" at 56 v. 66 and 68 v. 27, "Hindered from enjoying the fruits of our labour."—حَرَّمَ II. To forbid, make or declare unlawful (with acc. of the thing and عَلَى of the pers.). تَحْرِيمٌ n.a. Prohibition. مُحَرَّمٌ part. pass. That which is forbidden or unlawful, declared sacred.

حَرَى aor. i. *To decrease.*—تَحَرَّى V. To seek.

حَزَبَ *To touch.* حِزْبٌ Plur. أَحْزَابٌ A company,

troop, party, sect, Those who side with any one; أَىُّ ٱلْحِزْبَيْنِ 18 v. 11, "Which of the two parties;" Meaning probably The Companions of the Cave or the Companions of ٱلرَّقِيمُ mentioned in the 8th verse; ٱلْأَحْزَابُ The confederates mentioned in chap. 33 were a body of Infidels, who were leagued together against Moḥammad in the War of the Ditch; Those at 40 v. 31 are the People of Noah, etc. who appear in the next verse, and who were in league against the prophets of their day.

حَزَنَ aor. o. To grieve; حَزِنَ aor. a. To be sad; to be grieved about (with عَلَى of pers. or thing). حَزَنٌ and حُزْنٌ n.s.a. Grief, sorrow.

حَسَّ aor. o. *To parch up*, utterly destroy. حَسِيسٌ A sound (sc. hissing).—أَحَسَّ IV. To perceive, find, be aware of, feel (with مِنْ, or with acc. and مِنْ).—تَحَسَّسَ V. To make inquiry after (with مِنْ).

حَسَبَ aor. o. *To reckon;* حَسِبَ aor. a. and i. To think, imagine, to be of opinion, calculate (with acc. of thing, also with or without أَنْ before following verb); see D. S. Gr. T. 2, pp. 74, 296, and 580, also 127, *note.* حَسْبٌ n.a. One who suffices, a sufficiency, or that which one is obliged to regard as sufficient; Ex. فَحَسْبُهُ جَهَنَّمُ 2 v. 202, "And Hell shall be his sufficient reward;" حَسْبُنَا ٱللّٰهُ 9 v. 59, "God is all-sufficient for us." حَاسِبٌ part. act. One who reckons, or takes an account, an accomptant. حِسَابٌ Plur. حُسْبَانٌ A reckoning, computation, account; بِغَيْرِ حِسَابٍ 2 v. 208, "Without measure;" حِسَابِيَهْ 69 v. 20, "My account," for حِسَابِى; The هْ at the end of this word is called هَآءُ ٱلْوَقْفِ; The affixed pronoun ى is here written and pronounced يَ, as is frequently the case; D. S. Gr. T. 1, p. 459. حَسِيبٌ One who takes an account. The word حُسْبَانٌ besides being the plural of حِسَابٌ is also used as a collective noun meaning Darts or lightning, and it is in this sense that it is employed at 18 v. 38.—حَاسَبَ III. To call to account for (with acc. of pers. and بِ). إِحْتَسَبَ VIII. To calculate upon, expect.

حَسَدَ aor. i. and o. To envy (with acc. of pers. and عَلَى of thing). حَاسِدٌ part. act. One who envies. حَسَدٌ Envy.

حَسَرَ aor. i. *To lay bare, to be weary.* حَسْرَةٌ Plur. حَسَرَاتٌ D. S. Gr. T. 1, p. 355, Sighing, cause of sighing; يَا حَسْرَتَى 39 v. 57, "Ah! my sighing, (ah me!)" Expressions of this kind are spelt and pronounced in a variety of ways, D. S. Gr. T. 2, p. 90. حَسِيرٌ Fatigued. مَحْسُورٌ part. pass. Stripped, destitute.— إِسْتَحْسَرَ X. To be worn out with fatigue.

حَسَمَ aor. i. *To cut.* حُسُومٌ The usual acceptation of this word is A succession of unlucky nights; At 69 v. 7 the phrase ثَمَانِيَةَ أَيَّامٍ حُسُومًا may be interpreted "For eight days in miserable succession."

حَسُنَ and حَسُنَ To be good or beautiful; in the latter of these forms the verb is employed in a manner similar to the verbs of praise and blame نِعْمَ and بِئْسَ; Ex. حَسُنَ أُولَٰئِكَ رَفِيقًا 4 v. 71, "They are excellent (in point of) company;" At 18 vv. 28 and 30 two different forms of construction occur in the same sentence, as نِعْمَ ٱلثَّوَابُ وَحَسُنَتْ مُرْتَفَقًا "How delightful is their reward, and how delicious their couch;" D. S. Gr. T. 2, p. 223 *et seq.* حُسْنٌ Goodness, beauty, excellence, kindness. حَسَنٌ Beautiful, good, fair, gracious, handsome. حَسَنَةٌ A good thing, a benefit, good, a good work. حِسَانٌ masc. and fem. plur. of حَسِينٌ Beautiful; خَيْرَاتٌ حِسَانٌ 55 v. 70, "(Damsels) exquisite and beautiful." أَحْسَنُ (2nd declension) comp. form, not used adjectively in conjunction with a substantive, as رَجُلٌ أَحْسَنُ, but with the substantive understood; Better, best, more or most excellent. *Note.* Words of the second declension when in connexion with a complement take the three inflexions, thus بِأَحْسَنِهَا 7 v. 142, where the pronoun refers to ٱلْأَلْوَاحُ.

حُسْنَى fem. of أَحْسَنُ, when used substantively means a good action, good thing, happy state, happy end; Dual ٱلْحُسْنَيَانِ and in the oblique cases ٱلْحُسْنَيَيْنِ 9 v. 52, "The two most excellent things," viz. Victory and Martyrdom; For the Rules which govern adjectives in the comparative form I must refer the reader to D. S. Gr. T. 2, p. 301 *et seq.*—أَحْسَنَ IV. To do well, act uprightly, act with kindness (with بِ, or with إِلَى or لِ of the pers.); to render agreeable, make beautiful (with acc. of thing and لِ of pers.). إِحْسَانٌ n.a. A doing good, a kind action, kindness, well-doing. مُحْسِنٌ part. act. One who does well, acts righteously, a righteous man.

حَشَرَ aor. o. and i. To gather together, and hence, to raise from the dead, to banish (with acc. and إِلَى or عَلَى, used in the Pass. with لِ or إِلَى). حَشْرٌ n.a. An assembly, banishment, emigration; at 59 v. 2 the words لِأَوَّلِ ٱلْحَشْرِ refer to certain Jews who were banished by Mohammad. حَاشِرٌ part. act. One who assembles. مَحْشُورٌ part. pass. Gathered together.

حَصَبَ aor. i. *To scatter gravel, cast into the fire.* حَصَبٌ That which is cast into the fire, fuel. حَاصِبٌ A violent wind bringing with it a shower of stones.

حَصْحَصَ To become manifest.

حَصَدَ aor. o. and i. To reap. حَصَادٌ n.a. A reaping, harvesting. حَصِيدٌ Harvest, mown down, utterly destroyed.

حَصَرَ aor. o. *To bring into difficulty*, besiege; حَصِرَ aor. a. To be restricted, hindered (with أَنْ of the following verb). حَصُورٌ Chaste. حَصِيرٌ A Prison.—أَحْصَرَ IV. To prevent, keep back —from a journey, etc.—(with فِى).

حَصَلَ *To be over and above, to be manifest.*— حَصَّلَ II. To make manifest.

حَصُنَ *To be strongly fortified*; and حَصَنَ *To keep at home.* حُصُونٌ plur. of حِصْنٌ A fortress.— مُحَصَّنٌ part. pass. II. f. Fenced in, fortified.— أَحْصَنَ IV. To keep safe (with acc. and مِنْ), or in safe custody, to marry. مُحْصِنٌ part. act. One who is chaste or continent. مُحْصَنَةٌ part. pass. fem. A married woman, one who is chaste and modest.—تَحَصُّنٌ n.a. V. f. Chastity.

حَصَى aor. i. *To strike with a pebble.* أَحْصَى for أَحْصَى comparat. form, Clever in calculating (with لِ of the thing calculated); D. S. Gr. T. 2, p. 310.—أَحْصَى IV. To number, calculate, compute, take an account of, know.

حَضَّ aor. o. To incite any one, instigate (with عَلَى). —تَحَاضَّ VI. To urge one another (with عَلَى).

حَضَرَ aor. o. To be present to, or present at, stand in presence of (with acc. of pers. or thing); to hurt, as at 23 v. 100, أَنْ يَحْضُرُونِ (for يَحْضُرُونِى) "Lest they hurt me;" D. S. Gr. T. 1, p. 570. حَاضِرٌ part. act. One who is present at, present, close upon, as حَاضِرَةَ ٱلْبَحْرِ

7 v. 163, (The town) "close upon the sea," viz. The town of Elath, about which a fable is here told, and which is also referred to at 2 v. 61.—أَحْضَرَ IV. To present, bring into the presence of, cause to be present, put forward (with double acc.); أُحْضِرَتِ ٱلْأَنْفُسُ ٱلشُّحَّ 4 v. 127, "(Men's) souls are prone to—*Lit.* are made to be present with—covetousness:" see De Sacy's observations on the construction of the Passive Voice, Gr. T. 2, p. 123. مُحْضَرٌ part. pass. One who is made to be present, brought forward, given over to (punishment).—مُحْتَضَرٌ Made present, part. pass. VIII. f. This word occurs at 54 v. 28, كُلُّ شِرْبٍ مُحْتَضَرٌ; The passage is rather obscure, but it seems to imply that each portion of water should be divided among those who were present; viz. The She-Camel and the Tribe of Thamood on alternate days; see also 26 v. 155.

حَطَّ aor. o. *To put down.* حِطَّةٌ *A putting down,* remission (of sins), forgiveness; A word by some thought to signify the profession of faith لَا إِلٰهَ إِلَّا ٱللّٰهُ.

حَطَبَ aor. i. *To abound in wood.* حَطَبٌ Fire-wood, fuel.

حَطَمَ aor. i. To break into small pieces. حُطَامٌ That which crumbles away through dryness. ٱلْحُطَمَةُ A name of Hell.

حَظَّ aor. a. *To be in good circumstances.* حَظٌّ n.a. A part, portion, a fortune, good fortune.

حَظَرَ *To prohibit, hinder.* مَحْظُورٌ part. pass. Hindered.—مُحْتَظِرٌ part. act. VIII. f. One who builds a fold for cattle.

حَفَّ aor. i. To surround (with acc. and بِ). حَافٌّ part. act. One who goes round about.

حَفَدَ aor. i. *To run hastily, minister.* حَفَدَةٌ Daughters, Grandchildren: a collective noun; D. S. Gr. T. 1, p. 382; or it may be a plural of حَافِدٌ.

حَفَرَ *To dig.* حُفْرَةٌ A pit. حَافِرَةٌ *A beginning,* original state, former condition.

حَفِظَ aor. a. To keep, guard (with acc. and مِن); to take care of. حِفْظٌ n.a. A guarding, a keeping; حِفْظًا As a guard. حَافِظٌ part. act. One who guards, keeps watch; a guardian, keeper (with acc. or with لِ). حَفَظَةٌ an irregular plur. of حَافِظٌ Guardian (Angels). حَفِيظٌ same as حَافِظٌ, used with عَلَى in the sense of watching over evil doings; at 50 v. 31 it is used in the sense of one who keeps (God's commandments). مَحْفُوظٌ part. pass. Kept, well-guarded.—حَافَظَ III. To observe strictly (with عَلَى).—إِسْتَحْفَظَ X. To commit to one's keeping, or one's memory.

حَفِىَ aor. a. *To go barefoot, honour greatly.* حَفِىٌّ Thoroughly acquainted (with عَنْ); gracious, kind (with بِ).—أَحْفَى IV. To be importunate towards any one (with acc.).

حَقَّ aor. i. and o. To be right, just or fitting, worthy of, to be justly due to (with عَلَى); كَثِيرٌ حَقَّ عَلَيْهِ ٱلْعَذَابُ 22 v. 18, "Many deserve punishment;" *Literally,* "Many (a man), punishment is justly his due;" At 84 vv. 2 and 5 the verb appears in its passive form حُقَّتْ (pret. for fut.), which may mean "It shall be treated according to its deserts," or "shall be verified and certainly known;" the active voice having these significations as well as those above given. حَقٌّ That which is right and proper, just, true, justice, a right, just due, need, duty, such as payment of a debt; Ex. ٱلَّذِى عَلَيْهِ ٱلْحَقُّ 2 v. 282, "He upon whom is the duty (of payment of the debt);" it also means Truth, The Truth, One of the Names of God. حَقِيقٌ Fitting, just. أَحَقُّ (2nd declension) compar. More worthy, more just, truer. ٱلْحَاقَّةُ The Inevitable, the day of Judgment.—أَحَقَّ IV. To justify, verify (with acc. and بِ).—إِسْتَحَقَّ X. *To be worthy, adjudge worthy;* to be guilty of (with acc. of thing), or think guilty (with عَلَى of pers.), in both which senses it occurs at 5 v. 106.

حَقِبَ *To suffer from a retention of urine, to be withheld (rain, etc.).* حُقُبٌ A long space of time, space of eighty years; Plur. أَحْقَابٌ.

حَقَفَ *To lie among crooked or winding sands.* ٱلْأَحْقَافُ The winding sands; name of a province of Arabia, formerly inhabited by the tribe of 'Ād; plur. of حِقْفٌ.

حَكَمَ aor. o. *To exercise authority* (with عَلَى); to judge, judge between (with بَيْنَ of pers. and بِ of thing); to give judgment in favour of (with لِ of pers. and بِ of thing): when it means to give an *adverse* judgment it takes عَلَى of pers. حُكْمٌ judgment, wisdom; أَفَحُكْمَ ٱلْجَاهِلِيَّةِ يَبْغُونَ 5 v. 55, "Do they then desire the judgment of the days of ignorance?" *i.e.* To be judged according to the laws of Paganism; a rule of judgment, as أَنْزَلْنَاهُ حُكْمًا عَرَبِيًّا 13 v. 37, "We have sent it—the Korân—down as a rule of judgment in Arabic." حَكَمٌ A judge. حَاكِمٌ Plur. حُكَّامٌ and حَاكِمُونَ part. act. One who judges, a judge. حِكْمَةٌ Wisdom. حَكِيمٌ Wise, knowing. أَحْكَمُ comp. and super. More or most knowing or wise.—حَكَّمَ II. To take as judge (with acc. of pers. and فِي).—أَحْكَمَ IV. To confirm; The Passive أُحْكِمَتْ occurs at 11 v. 1, and has been variously interpreted; Sale renders it "Are guarded against corruption." مُحْكَمٌ part. pass. This word also admits of divers interpretations; a chapter is said to be مُحْكَمَةٌ when it is not abrogated by any subsequent revelation; it also means clear and perspicuous, void of ambiguity; at 3 v. 5 the verses called آيَاتٌ مُحْكَمَاتٌ, or those which are clear and are to be taken in their literal sense, are distinguished from those which are allegorical and figurative; the former are said to be أُمُّ ٱلْكِتَابِ "The mother—or ground-work—of the Book."—تَحَاكَمَ VI. To go together to judgment (with إِلَى).

حَلَّ aor. o. To untie—a knot—(with acc. and مِنْ); aor. i. and o. To fulfil the rites and ceremonies required of a pilgrim, to become حَلَالٌ after being أَحْرَمَ; to be lawful (with لِ of pers. and أَنْ of verb); to descend, alight (with عَلَى); to settle in a place. حِلٌّ Anything lawful, an inhabitant. حَلَالٌ Lawful, *One who has performed all the rites and ceremonies of a pilgrim.* حَلَائِلُ plur. of حَلِيلٌ A wife. تَحِلَّةٌ Dissolution of a vow. مَحِلٌّ Place of sacrifice.—أَحَلَّ IV. To render lawful, allow, allow to be lawful, allow to be violated (with acc. of thing and لِ of pers.); to violate; to cause to descend or settle (with double acc.). مُحِلٌّ part. act. One who considers lawful that which God has declared to be unlawful; Ex. غَيْرَ مُحِلِّي ٱلصَّيْدِ وَأَنْتُمْ حُرُمٌ 5 v. 1, "Not violating the prohibition against the chase while ye are on a pilgrimage:" مُحِلِّي being in conjunction with ٱلصَّيْدِ is here put for مُحِلِّينَ.

حَلَفَ aor. i. To swear (with لِ of pers. and بِ of object of the oath, also followed by إِنْ or لَوْ of verb, or by عَلَى of the thing sworn); Ex. يَحْلِفُونَ عَلَى ٱلْكَذِبِ 58 v. 15, "They swear to a falsehood." حَلَّافٌ A great swearer.

حَلَقَ aor. i. To shave.—مُحَلِّقٌ part. act. II. f. One who shaves.

حَلْقَمَ *To cut the throat.* حُلْقُومٌ The throat.

حَلَمَ *To dream.* حُلْمٌ A dream; Plur. أَحْلَامٌ. حِلْمٌ Understanding; Plur. أَحْلَامٌ. حُلُمٌ Puberty. حَلِيمٌ Kind, gracious, intelligent.

حَلَى aor. i. *To adorn with ornaments.* حِلْيَةٌ Ornaments, trinkets; This word is used in the Ḳorân as a collective noun, or it may be an irregular Plur. of حَلْىٌ, which also takes حُلِىٌّ, D. S. Gr. T. 1, p. 382.—حَلَّى II. same as حَلَى (with acc. of thing, or with مِنْ).

حمٓ Letters prefixed to the 40th and six following chapters of the Ḳorân, see آلم.

حَمَّ aor. o. *To heat.* حَمِيمٌ Boiling hot water, a near relative or friend.

حَمَأَ *To clean out mud from a well.* حَمَأٌ Mud. حَمِئَةٌ fem. of حَمِئٌ Muddy, composed of mud.

حَمِدَ aor. a. To praise. حَمْدٌ n.a. Praise. حَامِدٌ part. act. One who praises. حَمِيدٌ Worthy of praise. أَحْمَدُ A name of Moḥammad, Most praiseworthy, renowned. *Note.* By a perversion of the Gospel, the Mussulman Doctors teach that the Comforter promised under the name παράκλητος was the περικλυτὸς or Renowned Moḥammad; see Gr. Test. S. John xvi. v. 7. مَحْمُودٌ part. pass. Praised, lauded.—مُحَمَّدٌ part. pass. II. f. *Much-praised, highly lauded*, Moḥammad.

حَمَرَ aor. o. *To pare a thong of leather.* حِمَارٌ An ass; Plur. حُمُرٌ and حَمِيرٌ. حُمْرٌ plur. of أَحْمَرُ Red.

حَمَلَ aor. i. To carry, bear, bear away, load, charge with, impose a burthen (with acc. of thing and عَلَى or فِى); to attack any one (with عَلَى of pers.); to conceive, be with child, undertake (a duty), provide with carriage and other necessaries of a journey, as at 9 v. 93. حَمْلٌ n.a. Plur. أَحْمَالٌ A burthen, fœtus in the womb, time during which the fœtus is in the womb, as at 46 v. 14. حِمْلٌ A burthen, load. حَامِلٌ part. act. One who carries; فَٱلْحَامِلَاتِ وِقْرًا "And by those which bear a load," *i.e.* The clouds bearing a load of rain, or women bearing a burthen in their wombs, or the winds which bear the clouds, 51 v. 2. حَمَّالَةٌ A woman who carries much or frequently, a portress. حَمُولَةٌ A beast of burthen.—حَمَّلَ II. To impose a burthen on (with double acc.), charge one with (a duty).—إِحْتَمَلَ VIII. To take a burthen on one's-self, bear a burthen.

حَمَى aor. i. *To defend;* and حَمِىَ aor. a. To be hot. حَامٍ Ḥâmee, name of a camel concerning which certain superstitious usages were observed by the Pagan Arabs. حَامِيَةٌ fem. of part. act. That which is burning hot. حَمِيَّةٌ Affectation, cant.—أَحْمَى IV. To make hot; يُحْمَى عَلَيْهَا 9 v. 35, "It *i.e.* the money—ٱلدَّرَاهِمَ وَٱلدَّنَانِيرَ—shall be made hot;" *Literally*, It shall be made hot upon it, D. S. Gr. T. 2, p. 129.

حَنَّ aor. i. *To emit a sound as a she-camel towards her young; to be moved with pity.* حَنَانٌ Mercy. حُنَيْنٌ Ḥonein, Name of a valley near Mecca, where a battle was fought by Moḥammad.

حَنِثَ aor. a. To break one's oath. حِنْثٌ Wickedness.

حَنْجَرَ *To cut the throat.* حَنَاجِرُ (2nd declension) plur. of حَنْجَرَةٌ A throat.

حَنَذَ aor. i. *To roast.* حَنِيذٌ Roasted.

حَنَفَ aor. i. *To incline.* حَنِيفٌ Plur. حُنَفَاءُ (2nd declension) Inclining to the right Religion, orthodox.

حَنَكَ aor. i. and o. *To put a bit upon a horse.*—إِحْتَنَكَ VIII. To bring into subjection, utterly destroy; لَأَحْتَنِكَنَّ ذُرِّيَّتَهُ 17 v. 64, "Verily I will bring his posterity under my authority;" or, "I will destroy them utterly" (as locusts destroy everything where they alight).

حَابَ aor. o. *To sin.* حُوبٌ n.a. A sin.

حَاتَ aor. o. *To fly around.* حُوتٌ A fish; Plur. حِيتَانٌ.

حَاجَ aor. o. *To be in want of.* حَاجَةٌ Something necessary, a necessity, a thing, matter, wish, a want; إِلَّا حَاجَةً فِي نَفْسِ يَعْقُوبَ 12 v. 68, "Except for the sake of a wish (or to gratify a wish) in Jacob's mind."

حَاذَ aor. o. *To drive quickly.*—إِسْتَحْوَذَ X. To get the better of (with عَلَى). *Note.* Some verbs whose second Radical is و may be conjugated either regularly or irregularly in the 10th form.

حَارَ aor. o. To return. حُورٌ plur. of حَوْرَآءُ fem. of أَحْوَرُ both nouns of the 2nd declension, D. S. Gr. T. 1, p. 360; Houris, a name given to the Maids of Paradise on account of the splendour of their black eyes; the word is derived from حَوِرَ a form of حَارَ D. S. Gr. T. 1, p. 246, the exact meaning of which is somewhat a matter of dispute, but which is properly applied to the blackness of eye seen in a gazelle; The words حُورٌ عِينٌ which occur several times are generally translated "(Damsels) having large black eyes;" *Literally,* "Black-eyed (damsels) with large eyes," see عِينٌ. حَوَارِيٌّ Disciples or Apostles of Christ; This word is by some supposed to be of foreign origin; by others it is derived from حَارَ, one of the meanings of which is to whiten clothes by washing, the Arab commentators pretending that the Apostles were Fullers by trade.—حَاوَرَ III. To reply to in an argument (with acc.)—تَحَاوُرٌ n.a. VI. f. An argument between two or more persons.

حَازَ aor. o. *To gather together to one's-self.*—مُتَحَيِّزٌ for مُتَحَوِّزٌ D. S. Gr. T. 1, p. 105, part. act. V. f. One who goes aside or retreats (with إِلَى).

حَاشَ aor. o. *To beat for game;* حَاشَ in the Korân is used adverbially, and means far be it, as حَاشَ لِلّٰهِ "Far be it from God," or "God forbid," D. S. Gr. T. 1, p. 532.

حَاطَ aor. o. *To guard.*—أَحَاطَ IV. To surround, encompass, comprehend (knowledge), and hence to know (with بِ of thing); إِلَّا أَنْ يُحَاطَ بِكُمْ 12 v. 66, "Unless ye be prevented," or "compassed about (by some hindrance);" The verb is here impersonal with an ellipse of the subject, a common construction both in Arabic and Latin, D. S. Gr. T. 2, p. 129. مُحِيطٌ part. act. One who encompasses, or comprehends.

حَالَ aor. o. *To be changed,* to pass by, go between; Pass. حِيلَ ; وَحِيلَ بَيْنَهُمْ وَبَيْنَ مَا يَشْتَهُونَ 34 v. 53, "It (a bar) shall be passed between them and what they long for;" The verb is here used impersonally, D. S. Gr. T. 2, p. 129. حَوْلَ and مِنْ حَوْلِ adverbial expressions meaning round about, and from around, see دُونَ and مِنْ دُونِ. حَوْلٌ n.a. *Power,* a year. حِوَلٌ A change. حِيلَةٌ A plan, contrivance.—تَحْوِيلٌ n.a. II. f. A change, a turning off, or turning away.

حَوَى aor. i. *To collect.* حَوَايَا (2nd declension) for حَوَايِى D. S. Gr. T. 1, p. 111, plur. of حَوِيَّةٌ Intestines. أَحْوَى Dark-coloured, from حَوِىَ another form of حَوَى *To be dark-coloured as dead herbage; Fr. "Feuille morte."*

حَىَّ or حَيِىَ for حَيِوَ aor. i. a doubly imperfect verb, aor. يَحْيَا for يَحْيَوُ To live (with فِى). حَىٌّ Plur. أَحْيَآءٌ Living, He or that which liveth, alive. حَيَّةٌ A serpent. حَيَاةٌ or حَيَوةٌ, or more correctly حَيْوَةٌ Life. حَيَوَانٌ Life (eternal). يَحْيَى John. مَحْيَا for مَحْيَى for مَحْيَىٌ Life; مَحْيَاىَ My life, D. S. Gr. T. 1, p. 111.— حَيَّى II. To salute (with بِ). تَحِيَّةٌ n.a. A salutation.—أَحْيَى or أَحْيَا IV. To preserve one's life, restore to life, give life (with acc. and بِ or with double acc.); يُحْيِينِ for يُحْيِينِى 26 v. 81, "He will restore me to life." مُحْيِى for مُحْيِىٌ part. act. One who restores to life."—إِسْتَحْيَى X. To save alive; to be ashamed (with مِنْ of thing or with أَنْ of verb). إِسْتِحْيَآءٌ Bashfulness.

حَيْثُ Where, wherever, whither; مِنْ حَيْثُ From whence soever, from the place whence, or of the place where, from the time when, in a manner which; حَيْثُ مَا Wheresoever; حَيْثُ although strictly speaking a noun, is indeclinable, and is always found as an adverb and as antecedent to some complement either nominal or verbal, D. S. Gr. T. 2, p. 146.

حَادَ aor. i. To avert (with مِنْ).

حَارَ for حَيِرَ aor. a. *To be astonished.* حَيْرَانُ (2nd declension) Distracted.

حَاصَ aor. i. *To turn aside.* مَحِيصٌ A place or way of escape.

حَاضَ aor. i. To have her courses (a woman). مَحِيضٌ The monthly courses of a woman.

حَافَ aor. i. To be unjust (with عَلَى).

حَاقَ aor. i. To surround, hem in, compass about (with بِ of pers.).

حَانَ aor. i. *To arrive (the time).* حِينٌ Time, as 76 v. 1, حِينٌ مِنَ ٱلدَّهْرِ "A space of time;" 28 v. 14, عَلَى حِينِ غَفْلَةٍ "In a time of negligence," *i.e.* When the people were not mindful of him. حِينَ When, at the time of; throughout the Korân when used in this sense حِينَ is indeclinable, D. S. Gr. T. 2, p. 149; At 11 v. 5 the words أَلَا حِينَ belong properly to the next verse. حِينَئِذٍ Then, at that time, compounded of حِينَ and إِذْ or إِذًا, D. S. Gr. T. 1, p. 521.

خ

خَاسِئًا acc. part. act. of خَسَأَ q.v.

خَاوِيَةٌ fem. of خَاوٍ for خَاوِىٌ, see خَوَى.

خَبَأَ *To hide.* خَبْءٌ n.a. That which is hidden.

خَبَتَ *To humble one's-self (before God),* to acquiesce. —أَخْبَتَ IV. same as خَبَتَ (with إِلَى or لِ). مُخْبِتٌ part. act. One who humbles himself.

خَبُثَ To be bad. خَبِيثٌ Bad, evil, wicked. خَبَائِثُ plur. of خَبِيثَةٌ Impurities, filthy or wicked things or actions; sc. أَعْمَالٌ.

خَبَرَ *To prove;* and خَبُرَ aor. o. *To know.* خُبْرٌ n.a. Understanding, knowledge. خَبَرٌ Plur. أَخْبَارٌ News, tidings, report. خَبِيرٌ Knowing, One who knows, or is acquainted with.

خَبَزَ aor. i. *To make bread.* خُبْزٌ Bread.

خَبَطَ aor. i. *To stamp with the fore-feet.*—تَخَبَّطَ V. *properly, To strike with the fore-feet;* at 2 v. 276 it means to drive one mad, strike with confusion, to infect, or simply, to destroy.

خَبَلَ *To distract.* خَبَالٌ A hindrance, corruption, as لَا يَأْلُونَكُمْ خَبَالًا 3 v. 114, "They will not fail in corrupting you."

خَبَا aor. o. To be extinct.

خَتَرَ aor. i. and o. *To deceive.* خَتَّارٌ A perfidious man.

خَتَمَ aor. i. To seal (with عَلَى). خَاتَمٌ A seal; at 33 v. 40 Moḥammad is said to be خَاتَمَ ٱلنَّبِيِّين "The seal of the prophets." خِتَامٌ A sealing; the wax, clay, or other substance used in sealing. مَخْتُومٌ part. pass. Sealed.

خَدَّ aor. o. *To make an impression.* خَدٌّ A cheek. أُخْدُودٌ A pit or trench; The أَصْحَابُ ٱلْأُخْدُودِ spoken of at 85 v. 4, "The makers—or Lords—of the pit of fire" were the servants of ذُو ٱلنُّوَاسِ A Jewish tyrant who caused a number of Christians to be burnt alive.

خَدَعَ aor. a. *To cover over,* deceive. خَادِعٌ part. act. One who deceives.—خَادَعَ III. To endeavour to deceive.

خِدْنٌ Plur. أَخْدَانٌ *Equals, friends,* lovers; no verbal root.

خَذَلَ aor. o. To disappoint, leave without assistance. خَذُولٌ One who deserts his friends, a Traitor. مَخْذُولٌ part. pass. Destitute.

خَرَّ aor. i. and o. *To make a noise in flying (an eagle)*; to fall down (with مِنْ, عَلَى, or لِ).

خَرِبَ *To strike or pierce the ear, to lay waste.* خَرَابٌ A laying waste, a making desolate and ruinous.—أَخْرَبَ IV. To lay waste (with acc. and بِ).

خَرَجَ aor. o. To go out, go forth, come forth (with مِنْ, فِى, عَلَى, بِ, or إِلَى). خَرْجٌ and خَرَاجٌ Tribute, maintenance. خُرُوجٌ n.a. A getting or going forth; يَوْمُ ٱلْخُرُوجِ The Day of Resurrection. خَارِجٌ part. act. One who comes forth. مَخْرَجٌ An issue, place of exit.—أَخْرَجَ IV. To bring out, drive out, bring forth, produce, stretch forth, cast forth (with acc. and مِنْ, لِ, بِ, and فِى, also with أَنْ for بِأَنْ of following verb). إِخْرَاجٌ n.a. A driving out, expulsion, bringing forth. مُخْرِجٌ part. act. One who brings forth, etc. مُخْرَجٌ part. pass. One who is brought forth, etc.; also The place from whence, or time at which anything is brought forth; أَخْرِجْنِى مُخْرَجَ صِدْقٍ 17 v. 82, "Bring me forth (from the grave) with a favourable exit."—إِسْتَخْرَجَ X. To take out, take forth.

خَرْدَلَ quadriliteral, *To chop up meat.* خَرْدَلٌ Mustard-seed.

خَرَصَ aor. o. *To guess,* to tell lies. خَرَّاصٌ A liar.

خَرْطَمَ quadriliteral, *To strike on the nose.* خُرْطُومٌ A proboscis or nose.

خَرَقَ aor. i. and o. To rend, make a hole in, feign, falsely attribute.

خَزَنَ *To lay up in a storehouse, barn, or treasury.* خَزَائِنُ (2nd declension) plur. of خَزَانَةٌ A treasury, treasure, storehouse, magazine. خَازِنٌ part. act. One who lays in a store, or keeps a store of anything (with لِ of thing); Plur. خَزَنَةٌ Keepers.

خَزِىَ aor. a. To be disgraced. خِزْىٌ n.a. Shame, disgrace. أَخْزَى for أَخْزَىُ D. S. Gr. T. 1, pp. 110 and 403, comparative form, More disgraceful.—أَخْزَى IV. To cover with shame, disgrace (with acc. of pers. and فى). مُخْزٍ and in connexion with a complement مُخْزِى part. act. One who puts to shame.

خَسَأَ aor. a. *To drive away, to be dull—the senses;* to be driven away (with فى), as اِخْسَئُوا 23 v. 110, "Be ye driven away," imperat. plur. for اِخْسَأُوا, the hamza being changed into ؤ in consequence of the ḍamma, and the servile و being dropped, D. S. Gr. T. 1, pp. 95 and 104. خَاسِئٌ part. act. That which is dull, also that which is driven away (from society).

خَسِرَ aor. a. To wander from the right way, to be deceived, suffer loss, lose, perish. خُسْرٌ n.a. Loss, a losing concern. خَسَارٌ and خُسْرَانٌ ns.a. Perdition, loss. خَاسِرٌ part. act. One who wanders from the right way, a loser. أَخْسَرُ comparative form, The greatest loser, one who errs exceedingly.—تَخْسِيرٌ n.a. II. f. A loss.—أَخْسَرَ IV. To diminish (a quantity), give short measure. مُخْسِرٌ part. act. One who gives short measure.

خَسَفَ aor. i. To bury one beneath the earth, cause the earth to swallow up (with بِ of the person and acc. of أَرْضٌ); to be eclipsed (the moon).

خَشَبَ aor. i. *To mix together* (with بِ). خُشُبٌ plur. of خَشَبٌ Rough wood, timber.

خَشَعَ aor. a. *To be low or humble,* to humble one's-self (with لِ). خُشُوعٌ n.a. Humility. خَاشِعٌ part. act. One who humbles himself, or is dejected; at 41 v. 39 the passage تَرَى ٱلْأَرْضَ خَاشِعَةً must be rendered "Thou seest the earth barren and desolate;" Plur. خُشَّعٌ and خَاشِعُونَ.

خَشِىَ aor. a. To fear (with acc. or with أَنْ in the sense of lest). خَشْيَةٌ Fear.

خَصَّ *To distinguish as particular;* Pass. *To be in want.* خَاصَّةً Particularly, peculiarly. خَصَاصَةٌ n.a. Poverty.—إِخْتَصَّ VIII. To bestow upon any one in a peculiar manner, appropriate to (with بِ of thing and acc. of pers.).

خَصَفَ aor. i. To sew together—*prop. a sole*—(with acc. and عَلَى).

خَصَمَ aor. i. *To have the best in an altercation.* خَصْمٌ An adversary. *Note.* This word is used for both singular, dual, and plural, though the dual خَصْمَانِ is also found in the Korân, as at 38 v. 21, where there is an ellipse of the pronoun نَحْنُ. خَصِمٌ A contentious person. خَصِيمٌ A disputer.—خِصَامٌ n.a. III. f. Contention, dispute.—تَخَاصُمٌ n.a. VI. f. Mutual disputing and recrimination.—إِخْتَصَمَ and خِصِّمَ VIII. The reason for the latter form, which occurs at 36 v. 49, is given by De Sacy in his Grammar, T. 1, p. 223, To dispute, strive together by way of dispute or litigation (with فى, عِنْدَ, or لَدَى).

خَضَدَ aor. i. *To break wood,* cut off the thorns from a tree. مَخْضُودٌ part. pass. Deprived of thorns.

خَضِرَ aor. a. *To be green.* خَضِرٌ Green herbs. خُضْرٌ fem. plur. of أَخْضَرُ Green.—مُخْضَرَّةٌ fem. part. IX. f. That which is green.

خَضَعَ aor. a. To be humble and lowly (with بِ). خَاضِعٌ part. act. One who is submissive (with لِ).

خَطَّ aor. o. *To draw lines,* to write (with بِ).

خَطَأَ *To cast out scum—a pot;* خَطِئَ aor. a. *To do wrong.* خِطْأٌ n.a. An error, fault, sin. خَطَأً By mistake. خَطِيئَةٌ same as خِطْأٌ; خَطَايَا plur. of خَطِيئَةٌ D. S. Gr. T. 1, p. 370, the final ي being changed into ا because preceded by another ي; D. S. Gr. T. 1, p. 111. خَاطِئٌ part. act. One who sins, a sinner, sinful.—أَخْطَأَ IV.

To be in error, to sin (with بِ). خَاطِئَةٌ said to be a n.a. Habitual sinfulness; or it may be regarded as the fem. of خَاطِئٌ and agree with ٱلْأَفْعَالِ understood, as at 69 v. 9. *Note.* The ة is not unfrequently added to nouns to give intensity; D. S. Gr. T. 1, p. 322, *note* (3); see also T. 2, p. 279, *note.*

خَطَبَ aor. o. *To offer up the State Prayer called* خُطْبَةٌ. خَطْبٌ n.a. A matter, thing, business. خِطْبَةٌ n.a. The demanding a woman in marriage.—خَاطَبَ III. To speak to, address (with acc. of pers. and فِي of subject). خِطَابٌ n.a. A discourse; فَصْلَ ٱلْخِطَابِ 38 v. 19, "A sound judgment in legal matters."

خَطِفَ aor. a. *To march quickly* (*a camel*), To snatch, snatch away. خَطْفَةٌ Something snatched away by stealth.—تَخَطَّفَ V. To snatch away, carry off, despoil.

خَطَا aor. o. *To make a step forward.* خُطُوَاتٌ plur. of خُطْوَةٌ A step.

خَفَّ aor. i. To be light. خَفِيفٌ Plur. خِفَافٌ Light.—خَفَّفَ II. To make light, make things easier (with عَنْ of pers. and acc. of thing). تَخْفِيفٌ n.a. An alleviation.—إِسْتَخَفَّ X. To think or find light and easy, induce levity in any one (with acc. of pers.).

خَفَتَ *To be quiet or silent.*—خَافَتَ III. To speak in a low voice (with بِ).—تَخَافَتَ VI. To converse in a low tone.

خَفَضَ aor. i. *To remain in a place;* to lower (with acc. of thing and لِ of pers.), as إِخْفِضْ جَنَاحَكَ لِلْمُؤْمِنِينَ 15 v. 88, "Behave with humility,—*Literally*, lower thy wing—to the true believers." خَافِضٌ part. act. That which humbles.

خَفَى aor. i. *To make manifest*, and خَفِيَ aor. a. To be hidden (with عَلَي of pers.). خَفِيٌّ Hidden, as مِنْ طَرْفٍ خَفِيٍّ 42 v. 44, "Askance, or with a stealthy glance;" خَفِيًّا In secret. أَخْفَى for أَخْفَيُ comparative form, More hidden. خَافِيَةٌ A secret action. خُفْيَةً In secret.—أَخْفَى IV. To hide, conceal (with acc. and فِي or لِ); The words أَكَادُ أُخْفِيهَا at 20 v. 15 are by some translated "I want but little of concealing it," and by others "of making it manifest;" The iv. f. being used in both senses.—إِسْتَخْفَى X. To lie hid (with مِنْ). مُسْتَخْفٍ part. act. One who tries to hide himself.

خَلَّ aor. i. and a. *To be lean* (*meat*). خَلٌّ Plur. خِلَالٌ A camel entering his second year; see also under iii. f. خُلَّةٌ Friendship. خَلِيلٌ A friend, an epithet of Abraham, the friend of God; Plur. أَخِلَّاءُ (2nd declension), D. S. Gr. T. 1, p. 368.—خَالَّ III. *To be friendly towards any one.* خِلَالٌ n.a. Friendship; خِلَالٌ is also plur. of خَلَلٌ, in which sense it means the middle or inner parts, as خِلَالَ ٱلدِّيَارِ The inner apartments.

خَلَدَ aor. o. To be eternal, live for ever, remain for ever in a place (with فِي). خُلْدٌ and خُلُودٌ Eternity, eternal life. خَالِدٌ part. act. Living for ever, etc.—مُخَلَّدٌ part. pass. II. f. Made immortal, or eternal.—أَخْلَدَ IV. To render immortal; To incline towards (with إِلَى).

خَلَصَ aor. o. *To be pure and sincere*, to arrive at; خَلَصُوا نَجِيًّا 12 v. 80, "They held a secret conference." خَالِصٌ part. act. That which is pure; proper and peculiar; خَالِصَةً Peculiarly.—أَخْلَصَ IV. To purify (with acc. of pers. and

بِ), show sincerity in religion (with acc. of thing and لِ of pers.). إِخْلَاصٌ n.a. Faith pure and undefiled; The name of the 112th chapter, which is held in especial veneration. مُخْلِصٌ part. act. One who exhibits the sincerity and purity of his faith. مُخْلَصٌ part. pass. Purified, sincerely religious.—إِسْتَخْلَصَ X. To take entirely to one's-self (with acc. of thing and لِ of pers.).

خَلَطَ aor. i. To mix. خُلَطَآءُ plur. of خَلِيطٌ Those who are mixed up (in business).—خَالَطَ III. To mix one's-self up in the affairs of others (with acc.).—إِخْتَلَطَ VIII. To be mixed with (with بِ).

خَلَعَ aor. a. To draw off, put off.

خَلَفَ aor. o. *To be behind*, come after; to succeed (with فِى); to do a thing behind one's back (with acc. of pers. and thing), as at 7 v. 149; To act as deputy (with acc. of pers. and فِى), as أُخْلُفْنِى 7 v. 138, "Do thou act as my deputy." خَلْفٌ A succeeding generation; مِنْ خَلْفِ Behind, from behind, after, succeeding; ٱلَّذِينَ مِنْ خَلْفِهِمْ at 3 v. 164, "Those who are coming after them," refers to those for whom the honour of martyrdom is yet reserved. خَلْفَ After, behind; مَا خَلْفَهُمْ 2 v. 256, "That which is yet to come upon them." خَالِفٌ part. act. One who stays, or sits behind another. خِلَافٌ The contrary; مِنْ خِلَافٍ On opposite sides; خِلَافَ In opposition to. خِلْفَةٌ A difference; خِلْفَةً 25 v. 63, "For a distinction, or to follow one another;" see the corresponding passage in Genesis ch. 1, v. 14. خَوَالِفُ (2nd declension) plur. of خَالِفَةٌ, generally translated "Women," as being those who stay behind in case of war.

خَلِيفَةٌ A successor, lieutenant, vicar; a name given to sovereigns as Vicegerents of God, *also to the successors of Mohammad;* The termination ة adds energy or intensity to the expression, D. S. Gr. T. 1, p. 322; Plur. خَلَآئِفُ and خُلَفَآءُ both words of the 2nd declension, D. S. Gr. T. 1, p. 402.—خَلَّفَ II. To leave behind. مُخَلَّفٌ part. pass. Left behind.—خَالَفَ III. To oppose (with عَنْ), accede to (with acc. of pers. and إِلَى), as مَا أُرِيدُ أَنْ أُخَالِفَكُمْ إِلَى مَا أَنْهَاكُمْ عَنْهُ 11 v. 90, "I will not accede to you in what I forbid you." خِلَافٌ n.a. v. *suprà*.—أَخْلَفَ IV. To break the promise given to any one (with acc. of pers. and thing); At 34 v. 38 it means to restore (with acc.); In the Passive لَنْ تُخْلَفَهُ 20 v. 97, "It—the promise—shall not be broken for thee;" For the construction of doubly transitive verbs in the passive (or objective) voice, the learner may consult D. S. Gr. T. 2, p. 123. مُخْلِفٌ part. act. One who breaks his promise; for the construction مُخْلِفَ وَعْدِهِ رُسُلَهُ 14 v. 48 see D. S. Gr. T. 2, p. 187.—تَخَلَّفَ V. To remain behind (with عَنْ).—إِخْتَلَفَ VIII. To disagree, differ (with فِى). إِخْتِلَافٌ n.a. Diversity, vicissitude, contradiction. مُخْتَلِفٌ part. act. Differing one with another, various, diverse, different; For the construction مُخْتَلِفًا أُكُلُهُ 6 v. 142, "Whose food is of various kinds," see D. S. Gr. T. 2, pp. 79, 197, and 270.—إِسْتَخْلَفَ X. To make a successor, cause to succeed (with acc. and فِى). مُسْتَخْلَفٌ part. pass. Made a successor, or inheritor (with فِى).

خَلَقَ aor. o. *To measure accurately, and define the dimensions of anything,* to create, produce (with acc. and فِى, بِ, مِنْ, or لِ). خَلْقٌ n.a. collect.

noun, Creatures, created things, especially mankind, a creation, lying device; أَشَدُّ خَلْقًا 37 v. 11, "Stronger by nature;" At 36 v. 68 the word خَلْق would seem to stand for خَلَق "Old age." خُلُقٌ A natural disposition, manner or habit. خَالِقٌ part. act. One who creates; ٱلْخَالِقُ The Creator, one of the names of God. خَلَاقٌ A portion, full share of happiness. ٱلْخَلَّاقُ The Great Creator.—مُخَلَّقَةٌ fem. part. pass. II. f. Well and perfectly formed.—إِخْتِلَاقٌ n.a. VIII. f. A lying device.

خَلَا aor. o. *To be empty*, clear (with لِ), free, alone, alone with (with إِلَى); to pass away, to have been in existence or in force in former times; in the latter sense it appears at 48 v. 23, ٱلَّتِي قَدْ خَلَتْ مِنْ قَبْلُ; To be proper to or belong to (with لِ, also with فِي); to light on a vacant place (with فِي); this or the preceding would seem to be the *literal* meaning of the passage إِلَّا خَلَا فِيهَا نَذِيرٌ 35 v. 22. خَالِيَةٌ fem. of خَالٍ for خَالِيٌ part. act. That which has passed away.—خَلَّى II. *To empty*, make clear; خَلُّوا سَبِيلَهُمْ 9 v. 5, "Dismiss them," *Literally*, "Clear their road."—تَخَلَّى V. To be clear and empty.

خَمَدَ aor. o. *To get low* (*a fire*), *to faint away and die.* خَامِدٌ part. act. Extinct, dead.

خَمَرَ aor. i. and o. *To cover over, ferment.* خَمْرٌ fem. Wine. خُمُرٌ plnr. of خِمَارٌ A covering, and especially a woman's head and face veil.

خَمَسَ aor. o. *To take a fifth part.* خَمْسَةٌ masc. and خَمْسٌ fem. Five, see عَشْرَةٌ. خَمْسُونَ, Oblique خَمْسِينَ Fifty. خُمُسٌ A fifth part. خَامِسٌ The fifth.

خَمَصَ *To subside* (*a swelling*), *To be empty* (*the belly*). مَخْمَصَةٌ Hunger.

خَمَطَ aor. i. *To half-roast* (*meat*). خَمْطٌ n.a. Bitter.

خَنَزَ aor. a. *To stink.* خِنْزِيرٌ A pig; Plur. خَنَازِيرُ (2nd declension) Swine.

خَنَسَ aor. i. and o. *To remain behind, hide away.* خُنَّسٌ The Stars in general, or, according to some, the five Planets Saturn, Jupiter, Mars, Venus, and Mercury, because they have a retrograde as well as a direct motion. خَنَّاسٌ The Devil, because he hides himself at the name of God.

خَنَقَ *To strangle.*—مُنْخَنِقٌ part. act. VII. f. That which is strangled.

خَارَ aor. o. *To low like an ox.* خُوَارٌ A lowing.

خَاضَ aor. o. To plunge into, wade, enter into—a discourse,—engage in—a discussion, or vanity,—(with فِي). *Note.* After خَاضَ there is frequently an ellipse of the complement. خَوْضٌ n.a. A wading, engaging in (vain discourse). خَائِضٌ part. act. One who engages in vain discourse.

خَافَ for خَوِفَ aor. يَخَافُ for يَخْوَفُ, D. S. Gr. T. 1, pp. 113 and 115, To fear, dread, apprehend (with acc. and with عَلَى of pers. in sense of *for;* or with عَنْ or مِنْ in sense of *from;* it is likewise found with acc. of pers. and بِ of thing; also with أَنْ of following verb, or with acc. and إِنْ). خَوْفٌ n.a. Fear, dread. خَائِفٌ part. act. One who fears, afraid. خِيفَةٌ Fear; خِيفَةً Out of fear.—خَوَّفَ II. To cause to fear, frighten, terrify. تَخْوِيفٌ n.a. Terror; تَخْوِيفًا In order to terrify (them).—تَخَوَّفَ V. *To be frightened, to diminish by taking away a part.* تَخَوُّفٌ n.a. عَلَى تَخَوُّفٍ 16 v. 49 may be rendered "By taking away a portion of their goods or profits," or according to Sale's version, "By a gradual destruction."

خال aor. o. *To keep.* خَالَ Plur. أَخْوَالٌ A maternal Uncle. خَالَةٌ A maternal Aunt.—خَوَّلَ II. To bestow favours on (with double acc.).

خَانَ aor. o. To deceive, be unfaithful to (with acc. of pers. and ب); to violate (an engagement), as وَتَخُونُوا أَمَانَاتِكُمْ 8 v. 27, "Nor violate your covenants." N.B. وَ is here a disjunctive particle. خِيَانَةٌ n.a. A deceiving, treachery; وَإِنْ يُرِيدُونَ خِيَانَتَكَ 8 v. 72, "And if they desire to deceive thee;" the n.a. being here put for the verb; D. S. Gr. T. 2, p. 163. خَآئِنٌ part. act. One who deceives, a cheat, treacherous. خَآئِنَةٌ with ة added for sake of energy, D. S. Gr. T. 1, p. 322; same meaning as خَآئِنٌ; or it may agree with نَفْسٌ or نَظْرَةٌ understood, thus, يَعْلَمُ خَآئِنَةَ ٱلْأَعْيُنِ 40 v. 20, *Literally,* "He knoweth the deceitful of eyes;" For the construction of the Participle (verbal adjective) with the genitive, see D. S. Gr. T. 2, p. 183. خَوَّانٌ A perfidious person, a traitor. إِخْتَانَ— VIII. To deceive, defraud; ٱلَّذِينَ يَخْتَانُونَ أَنْفُسَهُمْ 4 v. 107, "Those who defraud one another;" *Literally,* "who mutually defraud themselves;" the eighth form being here put for the sixth, which is not used in this verb, D. S. Gr. T. 1, p. 138.

خَوَى aor. i. a doubly imperfect verb, *To be tumbled down (a house).* خَاوٍ for خَاوِىٌ, Fem. خَاوِيَةٌ part. act. That which is utterly ruinous, waste, and tumble-down; fallen down (with عَلَى).

خَابَ aor. i. To be disappointed, frustrated, to be in a hopeless state. خَآئِبٌ part. act. One who is in a hopeless state.

خَارَ aor. i. *To be in good circumstances, to be favourable to.* خَيْرٌ, Fem. خَيْرَةٌ Good, agreeable, Plur. أَخْيَارٌ; also Better, best, for أَخْيَرُ, the أ being omitted on account of the frequent use of the word; N.B. With these comparative significations it is common to all genders and numbers. ٱلْخَيْرَاتُ Good things, good works. خِيَرَةٌ Choice, selection.—تَخَيَّرَ V. To choose; at 68 v. 38 تَخَيَّرُونَ is for تَتَخَيَّرُونَ D. S. Gr. T. 1, p. 221.—إِخْتَارَ VIII. To choose, choose from out of (with double acc., also with acc. of pers. or thing chosen and عَلَى).

خَاطَ aor. i. *To sew.* خَيْطٌ A thread. خِيَاطٌ A needle.

خَالَ for خَيِلَ aor. a. D. S. Gr. T. 1, p. 243, *To imagine.* خَيْلٌ a collective noun, Horses, Horse, Cavalry.—خَيَّلَ II. To make to appear (with إِلَى of pers. and أَنْ).—مُخْتَالٌ a verbal adjective with the form of the passive part. of VIII. f. Proud, arrogant.

خَامَ aor. i. *To act the coward.* خِيَامٌ plur. of خَيْمَةٌ A pavilion.

د

دَأَبَ aor. a. and o. *To be diligent.* دَأْبٌ and دَأَبٌ A state, custom, manner, wont: دَأَبًا According to custom. دَآئِبَيْنِ oblique dual part. act. Both of whom diligently perform their work.

دَبَّ aor. i. *To go gently, crawl.* دَابَّةٌ Plur. دَوَابُّ Whatsoever moveth on the earth, especially beasts of burden; A miraculous Beast is spoken of at 27 v. 84, which is to be one of the Signs of the last Day.

دَبَرَ *To be behind.* دُبُرٌ The back, hinder part; مِنْ دُبُرٍ From behind. أَدْبَارٌ plnr. of دُبُرٌ The back, the last, extremity, that which comes after; نَرُدَّهَا عَلَى أَدْبَارِهَا 4 v. 50, "And we render them after the manner of their hinder parts," *i.e.* smooth and withont featnres; أَدْبَارَ ٱلسُّجُودِ 50 v. 39, "At the end of prayers;" alluding to certain supererogatory observances which may be made or not after the evening Prayer. دَابِرٌ The extreme, last remnant, uttermost part.—دَبَّرَ II. To dispose, manage, govern. مُدَبِّرٌ part. act. One who governs, etc. —أَدْبَرَ IV. To tnrn the back, retreat. إِدْبَارٌ n.a. إِدْبَارَ ٱلنُّجُومِ 52 v. 49, *Literally*, "At the waning of the Stars;" the words refer to certain observances after morning Prayer, see أَدْبَارٌ. مُدْبِرٌ part. act. One who turns his back and retreats.—تَدَبَّرَ and إِدَّبَّرَ V. D. S. Gr. T. 1, p. 220, To meditate upon, understand, consider.

دَثَرَ *To put forth leaves.*—مُدَّثِّرٌ part. act. V. f. One who wraps himself up in a garment; The name of the 74th chapter, in which Moḥammad is addressed by this name; He is said to have been thus wrapped up when accosted by the Angel Gabriel.

دَحَرَ aor. a. *To drive away.* دُحُورٌ n.a. A repelling; دُحُورًا 37 v. 9, "To drive (them) away." مَدْحُورٌ part. pass. Driven away, rejected.

دَحَضَ aor. a. *To examine into, slip, to be weak (an argument).* دَاحِضٌ part. act. That which has no force.—أَدْحَضَ IV. To weaken or nullify by an argument, condemn (with acc. and بِ). مُدْحَضٌ part. pass. One who is condemned or worthy of condemnation.

دَحَا aor. a. and o. To spread out, expand, *transitive.*

دَخَرَ aor. a. *To be small, vile, and of no value.* دَاخِرٌ part. act. That which is or becomes small, vile, or of no acconnt.

دَخَلَ aor. o. To enter (with acc. also with مِنْ, or with فِى); to go in nnto (with acc. of place and عَلَى of pers.); to join one's-self in company with (with بِ), as at 5 v. 66; دَخَلُوا بِٱلْكُفْرِ "They entered into—your society—with infidelity;" with بِ it also signifies to have connexion with, in which sense it occnrs at 4 v. 27. دَخَلٌ Vice, corrnption of either mind or body; دَخَلًا Falsely, fraudulently. دَاخِلٌ part. act. One who enters in.—أَدْخَلَ IV. To introduce, cause to enter, lead into (with acc. of pers. and فِى, or with donble acc.). مُدْخَلٌ part. pass. *Introduced*, also Time or place of entering in; D. S. Gr. T. 1, p. 305; أَدْخِلْنِى مُدْخَلَ صِدْقٍ 17 v. 82, "Cause me to enter (the grave) with a favonrable entrance," see مُخْرَجٌ. —مُدَّخَلٌ nonn of place VIII. f. A place of retreat, see مُدْخَلٌ *suprâ*.

دَخَنَ aor. a. and o. *To smoke.* دُخَانٌ Smoke.

دَرَّ aor. i. and o. *To give much milk (a camel), to shine.* دُرِّيٌّ Shining. مِدْرَارٌ An abundant rain.

دَرَأَ aor. a. To drive off, pnt off, avert (with عَنْ).— إِدَّارَأَ VI. for تَدَارَأَ D. S. Gr. T. 1, p. 220, To strive one with another (with فِى).

دَرَجَ aor. o. *To walk, go.* دَرَجَةٌ A step; in the Ḳorân it frequently means a step in rank, honour, or authority; a degree of honour or happiness; دَرَجَةٌ and دَرَجَاتٌ By degrees (of honour); أَعْظَمُ دَرَجَةً 9 v. 20, "Of higher degree," *Literally*, "Superior as to degree."— إِسْتَدْرَجَ X. *To move gradually;* consign to a gradual pnnishment.

دَرَسَ aor. o. *To be obliterated;* to study, read with attention (with acc. also with فِى). دِرَاسَةٌ Attentive stndy. إِدْرِيسُ Enoch, so called from his great learning; this word is found in the Korân of the 2nd declension, D. S. Gr. T. 1, p. 404; Freitag in his Dictionary spells it with the tanween.

دَرَكَ *To follow up, overtake.* دَرَكٌ n.a. The act of following np; لَا تَخَافُ دَرَكًا 20 v. 80, "Thou art in no fear of being overtaken (by the Egyptians);" دَرَكٌ also means the lowest bottom, sc. "Dregs" (of Hell).—أَدْرَكَ IV. To overtake, reach, attain unto, comprehend. مُدْرَكٌ part. pass. Overtaken.—تَدَارَكَ and إِدَّارَكَ VI. D. S. Gr. T. 1, p. 220, To overtake, follow one another (with فِى); to reach, comprehend; The passage at 27 v. 68 بَلِ ٱدَّارَكَ عِلْمُهُمْ فِى ٱلْآخِرَةِ is read in various ways and admits of several interpretations; it may either be rendered "Bnt their knowledge has comprehended (somewhat) of the life to come," or "Still less have they comprehended, etc.," see بَلْ.

دِرْهَمٌ Plur. دَرَاهِمُ (2nd declension) from the Pers. دِرَم, Money; a silver coin, the valne of which has varied considerably at different times and in different places; the weight of the *legal* dirhem is fixed at 50⅖ barleycorns.

دَرَى aor. i. To know; وَإِنْ أَدْرِى 21 vv. 109 and 111, "And I do not know;" for this negative use of إِنْ see D. S. Gr. T. 1, p. 520; the verb is nsed with acc., also with أَ whether.—أَدْرَى IV. To make to know, teach (with acc. of pers. and بِ).

دَسَّ aor. o. To hide (with acc. and فِى).

دَسَرَ aor. o. *To ram in.* دُسُرٌ plnr. of دِسَارٌ Oakum or Palm-tree fibres with which ships are canlked; according to others, Nails.

دَسَى aor. a. *To get no increase.*—دَسَّى II. To corrupt.

دَعَّ aor. o. To push, drive away with violence (with acc. and إِلَى). دَعٌّ n.a. A thrusting.

دَعَا aor. o. *To call out,* call, call npon; to call for, invoke (with acc. of pers., بِ of thing, and فِى of place); to pray to, invite (with acc. and لِ also with إِلَى, or with acc. and أَنْ); to attribnte (with acc. and لِ of pers.); دَعَانِ for دَعَانِى 2 v. 182, "He prays to me," D. S. Gr. T. 1, p. 459; أَدْعُوا "I invite," 1 pers. sing. aor. for أَدْعُو, the final Alif being an أَلِفُ ٱلْوِقَايَةِ or Alif of precaution, D. S. Gr. T. 1, p. 109; دَعَوُا, and when followed by Wesla, or Alif of union, دَعَوْا 3 pers. plur. pret. D. S. Gr. T. 1, pp. 69 and 112. دَعْوَى n.a. A cry, prayer; with an affixed pronoun it is written دَعْوَاهُمْ D. S. Gr. T. 1, p. 118. دُعَآءٌ A prayer, snpplication, invoking, asking for, calling upon or for. دَعْوَةٌ A supplication, prayer, invocation, summons; دَعْوَةً 30 v. 24, "By a summons." أَدْعِيَآءُ plur. of دَعِىٌّ An adopted or spurions Son. دَاعٍ for دَاعِىٌ part. act. One who prays, invites, summons, etc. a Preacher; at 2 v. 182 ٱلدَّاعِ is a poetic license for ٱلدَّاعِى D. S. Gr. T. 2, p. 497.—إِدَّعَى VIII. D. S. Gr. T. 1, p. 222, To claim, desire (with acc. or بِ).

دَفِئَ for دَفَأَ D. S. Gr. T. 1, p. 97, aor. a. *To be hot.* دِفْءٌ Warmth, warm clothing made of camel's hair; The food, milk and raiment derived from camels are all classed nnder the head of دِفْءٌ.

دَفَعَ aor. a. *To push,* pay over to (with acc. of

thing and (إِلَى); to repel, drive away, avert (with acc. and بِ). دَفْعٌ n.a. The act of prohibiting, prevention; لَوْلَا دَفْعُ ٱللّٰهِ ٱلنَّاسَ بَعْضَهُمْ بِبَعْضٍ 2 v. 252, "Unless God (had set) men to hinder one another;" The noun of action is here used instead of the verb, and governs the subject in the gen. and the object in the accus. case; D. S. Gr. T. 2, p. 166. دَافِعٌ part. act. One who averts.—دَافَعَ III. (with عَنْ) To defend.

دَفَقَ aor. o. and i. *To pour forth* (*water*). دَافِقٌ part. act. That which pours forth or is poured forth.

دَكَّ aor. o. To pound into dust. دَكٌّ Powder, a level bank of sand; دَكًّا Into powder. دَكَّةٌ Level sand. دَكَّآءُ (2nd declension) D. S. Gr. T. 1, p. 402, A flat mound of earth or dust.

دَكَرَ see ذَكَرَ.—إِدَّكَرَ VIII. f. of ذَكَرَ for إِذْتَكَرَ D. S. Gr. T. 1, p. 222. مُدَّكِرٌ part. act. see ذَكَرَ.

دَلَّ aor. o. To show, point out, guide (with acc. of pers. and عَلَى of thing). دَلِيلٌ *A proof*, a means of showing (with عَلَى), as جَعَلْنَا ٱلشَّمْسَ عَلَيْهِ دَلِيلًا 25 v. 47, "We made the sun to be a means of showing it—the shadow."

دَلَكَ *To rub, to incline downwards from the meridian* (*the sun*). دُلُوكٌ n.a. The declining of the sun from the meridian.

دَلَا aor. o. *To let down a bucket into a well.* دَلْوٌ comm. gend. A bucket.—دَلَّى II. To occasion a fall (with acc. of pers. and بِ).—أَدْلَى IV. To let down, offer as a bribe (with بِ of thing offered and إِلَى of pers.).—تَدَلَّى V. To approach closely.

دَمٌ for دَمَوٌ v. *infrà*.

دَمْدَمَ quadriliteral verb, *To plaster over*, obliterate, destroy (with عَلَى of pers. and بِ); Original root دَمٌّ *To plaster*.

دَمَرَ aor. o. *To destroy*.—دَمَّرَ II. same as دَمَرَ (with acc. also with عَلَى). تَدْمِيرٌ n.a. Destruction; فَدَمَّرْنَاهَا تَدْمِيرًا 17 v. 17, "Then we destroyed it with an utter destruction."

دَمَعَ aor. a. *To shed tears.* دَمْعٌ n.a. A tear; used with a plural signification, Tears.

دَمَغَ aor. a. and o. *To wound the brain;* hence, to destroy.

دَمٌ for دَمَوٌ; Plur. دِمَآءٌ Blood; the hamza here takes the place of final و, the word therefore retains the tanween; D. S. Gr. T. 1, pp. 113 and 402; لَا تَسْفِكُونَ دِمَآءَكُمْ 2 v. 78, "Ye shall not shed your blood," meaning "the blood of one another."

دِينَارٌ from the Persian دِنَّار, or more probably from the Greek δηνάριον, A gold coin, a ducat.

دَنَا aor. o. *To be near or low*, to draw near. دَانٍ for دَانِيٌ, Fem. دَانِيَةٌ part. act. That which is near at hand or low, like fruit hanging low and near at hand, as at 69 v. 23. أَدْنَى for أَدْنَيُ, Fem. دُنْيَا for دُنْيَى D. S. Gr. T. 1, pp. 110, 111, and 403, comp. and superl. form, Viler, worse, less, easier; *as it were*, more ready to hand, nearer, nearest; ٱلْحَيٰوةُ ٱلدُّنْيَا "The present life," as being nearer or perhaps viler; فِي أَدْنَى ٱلْأَرْضِ 30 v. 2, "In the nearest parts of the earth;" *where* is not decided, but it seems probable that the Victory spoken of in the text took place either in Syria or the Holy Land, possibly at Jerusalem; at 33 v. 59 أَدْنَى may be rendered "More convenient or suitable;" at 58 v. 8, "fewer;" and at 73 v. 20, "very near," or "somewhat less;" at 7 v. 168 it is used with an ellipse of the word

"يَأْخُذُونَ عَرَضَ هَٰذَا ٱلْأَدْنَى ,ٱلشَّىْء thus They take the goods of this baser thing (viz. the world)." دُنْيَا as a feminine substantive, The world, this world, this world's gear.—أَدْنَى IV. To bring near; at 33 v. 59 it means to fetch in order to put on (with عَلَى of pers.)

دَهَرَ *To happen.* دَهْرٌ Time; حِينٌ مِنَ ٱلدَّهْرِ 76 v. 1, "A space of time."

دَهَقَ *To cut in pieces, fill a cup.* دِهَاقٌ Full—a cup,—a bumper.

دَهَمَ aor. a. *To come suddenly upon.*—إِدْهَامٌ XI. To be of a blackish tint. مُدْهَامٌّ part. act. That which is of a dark green colour inclining to black, as gardens from being much watered.

دَهَنَ aor. o. *To anoint, dissimulate.* دِهَانٌ Red leather, also plur. of دُهْنٌ Butter, anointing oil; at 55 v. 37 it may be taken in either sense; if in the latter, it means that the heavens shall *melt away* and become like oil. —أَدْهَنَ IV. To use dissimulation, in modern phrase, to be a humbug. مُدْهِنٌ part. act. One who glosses over or holds in low estimation (with بِ), as أَفَبِهَٰذَا ٱلْحَدِيثِ أَنْتُمْ مُدْهِنُونَ 56 v. 80, "Will ye therefore gloss over this new revelation?" *i.e.* the Ḳorân.

دَهَى aor. i. *To happen to, injuriously affect any one.* أَدْهَى for أَدْهَىُ (see أَدْنَى) compar. form, More grievous.

دَاوُدُ or if written with the hamza دَاوُدُ for دَاوُودُ (2nd declension) David, D. S. Gr. T. 1, pp. 104 and 404.

دَارَ aor. o. To go round. دَارٌ fem. gender; Plur. دِيَارٌ A house, dwelling, mansion, abode; ٱلدَّارُ A name of Paradise; also of Medina, as at 59 v. 9. دَيَّارٌ Any. دَآئِرَةٌ Plur. دَوَآئِرُ (2nd declension) A change of fortune, turn of luck, especially of bad luck.—أَدَارَ IV. To transact (business).

دَالَ aor. o. *To change—as the times,—to undergo vicissitudes.* دُولَةٌ A change of time or fortune; دُولَةً 59 v. 7, "In one circuit."—دَاوَلَ III. To cause to interchange good and bad fortune (with acc. of thing and بَيْنَ of persons).

دَامَ aor. a. and o. To endure, continue, remain (with فِى); to persevere (with عَلَى). دَآئِمٌ part. act. That which endures perpetually, One who perseveres.

دَانَ aor. o. *To be inferior.* دُونَ and مِنْ دُونِ is properly a noun, signifying inferiority; as a preposition it is employed in a variety of senses, Besides, except, beneath, to the exclusion of, in preference to, contrary to, different to, in opposition to, without; at 16 v. 37 we find it used with two different meanings in the same verse, as مَا عَبَدْنَا مِنْ دُونِهِ مِنْ شَىْءٍ "We had not served anything besides him," and وَلَا حَرَّمْنَا مِنْ دُونِهِ مِنْ شَىْءٍ "Nor had we declared anything unlawful without him," *i.e.* without his permission; Lastly, it is used to express anything interposed between two objects, thus لَمْ نَجْعَلْ لَهُمْ مِنْ دُونِهَا سِتْرًا 18 v. 89, "We have given them nothing to act as a covering against it (the sun);" The people referred to in this passage having neither house nor clothing, but living in holes in the ground like the Earthmen of South Africa; So again at 19 v. 17, فَٱتَّخَذَتْ مِنْ دُونِهِمْ حِجَابًا "And she took a veil to cover herself from them;" see D. S. Gr. T. 1, p. 496.

دَانَ aor. i. *To be indebted, to judge,* profess the true faith (with acc.). دَيْنٌ A debt, that which one owes. دِينٌ Custom, institution, religion, the true faith, obedience, judgment; يَوْمُ ٱلدِّينِ

تَدَايَنَ VI. To become debtors one to another (with بِ).

دِينَارٌ for دِنَّارٌ, v. *suprà.*

The day of judgment; يُوَفِّيهِمُ ٱللّٰهُ دِينَهُمُ ٱلْحَقَّ 24 v. 25, "God will pay them their just due." مَدِينٌ One who receives payment of a debt.—

ذ

ذَا Plur. أُولَاءِ demonstrative pronoun, called also demonstrative article; This, that, He; to this pronoun the particle هَ or هَا is frequently prefixed, and it is then written هٰذَا or commonly هَذَا, Fem. هٰذِهِ, Plur. هٰؤُلَاءِ q.v. ذَا is frequently used with an ellipse of, or instead of ٱلَّذِى, and must then be translated "that which," or "he who," as مَا ذَا تَأْمُرُونَ 7 v. 107, "What then do ye order?" *Literally,* "What is that which ye order?" According to the system of the Arab grammarians these demonstratives are all indeclinable nouns, and totally independent of each other; D. S. Gr. T. 1, p. 441.—N.B. ذَا is likewise the acc. of ذُو q.v.

ذَأَبَ aor. a. *To collect.* ذِئْبٌ A wolf.

ذَاتٌ fem. of ذُو q.v.

ذَارِيَاتٌ fem. plur. part. act. of ذَرَا q.v.

ذَأَمَ aor. a. *To despise.* مَذْءُومٌ for مَذْؤُومٌ part. pass. Despised; D. S. Gr. T. 1, p. 104.

ذَبَّ aor. o. *To prohibit, wander to and fro.* ذُبَابٌ generic noun, A fly.

ذَبَحَ aor. a. *To split,* cut the throat, slay, sacrifice (with acc. and عَلَى). ذِبْحٌ That which is sacrificed, a victim.—ذَبَّحَ II. To slay in large numbers.

ذَبْذَبَ quadriliteral verb, *To be moved to and fro, as anything suspended in the air.* مُذَبْذَبٌ part. pass. Moved about, wavering to and fro (with بَيْنَ); Original root ذَبَّ q.v.

ذَخَرَ aor. a. *To select.*—إِذَّخَرَ VIII. To store up for future use (with acc. and فِى).

ذَرْ imperat. of وَذَرَ q.v.

ذَرَّ aor. o. *To scatter, strew.* ذَرَّةٌ noun of unity, One single ant. ذُرِّيَّةٌ Progeny, offspring, children, race; The following passage is rather obscure, فَمَا آمَنَ لِمُوسَى إِلَّا ذُرِّيَّةٌ مِنْ قَوْمِهِ 10 v. 83, "And none believed on Moses, save (certain) children of his people;" Some have imagined that Pharaoh's people are those referred to.

ذَرَأَ aor. a. To create, produce, multiply; as يَذْرَؤُكُمْ فِيهِ 42 v. 9, "He multiplies you by this means;" it is also used with the acc. and لِ.

ذَرَعَ *To measure with a cubit.* ذَرْعٌ A stretching forth of the hand, strength, power; ضَاقَ بِهِمْ ذَرْعًا 11 v. 79, "He was weak in power concerning them," *i.e.* He had no power to protect them; ذَرْعُهَا سَبْعُونَ ذِرَاعًا 69 v. 32, "The extension—length—of which is seventy cubits." ذِرَاعٌ comm. gend. A cubit, length of the arm from the elbow to the extremity of the middle finger. ذِرَاعَيْهِ 18 v. 17, oblique dual, "His two fore-legs;" *properly,* down to the knees.

ذَرَا aor. o. and i. To snatch away, scatter. ذَرْوٌ n.a. The act of scattering abroad. ذَارِوٌ for ذَارٍ

D. S. Gr. T. 1, p. 109, part. act.; Fem. Plur. ذَارِيَاتٌ, as وَٱلذَّارِيَاتِ ذَرْوًا 51 v. 1, "By the winds which scatter (the dust) in every direction;" or, by another interpretation, "By the women who scatter abroad (their offspring)."

ذَعِنَ *To obey.*—مُذْعِنٌ part. act. IV. f. One who is submissive (with إِلَى).

ذَقَنَ *To strike on the chin.* أَذْقَانٌ plur. of ذَقَنٌ A chin; at 17 vv. 108 and 109 it may be rendered "Faces."

ذَكَرَ aor. o. *To strike a man on the private parts*, to remember (with acc. and أَنْ); to commemorate, make mention of, bear in mind (with acc. and فِي or عَلَى). ذِكْرٌ A remembrance, record, commemoration, memoir, memorial, making mention, an exposition (of religion), admonition; The Ḳorân is frequently called ذِكْرٌ لِلْعَالَمِينَ "An admonition, or exposition of religion for all creatures;" أَهْلَ ٱلذِّكْرِ 16 v. 45, The Jews and Christians, as "Keepers of the oracles of God;" ذِكْرٌ also means fame, good report, as وَرَفَعْنَا لَكَ ذِكْرَكَ 94 v. 4, "And have we not exalted thy fame?" ذَكَرٌ Plur. ذُكُورٌ and ذُكْرَانٌ A male. ذَاكِرٌ part. act. One who remembers (God). ذِكْرَى (2nd declension) D. S. Gr. T. 1, p. 402, A remembering, admonition; ذِكْرَى ٱلدَّارِ 38 v. 46, "By their calling to mind the life to come;" فِيمَ أَنْتَ مِنْ ذِكْرَاهَا 79 v. 43, "What record of (or means of knowing) it do you possess?" *Note.* فِيمَ is here put for فِيمَا "In what?" see مَا. تَذْكِرَةٌ A warning, admonition, that which brings to one's recollection. مَذْكُورٌ part. pass. Remembered.—ذَكَّرَ II. To remind, warn (with acc. and بِ); to admonish. تَذْكِيرٌ n.a. A reminding, warning. مُذَكِّرٌ part. act. One who warns or admonishes.—تَذَكَّرَ or إِذَّكَّرَ V. D. S. Gr. T. 1, p. 220, To be admonished, to be reminded; أَوَلَمْ نُعَمِّرْكُمْ مَا يَتَذَكَّرُ فِيهِ مَنْ تَذَكَّرَ 35 v. 34, "And did we not give you (a sufficient) length of days, that whoso would be admonished might be admonished therein?"—إِدَّكَرَ VIII. D. S. Gr. T. 1, p. 222, To remember, remind one's-self. مُدَّكِرٌ part act. One who remembers or reminds himself, hence, who is reminded or admonished.

ذَكَا aor. o. *To burn furiously.*—ذَكَّى II. *To cause to burn*, to slay.

ذَلَّ aor. i. To be abject, humbled. ذُلٌّ n.a. Humility, abasement; جَنَاحَ ٱلذُّلِّ 17 v. 25, "The wing of humility," see جَنَحَ; At 17 v. 111 the words وَلَمْ يَكُنْ لَهُ وَلِيٌّ مِنَ ٱلذُّلِّ bear one or two interpretations; they may mean "Neither has he any friend, on account of the vileness (of all created things);" or they may be translated, "Neither has he any to protect him from ignominy," (as requiring no one). ذِلَّةٌ Abasement, ignominy, vileness. ذَلُولٌ Well-trained, tractable (a beast of burthen); commodious or easy, (the earth, or the paths of the earth); Plur. ذُلُلٌ. أَذِلَّةٌ plur. of ذَلِيلٌ Humble, submissive, mean, low-spirited, weak-hearted. أَذَلُّ comp. form (2nd declension), Viler, most vile.—ذَلَّلَ II. To humble, render submissive (with acc. and لِ); to bring low. تَذْلِيلٌ n.a. A bringing low.—أَذَلَّ IV. To abase.

ذَلِكَ Fem. تِلْكَ; Plur. أُولَئِكَ That, those; all of which are considered by Arab grammarians as indeclinable nouns, entirely distinct one from the other; they take as affixes the personal pronouns of the second person, as ذَٰلِكُمْ ,ذَٰلِكُمَا ,ذَٰلِكُنَّ ,تِلْكُمْ and تِلْكُمَا, according to the number and gender of the persons addressed; they are also fonnd with the nsnal prefixes, as كَذَٰلِكَ Thus, in that way; لِذَٰلِكَ For that reason, etc. See D. S. Gr. T. 1, p. 440.

ذَمَّ aor. o. *To revile.* ذِمَّةٌ A treaty, good faith. مَذْمُومٌ part. pass. Abnsed, disgraced.

ذَنَبَ aor. o. and i. *To follow closely.* ذَنْبٌ Plur. ذُنُوبٌ A crime, fanlt, sin. ذَنُوبٌ A portion, lot.

ذَهَبَ aor. a. To go (with إِلَى); go away, depart (with عَنْ); take away, or go away with (with بِ); D. S. Gr. T. 2, p. 121. ذَهَبٌ comm. gend. Gold. ذَاهِبٌ part. act. One who goes. ذَهَابٌ n.a. The act of taking away.—أَذْهَبَ IV. To take away, remove (with acc. and عَنْ), also to take, receive, as at 46 v. 19, where there is an ellipse of the words يُقَالُ لَهُمْ.

ذَهَلَ aor. a. To forget (with عَنْ).

ذُو Fem. ذَاتٌ, Gen. ذِى, Acc. ذَا; Dual ذَوَانِ, oblique ذَوَيْنِ, and in constr. with a complement ذَوَا and ذَوَىْ; Fem. Dnal ذَوَاتَانِ, obliqne ذَوَاتَيْنِ, and in constr. ذَوَاتَا and ذَوَاتَىْ; Plnr. ذَوُونَ, obliqne ذَوِينَ and in constr. ذَوُو and ذَوِى; Fem. Plur. ذَوَاتٌ; These words are never used but in connexion with a complement, it is therefore only in their abbreviated forms as ذَوَىْ ,ذَوَاتَا, etc. that they are to be fonnd in the Korân; their proper rendering depends very freqnently upon the sense of the words in connexion with which they occur; their most usual acceptation is Possessed of, Lord of, endowed with, or having; The following are a few of the instances where they may be paraphrased with advantage; Ex. ذُو عُسْرَةٍ 2 v. 280, "Under a difficulty;" فَذُو ذُو ٱنْتِقَامٍ 3 v. 3, "Mighty to avenge;" دُعَآءٍ عَرِيضٍ 41 v. 51, "Then is he given to much prayer; ذَوِى ٱلْقُرْبَىٰ 2 v. 172, "Relatives;" بِوَادٍ غَيْرِ ذِى زَرْعٍ 14 v. 40, "In an unfruitful valley;" ذَاتَ ٱلْيَمِينِ وَذَاتَ ٱلشِّمَالِ 18 v. 17, "To the right and left;" عَلَىٰ ذَاتِ أَلْوَاحٍ وَدُسُرٍ 54 v. 13, "On (a vessel) built with planks and oaknm" or nails, seo دَسَرَ; ذُو ٱلْقَرْنَيْنِ "The Lord of the two horns," either Alexander the Great, who is thus represented on his coins, or an older Hero who lived in the time of Ahraham; ذَا ٱلنُّونِ 21 v. 87, The prophet Jonah, see نُونٌ. In addition to tho meanings assigned to ذُو, ذَاتٌ has special significations, it may sometimes be rendered The essence of, the very identical, the thing itself; ذَاتُ ٱلصُّدُورِ 3 v. 148, "The very inmost thoughts of your breasts." For the rules of syntax which affect ذُو see D. S. Gr. T. 2, p. 145. *Note.* Instead of ذَوُونَ it is usual to employ the irregular Plural أُولُو, written أولوا q.v.

ذَادَ aor. o. To drive away; تَذُودَانِ 2 pers. fem. dual, 28 v. 23, "They drove away (their flocks)."

ذَاقَ aor. o. To taste, experience (with acc. and فِى or بِ). ذَآئِقٌ part. act. One who tastes.—أَذَاقَ IV. To causo to taste (with double acc.).

ذَانِكَ Those two; dual of ذَاكَ, generally written ذَلِكَ q.v.

ذُو see ذِى.

ذَاعَ aor. i. To become known.—أَذَاعَ IV. To divulge (with بِ).

ر

رَبَا see رَابِيَةٌ.

رَأَسَ aor. a. *To be the head of.* رَأْسٌ Plur. رُؤُسٌ A head, capital sum, as رُؤُسُ أَمْوَالِكُمْ 2 v. 279, "The capital of your money;" نُكِسُوا عَلَى رُؤُسِهِمْ 21 v. 66, "They fell back into idolatry," *Literally*, "They were turned upside down upon their heads."

رَابِيَاتٌ plur. of رَابِيَةٌ, rt. رَبَا q.v.

رَأَفَ aor. a. and o. *To be compassionate.* رَأْفَةٌ Compassion. رَؤُفٌ Compassionate, merciful.

رَأَى aor. a. To see, look (with إِلَى), behold, perceive, think (with أَنَّ); to know (with or without أَنَّ); with an affix رَآهُ is for رَأَاهُ, which again is for رَأَيَهُ D. S. Gr. T. 1, pp. 118 and 98; in the aorist and imperat. the أ is generally omitted, thus وَسَيَرَى ٱللّٰهُ عَمَلَكُمْ 9 v. 95, "And God will see your works;" أَرَأَيْتَكَ 17 v. 64, and أَرَأَيْتَكُمْ 6 v. 40; the personal pronoun كَ in these instances is purely a pleonasm, and adds nothing to the meaning; "What thinkest thou?" "What think ye?" D. S. Gr. T. 1, p. 544, and T. 2, p. 479; At 18 v. 37 تَرَنِ is for تَرَنِى D. S. Gr. T. 1, p. 459. رَأْىٌ Judgment, opinion; بَادِىَ ٱلرَّأْىِ 11 v. 29, "Upon first thoughts;" رَأْىَ ٱلْعَيْنِ 3 v. 11, "Judging by sight." رِئْىٌ That which pleases the eye. رُؤْيَا for رُؤْيَى (2nd declension) D. S. Gr. T. 1, pp. 111 and 402, A vision of the night. رِئَآءٌ Hypocrisy, ostentation; رِئَآءَ ٱلنَّاسِ 2 v. 266, "To be seen of men."—رَآءَى III. To deceive by hypocritically assuming a false appearance; يُرَآءُونَ for يُرَاءِيُونَ 3 pers. plur. aor. D. S. Gr. T. 1, p. 112, § 230.—أَرَى IV. for أَرْأَى To cause to see, show, make to appear (with double acc.); مَا أُرِيكُمْ إِلَّا مَا أَرَى 40 v. 30, "I only point out to you what I think (to be right)."—تَرَآءَى VI. To see one another, come in sight of one another; This word is written تَرَآءَ at 26 v. 61, the only place in the Korân where it occurs, but this seems to be a license, having for its object to avoid the concurrence of two quiescent letters; the following word ٱلْجَمْعَانِ commencing with a Wesla.

رَبَّ aor. o. *To be a lord and master.* رَبٌّ Plur. أَرْبَابٌ A Lord; رَبِّ for رَبِّى My Lord. رِبِّيُّونَ plur. of رِبِّىٌّ Myriads. رَبَآئِبُ (2nd declension) plur. of رَبِيبَةٌ A daughter-in-law. رَبَّانِىٌّ A Rabbi, a Doctor or one learned in Divine Law. رُبَّمَا Frequently, often, D. S. Gr. T. 1, p. 500.

رَبِحَ To be profitable (a trade or traffic).

رَبَصَ *To expect.*—تَرَبَّصَ V. To wait, wait for, expect, watch for something to befall any one (with acc. of thing and بِ of pers.). تَرَبُّصٌ n.a. The act of waiting, a period of waiting. مُتَرَبِّصٌ part. act. One who waits.

رَبَطَ aor. i. and o. *To tie*, confirm, strengthen (with عَلَى), as لِيَرْبِطَ عَلَى قُلُوبِكُمْ 8 v. 11, "That he might strengthen your hearts."—رَابَطَ III. To be firm and constant. رِبَاطًا A body of horse, consisting of five or more.

رَبَعَ *To be watered every fourth day (a camel)*; aor. a. i. and o. *To be the fourth.* رُبْعٌ The fourth part. رُبَاعَ Four by four; رُبَاعَ By fours (2nd declension), see ثُلَاثُ. أَرْبَعٌ fem. and أَرْبَعَةٌ masc. Four, see عَشْرٌ. أَرْبَعُونَ Forty. رَابِعٌ A fourth.

رَبَا aor. o. To increase, grow, swell, *mount up;* at 30 v. 38 لِيَرْبُوَا and يَرْبُوا are for لِيَرْبُو and يَرْبُو, the ا being an أَلِفُ ٱلْوِقَايَةِ or Alif of precaution, D. S. Gr. T. 1, p. 109. رَابٍ for رَابُوٌ Fem. رَابِيَةٌ part. act. That which mounts up; زَبَدًا رَابِيًا 13 v. 18, "The scum floating on the surface (of the water);" it also means severe, as فَأَخَذَهُمْ أَخْذَةً رَابِيَةً 69 v. 10, "And he inflicted on them a severe punishment." أَرْبَى comp. form, More numerous. رِبَوا or more correctly رِبًا Usury, the three cases being alike, D. S. Gr. T. 1, p. 106; with the Article it is sometimes spelt أَلرِّبَوا, the ا at the end being an Alif of precaution, v. *suprà.* رُبْوَةٌ or رَبْوَةٌ A hill, an elevated part of the Earth.—رَبَّى II. To nourish, nurse, educate (with acc. and فِى); رَبَّيَانِى 17 v. 25, "They two nourished me.—أَرْبَى IV. To cause to increase, grant an increase to.

رَتَعَ aor. a. *To feed in abundant pastures,* pass time pleasantly, enjoy one's-self.

رَتَقَ aor. o. *To mend anything by joining the broken parts.* رَتْقٌ n.a. Anything close, solid, impervious; The word occurs at 21 v. 31, where it is said that the Heavens and the Earth were originally رَتْقٌ, *i.e.* united together in one solid mass.

رَتِلَ *To be well and fairly arranged.*—رَتَّلَ II. To repeat (the Ḳorân) with a slow and distinct enunciation. تَرْتِيلٌ n.a. The act of repeating the Ḳorân in a slow and distinct manner.

رَجَّ aor. o. To move, shake. رَجٌّ n.a. A shaking, shock.

رَجَزَ *To compose a particular kind of verse called* رَجَزٌ. رِجْزٌ and رُجْزٌ Impurity, a plague, punishment, any abomination, especially Idolatry.

رَجَسَ aor. o. *To bellow loudly.* رِجْسٌ An abomination, punishment, indignation, doubt.

رَجَعَ aor. i. To return, turn back, turn off—blame—upon any one (with إِلَى), as لَعَلَّهُمْ إِلَيْهِ يَرْجِعُونَ 21 v. 59, "Perhaps they might turn it off upon him;" or, according to another version, "That they might return unto God;" to come back, فَرَجَعُوا إِلَى أَنْفُسِهِمْ 21 v. 65, "Then they came to themselves—returned to their senses;" to bring back, give back (with acc. and إِلَى); to turn again, as فَٱرْجِعِ ٱلْبَصَرَ 67 v. 3, "Turn again thine eyes (unto Heaven);" ٱرْجِعُونِ 23 v. 101, "Restore me (to life again)," A rare instance in the Ḳorân of the plural for the singular, used out of respect; D. S. Gr. T. 2, p. 237, *note.* رَجْعٌ and رُجْعَى ns.a. A return. رَاجِعٌ part. act. One who returns, etc. مَرْجِعٌ noun of time and place, A return.—تَرَاجَعَ VI. To return to one another.

رَجَفَ aor. o. To be in violent motion, to shake violently, tremble. رَجْفَةٌ An Earthquake, a mighty blast. رَاجِفَةٌ Name of the first blast of the trumpet which is to precede the general Resurrection.—مُرْجِفٌ part. act. IV. f. One who makes a commotion.

رَجَلَ aor. o. *To hurt one in the foot.* رَجْلٌ n.a. collective noun, Foot, Foot-soldiers. رِجْلٌ

fem.; Plur. أَرْجُلٌ A foot; وَلَا يَأْتِينَ بِبُهْتَانٍ يَفْتَرِينَهُ بَيْنَ أَيْدِيهِنَّ وَأَرْجُلِهِنَّ 60 v. 12, "And do not bring a calumny which they have invented between their hands and their feet;" The words are interpreted to mean, "Shall not lay their illegitimate offspring to their husbands." رَجُلٌ Plur. رِجَالٌ A man, as opposed to a woman; بِرِجَالٍ مِنَ ٱلْجِنِّ 72 v. 6, "With certain of the Jinn."

رَجَمَ aor. o. To stone. رَجْمٌ A doubt, conjecture; رَجْمًا بِٱلْغَيْبِ 18 v. 21, "Doubtfully guessing at that which is secret;" Plur. رُجُومٌ Things which are thrown. رَجِيمٌ Stoned, pelted or driven away with stones; an Epithet of Satan. مَرْجُومٌ part. pass. Stoned.

رَجَا aor. o. To hope (with acc. or with أَنْ); to hope for (with acc. and مِنْ or لِ); sometimes also to fear, but in this sense it is always found with a negative, thus كَانُوا لَا يَرْجُونَ نُشُورًا 25 v. 42, "They did not dread the Resurrection." أَرْجَآءٌ plur. of رَجًا The sides. مَرْجُوٌّ part. pass. Hoped for.—أَرْجَى IV. To put off, postpone; at 7 v. 108 أَرْجِهْ is for أَرْجِهِ "Put him off;" D. S. Gr. T. 1, p. 460. مُرْجَوْنَ plur. of مُرْجًى for مُرْجَوٌ part. pass. مُرْجَوْنَ لِأَمْرِ ٱللّٰهِ 9 v. 107, "Held in suspense (awaiting) the decree of God;" D. S. Gr. T. 1, p. 354.

رَحُبَ To be ample, spacious; بِمَا رَحُبَتْ 9 v. 25, "For all it was so spacious." مَرْحَبًا a form of salutation equivalent to Welcome! as مَرْحَبًا بِكُمْ "You are welcome."

رَحِيقٌ Pure Wine; no verbal root.

رَحَلَ aor. a. *To place saddle-bags on a camel.* رَحْلٌ n.a. A saddle-bag; Plur. رِحَالٌ. رِحْلَةٌ A journey, travelling; إِيلَافِهِمْ رِحْلَةَ ٱلشِّتَآءِ وَٱلصَّيْفِ 106 v. 2, "For their joining together (in fitting out) the Caravan in winter and summer."

رَحِمَ aor. a. To be merciful, have mercy upon (with acc. of pers.); In the passive تُرْحَمُونَ "Ye shall be treated with mercy," or "shall receive mercy." رَحْمَةٌ, sometimes spelt رَحْمَتٌ, D. S. Gr. T. 1, p. 276, *note*, Mercy, kindness. أَرْحَمُ compar. form, Most merciful. أَرْحَامٌ comm. gender, plur. of رَحِمٌ or رِحْمٌ A womb, relationship, as أُولُوا ٱلْأَرْحَامِ Blood relations. رُحْمٌ Kindness, affection. رَاحِمٌ part. act. One who shows mercy. رَحْمَانٌ or رَحْمٰنٌ D. S. Gr. T. 1, p. 404 (with the article usually spelt ٱلرَّحْمٰنُ), and رَحِيمٌ Merciful and compassionate; The two words are constantly found together, as if to add intensity one to the other, but the former conveys the more comprehensive meaning. رُحَمَآءُ (2nd declension) plur. of رَحِيمٌ. مَرْحَمَةٌ Mercy, kindness.

رَخِيَ aor. a. *To be soft and flabby.* رُخَآءٌ A gentle wind.

رَدَّ aor. o. To drive back, avert (with acc. and عَنْ, also with عَلَى); to restore, give back, bring back, refer, give again (with acc. and لِ, إِلَى, or عَلَى); فَرَدُّوا أَيْدِيَهُمْ فِي أَفْوَاهِهِمْ 14 v. 10, "Then they put their hands up to their mouths," either biting their own fingers in anger; or it may be, to close the mouths of the prophets; At 16 v. 72, and 22 v. 5 it means to keep back (with إِلَى); at 41 v. 47 (also with إِلَى) to reserve; and at 5 v. 107, To take (an oath). رَدٌّ n.a. 21 v. 41, The act of averting, bringing back, etc. رَادٌّ part. act.

One who averts, restores, etc.; فَمَا ٱلَّذِينَ فُضِّلُوا بِرَادِّى رِزْقِهِمْ 16 v. 73, "Nor do those who have been made superior (to others) give back their wealth, etc." Here بِرَادِّى is for بِرَادِّينَ, the participle—or noun of agency—being antecedent to a complement in the genitive; D. S. Gr. T. 2, p. 183; ب being an expletive after the negative مَا, see ب. مَرَدٌّ A place by which or to which we return; besides being a noun of time and place as above, مَرَدٌّ is also a noun of action, D. S. Gr. T. 1, p. 291, and then means the act of averting, restoring, etc. مَرْدُودٌ part. pass. Restored, averted, as غَيْرُ مَرْدُودٍ 11 v. 78, "Inevitable." —تَرَدَّدَ V. To be agitated, moved to and fro.— إِرْتَدَّ VIII. To be rendered, to return, turn again (with عَلَى), as فَٱرْتَدَّا عَلَى آثَارِهِمَا 18 v. 63, "And they retraced their steps;" or with إِلَى, as لَا يَرْتَدُّ إِلَيْهِمْ طَرْفُهُمْ 14 v. 44, "Their sight shall not return to them," being fixed with horror; at 27 v. 40 the same expression may be translated "In the twinkling of an eye," or "Before thou canst fix thine eye upon any object, and remove it;" with عَنْ it means to apostatize.

رَدَأَ *To prop a wall.* رِدْءٌ A helper.

رَدِفَ To come behind (with لِ). رَادِفٌ part. act. That which follows.—مُرْدِفٌ part. act. IV. f. same as رَادِفٌ; at 8 v. 9 it may either mean following one another, or causing (the believers) to follow one another.

رَدَمَ aor. i. *To shut* (*a gate*). رَدْمٌ n.a. A strong wall.

رَدَى aor. i. *To trample the earth with his feet* (*a horse*). رَدِىَ aor. a. To perish.—أَرْدَى IV. To bring to destruction.—تَرَدَّى V. To fall headlong. مُتَرَدِّيَةٌ fem. part. act. That which falls headlong, or is slain by a fall.

رَذُلَ aor. o. *To be base.* أَرْذَلُ Plur. أَرْذَلُونَ and أَرَاذِلُ comp. form, Vilest, most abject; إِلَى أَرْذَلِ ٱلْعُمُرِ 16 v. 72, "To the worst part of life," *i.e.* To a decrepit old age; the *Madidi infantia nasi.*

رَزَقَ aor. o. To supply with the necessaries of life, provide for, bestow upon (with double acc.); to sustain; لَا يَأْتِيكُمَا طَعَامٌ تُرْزَقَانِهِ 12 v. 37, "No food shall come to you with which ye shall be supplied;" For this use of the verb in the passive voice with a complement see D. S. Gr. T. 2, p. 124. رِزْقٌ A provision, maintenance, bounty, fortune, income, anything granted to another from which he derives benefit. رَازِقٌ part. act. One who provides for, or supplies with necessaries. ٱلرَّزَّاقُ The Great Provider, one of the names of God, as Providence.

رَسَّ aor. o. *To dig a well.* ٱلرَّسُّ Er-Rass; supposed to be the name of a well near Midian, or according to others near Antioch.

رَسَخَ *To be firm.* رَاسِخٌ part. act. One who is firmly established; ٱلرَّاسِخُونَ فِى ٱلْعِلْمِ 4 v. 160, "Those who are well grounded in learning."

رَسَلَ aor. o. *To send a messenger.* رَسُولٌ An apostle, a messenger; Plur. رُسُلٌ; at 33 v. 66 we find ٱلرَّسُولَا for ٱلرَّسُولَ, for the sake of the rhyme, by a license called إِشْبَاعٌ *saturation;* D. S. Gr. T. 2, p. 497; At 26 v. 15 the word رَسُولٌ is used with a plural signification thus إِنَّا رَسُولُ etc. as though it were "Verily we are a deputation;" several reasons are assigned for this; Freitag says, quoting the Kâmoos, that words of the form نَعُولٌ are both sing. and plur.; رَسُولٌ is by others considered to be a noun of action used adjectively, for this construction see D. S. Gr. T. 2, p. 280. رِسَالَةٌ A message, commission.—أَرْسَلَ IV. To send (with إِلَى, also with acc. and إِلَى or عَلَى); فَأَرْسِلُونِ 12 v. 45, for فَأَرْسِلُونِى, D. S. Gr. T. 1. p. 459. مُرْسِلٌ part. act. One who sends; فَلَا مُرْسِلَ لَهُ مِنْ بَعْدِهِ 35 v. 2, "There is no one who can send or bestow it, after he has withheld it." مُرْسَلٌ part. pass. One who is sent, a legate; أَلْمُرْسَلَاتُ 77 v. 1, Angels, winds, or the verses of the Korân, according to different interpretations.

رسا aor. o. *To be or stand firm.* رَوَاسِى (2nd declension) plur. of رَاسِيَةٌ fem. of رَاسٍ for رَاسِىٌ for رَاسِوٌ; D. S. Gr. T. 1, pp. 330 and 366, part. act. Things which are firmly and immovably fixed—mountains.—أَرْسَى IV. To fix firmly. مُرْسًى noun of time and place, That which is fixed with regard to time or place, as أَيَّانَ مُرْسَاهَا 7 v. 186, "When is its fixed time?"; a Port, harbour, or roadstead, as مَجْرَاهَا وَمُرْسَاهَا 11 v. 43, "Both whilst it is moving, and whilst it is at anchor, or at rest."

رَشَدَ aor. o. To walk in the right way, to be well directed. رَشَدٌ, رَشَادٌ, and رُشْدٌ nouns of action, A going in the right way, true direction, correct rule of action. رَاشِدٌ part. act. One who is well directed, or who walks in the right way. رَشِيدٌ A person of discernment, a guide to the right way.—مُرْشِدٌ part. act. IV. f. One who directs aright, a guide.

رَصَّ aor. o. *To cement or join together.* مَرْصُوصٌ part. pass. Firmly and compactly united.

رَصَدَ aor. o. *To observe, lie in wait.* رَصَدٌ n.a. A lying in wait; also as a collective noun, An ambush, band of watchers. مَرْصَدٌ A place of ambush. مِرْصَادٌ A place of observation, or of ambush.—إِرْصَادٌ n.a. IV. f. A means of preparation or fitting out.

رَضِعَ aor. a. and i. *To suck the mother's milk.* رَضَاعَةٌ n.a. The act of sucking milk: أَخَوَاتُكُمْ مِنَ ٱلرَّضَاعَةِ 4 v. 27, "Your foster sisters." مَرَاضِعُ (2nd declension) plur. of مَرْضَعٌ A breast.—أَرْضَعَ IV. To suckle (with acc. of child and لِ of father); to give suck to. مُرْضِعَةٌ fem. part. act. One who gives suck.—إِسْتَرْضَعَ X. To seek a nurse for (a child).

رَضِىَ aor. a. To be content, pleased (with عَنْ, with بِ, or with acc.); to choose (with بِ, also with acc. of thing and لِ of pers.). رَضِىٌّ Agreeable, acceptable. رَاضٍ for رَاضِىٌ part. act., Fem. رَاضِيَةٌ One who is content, well pleased; also pleasant, agreeable. رِضْوَانٌ Grace, acceptance, favour, that which is pleasing. مَرْضِىٌّ part. pass. Accepted, well pleased or contented. مَرْضَاتٌ n.a. for مَرْضَاةٌ D. S. Gr. T. 1, p. 276, *note;* The act of pleasing.—أَرْضَى IV. To content, please (with acc. of pers. and بِ).—تَرَاضَى VI. To be pleased with one another, to be mutually agreed (with بَيْنَ or بِ). تَرَاضٍ n.a. for تَرَاضِىٌ for تَرَاضُىٌ D. S. Gr. T. 1, p. 111, Mutual consent.—إِرْتَضَى VIII. To be pleased with, pleasing to (with لِ).

رَطَبَ *To be fresh and ripe (dates).* رُطْبٌ n.a. That which is green. رُطَبٌ collective noun, Fresh ripe dates.

رَعَبَ aor. a. *To frighten, fear.* رُعْبٌ n.a. Fear, terror.

رَعَدَ aor. a. and o. *To thunder.* رَعْدٌ Thunder.

رَعَى aor. a. on account of the guttural ع, D. S. Gr. T. 1, p. 250, To pasture, feed (cattle), to observe aright, as at 57 v. 27. رِعَايَةٌ n.a. A right observance. رِعَآءٌ plur. of رَاعٍ for رَاعِىٌ part. act. One who feeds flocks, a shepherd. مَرْعًى Pasture.—رَاعَى III. To observe, respect, look at (with acc. or with لِ); رَاعِنَا 2 v. 98, "Look at us;" a word to which Mohammad had a great objection, it having been derisively employed by some Jews, in whose language it had an uncomplimentary meaning.

رَغِبَ aor. a. To desire (with أَنْ); also to be unwilling (with أَنْ), or to dislike (with عَنْ); The passage at 4 v. 126 may be rendered either way; يَرْغَبُوا بِأَنْفُسِهِمْ عَنْ نَفْسِهِ 9 v. 121, "They should prefer themselves before him;" With إِلَى it means to supplicate. رَغَبٌ Love. رَاغِبٌ part. act. One who supplicates earnestly (with إِلَى); also one who is averse from (with عَنْ).

رَغِدَ *To abound in good things.* رَغَدًا Abundantly.

رَغَمَ aor. a. *To dislike, abhor.*—مُرَاغَمٌ noun of place III. form, A place of refuge.

رَفَتَ aor. o. and i. *To break in pieces.* رُفَاتٌ Dust, anything broken small.

رَفَثَ aor. o. *To be obscene.* رَفَثٌ Carnal intercourse.

رَفَدَ aor. i. *To give.* رِفْدٌ A gift. مَرْفُودٌ part. pass. Given.

رَفْرَفَ *To spread the wings.* رَفْرَفٌ A pillow.

رَفَعَ aor. a. To raise up, exalt, lift up (with acc. and إِلَى). رَافِعٌ part. act. Exalting, one who raises up. رَفِيعٌ High. مَرْفُوعٌ part. pass. Raised on high, exalted.

رَفَقَ *To help.* رَفِيقٌ A companion, friend. مِرْفَقٌ *An elbow, utility, comfort;* مِرْفَقًا Comfortably; Plur. مَرَافِقُ (2nd declension) Elbows.—مُرْتَفَقٌ A couch, noun of place derived from the VIII. f. which means *To recline on the elbow.*

رَقَّ *To be thin.* رَقٌّ A volume or scroll, *generally* of parchment.

رَقَبَ aor. o. To observe, respect, regard (with acc. and فِى). رَقِيبٌ A watcher, an observer. رَقَبَةٌ Plur. رِقَابٌ A neck, a slave; تَحْرِيرُ رَقَبَةٍ 4 v. 94, "The freeing of a neck (from the yoke of slavery)."—تَرَقَّبَ V. To look about one.—إِرْتَقَبَ VIII. To observe, watch. مُرْتَقِبٌ part. act. One who watches.

رَقَدَ aor. o. *To sleep.* رُقُودٌ n.a. Sleeping. مَرْقَدٌ A bed.

رَقَمَ *To write, mark with diacritical points.* أَلرَّقِيمُ Er-Rakeem, a word, the meaning of which is in dispute; according to one interpretation it was the name of a leaden plate, on which were inscribed the names of the seven sleepers. مَرْقُومٌ part. pass. Written.

رَقِىَ aor. a. To mount a ladder (with فِى); *to enchant.* رُقِىٌّ n.a. An ascent. رَاقٍ for رَاقِىٌ part. act. An enchanter; وَقِيلَ مَنْ رَاقٍ 75 v. 27, "And it is said, who is the magician (to drive away his agony)?" تَرَاقِىَ acc. plur. of تَرْقُوَةٌ A breast-bone; see this word under ت, see also مَثَانِىَ, rt. ثنى.—إِرْتَقَى VIII. To ascend (with فِى).

رَكِبَ aor. a. To ride (with acc.); to be carried, go on board a ship (with فِى). رَكْبٌ A company of 10 or more mounted on camels, a small caravan. رُكْبَانٌ plur. of رَاكِبٌ part. act. One who rides, mounted. رِكَابٌ collective noun, Camels. رَكُوبٌ Use of a camel in riding.—رَكَّبَ II. To put together.—مُتَرَاكِبٌ part. act. VI. f. Lying in heaps.

ركد *To be still.* رَوَاكِدُ (2nd declension) fem. plur. of رَاكِدٌ part. act. That which is still.

ركز aor. o. and i. *To fix a spear in the ground.* رِكْزٌ A low sonnd, a whisper.

ركس *To invert.*—أَرْكَسَ IV. To overtnrn, upset.

ركض aor. o. *To move the feet*, stamp on the ground; to fly (with عَنْ); Before the words أُرْكُضْ بِرِجْلِكَ at 38 v. 41 we mnst understand قِيلَ لَهُ, and between the first and last parts of the verse, we have to imagine the springing up of a fonntain, or *two*, according to the fancy of the Commentators.

ركع aor. a. *To have the back bent*, to bow down in prayer. رَاكِعٌ Plur. رَاكِعُونَ and رُكَّعٌ part. act. One who bows down.

ركم aor. o. To gather together in a heap. رُكَامٌ A heap; رُكَامًا In heaps. مَرْكُومٌ part. pass. Gathered in a heap.

ركن aor. a. To incline one's-self (with إِلَى). رُكْنٌ a stay, snpport, prop; hence, Princes or chiefs of the people.

رم aor. o. and i. *To repair*; also aor. i. *To be rotten.* رَمِيمٌ Rotten; adjective of common gender.

رُمَّانٌ generic nonn, Pomegranates.

رمح aor. a. *To pierce with a lance.* رِمَاحٌ plur. of رُمْحٌ A lance.

رمد aor. o. and i. *To invade an enemy's country.* رَمَادٌ Ashes.

رمز aor. o. and i. *To nod, wink.* رَمْزٌ n.a. A sign, such as a wink or nod.

رمض aor. i. *To bake a sheep in its skin.* رَمَضَانُ (2nd declension) Ramaḍân, the ninth month of the Arabian year, said to be so named, because it originally fell in the height of summer.

رمى aor. i. To throw, cast, throw out (with acc. or with بِ of thing); to cast aspersions upon any one (with acc. of pers.), as at 24 vv. 4, 6, aud 23; At 8 v. 17 allusion is made to a miracle which was wronght at Bedr in favour of Moḥammad, who, by throwing a handful of gravel into the faces of the Ḳoreish, bronght about a victory in his favour.

رهب aor. a. To fear (with acc. or with لِ of pers.). رَهْبٌ, رَهَبٌ, and رَهْبَةٌ ns.a. Fear; رَهْبَةً فِي صُدُورِهِمْ 59 v. 13, "On account of the fear inspired in their breasts by God." رُهْبَانٌ plnr. of رَاهِبٌ A monk. رَهْبَانِيَّةٌ Monasticism.—أَرْهَبَ IV. To frighten, canse terror (with acc. of pers. and بِ of thing).—إِسْتَرْهَبَ X. To terrify.

رهط *To take large mouthfuls.* رَهْطٌ n.a. A family; تِسْعَةُ رَهْطٍ 27 v. 49, "Nine men of a family;" D. S. Gr. T. 2, p. 316; This word is not generally used when more than 10 men are spoken of, bnt in any case they must be the sons of one man.

رهق aor. a. To follow closely, cover; aor. i. To oppress, cause to suffer; to be given to evil practices towards (with double acc.). رَهَقٌ n.a. Folly, oppression.—أَرْهَقَ IV. To impose a difficult task on any one, afflict with troubles and difficulties (with double acc.).

رهن *To give in pledge.* رَهِينٌ Given in pledge. رِهَانٌ plnr. of رَهْنٌ A pledge.

رها aor. o. *To go softly.* رَهْوٌ n.a. A ditch or furrow.

رَوَاسِي see رَسَا.

راح aor. o. *To do anything in the evening or at sun-set.* رَوْحٌ n.a. Rest, mercy. رُوحٌ comm. gend. A spirit, sonl; رُوحُ ٱلْقُدُسِ 16 v. 104, "The Spirit of Holiness," or "the Holy Spirit," viz. The Angel Gabriel, who alone is intended by this name; At 16 v. 2 it may be translated the Inspiration or Revelation, viz. the Korân. رِيحٌ fem., Plnr. رِيَاحٌ A wind, smell, prosperity, power. رَوَاحٌ The evening, as رَوَاحُهَا شَهْرٌ 34 v. 11, "(It blew) for a month in the evening." *Note.* At the commencement of this verse we must understand the word سَخَّرْنَا q.v. رَيْحَانٌ Victuals, things necessary to support life.— أَرَاحَ IV. To drive home (flocks) in the evening.

رَادَ aor. o. *To seek.* رُوَيْدًا Gently; رُوَيْدَ is said to be equivalent to أَمْهِلْ Grant a respite; D. S. Gr. T. 1, p. 546; at 86 v. 17 the words are found in conjunction أَمْهِلْهُمْ رُوَيْدًا "Grant them a gentle respite," or "respite them for a while." رَاوَدَ— III. To long after, desire to have intercourse with (with acc. and عَنْ); thus رَاوَدَتْنِي عَنْ نَفْسِي 12 v. 26, "She desired to lie with me;" At 12 v. 61 it means simply to solicit. أَرَادَ IV. To be willing, wish, desire, intend, mean (with acc. and بِ, also with أَنْ); يُرِدْنِ 36 v. 22 for يُرِدْنِي aor. conditional and نِي.

رَاضَ aor. o. *To exercise, or break in a colt.* رَوْضَةٌ A rich and well-watered meadow.

رَاعَ aor. o. *To frighten.* رَوْعٌ n.a. Fear, timidity.

رَاغَ aor. o. To turn furtively from one thing to another (with إِلَى); to turn upon (with عَلَى).

رَامَ aor. o. *To seek.* أَلرُّومُ collective noun, The Greeks, as being subject to the Roman Empire. *Note.* The events mentioned at the beginning of the 30th chapter relate to the wars between the Greeks and Persians under Heraclius and Chosroes.

رَابَ aor. i. *To make uncertain.* رَيْبٌ n.a. A doubt, calamity, as رَيْبَ ٱلْمَنُونِ 52 v. 30, "Adverse fortune," *literally,* "the calamity of the time." رِيبَةٌ Suspicion, uncertainty.— مُرِيبٌ part. act. IV. f. Disquieting, he or that which inspires doubt or suspicion; also one who is guilty of a crime.—إِرْتَابَ VIII. To be in doubt. مُرْتَابٌ part. act. One who is in doubt, a sceptic.

رَاشَ aor. i. *To fit feathers to an arrow.* رِيشٌ generic noun, Feathers; fine clothing.

رَاعَ aor. i. *To grow.* رِيعٌ A high hill.

رَانَ aor. i. To take possession—of the heart—(with عَلَى).

ز

زَبَدَ aor. o. *To give anyone cream to eat.* زَبَدٌ Froth, scum.

زَبَرَ aor. o. *To pelt with stones.* زَبُورٌ A book, The Book of Psalms; Plnr. زُبُرٌ Books, writings, Scriptures; زُبُرٌ and زُبَرٌ are also Plurals of زُبْرَةٌ A lump or large piece of iron, a divided portion, sect; زُبَرٌ occurs with the first of these meanings at 18 v. 95, and زُبُرٌ with the last, at 23 v. 55.

زَبَنَ aor. i. *To sell dates on the tree by guess.* زَبَانِيَةٌ plur. of زِبْنِيَةٌ, or wanting the singular, Rebels (against God), Prætorian Guards; at 96 v. 18 it appears to refer to the Angels who keep guard over Hell.

زَجَّ aor. o. *To pierce with the ferule of a spear;* زُجَاجَةٌ noun of unity, A thing made of glass, as a glass vessel.

زَجَرَ aor. o. *To prohibit, drive away.* زَجْرٌ n.a. The act of driving or prohibiting. أَلزَّاجِرَاتُ fem. plur. part. act. Those who drive; فَٱلزَّاجِرَاتِ زَجْرًا

37 v. 2, "And the Angels who drive forward the clouds, or drive away evil spirits, or keep men from sin." زَجْرَةٌ A single cry.—إِزْدَجَرَ VIII. for إِزْتَجَرَ To drive away with cries, reject. مُزْدَجَرٌ part. pass. Forbidden.

زجا aor. o. *To be easy.*—أَزْجَى IV. To propel, drive forward (with acc. and لِ or فِى). مُزْجَاةٌ fem. of مُزْجًى Few, small.

زَحْزَحَ To remove far from a place (with عَنْ). مُزَحْزِحٌ part. act. One who removes, as وَمَا هُوَ بِمُزَحْزِحِهِ مِنَ ٱلْعَذَابِ 2 v. 90, "But he shall not free himself from the punishment." Derived from زَحٌّ which has the same meaning.

زَحَفَ aor. a. *To proceed towards.* زَحْفٌ n.a. An army marching in a hostile manner.

زُخْرُفٌ Anything highly embellished, as with gilding, decoration by gilding, gold, embellishment, either real, as the flowers of the earth, 10 v. 25; or figurative, as a flowery disconrse, 6 v. 112; verbal rt. زَخْرَفَ To gild.

زَرَبَ aor. o. *To construct a pen or fold for sheep.* زَرَابِىُّ (2nd declension) plur. of زِرْبِيَّةٌ A rich carpet.

زَرَعَ aor. a. To sow seed, give increase to, as أَأَنْتُمْ تَزْرَعُونَهُ أَمْ نَحْنُ ٱلزَّارِعُونَ 56 v. 64, "Do ye give it its increase, or are We the givers of it?" زَرْعٌ Plur. زُرُوعٌ Seed, corn, land sown with corn. زُرَّاعٌ plur. of زَارِعٌ part. act. A sower.

زَرِقَ aor. o. and i. *To drop dung (a bird); to have blue eyes.* زُرْقٌ plur. of أَزْرَقُ One who has blne eyes; an enemy, such as the Greeks, whose eyes were freqnently of that colour.

زَرَى aor. i. *To abuse.*—إِزْدَرَى VIII. for إِزْتَرَى D. S. Gr. T. 1, p. 222, To despise.

زَعَمَ aor. o. *To speak*, assert, generally used in doubtful matters; to suppose, think, imagine, fancy, to be of opinion (with acc. or with أَنْ). زَعْمٌ n.a. Fancy, imagination. زَعِيمٌ A snrety, one who vouches for or guarantees another.

زَفَّ aor. o. *To carry home the bride in procession;* aor. i. To hasten, go with hurried steps.

زَفَرَ aor. i. *To send forth a deep breath.* زَفِيرٌ A deep sob; *properly*, the first part of the braying of an ass, as شَهِيقٌ is the second; at 11 v. 108 these words may be rendered "Sobbing and sighing;" at 25 v. 13 the term زَفِيرًا is applied to the roaring of flames.

زَقَمَ *To swallow speedily.* أَلزَّقُّومُ A tree growing in the midst of Hell, for a description see ch. 37 v. 60; The tree after which this infernal prodnction was named bears a kind of intensely bitter almond.

زَكَرِيَّاءُ Zacharias.

زَكَى or more properly زَكَا aor. o. *To grow*, to be pure, or purified. زَكَوةٌ pronounced, and sometimes written زَكَاةٌ or زَكَوةٌ like صَلَوةٌ or صَلَاةٌ, D. S. Gr. T. 1, p. 36, Purity, a portion of one's substance given in order to purify the rest, *i.e.* Alms; خَيْرًا مِنْهُ زَكَوةً 18 v. 80, "One more righteons than he," *literally*, "Better as to purity." زَكِىٌّ Pious, righteous. أَزْكَى for أَزْكَىُ comp. form, Purer, more righteons; أَزْكَى طَعَامًا 18 v. 18, "The purest and best food."—زَكَّى II. To purify, justify (with acc. of pers. and بِ of thing).—تَزَكَّى and إِزَّكَّى V. To endeavour to be pnre and holy, to give part of one's substance in alms, as at 92 v. 18.

زَلَّ aor. i. To slip.—أَزَلَّ IV. To cause to slip or fall (with acc. and عَنْ).—إِسْتَزَلَّ X. same as أَزَلَّ, but with acc. of pers. and بِ.

زَلْزَلَ To shake, shake to and fro. زِلْزَالٌ n.a. The act of shaking; إِذَا زُلْزِلَتِ ٱلْأَرْضُ زِلْزَالَهَا 99 v. 1, "When the earth is shaken by an earthquake;" *literally*, "by its shaking." زَلْزَلَةٌ A shock—of an earthquake.

زَلَفَ *To draw near.* زُلْفَةٌ Nearness, proximity, a near approach; زُلْفَةٌ Near at hand; Plur. زُلَفٌ; The phrase زُلَفًا مِنَ ٱللَّيْلِ at 11 v. 116 signifies those hours of the night which commence at the close of day, and those of the day which commence at the close of night; There are other ways of spelling this word, such as زُلْفًا. زُلُفًا and زُلْفَى, the last being a noun in the singular, having the same signification as زُلْفَةٌ, and of the second declension, D. S. Gr. T. 1, p. 402.—أَزْلَفَ IV. To bring near, cause to approach (with acc. and لِ).

زَلَقَ aor. o. *To slip.* زَلَقٌ A place in which the feet are liable to slip.—أَزْلَقَ IV. To cause to slip or fall (with acc. of pers. and بِ).

زَلَمَ *To wander about.* زَلَمٌ Plur. أَزْلَامٌ Headless arrows used by the ancient Arabs for purposes of divination, a superstition forbidden by the Korân; for a curious illustration of this custom see Ezekiel ch. xxi. v. 21.

زَمَرَ aor. i. *To play upon a wind instrument.* زُمَرٌ plur. of زُمْرَةٌ A crowd of men; زُمَرًا In crowds.

زَمَلَ aor. i. and o. *To limp.*—مُزَّمِّلٌ part. act. of إِزَّمَّلَ for تَزَمَّلَ V. f. D. S. Gr. T. 1, p. 220, To wrap one's-self in a garment. The epithet ٱلْمُزَّمِّلُ is applied to Mohammad in the 73rd ch. because at the moment it was communicated to him he was wrapped in a mantle either asleep or at prayers; so say the commentators.

زَمْهَرَ *To flash with anger* (*an eye*). زَمْهَرِيرٌ Excessive cold, by some interpreted to mean the Moon; original root زَمِهَ *To be violent.*

زَنْجَبِيلٌ Ginger, with which the water of Salsabeel, a fountain in Paradise, is to be flavoured.

زَنَمٌ no verbal root, *An excrescence behind the hoofs of goats.* زَنِيمٌ Spurious, illegitimate.

زَنَى aor. i. To be guilty of fornication. زِنًا n.a. Fornication. زَانٍ and with the article ٱلزَّانِي and ٱلزَّانِيَةُ part. act. One who is guilty of fornication.

زَهَدَ aor. a. *To abstain;* aor. i. *To have in low estimation.* زَاهِدٌ part. act. One who esteems lightly, or holds in low estimation (with فِي of thing).

زَهَرَ aor. a. *To be resplendent.* زَهْرَةٌ *A flower,* splendour.

زَهَقَ aor. a. *To be full of marrow* (*a bone*); to vanish, disappear, perish. زَاهِقٌ part. act. That which vanishes away. زَهُوقٌ Vain, perishable.

زَاجَ aor. o. *To stir up strife.* زَوْجٌ Plur. أَزْوَاجٌ A companion, mate, spouse, husband or wife, an individual when consorting with another; that in which individuals are united, as a kind, species, class, or sex, also a pair, a couple; Examples, فَأَنْبَتْنَا فِيهَا مِنْ كُلِّ زَوْجٍ كَرِيمٍ 31 v. 9, "And we have caused (vegetables) to spring up in it of every generous species;" فِيهِمَا مِنْ كُلِّ فَاكِهَةٍ زَوْجَانِ 55 v. 52, "In each (garden) there shall be two kinds of every fruit," or it may be "Two pairs of every kind;" thus at 11 v. 42 the words مِنْ كُلِّ زَوْجَيْنِ ٱثْنَيْنِ may either be rendered two, or two pair, of every kind, so also at 13 v. 3, 6 v. 144 and elsewhere; for the use of إِثْنَيْنِ with the dual see D. S. Gr.

T. 2, p. 315, where he translates زَوْجَيْنِ ٱثْنَيْنِ "Two individuals," a reading which is supported by the passages at 51 v. 49, where زَوْجَيْنِ must of necessity have the meaning of two individuals paired together, and at 15 v. 88, where أَزْوَاجًا means simply "individuals," or "certain of them;" وَآخَرُ مِنْ شَكْلِهِ أَزْوَاجٌ 38 v. 58, "And other (matters) of a similar kind shall be in conjunction with it;" In this passage there appears to be an ellipse, آخَرُ for أَأْخَرُ in virtue of its comparative form being pnt in the singular, D. S. Gr. T. 2, p. 304; it is also written أُخَرُ, see 3 v. 5.—زَوَّجَ II. To give in marriage (with donble acc.); to wed to (with acc. and بِ); to join together; وَإِذَا ٱلنُّفُوسُ زُوِّجَتْ 81 v. 7, "And when the souls shall be joined (to their bodies);" At 42 v. 49 it means to make of two kinds, to make or give conjointly.

زَادَ aor. o. *To take provisions.* زَادٌ Provision for a journey.—تَزَوَّدَ V. To provide one's-self for a jonrney.

زَارَ aor. o. To visit. زُورٌ False, a falsehood.—تَزَاوَرَ VI. To decline (with عَنْ); تَزَاوَرُ 18 v. 16 is for تَتَزَاوَرُ 3 pers. fem. sing. aor.

زَالَ aor. o. To cease, cease to be in a place, fail, perish, as أَنْ تَزُولَا 35 v. 39, "Lest they fail;" to decline, as إِنْ كَانَ مَكْرُهُمْ لِتَزُولَ مِنْهُ ٱلْجِبَالُ 14 v. 47, "Even though their craftiness were such that the mountains should be moved by it;" *literally*, "shonld cease to remain in their places, or incline downwards (like the Sun)." زَوَالٌ n.a. A declining, declination as of the sun from the meridian, in which sense it is figuratively employed at 14 v. 46.

زَاتَ aor. i. *To dress food with oil.* زَيْتٌ Oil. زَيْتُونٌ collective noun, The olive, olives. زَيْتُونَةٌ nonn of unity, An olive, an olive-tree.

زَادَ aor. i. *To be increased*, to increase, canse to increase, give an increase to (with acc. of pers. and فِي or with donble acc.); to exceed in number; أَوْ يَزِيدُونَ 37 v. 147, "Or there were more in nnmber;" to make an addition to (with عَلَى). زَيْدٌ Zeid, Moḥammad's freedman and adopted son, whose wife Zeinab Moḥammad married after her divorce from Zeid; see ch. 33. زِيَادَةٌ An increase, addition. مَزِيدٌ An accession, increase, addition.—إِزْدَادَ for إِزْتَادَ VIII. D. S. Gr. T. 1, p. 222, To increase, suffer an increase, or be increased by (with acc.); as وَٱزْدَادُوا تِسْعًا 18 v. 24, "And they suffered an increase of nine (years)."

زَاغَ aor. i. To be inclined downwards, to become dim (the sight), turn aside, deviate (with عَنْ). زَيْغٌ n.a. Perversity.—أَزَاغَ IV. To cause to deviate, render perverse.

زَالَ aor. i. and a. To cease (with فِي).—زَيَّلَ II. To make a separation (with بَيْنَ).—تَزَيَّلَ V. To be separated one from the other.

زَانَ aor. i. *To adorn.* زِينَةٌ An ornament, as apparel at 7 v. 29, or trinkets, etc., pomp; sometimes used collectively for ornaments, as at 20 v. 90 and elsewhere; At 20 v. 61 يَوْمُ ٱلزِّينَةِ means the day of the solemn feast, when the temples and other bnildings were decked ont in olden times.—زَيَّنَ II. To adorn, prepare (with acc. and بِ or فِي); to deck a thing ont (with specious arguments, or otherwise), to make it appear pleasing (with acc. and لِ); لَأُزَيِّنَنَّ لَهُمْ فِي ٱلْأَرْضِ 15 v. 39, "Verily I will make (their disobedience) appear pleasing to them on the Earth."—إِزَّيَّنَ for تَزَيَّنَ V. D. S. Gr. T. 1, p. 220, To be adorned.

س

س an adverb prefixed to the aorist tense of verbs, and giving them a future signification; it is considered as an abbreviation of سَوْفَ q.v.; thus سَآوِى إِلَى جَبَلٍ 11 v. 45, "I will betake myself to a mountain," see أَوَى; it is likewise used in conjunction with other prefixes, as فَسَيَكْفِيكَهُمُ ٱللّٰهُ 2 v. 131, "And God will suffice thee (as a protection against) them," see كَفَى.

سَأَلَ aor. a. To ask, interrogate, ask for, demand (with acc. of pers. and أَنْ, also with double acc. or with acc. of pers. and بِ or عَنْ); to pray to (with acc.), as at 55 v. 29; Imperat. إِسْأَلْ and سَلْ. *Note.* Verbs whose second radical is hamzated are frequently declined after the manner of concave verbs. سُؤْلٌ A request, petition. سُؤَالٌ n.a. The act of demanding. سَائِلٌ part. act. One who asks, demands, etc., a beggar, as at 93 v. 10. مَسْؤُولٌ part. pass. That which is demanded or inquired into; at 17 vv. 36 and 38 it refers to those things which shall be inquired into at the day of judgment.—تَسَآءَلَ VI. To ask or make inquiries of one another (with عَنْ), as ٱلَّذِى تَسَّآءَلُونَ بِهِ 4 v. 1, "About whom ye have discussions one with another, or in whose name ye beseech one another;" تَسَّآءَلُونَ which may also be spelt تَسَآءَلُونَ is here put for تَتَسَآءَلُونَ, D. S. Gr. T. 1, p. 220.

سَئِمَ aor. a. To disdain, dislike, scorn (with أَنْ, or with مِنْ of thing).

سَبَّ aor. o. *To cut*, revile. سَبَبٌ Plur. أَسْبَابٌ A rope, cord, lien or that by which one thing is connected with another, as a path, way, means to an end, *a cause*; وَآتَيْنَاهُ مِنْ كُلِّ شَىْءٍ سَبَبًا فَأَتْبَعَ سَبَبًا 18 v. 83, "And we gave him a means to accomplish every end, so he followed his way;" فَلْيَرْتَقُوا فِى ٱلْأَسْبَابِ 38 v. 9, "Let them then ascend into the tracts (of Heaven)."

سَبَأٌ Sabâ', v. سَبَى.

سَبَتَ aor. o. and i. *To rest*, celebrate the Sabbath. سَبْتٌ The Sabbath; at 7 v. 163 and elsewhere reference is made to the story of certain Jews who resided at Elath on the Red Sea in the time of David, and who were turned into apes for catching fish on the Sabbath day. سُبَاتٌ Rest.

سَبَحَ aor. a. *To swim*, roll onwards, perform a daily course (with فِى). سَبْحٌ n.a. The act of swimming, occupation in worldly affairs. سَابِحٌ part. act. One who swims or moves with a swimming motion, applied to Angels at 79 v. 3, or, according to another of several interpretations, to ships. سُبْحَانٌ Praise; سُبْحَانَ ٱللّٰهِ and سُبْحَانَهُ are adverbial expressions in which there is an ellipse of the verb أُسَبِّحُ, as "The praise of God," or "by praising him," for "I celebrate the Praise of God," etc., hence it is that the word سُبْحَانَ appears in the accus., see D. S. Gr. T. 1, p. 502, and T. 2, p. 82; سُبْحَانَ ٱللّٰهِ عَمَّا يَصِفُونَ 37 v. 159; In this and similar passages there would appear to be also an ellipse of the verb تَعَالَى; At 28 v. 68 this deficiency is supplied, and the passage then reads thus, "I celebrate the Praise of God, and may He be far exalted above that which they impute to Him."—سَبَّحَ II. To sing praises (with لِ of pers.), celebrate praises (with بِ), laud and magnify (with acc.). تَسْبِيحٌ n.a.

The act of praise. مُسَبِّحٌ part. act. One who celebrates praises.

سَبَطَ aor. a. *To be lank (hair).* سِبْطٌ Plur. أَسْبَاطٌ A tribe (of the children of Israel).

سَبَعَ aor. a. and i. *To make a number up to seven.* سَبْعٌ fem., سَبْعَةٌ masc. Seven, see عَشَرٌ. سَبْعُونَ Seventy. سَبُعٌ A wild-beast.

سَبَغَ aor. o. *To be long and trailing on the ground (a garment).* سَابِغَةٌ A coat of mail.—أَسْبَغَ IV. To cause to abound (with acc. and عَلَى of pers.).

سَبَقَ aor. i. and o. To be in advance of (with acc.); precede (with لِ); to go before (with acc. and بِ or إِلَى); pass before, go forth previously, as a sentence of condemnation (with عَلَى of pers. and مِنْ), with which meaning it appears at 11 v. 42; or a promise of eternal happiness (with لِ of pers. and مِنْ), as at 21 v. 101; to happen previously, pass by, surpass, get the better of (with acc.); With بِ it may sometimes be rendered to do previously, as مَا سَبَقَكُمْ بِهَا مِنْ أَحَدٍ مِنَ ٱلْعَالَمِينَ 7 v. 78, "No created being has committed this (crime) before you;" to prevent, in the old sense of to be beforehand with (with acc. of pers. and بِ); thus at 21 v. 27 لَا يَسْبِقُونَهُ بِٱلْقَوْلِ "They do not prevent him in their speech." سَبْقٌ n.a. The act of preceding. سَابِقٌ part. act. One who precedes or outstrips in a race; At 56 v. 10 we find the word ٱلسَّابِقُونَ repeated, probably to give force and dignity to the expression, which may there be rendered "The leaders on earth and in Heaven," viz. those who having been the first to embrace the Faith, shall be the first in Paradise. مَسْبُوقٌ part. pass. One who is surpassed or beaten in a race; Sale translates this word "prevented," a meaning it may well bear in the two instances in which it occurs.—سَابَقَ III. To strive to excel or reach before another (with إِلَى).—إِسْتَبَقَ VIII. To strive one with another in a race, or to reach a goal (with acc.).

سَبَلَ *Rain,* no verbal root. سَبِيلٌ Plur. سُبُلٌ (com. gend.) A way, road; a cause or reason, as at 9 vv. 92 and 94, where it means "a cause of reproach;" إِبْنُ ٱلسَّبِيلِ A traveller; سَبِيلُ ٱللّٰهِ The path of duty to God; it frequently means an expedition or war made by believers to propagate the Mohammadan faith; a necessity, as لَيْسَ عَلَيْنَا فِى ٱلْأُمِّيِّينَ سَبِيلٌ 3 v. 69, "There is no necessity incumbent upon us (to pay or observe justice) towards the Heathen."

سَبَى aor. i. *To take captive.* سَبَأٌ Sabâ', called in Scripture "Sheba," a city of Yeman destroyed by the inundation of El 'Arem; it took its name from Sabâ', the great grandson of Kaḥṭàn or Joctan.

سِتٌّ for سِدْسٌ fem. Six; masc. سِتَّةٌ, see عَشَرٌ. سِتُّونَ, Oblique سِتِّينَ Sixty.

سَتَرَ aor. o. *To cover.* سِتْرٌ A veil, covering. مَسْتُورٌ part. pass. Spread over as a veil.—إِسْتَتَرَ VIII. To hide one's-self.

سَجَدَ aor. o. *To be humble,* submit one's-self, bow down in adoration with the forehead touching the ground, to worship (with لِ). سَجْدَةٌ Adoration. سَاجِدٌ Plur. سُجُودٌ and سُجَّدٌ part. act. One who bows down. مَسْجِدٌ Plur. مَسَاجِدُ (2nd declension) A place of adoration, mosque; مِنَ ٱلْمَسْجِدِ ٱلْحَرَامِ إِلَى ٱلْمَسْجِدِ ٱلْأَقْصَى 17 v. 1, "From the sacred temple at Mecca to the further mosque at Jerusalem," or as Beidâwëe explains it, to the Holy House there; for at that time there was no mosque behind it.

سَجَرَ aor. o. *To utter a cry, as a camel to her foal; to pour forth, fill with water*, to burn (with فِى). مَسْجُورٌ part. pass. وَٱلْبَحْرِ ٱلْمَسْجُورِ 52 v. 6, "By the ocean poured forth over the earth." سَجَّرَ— II. To swell and become turgid (the ocean).

سَجَلَ *To pour forth.* سِجِلٌّ which is spelt in various ways, has also sundry significations; by some it is supposed to mean the Angel who inscribes men's actions in a book, rolling it up at their death; or it may be the name of a certain scribe of Moḥammad, or a written scroll; for the construction of the words كَطَىِّ ٱلسِّجِلِّ لِلْكُتُبِ 21 v. 104, see D. S. Gr. T. 2, p. 164; see also his Chrestomathie Arabe, T. 3, p. 231. سِجِّيلٌ Baked clay of which the stones were formed which were said to have been rained down from Heaven upon Sodom, and also upon the "Companions of the Elephant" mentioned in chap. 105.

سَجَنَ aor. o. To imprison. مَسْجُونٌ part. pass. Imprisoned. سِجْنٌ A prison. سِجِّينٌ The register in which the actions of the wicked are recorded, or the place where it is kept.

سَجَا aor. o. (also written سَجَى) To be quiet, tranquil or dark (the night).

سَحَبَ aor. a. To drag along the ground (with فِى). سَحَابٌ A cloud, clouds, sometimes used as a collective noun.

سَحَتَ *To destroy utterly, eradicate.* سُحْتٌ Unlawful, forbidden by law.—أَسْحَتَ IV. same as primitive form (with acc. of pers. and بِ).

سَحَرَ aor. a. *To gild*, enchant, bewitch (with acc. and بِ). سِحْرٌ Sorcery, enchantment. سَحَرٌ Plur. أَسْحَارٌ The early dawn. سَاحِرٌ Plur. سَحَرَةٌ part. act. A magician, sorcerer. سَحَّارٌ A great magician. مَسْحُورٌ part. pass. One bewitched, deluded by sorcery.—مُسَحَّرٌ part. pass. II. f. Bewitched.

سَحَقَ *To beat small*, and سَحِقَ *To be far off.* سُحْقٌ n.a. The act of being far off; فَسُحْقًا 67 v. 11, "Far then be (pardon) from them;" an ellipse for فَأَسْحَقَهُمُ ٱللّٰهُ سُحْقًا "God has removed them far away in respect of pardon." سَحِيقٌ Far distant. إِسْحَقُ Isaac (2nd declension) D. S. Gr. T. 1, p. 404.

سَحَلَ *To strip off the bark.* سَاحِلٌ Shore of a river or sea.

سَخِرَ aor. a. To ridicule (with مِنْ of pers.). سَاخِرٌ part. act. One who turns to ridicule. سِخْرِىٌّ A jeer, ridicule; at 43 v. 31 it means One who is compelled to serve without payment.—سَخَّرَ II. To subject (with acc. and لِ); to compel any one to work without payment; at 69 v. 7 it is used with the acc. and عَلَى of pers. and may there be rendered "He caused it to assail them." مُسَخَّرٌ part. pass. Subjected, compelled to serve or work.—إِسْتَسْخَرَ X. To turn anything to ridicule.

سَخِطَ aor. a. To be angry (with عَلَى). سَخَطٌ Wrath. —أَسْخَطَ IV. To incense.

سَدَّ aor. o. *To obstruct, stop up.* سَدٌّ n.a. or سُدٌّ A mountain, an obstacle, rampart, bar; ٱلسَّدَّيْنِ 18 v. 92 oblique dual, "The two mountains," supposed to be situated in Armenia, or on the borders of Turkistan. سَدِيد Well-directed, convenient or opportune.

سَدَرَ *To let down the hair.* سِدْرٌ generic noun, The Lote-tree. سِدْرَةٌ noun of unity, A single Lote-tree; سِدْرَةُ ٱلْمُنْتَهَى 53 vv. 14 and 16, The Lote-tree, beyond which no creature can pass;

allusion is made to it in Moore's Lalla Rookh.

"Farewell, ye vanishing flowers, that shone,
In my fairy wreath, so bright and brief;
Oh! what are the brightest that e'er have blown,
To the Lote tree springing by Allah's throne,
Whose flowers have a soul in every leaf."

سَدَسَ aor. o. *To take a sixth part.* سُدُسٌ A sixth part. سَادِسٌ The sixth.

سَدَا aor. o. *To stretch out the hand towards any one.* سُدًى Neglected, uncared for.

سَرَّ aor. o. *To cut the navel string*, to make glad, rejoice. سُرُورٌ n.a. Joy. سِرٌّ A secret; سِرًّا Secretly, in private. سُرُرٌ plur. of سَرِيرٌ A couch, throne. سَرَّآءُ Joy, joyful state. سَرَآئِرُ (2nd declension) plur. of سَرِيرَةٌ A secret. مَسْرُورٌ part. pass. Rejoiced.—أَسَرَّ IV. To conceal, and also to reveal or manifest (with acc.); At 10 v. 55 and 34 v. 32 it seems doubtful which of these meanings is intended to be conveyed; to entrust a secret (with إِلَى), hold a secret conversation (with acc. or with لِ of pers.). إِسْرَارٌ n.a. A secret.

سَرَبَ aor. o. *To enjoy free pasture (a camel).* سَرَبٌ A pipe for the conveyance of water; سَرَبًا 18 v. 60 may be translated "as it were in a tunnel;" the fish there mentioned being supposed to have swum in that manner under the sea. سَرَابٌ A mirage, deceitful appearance, as of water in the desert. سَارِبٌ part. act. One who goes forth freely and carelessly.

سَرْبَلَ *To put on the garment called* سِرْبَالٌ. سَرَابِيلُ (2nd declension) plur. of سِرْبَالٌ A garment, either generally, or a coat of mail; at 16 v. 83 it is used in both senses.

سَرَجَ aor. o. *To saddle;* and سَرِجَ *To shine.* سِرَاجٌ A lamp, or rather a candle, the receptacle being called قِنْدِيلٌ.

سَرَحَ aor. a. *To let (a flock) go free to pasture at liberty;* to lead out to pasture in the morning. سَرَاحٌ Dismissal.—سَرَّحَ II. To dismiss freely, divorce (with acc. of pers. and بِ). تَسْرِيحٌ n.a. Dismissal, divorce.

سَرَدَ aor. o. *To perforate.* سَرْدٌ n.a. Work made of rings woven together, as chain armour.

سَرْدَقَ *To cover with an awning.* سُرَادِقٌ 18 v. 28, Smoke which surrounds and covers after the manner of a tent.

سَرُعَ *To be quick.* سَرِيعٌ Plur. سِرَاعٌ Swift, prompt, hastening; سَرِيعُ ٱلْحِسَابِ Swift at taking account; سِرَاعًا Suddenly, hastily. أَسْرَعُ (2nd declension, comp. form) D. S. Gr. T. I, p. 403, Very swift, swiftest.—سَارَعَ III. To hasten emulously, or in company with others (with لِ or فِى of pers. or thing, also with إِلَى).

سَرَفَ aor. o. *To eat away (the leaves of a tree).*—أَسْرَفَ IV. To be prodigal, extravagant, to exceed bounds, transgress (with فِى or عَلَى). إِسْرَافٌ n.a. The act of exceeding bounds, extravagance, transgression. مُسْرِفٌ part. act. One who is guilty of excess, extravagant, a transgressor.

سَرَقَ aor. i. To steal. سَارِقٌ part. act. One who steals.—إِسْتَرَقَ VIII. To take away by stealth, as ٱسْتَرَقَ ٱلسَّمْعَ 15 v. 18, "He listened by stealth," as the Genii to the conversation of the angels.

سَرْمَدٌ Perpetual; سَرْمَدًا Perpetually, a word apparently of mixed Persian and Arab origin.

سَرَى aor. i. To travel by night; وَٱللَّيْلِ إِذَا يَسْرِ 89 v. 3, "By the night when it passeth away;" يَسْرِ is here written by poetic licence for يَسْرِى on account of the pause—وَقْف—at the end of the verse; D. S. Gr. T. 2, p. 496. سَرِىٌّ A rivulet.—أَسْرَى IV. To travel by night; with بِ it becomes transitive, To cause to travel, thus at 20 v. 79 أَنْ أَسْرِ بِعِبَادِى "(saying) Take my servants for a journey by night," see أَنْ.

سَطَحَ aor. a. To spread out.

سَطَرَ aor. o. To write. أَسَاطِيرُ Fables, idle tales; This word, a plural of the 2nd declension, seems to be derived from the Greek ἱστορία, but the sing. is doubtful. مَسْطُورٌ part. pass. Written. مُسَيْطِرٌ also spelt مُصَيْطِرٌ One who presides over, a manager of affairs.—مُسْتَطَرٌ part. pass. VIII. f. Written.

سَطَا aor. o. To attack with violence (with بِ of pers.).

سَعَةٌ see وَسِعَ.

سَعَدَ aor. a. *To be fortunate* (*a day*); and سَعِدَ To be happy (a man). سَعِيدٌ Happy, blessed.

سَعَرَ aor. a. *To light a fire.* سَعِيرٌ fem. A burning fire, Hell. سُعُرٌ Madness.—سَعَّرَ II. To cause to burn fiercely.

سَعَى aor. a. on account of the guttural ع, To go hastily (with إِلَى); to run, be diligent, purpose, to endeavour labour or strive after (with acc. also with لِ or فِى); وَأَمَّا مَنْ جَآءَكَ يَسْعَى 80 v. 8, "But as for him who comes to thee striving after (good)." سَعْىٌ n.a. The act of going quickly or hastily, an endeavour; فَلَمَّا بَلَغَ مَعَهُ ٱلسَّعْىَ 37 v. 100, "And when he had attained such an age that he could assist him in his work;" وَسَعَى لَهَا سَعْيَهَا 17 v. 20, "And diligently strives after it;" *Literally*, "And endeavours after it with its endeavour;" the noun of action being added to the verb to give energy to the expression—لِلتَّأْكِيدِ.

سَغَبَ aor. o. *To suffer from hunger and want.* مَسْغَبَةٌ Famine.

سَفَحَ aor. a. *To pour forth.* مَسْفُوحٌ part. pass. Poured forth.—مُسَافِحٌ part. act. III. f. One who commits fornication.

سَفَرَ aor. i. *To sweep* (*a house*), *go on a journey.* سَفَرٌ Plur. أَسْفَارٌ A journey; أَسْفَارٌ is also the plur. of سِفْرٌ A large Book or Tome. سَفَرَةٌ plur. of سَافِرٌ A scribe.—أَسْفَرَ IV. To shine, brighten (the dawn). مُسْفِرٌ part. act. Shining.

سَفَعَ aor. a. *To strike with the wings* (*a bird when fighting*), to drag along (with بِ), as at 96 v. 15, لَنَسْفَعًا بِالنَّاصِيَةِ "Verily we will drag him by the forelock;" where instead of the نّ of the second energetic form of aorist, the tanween of the fatha اً is used, see D. S. Gr. T. 1, p. 156.

سَفَكَ aor. i. To shed (blood).

سَفَلَ aor. o. *To be low.* سَافِلٌ part. act. One who is low, vile, abject; عَالِيَهَا سَافِلَهَا 11 v. 84, "Upside down." أَسْفَلُ Fem. سُفْلَى comp. form, Very low, lower, lowest.

سَفَنَ aor. i. *To scrape off the skin.* سَفِينَةٌ A bark, ship; at 29 v. 14 The Ark.

سَفَهَ and سَفِهَ To make a fool of (any one), render foolish, as مَنْ سَفِهَ نَفْسَهُ 2 v. 124, "He who has made a fool of himself." سَفَهٌ n.a. Folly; سَفَهًا Foolishly. سَفِيهٌ Plur. سُفَهَآءُ (2nd declension) A fool, foolish, silly, ignorant; سَفِيهُنَا 72 v. 4, "The foolish individual amongst us," viz. Iblees, or a rebellious spirit. سَفَاهَةٌ Folly.

سَقَرَ *To injure by heat* (*the sun*). سَقَرُ fem. Hell-fire (2nd declension), supposed to be of foreign origin, D. S. Gr. T. 1, p. 405.

سَقَطَ aor. o. To fall (with فِي ; سُقِطَ فِي أَيْدِيهِمْ 7 v. 148, an instance of a كِنَايَة or vague expression substituted for another, and meaning "They grievously repented." سَاقِط part. act. Falling. —سَاقَطَ III. To let fall (with acc. and عَلَى).— أَسْقَطَ IV. To cause to fall (with acc. and عَلَى).

سَقَفَ aor. o. *To roof over.* سَقْف Plur. سُقُف A roof.

سَقِمَ aor. a. *To be ill.* سَقِيم Sick, ill.

سَقَى aor. i. To water, give drink to (with double acc.); In the Pass. to be given (water, etc.) to drink, see D. S. Gr. T. 2, p. 123; When meaning simply to be watered, as at 13 v. 4, the Passive verb governs its complement by means of the preposition بِ, as يُسْقَى بِمَآءٍ وَاحِدٍ, or the verb may here be taken in an impersonal sense "Rigatum est," with an ellipse of عَلَيْهَا; by some however it is written تُسْقَى; so again at 14 v. 19, and similar passages, وَيُسْقَى مِنْ مَآءٍ صَدِيدٍ "And he shall be given to drink of a putrid liquid," where we may understand an ellipse of the word شَيْئًا. سِقَايَة n.a. The act of giving drink to, also a drinking cup. سُقْيَا for سُقْيَى (2nd declension), final ي when preceded by يَ being changed into short alif, D. S. Gr. T. 1, p. 111, A watering; At 91 v. 13 where this word occurs there is a considerable ellipse, فَقَالَ لَهُمْ رَسُولُ ٱللّٰهِ نَاقَةَ ٱللّٰهِ وَسُقْيَاهَا "And the apostle of God said unto them (let alone—ذَرُوا) God's she-camel and (do not hinder) her drinking."—أَسْقَى IV. To give drink to, to water (with double acc.).—إِسْتَسْقَى X. To ask any one for drink (with acc. of pers.).

سَكَبَ To pour forth. مَسْكُوب part. pass. Poured forth, flowing.

سَكَتَ aor. o. *To be silent,* appeased—anger—(with عَنْ of person).

سَكَرَ aor. i. *To fill a vessel;* and سَكِرَ aor. a. *To be drunk.* سَكَر Intoxicating drink, especially Date-wine. سَكْرَة *properly, Drunkenness,* stupefaction; سَكْرَةُ ٱلْمَوْتِ 50 v. 18, "The agonies of death." سُكَارَى plur. of سَكْرَانُ Drunken.—سَكَّرَ II. To make drunken; سُكِّرَتْ أَبْصَارُنَا 15 v. 15, "Our eyes are intoxicated," *i.e.* bewildered.

سَكَنَ aor. o. To be quiet, rest, dwell (with فِي); dwell with (with إِلَى); inhabit (with acc.). سَكَن Any means of rest or quiet, a habitation. سَاكِن part. act. That which remains quiet; at 25 v. 47 speaking of the Shadow at daybreak it means "fixed," either by the Sun's neglecting to rise, or rising always in the same place. سِكِّين comm. gend. A knife. سَكِينَة Tranquillity, security; a word variously interpreted, but probably referring to the Hebrew *Schechinah* שכינא The Divine presence which appeared on the Mercy seat of the Ark. مَسَاكِن (2nd declension) plur. of مَسْكَن A habitation. مَسْكَنَة Poverty, misery. مَسْكُون part. pass. Inhabited. مِسْكِين Plur. مَسَاكِين (2nd declension) Poor.—أَسْكَنَ IV. To make to dwell, cause to abide (with double acc. also with بِ or فِي of place); to quiet.

سَلَّ aor. o. *To bring out.* سُلَالَة An extract.— تَسَلَّلَ V. To withdraw one's-self privately.

سَلْسَلَ see سَلَاسِل.

سَلَبَ aor. o. To snatch away from (with acc. of pers. and thing).

سَلَحَ aor. a. *To void excrement.* أَسْلِحَة plur. of سِلَاح comm. gend. Arms, weapons.

سَلَخَ aor. o. *To flay*, pluck off, withdraw (with acc. and مِنْ). إِنْسَلَخَ VII. To pass away, pass by (with مِنْ).

سَلْسَبِيل Salsabeel, name of a fountain in Paradise.

سَلْسَلَ *To join chainwise one thing to another.* سِلْسِلَةٌ Plur. سَلَاسِل (2nd declension) A chain.

سَلِطَ aor. a. *To be hard.* سُلْطَان comm. gend. Power, authority, demonstration, argument, convincing proof; سُلْطَانِيَهْ 69 v. 29 for سُلْطَانِي "My power;" the final ة is called هَاءُ ٱلْوَقْف, for which see D. S. Gr. T. 1, p. 459.—سَلَّطَ II. To give power or authority, to make victorious (with acc. and عَلَى).

سَلَفَ aor. o. *To harrow*, to pass or be past, to go or happen previously; فَلَهُ مَا سَلَفَ 2 v. 276, "Then shall that which is past be (forgiven) to him," or no account shall be required of him. سَلَفٌ n.a. A precedent.—أَسْلَفَ IV. *properly, to pay for goods beforehand*, but in the Korân it must be understood of the actions done in this life, which are, as it were, sent before us.

سَلَقَ aor. i. *To throw on the back, throw down backwards*, to abuse (with acc. and بِ).

سَلَكَ aor. o. To cause to go or walk, as وَسَلَكَ لَكُمْ فِيهَا سُبُلًا 20 v. 55, "And has made you to walk in it by paths;" to cause to enter (with acc. of pers. or thing, and فِي of place, or with double acc.); سَلَكْنَاهُ 26 v. 200, "We have caused it to enter;" both here and at 15 v. 12 the word ٱلْكُفْر "unbelief" must be understood; سَلَكَ also means simply to walk (with acc. of place), thus لِتَسْلُكُوا مِنْهَا سُبُلًا فِجَاجًا 71 v. 19, "That ye may walk in its spacious paths."

سَلِمَ aor. a. *To be safe and sound.* سَلْمٌ Peace. سِلْمٌ comm. gend. Obedience to the doctrines of El Islâm. سَلَمٌ A treaty of peace or submission, a captive. سَالِمٌ part. act. One who is safe. سَلَامٌ Peace, safety, a greeting of peace, security; ٱلسَّلَامُ One of the names of God; دَارُ ٱلسَّلَامِ Paradise, the abode of peace; at 21 v. 69 it may be interpreted "a means of security;" the fire into which Abraham had been thrown by Nimrod not only having left the former uninjured, but also destroyed his enemies. سُلَّمٌ comm. gend. A ladder. سَلِيمٌ Perfect, sincere. سُلَيْمَان (2nd declension) Solomon.—سَلَّمَ II. To preserve, give salvation, deliver, hand over (with acc. and لِ or إِلَى of pers.); to submit to a judgment, salute (with عَلَى); فَسَلِّمُوا عَلَى أَنْفُسِكُمْ 24 v. 61, "Salute the people of the House" (as being of your own people), *literally*, "Salute yourselves." تَسْلِيمٌ n.a. A salutation, submission, resignation. مُسَلَّمَةٌ fem. part. pass. Handed over, sound.—أَسْلَمَ IV. To submit, commit (with acc. and إِلَى); to resign one's self (with لِ); to profess El Islâm. إِسْلَامٌ n.a. The act of resignation to God; ٱلْإِسْلَامُ El Islâm, the only true Religion which according to Mohammad was professed by all the Prophets from Adam downwards; from the words of the Korân 49 v. 14 it would appear to be rather the profession of faith than the faith itself; the latter, which is from the heart, is called ٱلْإِيمَانُ; upon this point however there are differences of opinion among the Moslems. مُسْلِمٌ part. act. One who resigns himself to God, a Moslem, one who professes the faith of El Islâm.—مُسْتَسْلِمٌ part. act. X. f. One who submits to judgment.

سَلَا aor. o. *To be careless about a thing.* سَلْوَى for سَلْوَى (2nd declension) generic noun, Quails.

سَمَّ aor. o. *To poison, penetrate.* سَمٌّ n.a. A hole; سَمُّ ٱلْخِيَاطِ The eye of a needle; this name is given in the East to the small doorway for foot passengers at the side of a large gateway; see S. Matthew chap. xix. v. 24. سَمُومٌ fem. generic noun, *The Simoom;* a pestilential scorching wind, which it is said shall penetrate into the bodies of the damned; it was from the fire of this wind that the Jinn or dæmons were created, see 15 v. 27.

سَمَدَ *To stand in astonishment, to idle.* سَامِدٌ part. act. One who passes his time in vanities.

سَمَرَ aor. o. *To pass the night in conversation.* سَامِرٌ part. act. One who converses by night. ٱلسَّامِرِيُّ or سَامِرِيٌّ The Samaritan, a name given to an individual who is said to have made the Golden Calf for the Children of Israel.

سَمِعَ aor. a. To hear (with acc.); hear of (with بِ); to hearken, listen, hearken to (with لِ); فَٱسْمَعُونِ for فَٱسْمَعُونِى 36 v. 24, "Then hear me;" D. S. Gr. T. 1, p. 459. سَمْعٌ n.a. The act of hearing, hearing. سَمِيعٌ One who hears. سَمَّاعٌ One who is in the habit of hearkening, D. S. Gr. T. 1, p. 322.—أَسْمَعَ IV. To make to hear (with double acc.); at 19 v. 39 أَسْمِعْ بِهِمْ is by some understood as a verb of admiration, "How sharp shall be their hearing," viz. that of the Infidels; D. S. Gr. T. 2, p. 585; according to another interpretation أَسْمِعْ is here the imperative of the iv. f. "Do thou cause them to hear;" the same remark applies to 18 v. 25, where however the expression, if understood in the imperative, must be taken as ironical, "Do thou cause (God) to hear." مُسْمِعٌ part. act. One who makes to hear. مُسْمَعٌ part. pass. One who is made to hear; وَٱسْمَعْ غَيْرَ مُسْمَعٍ 4 v. 48, "And hear without being made to (hear or) understand;" out of numerons explanations of this passage none seem quite satisfactory; possibly the words being used by Jews to annoy Mohammad conveyed a *double entendre.*—تَسَمَّعَ or إِسَّمَّعَ V. To listen to (with إِلَى), D. S. Gr. T. 1, p. 220.—إِسْتَمَعَ VIII. To hear, listen, hearken to (with لِ or إِلَى); to overhear. مُسْتَمِعٌ part. act. One who hears or listens.

سَمَكَ *To raise on high.* سَمْكٌ A roof, or the highest part of the interior of a building.

سَمِنَ aor. a. *To be fat.* سَمِينٌ Plur. سِمَانٌ Fat.—أَسْمَنَ IV. To fatten.

سَمَا aor. o. *To be lofty.* سَمَآءٌ comm. gend., Plur. سَمَوَاتٌ Heaven, of which the Korân says there are seven, *vide* 2 v. 27. إِسْمٌ Plur. أَسْمَآءٌ A name; when following another word إِسْمٌ is always written with the وَصْلَةٌ thus ٱسْمٌ; In the formula بِسْمِ ٱللّٰهِ, when commencing a sentence, and not following a verb, the ا is omitted on acconnt of its freqnent nse, in all other instances it is retained; thus when at 11 v. 43 we find بِسْمِ in the middle of a sentence, we know that there is an ellipse of the word قَآئِلِينَ; see De Sacy's Anthologie Grammaticale Arabe, p. 112. سَمِيٌّ A namesake.—سَمَّى II. To name, call by name. تَسْمِيَةٌ n.a. The act of naming, an appellation. مُسَمًّى for مُسَمَّىٌ D. S. Gr. T. 1, p. 111, part. pass. Named, fixed, determined.

سَنَّ aor. o. *To form.* سِنٌّ fem. A tooth. سُنَّةٌ sometimes spelt سُنَّتٌ, D. S. Gr. T. 1, p. 276, *note;*

Plnr. سُنَنٌ A law, ordinance, line of conduct, mode of life, punishment. مَسْنُونٌ part. pass. Formed, made into shape.

سُنْبُلٌ Plur. سَنَابِلُ (2nd declension) An ear of corn. سُنْبُلَةٌ noun of unity, One ear of corn; this word is by some derived from سَبَلَ.

سِنَةٌ Drowsiness, rt. وَسِنَ q.v.

سَنَدَ aor. o. *To lean upon.*—مُسَنَّدٌ part. pass. II. f. Propped up.

سُنْدُسٌ a word of Persian origin, meaning Fine silk.

سَنِيمَةٌ see وَسَمَ.

سَنِهَ *To be full of years.*—تَسَنَّهَ V. To be musty, mouldy through age.

سَنَا aor. o. *To water the ground with a Persian wheel, to shine.* سَنًا for سَنَوٌ D. S. Gr. T. 1, p. 106, Splendour. سَنَةٌ Plur. سَنَوَاتٌ or سِنُونَ, Oblique سِنِينَ A year, a barren year, barrenness, dearth; for the use of the masculine form of plur. with certain feminine nouns see D. S. Gr. T. 1, p. 358; this word is by some derived from سَنِهَ; in either case the last radical is dropped, and the ة taken in its place, see D. S. Gr. T. 1, pp. 358 and 317.*

سَهِرَ aor. a. *To be watchful.* سَاهِرَةٌ The face of the Earth, or according to another interpretation, the place of the last Judgment; it is also one of the names of Hell.

سَهُلَ *To be smooth, level.* سُهُولٌ plur. of سَهْلٌ A plain.

سَهَمَ aor. a. *To be lean.*—سَاهَمَ III. To cast lots.

سَهَا aor. o. *To forget, neglect.* سَاهٍ for سَاهِيٌ D. S. Gr. T. 1, p. 330, part. act. Neglecting, negligent (with عَنْ).

* At page 358 in the second edition, § 838, there is a misprint in the second line of the paragraph, where ة should be read for ة.

سَآءَ aor. o. *To do evil,* be evil, wretched or grievous; very frequently used with the acc. as سَآءَ سَبِيلًا "It is an evil way," *Literally,* "It is evil as to its way;" to grieve, afflict (with acc.), as لِيَسُوْءُا وُجُوهَكُمْ 17 v. 7, "To vex you," *literally,* "your faces;" The language is here more than usually obscure; according to the commentators the sense of the passage is somewhat as follows, "And when there came the punishment with which ye were threatened for your latter offence (we sent against you certain foes) to vex you," etc. There are numerous readings and interpretations of the above, from all which it appears that while Moḥammad himself was not very strong on ancient history, his commentators have only "made that darker which was dark enough before;" Pass. سِيءَ or سِيٓءَ for سُوِءَ To be made sad, to be vexed for (with بِ). سُوْءٌ n.a. and سُوْءٌ Evil. سَيِّئٌ Bad, wicked, evil, used both as substantive and adjective. سَيِّئَةٌ Evil, a sin, evil action. سَوْءَةٌ Plur. سَوْآتٌ Shame, secret parts. أَسْوَأُ comp. form, Worse, worst.—أَسَآءَ IV. To do evil. مُسِيٓءٌ part. act. An evil doer.

سَاحَةٌ A courtyard open to the sky, no verbal root.

سَادَ aor. o. *To be Lord;* and سَوِدَ *To be black.* سَيِّدٌ Plur. سَادَةٌ A Lord, a person of distinction. أَسْوَدُ Plur. سُودٌ Black; Words expressive of colour although in the comparative form are generally used with a positive meaning, D. S. Gr. T. 1, p. 324.—إِسْوَدَّ IX. To become black. مُسْوَدٌّ part. act. Become black.

سَارَ aor. o. *To mount a wall.* سُورٌ A wall. سُورَةٌ Plur. سُوَرٌ *A degree of rank, a sign,* a chapter of the Korân. سِوَارٌ A bracelet; Plur. أَسْوِرَةٌ and

أَسَاوِرُ (2nd declension).—تَسَوَّرَ V. To climb over a wall (with acc.); تَسَوَّرُوا ٱلْمِحْرَابَ 38 v. 20, "They climbed over the wall of the private apartment."

ساط aor. o. *To mingle.* سَوْطٌ n.a. A mixture, a scourge; at 89 v. 12 the words سَوْطَ عَذَابٍ may be rendered "A mixture of varions punishments resembling a scourge."

ساع aor. o. *To let (camels) run free.* سَاعَةٌ An hour, time; ٱلسَّاعَةُ The hour of Resurrection, the last Day; سَاعَةً *adverbially*, By a single hour. سُوَاعٌ Soowá', name of an idol said to have been worshipped by the Antedilnvians, and again after the Flood by certain tribes of Arabs.

ساغ aor. o. *To pass easily and pleasantly down the throat.* سَائِغٌ part. act. That which passes pleasantly down the throat, agreeable to drink. —أَسَاغَ IV. To causo to pass easily down the throat.

ساف aor. o. *To try by smelling.* سَوْفَ a particle prefixed to the Indicative and Energetic Moods of the Aorist tense in order to give them a future signification, occasionally joined to other prefixes as فَلَسَوْفَ, and sometimes contracted into سَ q.v.

ساق aor. o. To drive; Pass. سِيقَ (with acc. and إِلَى). سَاقٌ fem., Plur. سُوقٌ A leg, stalk. أَسْوَاقٌ plnr. of سُوقٌ comm. gend. A market-place. سَائِقٌ part. act. A driver; سَائِقٌ وَشَهِيدٌ 50 v. 20, "A driver and a witness," Two Angels who shall attend every man at the last day. مَسَاقٌ n.a. The act of driving.

سال for سَأَلَ aor. a. D. S. Gr. T. 1, p. 236. *To ask.* —سَوَّلَ II. To contrive, snggest, prepare (with acc. and لِ of pers.).

سام aor. o. *To go to pasture*, afflict, impose a hard task or pnnishment upon (with double acc.). سِيمَا A sign, mark (2nd declension) D. S. Gr. T. 1, p. 402. *Note.* Some suppose this word to be derived from وسم q.v.—مُسَوِّمٌ part. act. II. f. One who makes a mark of distinction, a person of mark or distinction; at 3 v. 121 the word is somtimes read مُسَوَّمِينَ part. pass. "(Angels) distinguished by their appearance;" at 3 v. 12 it means "marked with a سِيمَةٌ or brand."—أَسَامَ IV. To tnrn out to graze (with فِى).

سوى aor. a. *To intend.* سُوًى Equal, middle. مَكَانًا سُوًى 20 v. 60, "In an equal place, or in a place in the midst," *i.e.* half way between yon and us. *Note.* In Flnegel's Korân, edition of 1834, there is a misprint in this placc, مَكَانًا for مَكَانًا. سَوَآءٌ Eqnal, the same, even, equality, correctness, rectitude, the middle, the midst; سَوَآءَ ٱلسَّبِيلِ The right way; سَوَآءً لِلسَّآئِلِينَ 41 v. 9, "Correctly (fixing the time) for those who inquire about it." سَوِىٌّ Even, right, sound in mind and body; سَوِيًّا 19 v. 11, "Being in sound health," *i.e.* althongh not being dumb. —سَوَّى II. To proportion, fashion, perfect, make level or equal (with بِ); فَسَوَّاهَا 91 v. 14, "And (God) sent an eqnal destrnction npon them all;" the word دَمْدَمَةٌ is here understood.—سَاوَى III. To make level (with بَيْنَ).—إِسْتَوَى VIII. To be equal, to ascend, intend, set one's self to do a thing (with إِلَى); to sit firm and square npon (with عَلَى); to attain maturity as at 28 v. 13; At 53 v. 6 فَٱسْتَوَى is by some rendered "And he (the Angel Gabriel) stood erect in his proper form," in which he had appeared to none of the Prophets before Moḥammad.

سَابَ aor. i. *To flow.* سَآئِبَةٌ Sâ-iba, name of a she-camel concerning which the Pagan Arabs held certain superstitions, among others the right of free pasture.

سَاحَ aor. i. *To flow over the ground (water)*; to run backwards and forwards (with فِى). سَآئِحٌ One who wanders about in the cause of religion, and especially one who fasts, hence, devout.

سَارَ aor. i. To go, travel, journey (with فِى). سَيْرٌ n.a. The act of going, a journey. سِيرَةٌ State, condition. سَيَّارَةٌ A company of travellers.—سَيَّرَ II. To make to go, cause to pass away.

سَالَ aor. i. To flow. سَيْلٌ n.a. A brook, torrent. سَيْلُ ٱلْعَرِمِ 34 v. 15, The inundation of El 'Arem, see عَرَمٌ.—أَسَالَ IV. To cause to flow (with acc. and لِ of pers.).

سَيْنَآءُ or سِينَآءُ (2nd declension) Mount Sinai.

سِينِينَ A synonym of Sinai (2nd declension, on account of its feminine gender and foreign origin); طُورُ سِينِينَ, طُورُ سَيْنَآءَ, طُورُ سِينَآءَ and are all different names of the mountain which stands in the territory of Sinai; some have supposed these words to be derived from سَنًا Splendour, or سَنَآءٌ An eminence; for the termination ينَ see إِلْيَاسُ.

ش

شَأَمَ aor. a. *To be unlucky, sinister.* مَشْأَمَةٌ The left hand; أَصْحَابُ ٱلْمَشْأَمَةِ 56 v. 9, "The companions of the left hand," *i.e.* The damned; either because the Books containing their actions in life will be given into their left hands, or because they will be companions in misfortune,—مَشَائِيمُ.

شَأَنَ aor. a. *To know, care for.* شَأْنٌ A matter, business, thing.

شَنَأَ see شَانِئَكَ.

شِبْهٌ *A likeness.* The verb is not used in the primitive form.—شَبَّهَ II. To liken; Pass. شُبِّهَ To be made like; شُبِّهَ لَهُمْ 4 v. 156, "A likeness or similitude (of Christ) was made for them;" it being believed by the Mohammedans that Judas or some other person was substituted for our Blessed Lord, and crucified in his stead.—تَشَابَهَ VI. To have a mutual resemblance to each other, used with عَلَى of pers., thus at 2 v. 65, إِنَّ ٱلْبَقَرَ تَشَابَهَ عَلَيْنَا "Verily the cows appear to us to have a resemblance one to another;" to be figurative or allegorical. مُتَشَابِهٌ part. act. Mutually resembling one another; كِتَابًا مُتَشَابِهًا مَثَانِىَ 39 v. 24, "A Book conformable to itself in (or as to its) repeated portions," or "twofold qualities," viz. those mentioned at 3 v. 5, where مُتَشَابِهَاتٌ may be rendered open to conjecture, metaphorical or ambiguous, see مُحْكَمَاتٌ, rt. حَكَمَ.—مُشْتَبِهٌ part. act. VIII. f. That which is similar.

شَتَّ aor. i. *To separate.* شَتٌّ n.a. Plur. أَشْتَاتٌ Separate; أَشْتَاتًا 99 v. 6, "Divided into classes." شَتَّى indeclinable, sing. and plur. Separate, divided; in an adverbial form, Separately; It is said by Beiḍâwee to be a plur. of شَتِيتٌ.

شَتَا aor. o. *To winter.* شِتَآءٌ Winter.

شَجَرَ *To avert*, to be a matter of controversy (with بَيْنَ). شَجَرٌ generic noun, A plant having a trunk or stem, a tree, trees; جَعَلَ لَكُمْ مِنَ ٱلشَّجَرِ ٱلْأَخْضَرِ نَارًا 36 v. 80, "He giveth you fire out of the green tree;" Fire is obtained by rubbing together the wood of the مَرْخٌ and عَفَارٌ, even when green. شَجَرَةٌ noun of unity, A tree, a plant.

شَحَّ aor. o. and i. *To be avaricious.* شُحٌّ Avarice. أَشِحَّةٌ plur. of شَحِيحٌ Avaricious, covetous.

شَحَمَ aor. a. *To give any one fat to eat.* شُحُومٌ plur. of شَحْمٌ Fat.

شَحَنَ aor. a. *To fill.* مَشْحُونٌ part. pass. Filled, loaded (a ship).

شَخَصَ aor. a. *To be raised up,* to be fixed (the eyes) in horror. شَاخِصٌ part. act. That which is fixed in horror, as the sight of the eyes.

شَدَّ aor. o. *To run,* establish, bind firmly, strengthen (with acc. and بِ); وَٱشْدُدْ عَلَى قُلُوبِهِمْ 10 v. 88, "Harden their hearts." شَدِيدٌ Plur. شِدَادٌ and أَشِدَّآءُ (2nd declension) Vehement, strong, violent, severe, grievous. *Note.* Adjectives of the forms فَعِيلٌ and فِعَالٌ are used indifferently for both masc. and fem., thus at 12 v. 48 before the words سَبْعٌ شِدَادٌ we must understand the fem. plur. سِنُونَ; so also at 72 v. 12, where سَمٰوَاتٌ is the word to be supplied. أَشَدُّ for أَشْدَدُ comp. form, more or most strong, etc., as أَشَدُّ قَسْوَةً 2 v. 69, *lit.* "More strong in hardness," for أَقْسَى Harder, D. S. Gr. T. 1, p. 325. أَشُدٌّ The age of full strength, viz. from 18 to 30.—إِشْتَدَّ VIII. To act with violence against (with بِ).

شَرَّ aor. o. and i. *To do evil.* شَرٌّ Plur. أَشْرَارٌ Evil, bad, wicked. شَرَرٌ collective noun, Sparks of fire.

شَرِبَ aor. a. To drink (with acc. or with بِ). شِرْبٌ n.a. A portion of water, time of drinking. شُرْبٌ n.a. A drinking. شَارِبٌ part. act. One who drinks. شَرَابٌ Drink, a beverage, potion. مَشْرَبٌ A drinking place; it is also a noun of action, meaning simply the act of drinking, or drink; Plur. مَشَارِبُ (2nd declension).—أَشْرَبَ IV. To give to drink, make to drink; وَأُشْرِبُوا فِي قُلُوبِهِمُ ٱلْعِجْلَ 2 v. 87, "And they were made to drink the calf into their hearts;" for the construction see D. S. Gr. T. 2, pp. 124 and 453.

شَرَحَ aor. a. To open, enlarge, expand (with acc. and لِ or بِ).

شَرَدَ aor. o. *To become a fugitive.*—شَرَّدَ II. To disperse (with بِ).

شِرْذِمَةٌ A small band of men; possibly derived from شَرَذَ for شَرَدَ.

شَرَطَ aor. o. and i. *To impose a condition.* أَشْرَاطٌ plur. of شَرَطٌ A sign.

شَرَعَ aor. a. To lay down a law, appoint a religion for any one (with acc. and لِ of pers.). شُرَّعٌ plur. of شَارِعٌ part. act. Holding up (their heads), or appearing manifestly, both of which meanings belong to the verb; for the story alluded to at 7 v. 163 see سَبْتٌ. شِرْعَةٌ and شَرِيعَةٌ A law or institution prescribed by God, the right way or mode of action; ثُمَّ جَعَلْنَاكَ عَلَى شَرِيعَةٍ مِنَ ٱلْأَمْرِ 45 v. 17, "Then we put you in the right way concerning the matter (of faith)."

شَرَقَ aor. o. *To split, rise (as the sun).* شَرْقِيٌّ Of or pertaining to the East, Eastern. مَشْرِقٌ The place of sunrise, the East. ٱلْمَشْرِقَيْنِ oblique dual, *Literally,* The two Easts, or the two places where the snn rises in winter and summer; at 43 v. 37 the words بُعْدَ ٱلْمَشْرِقَيْنِ are by some interpreted to mean the distance from East to West; Plur. مَشَارِقُ (2nd declension) The Eastern parts, the different points of sunrise.—أَشْرَقَ IV. To shine, rise (the sun). إِشْرَاقٌ n.a. The sunrise. مُشْرِقٌ part. act. One on whom the sun has risen, or who does anything at sunrise.

شَرِكَ aor. a. *To be a companion or sharer.* شِرْكٌ A share, participation; at 31 v. 12 it means polytheism or idolatry; يَكْفُرُونَ بِشِرْكِكُمْ 35 v. 15, "They will disclaim your having associated them with God." شَرِيكٌ An associate, partner, sharer; Plur. شُرَكَآءُ (2nd declension) شُرَكَآءُ لِلّٰهِ All those to whom the idolaters rendered a share of Divine honours, such as Angels, Genii, Devils, idols, etc., it is to these that allusion is made at 6 v. 137 and elsewhere. *Note.* Nouns of the second declension when followed by the affixed pronouns take the three inflexions; thus شُرَكَآؤُهُمْ, شُرَكَآئِهِمْ, and شُرَكَآءَهُمْ.—شَارَكَ III. To share with (with acc. of pers. and فِى).—أَشْرَكَ IV. To make a sharer or associate (with acc. of pers. and بِ or فِى); to give companions—to God—(with acc. of pers. and بِ); to be a polytheist or idolater; أَشْرَكْتُمُونِ 14 v. 27, "Ye associated me," D. S. Gr. T. 1, p. 459. مُشْرِكٌ part. act. One who gives associates to God, an idolater.—مُشْتَرِكٌ part. act. VIII. f. One who partakes or shares (with فِى).

شَرَى aor. i. *To buy*, sell, barter (with acc. of thing sold or bartered and بِ of thing taken in exchange).—إِشْتَرَى VIII. To buy, barter, take in exchange (with acc. and بِ); it is also found at 2 v. 84 with the sense of to sell or give in exchange (with acc. and بِ); at 2 v. 15 and elsewhere the word ٱشْتَرَوُا is written with a Damma instead of Jezm over the و on account of the Wesla which follows it; D. S. Gr. T. 1, p. 69.

شَطَّ aor. o. and i. *To be far off.* شَطَطًا An extravagant lie.—أَشَطَّ IV. To act unjustly.

شَطَأَ aor. a. *To walk on the bank of a river.* شَطْأٌ The stalk of a plant. شَاطِئٌ Bank of a river or valley.

شَطَرَ aor. o. *To part in two.* شَطْرٌ n.a. A side. شَطْرَ In the direction of.

شَطَنَ aor. o. *To be obstinate, perverse.* شَيْطَانٌ Plur. شَيَاطِينُ (2nd declension) Satan, a Devil.

شَعَبَ *To collect.* شُعُوبٌ plur. of شَعْبٌ n.a. A large tribe, a nation. شُعَبٌ plur. of شُعْبَةٌ A forked branch. شُعَيْبٌ Sho'aib, name of a prophet sent to the Midianites.

شَعَرَ aor. o. To know, perceive, understand, *to make verses.* شِعْرٌ n.a. Poetry, the art of Poetry. شَعْرٌ Plur. أَشْعَارٌ Hair. شَاعِرٌ Plur. شُعَرَآءُ (2nd declension) part. act. A Poet. شِعْرَى Sirius, the Dog-star, which was worshipped by the Arabs in Pagan times. شَعَآئِرُ (2nd declension) plur. of شِعَارَةٌ A sign, rite, ceremony performed by the pilgrims at Mecca, one of which was the offering of victims; hence some understand the words يُعَظِّمْ شَعَآئِرَ ٱللّٰهِ 22 v. 33, "Holds in honour the offerings made to God," viz. by choosing for slaughter victims of great value. مَشْعَرٌ A place appointed for sacred rites; ٱلْمَشْعَرُ ٱلْحَرَامُ A mountain called Ḳuzaḥ in the neighbourhood of Mecca.—أَشْعَرَ IV. To make any one understand (with acc. of pers. and (أَنْ); to make known to (with بِ of pers. or thing made known, and acc. of pers. to whom the discovery is made).

شَعَلَ *To light a fire.*—إِشْتَعَلَ VIII. *To be lighted*, to become shining.

شَغَفَ aor. a. To affect in the heart's core, inspire with violent love.

شَغَلَ aor. a. To employ, occupy. شُغُلٌ plur. of شُغْلٌ n.a. Work, occupation, employment.

شَفَعَ aor. a. *To make even that which was odd*, to intercede, be an intercessor (with عِنْدَ of pers to whom, and لِ of pers. for whom intercession is made). شَفْعٌ n.a. A pair, double; وَٱلشَّفْعِ وَٱلْوَتْرِ 89 v. 2, "By the double and the single;" numerous interpretations are given; according to one of the most plausible it may mean, All created things,—which are said to have been made in pairs,—and The Creator, who is One and Single. شَافِعٌ part. act. One who intercedes. شَفِيعٌ Plur. شُفَعَآءُ (2nd declension) An intercessor. شَفَاعَةٌ Intercession.

شَفَقَ *To fear, pity.* شَفَقٌ Redness of the sky after sunset.—أَشْفَقَ IV. To be afraid (with مِنْ or with أَنْ of verb). مُشْفِقٌ part. act. One who is afraid or in terror.

شَفَهَ aor. a. *To strike any one on the lip.* شَفَةٌ for شَفَهَةٌ (see سَنَةٌ, rt. سَنَا), A lip; Dual شَفَتَانِ and Oblique شَفَتَيْنِ The two lips.

شَفَا aor. o. *To be near setting* (*the sun*); and شَفَى aor. i. To heal, cure. شَفَا A brink. شِفَآءٌ Medicine, remedy, means of cure.

شَقَّ aor. o. To split, cleave, place under a difficulty, or impose a hard condition (with عَلَى). شَقٌّ n.a. The act of splitting, a fissure, difficulty, labour, trouble. شِقٌّ Difficulty, trouble. شُقَّةٌ A distance, a tract, a long way. أَشَقُّ comp. form (2nd declension for أَشْقَقُ) More troublesome, more difficult to be borne.—شَاقَّ III. To contend with, oppose, resist, separate one's-self from (with acc.); ٱلَّذِينَ كُنتُمْ تُشَاقُّونَ فِيهِمْ 16 v. 29, "Concerning whom ye used to contend (with the believers)." شِقَاقٌ n.a. The act of separating one's-self, schism, heresy, dissent, contention; شِقَاقِى 11 v. 91, "Your contending with me."—إِشَّقَّقَ or تَشَقَّقَ V. D. S. Gr. T. 1, p. 220, To be split open, cleft asunder (with بِ); at 25 v. 27 تَشَقَّقُ is for تَتَشَقَّقُ, D. S. Gr. T. 1, p. 221, and the meaning of the passage is that the Heavens shall be cloven asunder by the clouds on which the Angels shall descend.—إِنْشَقَّ VII. To be cloven asunder; وَٱنْشَقَّ ٱلْقَمَرُ 54 v. 1, "And the moon hath been (or shall be) cloven asunder;" the former meaning having reference to a miracle said to have been wrought by Mohammad, and the latter to one of the signs of the last day. إِنْشِقَاقٌ n.a. The act of cleaving asunder.

شَقَا aor. o. *To make miserable;* and شَقِىَ aor. a. To be miserable, wretched, unhappy. شَقِىٌّ Miserable; at 19 vv. 4 and 49 it may be rendered "disappointed." أَشْقَى comp. form, Most wretched; أَشْقَاهَا 91 v. 12, "The greatest wretch among them," whose name was قُدَارُ بْنُ سَالِفٍ, see 54 v. 29. شِقْوَةٌ Misery, wretchedness.

شَكَّ *To doubt.* شَكٌّ A doubt.

شَكَرَ aor. o. To give thanks, to be grateful (with لِ); فَإِنَّمَا يَشْكُرُ لِنَفْسِهِ 27 v. 40, "He is only grateful to the benefit of his own soul;" to thank, show or feel gratitude for (with acc.); أَنْ أَشْكُرَ

نِعْمَتَكَ 27 v. 19, "That I may show my gratitude for thy favour." شُكْرٌ Plur. شُكُورٌ n.a. The giving thanks, gratitude, thanks. شَاكِرٌ part. act. One who gives thanks or is grateful; God is said to be grateful in the sense of giving rewards to men for their obedience. شَكُورٌ Thankful; a distinction is made between this word and شَاكِرٌ; the former is said to denote a person who is thankful for little or for nothing, the latter grateful for large favours; in the Ḳorân we find both epithets applied to God. مَشْكُورٌ part. pass. Gratefully accepted, acceptable.

شَكِسَ *To be cross-grained and ill-tempered* (*a man*). —مُتَشَاكِسٌ part. act. VI. f. Quarrelling, or at variance with each other.

شَكَلَ aor. o. *To shackle, fasten by a tether.* شَكْلٌ A similitude, likeness. شَاكِلَةٌ Likeness, mode; عَلَى شَاكِلَتِهِ 17 v. 86, "According to his own way."

شَكَا aor. o. To utter a complaint (with acc. and إِلَى); at 12 v. 86 we find an *alif of precaution* added to the word أَشْكُو, see D. S. Gr. T. 1, p. 109. مِشْكَاةٌ A niche in a wall.—إِشْتَكَى VIII. To make a complaint (with إِلَى).

شَمِتَ aor. a. *To rejoice at the misfortunes of others.* —أَشْمَتَ IV. To cause to rejoice over another's misfortunes (with acc. and بِ of pers.).

شَمَخَ *To be lofty and long.* شَامِخٌ part. act. That which is lofty.

شَمَزَ *To be seized with horror.*—إِشْمَأَزَّ IV. f. of شَمْأَزَ a quadriliteral verb not found in the 1st form, To creep or contract with horror.

شَمَسَ aor. i. and o. *To be bright with sunshine.* شَمْسٌ fem. The Sun.

شَمَلَ aor. o. *To comprehend, contain.* شِمَالٌ Plur. شَمَآئِلُ (2nd declension) The left hand; for an explanation of 56 v. 40 see شَأْمٌ.—إِشْتَمَلَ VIII. To contain, conceive (with acc. and عَلَى), as أَمَّا ٱشْتَمَلَتْ عَلَيْهِ أَرْحَامُ ٱلْأُنْثَيَيْنِ 6 v. 144, "Or that which the wombs of the two females have conceived."

شَنَأَ aor. a. *To hate.* شَنَآنٌ for شَنْآنٌ n.a. Hatred. شَانِئٌ for شَانِئٌ, D. S. Gr. T. 1, p. 97, part. act. One who hates.

شَهَبَ aor. a. *To burn, scorch.* شِهَابٌ Plur. شُهُبٌ A flaming fire.

شَهِدَ aor. a. To be present at, in, or with (with acc.); to bear witness that (with أَنَّ or بِأَنَّ), against (with عَلَى), or of (with بِ); to bear testimony to a fact (with إِنَّ); as نَشْهَدُ إِنَّكَ لَرَسُولُ ٱللّٰهِ 63 v. 1, "We bear testimony to the fact that thou art indeed the apostle of God; to bear witness by an oath (with acc. and بِ), as أَنْ تَشْهَدَ أَرْبَعَ شَهَادَاتٍ بِٱللّٰهِ 24 v. 8, "That she make four asseverations by God;" It is also found with the simple acc., as لَا يَشْهَدُونَ ٱلزُّورَ 25 v. 72, "They bear no false witness," and again at 22 v. 29 لِيَشْهَدُوا مَنَافِعَ لَهُمْ, "That they may witness the benefits accruing to them." شَاهِدٌ Plur. شُهُودٌ and أَشْهَادٌ part. act. One who is present, or who bears witness, a witness; at 11 v. 20 the word is generally supposed to mean the Ḳorân; وَشَاهِدٍ وَمَشْهُودٍ 85 v. 3, "By a witness and a thing witnessed;" a vague and indefinite expression, of which a great number of explanations have been suggested by the commentators; according to one it means the Creator and Creation, or *vice versâ*; several others are given in Sale's Ḳorân; وَبَنِينَ شُهُودًا 74 v. 13, "And sons remaining in his presence (at Mecca)." شَهِيدٌ

Plur. شُهَدَآءُ (2nd declension) A witness; 50 v. 20, *vide* سَاقٍ; One who bears سَآئِقٌ وَشَهِيدٌ witness to the truth by suffering martyrdom, a martyr, as at 4 v. 71 and 39 v. 69. شَهَادَةٌ n.a. of شَهِدَ To testify, the act of bearing witness, evidence, a taking of evidence, testimony; أَرْبَعُ شَهَادَاتٍ بِٱللّٰهِ 24 v. 6, "Evidence given by swearing four times by God;" عَالِمُ ٱلْغَيْبِ وَٱلشَّهَادَةِ 9 v. 95, "He who knoweth that which ye keep secret, and that which ye make known." مَشْهَدٌ Time or place of being present, or of giving or hearing evidence; the word occurs at 19 v. 38, and is susceptible of any of the above meanings. مَشْهُودٌ part. pass. That which is witnessed; يَوْمٌ مَشْهُودٌ 11 v. 105, "A day on which evidence shall be given," or it may be "a day which shall be witnessed by all," or "of which testimony has been given;" إِنَّ قُرْآنَ ٱلْفَجْرِ كَانَ مَشْهُودًا 17 v. 80, "Verily the prayer (or reading) at daybreak is borne witness to" (by the guardian angels).—أَشْهَدَ IV. To take as witness, call to witness (with acc. and عَلَى); to call upon any one to be present at or to witness (with acc. of pers. and thing); to cause evidence to be taken of or against (with عَلَى).—إِسْتَشْهَدَ X. To call as witness (with acc. and عَلَى).

شَهَرَ aor. a. *To publish abroad.* شَهْرٌ Plur. أَشْهُرٌ and شُهُورٌ A month; originally *A moon, either new, or according to others, a full moon;* ٱلْحَجُّ أَشْهُرٌ مَعْلُومَاتٌ 2 v. 193, "The (time for the) pilgrimage is (the) known months," viz. Shawâl, Dhu'l Ḳa'da, and part of Dhu'l Ḥajja; The word وَقْتُ must here be understood; *Lit.* "The pilgrimage (its time) is," etc., ٱلْحَجُّ being what the grammarians call مُبْتَدَآءٌ مَرْفُوعٌ بِٱلْإِبْتِدَآءِ, put in the nominative case as being an inchoative; see D. S. Gr. T. 2, p. 594.

شَهَقَ aor. a. and i. *To draw in the breath in sighing.* شَهِيقٌ properly, *The drawing in of the breath of an ass in braying,* A sigh, see زَفِيرٌ; at 67 v. 7 it is applied to the roaring of Hell-fire.

شَهَا aor. o. *To desire, long for.* شَهْوَةٌ n.a. Plur. شَهَوَاتٌ Lust, desire.—إِشْتَهَى VIII. same as شَهَا.

شَابَ aor. o. *To mingle.* شَوْبٌ n.a. A mixture; لَشَوْبًا مِنْ حَمِيمٍ 37 v. 65, "A mixture of boiling water and other delicacies," with which evildoers are to be allowed to wash down the fruit of the infernal tree Ez-Zaḳḳoom.

شَارَ aor. o. *To gather honey from the comb.* شُورَى (2nd declension) A consultation; وَأَمْرُهُمْ شُورَى بَيْنَهُمْ 42 v. 36, "And their business is (a matter of) consultation among them."—شَاوَرَ III. To consult.—أَشَارَ IV. To make signs (with إِلَى of pers.).—تَشَاوُرٌ n.a. VI. f. Consultation with one another.

شُوَاظٌ Flame without smoke; no verbal root.

شَاكَ aor. o. *To prick.* شَوْكَةٌ *A single thorn,* weapons, arms.

شَوَى aor. يَشْوِي a doubly imperfect verb, To roast, scald. شَوًى plur. of شَوَاةٌ The scalp.

شَآءَ for شَيِئَ or شَيَأَ, aor. يَشَآءُ To will, be willing, wish (with acc. or أَنْ of verb). شَيْءٌ n.a. Plur. أَشْيَآءُ (2nd declension, see D. S. Gr. T. 1, p. 364, *note*) A thing, matter, affair; شَيْئًا *adverbially,* In any way, at all.

شَابَ aor. i. *To be hoary* (*the head*). شَيْبٌ and شَيْبَةٌ n.a. Hoariness. شِيبٌ plur. of أَشْيَبُ Hoary, grey-headed; this word may be regarded as a contracted form of شُيُبٌ or شُيْبٌ, like بِيضٌ for بُيْضٌ, or سِيَلٌ for سُيُلٌ, D. S. Gr. T. 1, p. 360.

وَشَى see شِيَةٌ.

شَاخَ aor. i. *To be old.* شَيْخٌ Plur. شُيُوخٌ An old man.

شَادَ aor. i. *To plaster a wall.* مَشِيدٌ part. pass. *properly*, Plastered with gypsum; according to El Beidâwee it may also be rendered lofty.—مُشَيَّدٌ part. pass. II. f. Built up on high.

شَاعَ aor. i. To be published abroad; with فِي of pers. it is used in a bad sense, as أَنْ تَشِيعَ ٱلْفَاحِشَةُ فِي ٱلَّذِينَ آمَنُوا 24 v. 18, "That filthy rumours should be spread abroad about the true believers." شِيعَةٌ Plur. شِيَعٌ and أَشْيَاعٌ A sect, party; أَشْيَاعُهُمْ Those of a like persuasion, or of their party.

ص

صٓ The name and initial letter of the 38th chapter, see آلٓمٓ.

صَبَّ aor. o. To pour (with acc. and عَلَى); at 44 v. 48 it is used with فَوْقَ, "Pour over," and at 22 v. 20 with مِنْ فَوْقِ. صَبٌّ n.a. The act of pouring.

صَبَأَ aor. a. *To rise (a star).* صَابِئُونَ The Ṣabeans, who thought themselves followers of the religion of Noah, and worshipped the heavenly bodies.

صَبَحَ aor. a. *To give one a morning draught.* صُبْحٌ صَبَاحٌ and إِصْبَاحٌ The morning. مِصْبَاحٌ Plur. مَصَابِيحُ (2nd declension) A lamp.—صَبَّحَ II. To come to or come upon in the morning.—أَصْبَحَ IV. To be, become, happen, or do anything in the morning; This word is one of the أَخَوَاتُ كَانَ or sisters of كَانَ, which govern their attributes in the acc., D. S. Gr. T. 2, p. 60; أَصْبَحَ may frequently be rendered simply "he was, or became," and sometimes "he began," as فَأَصْبَحَ يُقَلِّبُ 18 v. 40, "And he began to turn down." مُصْبِحٌ part. act. One who does anything in, or enters upon, the morning.

صَبَرَ aor. i. *To bind,* to be patient or constant, to endure patiently or be constant towards (with acc. or with عَلَى). صَبْرٌ n.a. Patience. صَابِرٌ part. act. One who is patient or constant, persevering. صَبَّارٌ Very patient, constant.—صَابَرَ III. To excel in patience.—أَصْبَرَ IV. To suffer misfortune; فَمَا أَصْبَرَهُمْ عَلَى ٱلنَّارِ 2 v. 170, "How great will be their sufferings in the Fire." For the construction of verbs of admiration see D. S. Gr. T. 2, p. 218.—إِصْطَبَرَ VIII. D. S. Gr. T. 1, p. 222, To be patient or constant (with لِ or عَلَى).

صَبَعَ aor. a. *To point the finger at any one.* أَصَابِعُ (2nd declension) comm. gend. plur. of أُصْبُعٌ A finger.

صَبَغَ aor. a. o. and i. *To dye.* صِبْغٌ Sauce. صِبْغَةٌ Baptism; صِبْغَةَ ٱللّٰهِ 2 v. 132, an elliptical expression meaning "God has baptized us with his baptism," or "his religion;" the visible signs of which appear in the believer, as water is seen on the person of one baptized; the word صِبْغَةً is said to be put in the acc. as being the corroborative, ٱلْمُؤَكِّدُ of آمَنَّا v. 130, and the substitute or equivalent, ٱلْبَدَل of مِلَّةَ إِبْرٰهِيمَ D. S. Gr. T. 2, p. 526, see also p. 85 of the same volume.

صَبَا aor. o. *To be puerile*, to feel a youthful propensity towards (with إِلَى). صَبِيٌّ A male child, a boy.

صَحَبَ *To flay an animal;* and صَحِبَ aor. a. *To be a companion to any one.* صَاحِبٌ Plur. صَحْبٌ, Plur. of Plur. أَصْحَابٌ D. S. Gr. T. 1, p. 376, A companion, associate; it frequently means Lord of, or the possessor of any quality or thing; one in intimate relation with anything, as صَاحِبُ ٱلْحُوتِ Jonah; as it were, "He of the fish or the man of the fish;" أَصْحَابُ ٱلنَّارِ "The men, or companions of the fire,—the Damned;" أَصْحَابُ ٱلْمَشْأَمَةِ and أَصْحَابُ ٱلْمَيْمَنَةِ 56 vv. 8 and 9, "The companions of the Right and Left hands," viz. The Righteous and the Wicked, so called because they shall receive the Books containing a register of their actions, the former in their right hands, and the latter in their left; يَا صَاحِبَيِ ٱلسِّجْنِ 12 v. 39 oblique dual, D. S. Gr. T. 1, p. 415, "O my two fellow prisoners!": as in the case of ذُو, the proper rendering of this word may best be gathered from the context, thus at 51 v. 59, where أَصْحَابِهِمْ refers to "Those who resembled them in former days." صَاحِبَةٌ A consort, wife.—صَاحَبَ III. To bear company with (with acc.).—أَصْحَبَ IV. To preserve, hinder, keep from (with مِنْ).

صَحَفَ *To dig with an instrument called* مِصْحَفَةٌ. صِحَافٌ plur. of صَحْفَةٌ A dish. صُحُفٌ plur. of صَحِيفَةٌ A leaf or page of a book, a book; صُحُفًا مُنَشَّرَةً 74 v. 52, "Open Books" from Heaven, in which should be written each man's name, with an order to follow Moḥammad.

صَخَّ aor. o. *To strike anything solid.* صَاخَّةٌ A deafening noise.

صَخْر generic noun, Rocks. صَخْرَةٌ noun of unity, A rock; no verbal root.

صَدَّ aor. o. To turn away the face (with عَنْ); turn away, divert, hinder (with acc. and عَنْ); aor. o. and i. To cry aloud (with مِنْ of object), as at 43 v. 57; the words in the text refer to a passage at 21 v. 98, where judgment is denounced against all objects of idolatrous worship; but the Meccans contending that Jesus must be included with the rest, the blunder was corrected by the 101st verse. صَدٌّ n.a. The act of hindering, diverting, or turning away from. صُدُودٌ n.a. The act of turning away the face. صَدِيدٌ Boiling (water), the serum in a wound, purulent matter, see شَوْبٌ.

صَدَرَ aor. o. and i. *To return from watering*, to proceed, go forward. صَدْرٌ n.a. Plur. صُدُورٌ comm. gend. The bosom, breast.—أَصْدَرَ IV. To bring back, as حَتَّى يُصْدِرَ ٱلرِّعَآءُ 28 v. 23, "Till the shepherds have brought away (their flocks)."

صَدَعَ aor. a. *To split*, expound, profess openly (with بِ). صَدْعٌ A fissure.—صَدَّعَ II. Pass. صُدِّعَ To oppress with, or suffer from headache.—إِصَّدَّعَ for تَصَدَّعَ V. D. S. Gr. T. 1, p. 220, To be split up or divided in two. مُتَصَدِّعٌ part. act. That which is cloven or splits itself in two.

صَدَفَ aor. i. To turn aside (with عَنْ). صَدَفٌ The steep side of a mountain.

صَدَقَ aor. o. To be truthful, true or sincere, to speak

the truth, to establish or confirm the truth of what another has said, to verify (with double acc.), as صَدَقَ ٱللّٰهُ رَسُولَهُ ٱلرُّؤْيَا 48 v. 27, "God hath confirmed for his Apostle the truth of the vision;" to keep faith (with acc.); observe a promise faithfully (with double acc.). صِدْقٌ Truth, veracity, sincerity, soundness, excellence in a variety of different objects; thus مُبَوَّأَ صِدْقٍ 10 v. 93, "A salubrious and agreeable dwelling;" مُدْخَلَ صِدْقٍ 17 v. 82, "With a favourable entrance (into the grave);" لِسَانًا صِدْقٍ عَلِيًّا 19 v. 51, *Literally*, "A lofty tongue of veracity;" meaning that they should receive the highest praise; a similar phrase occurs at 26 v. 84. صَادِقٌ part. act. One who, or That which is true, sincere, one who speaks the truth. صَدَقَةٌ Whatever is given and sanctified to God's service, as alms or tithes, etc. صَدُقَةٌ A dowry given by the husband to his wife. صَدِيقٌ comm. gend. A sincere friend. أَصْدَقُ (2nd declension) comp. form, More true. صِدِّيقٌ Very truthful, a man of veracity.—صَدَّقَ II. To be very sincere and truthful, to verify, to prove the truth of, as صَدَّقَ عَلَيْهِمْ إِبْلِيسُ ظَنَّهُ 34 v. 19, "Iblees proved the truth of his opinion of them;" to give credit to, or believe in the truth of (with بِ). تَصْدِيقٌ n.a. A verification. مُصَدِّقٌ part. act. One who verifies, confirms, or bears witness to the truth.—تَصَدَّقَ or إِصَّدَّقَ V. D. S. Gr. T. 1, p. 220, To give alms (with عَلَى of pers.); فَمَنْ تَصَدَّقَ بِهِ 5 v. 49, "And whosoever remits it (the penalty, or the retaliation) as alms;" the word is also found with this signification at 2 v. 280 and 4 v. 94. مُتَصَدِّقٌ and مُصَّدِّقٌ part. act. One who gives alms.

صَدَا aor. o. *To clap the hands.*—تَصْدِيَةٌ n.a. II. f. A clapping of hands.—تَصَدَّى V. To receive with honour; at 80 v. 6 this word is put for تَتَصَدَّى D. S. Gr. T. 1, p. 221.

صَرَّ aor. o. *To tie up a purse;* aor. i. *To cry aloud.* صِرٌّ Excessive cold that scorches plants. صَرَّةٌ A loud cry.—أَصَرَّ IV. To be obstinate, persist obstinately (with عَلَى).

صَرَحَ *To make manifest.* صَرْحٌ n.a. A palace, a high tower, or other lofty structure.

صَرَخَ *To cry aloud.* صَرِيخٌ One who brings help.—مُصْرِخٌ part. act. IV. f. same as صَرِيخٌ; وَمَا أَنْتُمْ بِمُصْرِخِيَّ 14 v. 27, "Neither can ye help me," for مُصْرِخِينَ oblique plural with personal pronoun يِ, D. S. Gr. T. 1, p. 459.—إِصْطَرَخَ VIII. for إِصْتَرَخَ D. S. Gr. T. 1, p. 222, To cry aloud.—إِسْتَصْرَخَ X. To implore assistance of any one (with acc. of pers.).

صَرْصَرَ quadriliteral verb, derived from صَرَّ q.v. *To make a chattering noise (as a green woodpecker).* صَرْصَرٌ A loud roaring and furious wind, or according to another interpretation, a blast of cold wind.

صِرَاطٌ comm. gend. A way, and especially an open way; *the name of a bridge over Hell;* no verbal root.

صَرَعَ aor. a. *To prostrate.* صَرْعَى plur. of صَرِيعٌ Lying prostrate.

صَرَفَ aor. i. To turn, turn away, divert, avert (with acc. and عَنْ); to turn towards (with acc. and إِلَى); صَرَفَكُمْ عَنْهُمْ 3 v. 146, "He put you to flight before them." صَرْفٌ n.a. The act of averting. مَصْرِفٌ A place to turn to, a refuge. مَصْرُوفٌ part. pass. Averted.—صَرَّفَ II. To explain, give an explanation of (with مِنْ); at

25 v. 52 the words صَرَّفْنَاهُ بَيْنَهُمْ may either refer to the water, and must then be rendered "We cause it to flow amongst them (by different channels)," or it may be translated "We have explained the matter to them (in the Korân)." تَصْرِيفٌ n.a. Change (of wind). إِنْصَرَفَ VII. To turn aside.

صَرَمَ aor. i. To cut off—dates (from a tree). صَارِمٌ part. act. One who cuts or gathers fruit. صَرِيمٌ A garden whose fruit has all been gathered; also a dark night, as though it were burnt up and black; both meanings have been assigned at 68 v. 20.

سَطَرَ see صَطَرَ.

صَعِدَ aor. a. To mount (a ladder); ascend (with إِلَى). صَعَدٌ A severe torment. صَعِيدٌ Earth, sand, or dust. صَعُودٌ A calamity, torment, name of a mountain of fire in Hell; سَأُرْهِقُهُ صَعُودًا 74 v. 17, "I will afflict him with torment," or "I will compel him to climb a peak of fire;" the words may be taken in either sense.—أَصْعَدَ IV. To mount up.—إِصَّعَّدَ for تَصَعَّدَ V. D. S. Gr. T. 1, p. 220, To climb up (with فِي).

صَعِرَ *To have the face distorted.*—صَعَّرَ II. To make a wry face at (with acc. and لِ of pers.).

صَعَقَ aor. a. *To strike with lightning;* and صَعِقَ To swoon, expire. صَعِقٌ One in a swoon. صَاعِقَةٌ Plur. صَوَاعِقُ (2nd declension) A stunning noise as of a thunderbolt, a punishment from Heaven, a thunderbolt.—أَصْعَقَ IV. To cause to swoon.

صَغُرَ aor. o. *To be younger than another;* and صَغِرَ *To be small.* صَاغِرٌ part. act. One who is small, vile, contemptible. صَغِيرٌ Small. أَصْغَرُ (2nd declension) comp. form, Smaller. صَغَارٌ Vileness, contempt.

صَغَا aor. o. and i. *To incline,* swerve; and صَغِيَ aor. a. To incline towards (with إِلَى).

صَفَّ aor. o. *To set, arrange in a row or rank, to extend the wings in flying.* صَفٌّ A row, rank; صَفًّا In order, in line of battle; وَٱلصَّافَّاتِ صَفًّا 37 v. 1, "By (the Angels) standing in rank." صَافٌّ part. act. Extending its wings. صَوَافُّ for صَوَافِفُ (2nd declension) plur. of صَافَّةٌ for صَافِفَةٌ A camel standing with its fore-feet in line, or with three feet on the ground and one fore-foot tied up. مَصْفُوفٌ part. pass. Arranged in order.

صَفَحَ aor. a. *To turn one's-self away from, repel;* to pardon, forgive (with عَنْ); at 64 v. 14 this word is found in combination with عَفَا and غَفَرَ, the meaning of all three is nearly identical, but a slight distinction may be made by consulting the primary signification of each word; a somewhat similar passage occurs in the 51st Psalm, "Turn thy face from my sins, and put out all my misdeeds." صَفْحٌ n.a. Pardon, the act of repelling a suitor; with the latter meaning it is found at 43 v. 4.

صَفَدَ aor. i. *To bind.* أَصْفَادٌ Fetters, plur. of صَفَدٌ *A present,* and hence *an obligation.*

صَفِرَ aor. i. *To whistle.* صَفْرَآءُ (2nd declension) fem. of أَصْفَرُ Yellow; Plur. صُفْرٌ comm. gend.—مُصْفَرٌّ part. IX. f. That which is or becomes yellow.

صَفْصَفَ quadriliteral, *To pass alone over a level plain.* صَفْصَفٌ A level plain.

صَفَنَ aor. i. *To stand on three feet—as a horse—with the toe of one of the hind feet just touching the ground.* ٱلصَّافِنَاتُ fem. plur. part. act. Horses standing as above; at 38 v. 30

the word ٱلْخَيْلَ is to be understood, D. S. Gr. T. 2, pp. 233 and 267.

صَفَا aor. o. *To be clear.* ٱلصَّفَا Name of a mountain near Mecca. صَفْوَانٌ A hard stone.—مُصَفًّى part. pass. II. f. Clarified.—أَصْفَى IV. To choose in preference to, or grant to another a preference in the choice of anything (with acc. of pers. and بِ of thing).—إِصْطَفَى VIII. for إِصْتَفَى D. S. Gr. T. 1, p. 222, To choose, select; to choose in preference to (with acc. and عَلَى); at 37 v. 153 we find أَصْطَفَى for أَٱصْطَفَى "Hath he chosen?" D. S. Gr. T. 1, p. 71. مُصْطَفًى part. pass. Chosen.

صَكَّ To strike violently.

صَلَبَ aor. i. To crucify. صُلْبٌ The back-bone or loins; Plnr. أَصْلَابٌ.—صَلَّبَ II. To cause to be crucified.

صَلَحَ aor. a. *To be right,* good, honest, upright. صُلْحٌ Peace, reconciliation; صُلْحًا Peaceably. صَالِحٌ part. act. One who or that which is good, sound, free from blemish, perfect, upright, righteous, a man of integrity; also a proper name, Ṣâleḥ, a prophet said to have been sent to the tribe of Thamood; ٱلصَّالِحَاتُ Good works.—أَصْلَحَ IV. To make whole and sound, amend, reconcile; to make a reconciliation or peace (with بَيْنَ); to dispose aright (with acc. and لِ of pers.); to render fit, as at 21 v. 90, وَأَصْلَحْنَا لَهُ زَوْجَهُ "And we rendered his wife fit (for child-bearing);" instances occur, as at 27 v. 49, where the meaning seems to approach very closely to that of the primitive form, to be upright, or act with integrity; at 46 v. 14 it means to show kindness (with لِ of pers. and فِى of thing). إِصْلَاحٌ n.a. Uprightness, righteousness, reconciliation, amendment, reformation. مُصْلِحٌ part. act. One who is upright, righteous, a person of integrity, a reformer; at 28 v. 18 it may be translated "Peacemaker."

صَلَدَ aor. i. *To be hard.* صَلْدٌ Hard.

صَلْصَلَ *To sound.* صَلْصَالٌ Dry clay. Derived from صَلَّ aor. i. *To sound.*

صَلَا aor. o. *To hurt in the small of the back;* and صَلِىَ for صَلِوَ aor. a. *To have the centre of the back bent in, as a mare before foaling.* صَلَوٰةٌ pronounced, and sometimes written صَلَاةٌ D. S. Gr. T. 1, p. 36; Plnr. صَلَوَاتٌ A prayer; صَلَوَاتٌ مِنْ رَبِّهِمْ 2 v. 152, "Mercies from their Lord;" at 22 v. 41 it means "Synagogues."—صَلَّى II. To pray, *properly,* by bending the knees and whole body in adoration, or generally, to offer prayer to God (with لِ); with عَلَى it means to pray for, also to bless, as in the formula صَلَّى ٱللّٰهُ عَلَيْهِ وَسَلَّمَ "*God bless and keep him.*" مُصَلٍّ for مُصَلِّىٌ part. act. One who prays. مُصَلًّى A place of prayer.

صَلَى aor. i. *To roast;* and صَلِىَ aor. a. To undergo roasting in the fire (with acc. of fire); Instead of يَصْلَى another reading of several passages is يُصْلَى etc. in the Pass. or يُصَلَّى in the ii. f. and they must then be translated "He shall be burnt" or "roasted." صَالٍ part. act. One who suffers the pain of being roasted; صَالُوا ٱلنَّارِ for صَالُونَ as antecedent to the complement ٱلنَّارِ 38 v. 39, *Literally,* "Sufferers of the roasting of the fire," or "entering Hell-fire to be roasted therein." صِلِىٌّ n.a. Roasting.—صَلَّى II. To cause to be burnt, submit to the action of fire (with acc. of pers. and of the fire), thus

ثُمَّ ٱلْجَحِيمَ صَلُّوهُ 69 v. 31, "Then cause him to be bnrnt in Hell." تَصْلِيَةٌ n.a. A burning.—أَصْلَى IV. To thrust into the fire to be bnrnt (witb donble acc.).—إِصْطَلَى for إِصْتَلَى VIII. D. S. Gr. T. 1, p. 222, To be warmed at the fire.

صَمَّ *To cork a bottle;* aor. a. To become deaf. صُمٌّ Deaf, plur. of أَصَمُّ (2nd declension).—أَصَمَّ IV. To make deaf.

صَمَتَ aor. o. *To be silent.* صَامِتٌ part. act. One wbo bolds bis peace.

صَمَدَ aor. o. *To wish to approach any one.* صَمَدٌ A Lord, one to whom reference is made in matters of importance; as an adjective it means snblime, everlasting.

صَمَعَ aor. a. *To beat with a cudgel.* صَوَامِعُ (2nd declension) plur. of صَوْمَعٌ A monastery.

صَنَعَ aor. a. To make, do; chiefly used in tbings wbere art is employed; to nourisb or bring up; وَلِتُصْنَعَ عَلَى عَيْنِي 20 v. 40, "And that tbou mightest be brougbt up under my eye;" a similar meaning also pertains to tbe IV. f. صُنْعٌ n.a. An act, that wbicb is done; For tbe elliptical expression صُنْعَ ٱللّٰهِ at 27 v. 90 see وَصِيَّةٌ; see also a similar ellipse at 4 v. 121. صَنْعَةٌ An art. مَصَانِعُ (2nd declension) plur. of مَصْنَعٌ A cistern, also a palace, citadel or other fine building.—إِصْطَنَعَ for إِصْتَنَعَ VIII. D. S. Gr. T. 1, p. 222, To appoint as agent (witb acc. and لِ).

صَنِمَ *To be foul (a smell).* أَصْنَامٌ plnr. of صَنَمٌ An idol.

صِنْوٌ or صُنْوٌ A palm or otber tree springing from tbe same root as others; Plur. صِنْوَانٌ; no verbal root.

صَهَرَ aor. a. *To injure by its heat (the sun),* to dissolve. صِهْرٌ Relationship by marriage.

صَابَ aor. o. *To pour forth, hit the mark.* صَوَابٌ That whicb is right. صَيِّبٌ A rain-cloud.—أَصَابَ IV. To overtake, happen to, befall, fall upon (witb acc.); To will, as at 38 v. 35; to happen, 57 v. 22; To affect injuriously, as at 3 v. 113 أَصَابَتْ حَرْثَ, "It strikes (or injures) the corn;" To meet witb, as at 3 v. 159 قَدْ أَصَبْتُمْ مِثْلَيْهَا, "Ye had already met with two pieces of good fortune eqnivalent to it," viz. at Bedr, wbere the forces under Moḥammad bad not only slain seventy of tbe Ḳoreish, but had also taken an equal nnmber prisoners; of this tbey are reminded when murmuring at the loss tbey sustained at Oḥod; To send down, pour down upon, afflict or pnnish (witb acc. and بِ), as أَصَبْنَاهُمْ بِذُنُوبِهِمْ 7 v. 98, "We conld pnnisb them for tbeir sins;" نُصِيبُ بِرَحْمَتِنَا مَنْ نَشَآءُ 12 v. 56, "We pour down our mercy upon whom we please." مُصِيبٌ part. act. That whicb bappens. مُصِيبَةٌ An accident, misfortnne, calamity.

صَاتَ aor. o. and a. *To emit a sound.* صَوْتٌ n.a. A sonnd, voice; Plnr. أَصْوَاتٌ.

صَارَ aor. o. To incline or tnrn—a thing—towards (witb إِلَى); *To divide, dissect.* صُورٌ A trumpet. صُورَةٌ Plnr. صُوَرٌ A form.—صَوَّرَ II. To form, fashion (with acc. and فِي). مُصَوِّرٌ part. act. One wbo forms. ٱلْمُصَوِّرُ Tbe Fashioner, a name of God.

صَاعَ aor. o. *To measure with a* صَاعٌ *containing about four pints.* صُوَاعٌ A drinking cnp.

صَافَ aor. o. *To bear wool.* أَصْوَافٌ plur. of صُوفٌ Wool, a fleece.

صَامَ aor. o. To fast; فَلْيَصُمْهُ 2 v. 181, "Let bim fast (during) it," for فِيهِ, D. S. Gr. T. 2, p. 389. صَوْمٌ and صِيَامٌ ns.a. A fast, tbe act of fasting. صَآئِمٌ part. act. One who fasts.

صَاحَ aor. i. *To shout.* صَيْحَةٌ n.a. A shout, a blast, a terrible and mighty noise, also a punishment from Heaven.

صَادَ aor. i. and a. *To hunt.* صَيْدٌ Game, the produce of the chase, including fish.—إِصْطَادَ for إِصْتَادَ VIII. D. S. Gr. T. 1, p. 222, To hunt.

صَارَ aor. i. *To become;* to go, tend towards (with إِلَى). مَصِيرٌ n.a. The act of going, a journey, departure; also as a noun of time and place, the place to which any one goes, or at which one arrives; at 25 v. 16 it may be rendered "a retreat."

صَاصَ aor. i. *To produce imperfect dates (a palm-tree).* صَيَاصٍ for صَيَاصِيُ plur. of صِيصَةٌ or صِيصِيَةٌ A castle, or defensive work.

صَافَ aor. i. *To pass the summer.* صَيْفٌ n.a. The summer.

ض

ضَائِنٌ Plur. ضَأْنٌ Sheep; no verbal root.

ضَبَحَ aor. a. *To breathe hard in running.* ضَبْحٌ n.a. The act of panting.

ضَجَعَ aor. a. *To lie on the side.* مَضَاجِعُ (2nd declension) plur. of مَضْجَعٌ A sleeping place, resting place; at 3 v. 148 it alludes to the sleep of death.

ضَحِكَ aor. a. To laugh, laugh at, ridicule (with مِنْ). ضَاحِكٌ part. act. Laughing, one who laughs.

ضَحَا aor. o. *To appear conspicuously;* and ضَحِيَ aor. a. To suffer from the heat of the snn. ضُحًا or ضُحَى comm. gend. said by some to be the plur. of ضَحْوَةٌ Those hours of the morning which follow shortly after sunrise; at 91 v. 1 and 79 v. 29 it means the full brightness of the sun.

ضَدَّ aor. o. *To gain a law-suit.* ضِدٌّ Contrary, an adversary.

ضَرَّ aor. o. To hurt, harm, iujnre. ضَرٌّ n.a. Harm, hurt, injury, affliction. ضُرٌّ Harm, affliction, evil, adversity, famine, as at 12 v. 88. ضَرَرٌ Hurt, inconvenicnce. ضَارٌّ part. act. One who hurts. ضَرَّآءُ fem. (2nd declension) D. S. Gr. T. 1, p. 402, Adversity, loss, tribulation.—ضَارَّ III. To hurt, annoy; to pnt to inconvenieuce on account of (with acc. of pers. and بِ). *Note.* In Surd verbs of this form there is no difference between the act. and pass. in the Aorist tense. ضِرَارٌ n.a. Injury; ضِرَارًا By violence. مُضَارٌّ part. act. Iujuring.—إِضْطَرَّ for إِضْتَرَّ VIII. D. S. Gr. T. 1, p. 222, To compel; to drive forcibly (with acc. and إِلَى); Pass. أُضْطُرَّ To be driven by necessity (with فِى or إِلَى). مُضْطَرٌّ part. act. or pass. One compelled by necessity; أَلْمُضْطَرُّ 27 v. 63, "Him who is compelled by his necessities" (to ask relief of God).

ضَرَبَ aor. i. To beat, strike (with acc. and بِ); This is the primary meaning, but the verb admits of a great variety of interpretations, thus ضَرَبَ ٱللَّهُ مَثَلًا 14 v. 29, "God propounds as an example," or "puts forth a parable" (with لِ); thus also at 43 v. 16 مَا ضَرَبَ لِلرَّحْمٰنِ مَثَلًا, "That which they pass off upon the Merciful as being his similitnde," viz. female children; in allusion to the angels, who were considered to be the daughters of God; ضَرَبُوا فِي ٱلْأَرْضِ 3 v. 150, "They travelled in the earth;" here we may suppose an ellipse of بِأَرْجُلِهِمْ or some similar word; so likewise in the expression إِذَا ضَرَبْتُمْ فِي سَبِيلِ ٱللّٰهِ 4 v. 96, "When ye are on the march in the cause of God's religion;" مَا ضَرَبُوهُ لَكَ إِلَّا جَدَلًا 43 v. 58, "They have only set this question before thee for the sake of disputation;" وَلْيَضْرِبْنَ بِخُمُرِهِنَّ عَلَى جُيُوبِهِنَّ 24 v. 31, "And let them draw their veils over their bosoms;" أَفَنَضْرِبُ عَنْكُمُ ٱلذِّكْرَ 43 v. 4, "Shall we then turn away from you our admonition;" فَضُرِبَ بَيْنَهُمْ بِسُورٍ 57 v. 13, "And a separation shall be made between them by a wall;" وَضُرِبَتْ عَلَيْهِمُ ٱلذِّلَّةُ 2 v. 58, "And vileness was stamped upon them." ضَرْبٌ n.a. The act of striking, a blow, a going from place to place; at 47 v. 4 there is an ellipse of a verb, see D. S. Gr. T. 2, p. 460.

ضَرَعَ aor. a. *To be humble.* ضَرِيعٌ A plant growing in Hell, said to be more bitter than aloes, more fetid than a putrid corpse, and more burning than fire.—تَضَرَّعَ and إِضَّرَّعَ D. S. Gr. T. 1, p. 222, V. To humble one's-self, submit one's-self humbly to God. تَضَرُّعٌ n.a. Humility.

ضَعُفَ and ضَعَفَ aor. o. To be weak. ضَعْفٌ and ضُعْفٌ ns.a. Weakness, infirmity. ضِعْفٌ Plur. أَضْعَافٌ Like, an equal portion, a portion equal to another, or as much again, double; إِذًا لَأَذَقْنَاكَ ضِعْفَ ٱلْحَيٰوةِ وَضِعْفَ ٱلْمَمَاتِ 17. v. 77, "Then we should verily have caused thee to taste an equal share (of the punishment) of this life, and an equal share (of the punishment) of death," *i.e.* a double punishment, the word عَذَابٌ being in both cases understood; D. S. Gr. T. 2, p. 279; Dual ضِعْفَانِ, Oblique ضِعْفَيْنِ Two equal portions, twofold. ضِعَافٌ plur. of ضَعُوفٌ comm. gend. Weak. ضَعِيفٌ Plur. ضُعَفَآءُ (2nd declension) Weak, infirm. أَضْعَفُ (2nd declension) comp. form, Weaker.—ضَاعَفَ III. To double, give double (with acc. and لِ). مُضَاعَفٌ part. pass. Doubled.—مُضْعِفٌ part. act. IV. f. One who makes double.—إِسْتَضْعَفَ X. To think, repute, or esteem weak, and hence to ill-treat a person as if he were weak, to take advantage of his weakness, thus at 7 v. 149. مُسْتَضْعَفٌ part. pass. One who is found or held to be weak.

ضَغَثَ aor. a. *To repeat in a confused and jumbled manner.* ضِغْثٌ A handful of green and dry grass or other herbs; Plur. أَضْغَاثٌ Things confusedly mixed together; أَضْغَاثُ أَحْلَامٍ 12 v. 44, "Confused dreams."

ضَغِنَ aor. a. *To dislike.* أَضْغَانٌ plur. of ضِغْنٌ Ill-feeling, hatred.

ضَفْدَعٌ A frog; Plur. ضَفَادِعُ (2nd declension); The grammatical root is ضَفْدَعَ *To contain frogs (water).*

ضَلَّ aor. i. To err (with بِ); to wander away, go astray from (with acc. or with عَنْ); to err against (with عَلَى); to go from the thoughts or be forgotten, as at 17 v. 69; to leave in the lurch (with عَنْ); to lie hidden (with فِي), as at 32 v. 9. ضَالٌّ part. act. One who errs or goes astray. ضَلَالٌ and ضَلَالَةٌ Error, mistake. أَضَلُّ (2nd declension) comp. form, One who goes more astray; For the Rules of Syntax affecting the comparative and superlative forms see D. S. Gr. T. 2, p. 301.—تَضْلِيلٌ n.a. II. f. Error.—أَضَلَّ IV. To cause to err, seduce, lead astray from (with double acc. or acc. and

(عَنْ), as فَأَضَلُّونَا ٱلسَّبِيلَا 33 v. 67, "And they have seduced us from the right path;" The ا is here added to ٱلسَّبِيلَ to assist the rhyme; D. S. Gr. T. 2, p. 497; أَضَلَّ أَعْمَالَهُمْ 47 v. 1, "He has made their (good) works to be of none effect;" to seduce through or by means of (with بِ). مُضِلٌّ part. act. One who seduces.

ضَمَّ aor. o. To draw close, to hug (with acc. and إِلَى); وَٱضْمُمْ يَدَكَ إِلَى جَنَاحِكَ 20 v. 23, "Draw thine hand close under thine arm."

ضَمَرَ aor. o. *To be slender.* ضَامِرٌ part. act. That which is slender, or tucked up in the belly.

ضَنَّ aor. a. and i. *To be tenacious or grasping.* ضَنِينٌ Greedy, avaricious, grudging; وَمَا هُوَ عَلَى ٱلْغَيْبِ بِضَنِينٍ 81 v. 24, "And he does not act grudgingly in the communication of the secrets;" some copies have بِظَنِينٍ, "He had no suspicion of the secrets."

ضَنَكَ *To be narrow.* ضَنْكٌ n.a. comm. gend. Narrow, wretched.

ضَهِىَ *To be without breasts and barren (a woman), and therefore like a man.*—ضَاهَى III. for ضَاهَأَ (the primitive form ضَهَأَ is not found), To resemble, D. S. Gr. T. 1, p. 236. *Note.* The word يُضَاهِئُونَ 9 v. 30 is also spelt يُضَاهِئُونَ, and يُضَاهُونَ without the hamza.

ضَآءَ aor. o. *To shine.* ضِيَآءٌ Light.—أَضَآءَ IV. To enlighten, illuminate.

ضَارَ aor. i. *To injure.* ضَيْرٌ n.a. Harm, injury.

ضَازَ aor. i. *To defraud.* ضِيزَى for ضُيْزَى D. S. Gr. T. 1, p. 112 (2nd declension), An unfair apportionment.

ضَاعَ aor. i. *To perish.*—أَضَاعَ IV. To suffer to perish, neglect, be unmindful of.

ضَافَ aor. i. *To become a guest.* ضَيْفٌ n.a. sing. and plur. A guest, guests.—ضَيَّفَ II. To entertain a guest.

ضَاقَ aor. i. To be narrow, straitened; وَضَاقَ بِهِمْ ذَرْعًا 11 v. 79, "And he was powerless to (protect) them;" ضَاقَتْ عَلَيْهِمُ ٱلْأَرْضُ 9 v. 119, "The earth became straitened for them." ضَيْقٌ n.a. Trouble, grief. ضَيِّقٌ Strait, narrow. ضَآئِقٌ part. act. That which becomes narrow or straitened.—ضَيَّقَ II. To reduce to straits (with عَلَى of pers.).

ط

طَالُوتُ (2nd declension) Saul, king of Israel.

طَبَعَ aor. a. To seal, seal up (with عَلَى).

طَبَقَ aor. i. *To cover.* طَبَقٌ A state, condition. طِبَاقٌ plur. of طَبَقَةٌ The order of the Heavens, one above another; طِبَاقًا In order one above another.

طِبْنَ 3rd pers. fem. plur. of طَابَ for طَيَبَ q.v.

طَحَى aor. a. D. S. Gr. T. 1, p. 250, To expand, spread out.

طَرَحَ aor. a. To cast forth (with double acc.), as ٱطْرَحُوهُ أَرْضًا 12 v. 9, "Cast him forth into a (distant or unknown part of the) earth."

طَرَدَ aor. o. To drive away; the word فَتَطْرُدَهُمْ is put in the subjunctive at 6 v. 52 as being what the grammarians call جَوَابُ ٱلنَّفْيِ; for this use of the subjunctive after فَ see D. S. Gr. T. 2, p. 26, where the above-named passage is quoted. طَارِدٌ part. act. One who drives away.

طَرَفَ aor. i. *To avert.* طَرْفٌ n.a. An eye, a glance, sight of the eyes. طَرَفٌ Plur. أَطْرَافٌ The extremity, extreme part or verge, border; طَرَفَيِ ٱلنَّهَارِ 11 v. 116, "The two extremities of the day," morning and evening.

طَرَقَ aor. o. *To come by night.* طَارِقٌ part. act. That which appears by night. طَرِيقٌ comm. gend. A way, a road. طَرِيقَةٌ Plur. طَرَآئِقُ (2nd declension) A path, line of conduct, behaviour; أَمْثَلُهُمْ طَرِيقَةً 20 v. 104, "Those most eminent for their good conduct;" سَبْعَ طَرَآئِقَ 23 v. 17, "Seven tracts," meaning the seven Heavens; طَرِيقَةٌ is also used with a plur. signification for Chiefs, Princes; thus at 20 v. 66.

طَرَا aor. o. *To come from afar;* and طَرِيَ aor. a. *To be recent.* طَرِيٌّ Fresh.

طس Initial letters of the 27th chapter, pronounced Ṭà' Seen, see الٓمٓ.

طسٓمٓ Initial letters of the 26th and 28th chapters, see طس.

طَعِمَ aor. a. To eat, taste; لَيْسَ جُنَاحٌ فِيمَا طَعِمُوا 5 v. 94, "There is no sin in that they have tasted" (that which had not at that time been forbidden them). طَاعِمٌ part. act. One who eats. طَعْمٌ n.a. Taste, and طَعَامٌ n.a. Food, the act of eating, as at 5 v. 97.—أَطْعَمَ IV. To feed, give food to (with double acc.); أَطْعَمَهُمْ مِنْ جُوعٍ 106 v. 3, "Who hath provided them with food against hunger." إِطْعَامٌ n.a. The act of feeding; At 2 v. 180 and 5 v. 96 طَعَامٌ also appears to bear this meaning, and may then be considered as another noun of action of the IV. f.—إِسْتَطْعَمَ X. To ask for food (with double acc.).

طَعَنَ aor. a. and o. *To pierce with a spear,* to speak ill of (with فِى of pers.). طَعْنٌ n.a. Evil speaking.

طَغَا aor. o. and طَغَى or طَغِيَ aor. a. To transgress, exceed all bounds (in wickedness); to wander from its orbit, applied at 53 v. 17 to the eye-sight; to overflow, as at 69 v. 11. طُغْيَانٌ n.a. Transgression, the being exceedingly wicked. طَاغٍ for طَاغِىٌ part. act. One who is excessively impious, a transgressor. طَاغِيَةٌ A storm of thunder and lightning of extreme severity. أَطْغَى comp. form for أَطْغَىُ (2nd declension) Most extravagant in wickedness. طَغْوَى Excess of impiety, as كَذَّبَتْ ثَمُودُ بِطَغْوَاهَا 91 v. 11, "The tribe of Thamood accused (Ṣàleḥ) of falsehood by reason of their extreme wickedness." *Note.* The names of Arab tribes are feminine. طَاغُوتٌ Ṭàghoot, a word which with the sing. form has sometimes a plur. signification, and then means Idols, dæmons, or whatever is worshipped besides God, and particularly the two Idols worshipped by the people of Mecca; at 4 v. 63 it is used in the sing., and is there said to refer to a certain Jew named كَعْبُ بْنُ ٱلْأَشْرَفِ, either from his exceeding wickedness, or because a judgment given by him would be prompted by the Devil. —أَطْغَى IV. To cause to transgress, to make one a transgressor.

طَفَّ *To be near.*—تَطْفِيفٌ n.a. II. f. The giving short measure. مُطَفِّفٌ part. act. One who gives short measure.

طَفِئَ aor. a. *To be extinguished.*—أَطْفَأَ IV. To extinguish (with acc. and بِ).

طَفِقَ aor. a. To begin.

طَفَلَ *To be of a tender age.* طِفْلٌ sing. and plur., though we also find the plur. أَطْفَالٌ Very young children, infants.

طَلَّ *To moisten the ground* (*dew*). طَلٌّ Dew.

طَلَبَ aor. o. *To seek;* at 7 v. 52 it means to follow up. طَلَبٌ n.a. The act of searching for. طَالِبٌ part. act. A petitioner. مَطْلُوبٌ part. pass. Petitioned.

طَلَحَ aor. a. *To be weary.* طَلْحٌ n.a. A Plantain or Banana tree, according to some the Acacia or Egyptian thorn.

طَلَعَ aor. a. and o. To ascend, rise—the sun,—(with عَلَى). طَلْعٌ The spathe or sheath in which the flowers of the date-palm are enclosed, also the fruit when it first appears, or simply fruit, as at 37 v. 63. طُلُوعٌ n.a. The rising. مَطْلَعٌ n.a. The time of rising (of the dawn). مَطْلِعٌ n.a. Place of the sun's rising.—أَطْلَعَ IV. To make manifest to any one, cause one to understand (with acc. of pers. and عَلَى of thing).—إِطَّلَعَ for إِطْتَلَعَ VIII. D. S. Gr. T. 1, p. 222, To mount up (with إِلَى); to penetrate (with acc.) as at 19 v. 81, where we have أَطَّلَعَ "Has he penetrated?" for أَاطَّلَعَ, the ا of union being omitted after the interrogative أ D. S. Gr. T. 1, p. 71; At 37 v. 52 is a passage which is read and interpreted in various ways, see D. S. Gr. T. 2, p. 185, but adopting the reading given by Flügel هَلْ أَنْتُمْ مُطَّلِعُونَ فَاطَّلَعَ, the meaning will be "Will ye look down (upon the inhabitants of Hell)?—and he shall look down," (pret. for fut.); in this sense the verb governs its complement with عَلَى; so likewise when it means to mount above, come upon, or meet with. مُطَّلِعٌ part. act. One who looks down upon.

طَلَقَ aor. o. *To be divorced.* طَلَاقٌ n.a. Divorce.—طَلَّقَ II. To divorce. مُطَلَّقَةٌ fem. part. pass. A woman who is divorced.—إِنْطَلَقَ VII. To depart, go one's way, to be free or loose, as at 26 v. 12.

طَمَّ aor. o. and i. *To be much.* طَامَّةٌ A calamity; ٱلطَّامَّةُ ٱلْكُبْرَى 79 v. 34, "The very great calamity," viz. The last Judgment.

طَمَثَ aor. o. and i. To deflower a virgin.

طَمَسَ aor. o. and i. To obliterate, put out (the eyes), as at 54 v. 37; At 4 v. 50 it means to deface the features; to destroy utterly (with عَلَى).

طَمِعَ aor. a. To desire (with أَنْ). طَمَعٌ n.a. Desire, a hoping or longing for; at 13 v. 13 طَمَعًا means "causing you to be full of hope (for rain)."

طَمَنَ *Quiet;* whence comes طَمْأَنَ (quadriliteral) *To rest.*—إِطْمَأَنَّ IV. To be quiet, rest securely in, or satisfied with (with بِ); فَإِذَا ٱطْمَأْنَنْتُمْ 4 v. 104, "And when ye are secure (from danger);" 2 pers. plur. pret. D. S. Gr. T. 1, p. 231. مُطْمَئِنٌّ part. act. One who rests securely, or enjoys peace and quiet.

طه Initial letters and name of the 20th chapter, pronounced Ṭâ' Hâ', see الم.

طَهَرَ *To remove;* aor. o. *To be pure,* free from her courses (a woman). طَهُورٌ n.a. Pure. أَطْهَرُ (2nd declension) comp. form, More pure, see D. S. Gr. T. 2, p. 304.—طَهَّرَ II. To purify, cleanse. تَطْهِيرٌ n.a. Purification. مُطَهِّرٌ part. act. One who frees from impurity. مُطَهَّرٌ part. pass. Purified, freed from impurity, clean, pure.—تَطَهَّرَ or إِطَّهَّرَ V. D. S. Gr. T. 1, p. 220, To purify one's-self, keep one's-self pure; فَاطَّهَّرُوا 5 v. 9, imperat. "Then purify yourselves" (by washing the entire body). مُتَطَهِّرٌ or مُطَّهِّرٌ part. act. Those who purify themselves, or are clean, pure.

طَادَ aor. o. *To be firm and immoveable.* طَوْدٌ A mountain.

طَارَ aor. o. *To approach.* طُورٌ A mountain; طُورُ

طَاقَ aor. o. To go round about, encompass (with عَلى); to go about, circulate (with بَيْنَ). طَآئِف part. act. One who goes round about or encompasses; at 68 v. 19 it means a common destruction surrounding all; see also طَافَ for طَيْف. طَآئِفَةٌ A part, some, a party, a people, a company or band of men from 2 to 1000, according to different authorities. طُوفَانٌ The Deluge, a common destruction or calamity which embraces all. طَوَّافٌ One who goes about (to serve another).—إِطَّوَّفَ V. D. S. Gr. T. 1, p. 220, To go round about (with بِ).

طَاقَ aor. o. *To be able.* طَاقَةٌ Power, strength.— طَوَّقَ II. To twist a collar; سَيُطَوَّقُونَ مَا بَخِلُوا بِهِ 3 v. 176, "They shall have that which they have covetously withheld twisted as a collar about their necks," *lit.* "they shall be bound with it for a collar."—أَطَاقَ IV. To be able (to do a thing, with acc.).

طَالَ aor. o. To be long, to last long, or be prolonged (with عَلَى of pers.). طَوْلٌ Plenty of wealth, a sufficiency of means, Power, as at 40 v. 3. طُولٌ n.a. Height. طَوِيلٌ Long.— تَطَاوَلَ VI. To be prolonged (with عَلَى of pers.).

طَوَى aor. i. To roll up. طَيٌّ n.a. The act of rolling up. طُوًى Ṭoowa, name of a valley near Mount Sinai. مَطْوِيٌّ part. pass. Rolled up.

طَابَ aor. i. To be good, pleasing (with لِ); فَإِنْ طِبْنَ لَكُمْ عَنْ شَيْءٍ مِنْهُ نَفْسًا 4 v. 3, "And if they kindly give you up any portion of it of their own free will," *lit.* "if they are good to you concerning any portion," etc. طُوبَى. (2nd declension) Good fortune, happiness. طَيِّبٌ Good, agreeable, sweet and clean, happy, favourable.

طُورُ سِينِينَ or سَيْنَآءَ Mount Sinai; it is also called الطُّور. أَطْوَارٌ plur. of طَوْرٌ A condition or state; خَلَقَكُمْ أَطْوَارًا 71 v. 13, "He created you after a variety of states or stages of existence;" beginning with the formation of Adam.

طَاعَ aor. o. and a. *To be obedient;* to hearken to (intercession), as at 40 v. 19. طَوْعٌ Obedient; طَوْعًا With willing obedience. طَاعَةٌ Obedience. طَآئِعٌ part. act. One who is obedient, obedient. —طَوَّعَ II. To permit, consent to (with acc. and لِ of pers.).—أَطَاعَ IV. To obey. مُطَاعٌ part. pass. Obeyed.—تَطَوَّعَ V. To give one's-self obediently or willingly to perform (a good work). مُطَّوِّعٌ part. act. D. S. Gr. T. 1, p. 327, One who gives himself willingly to perform (a good or charitable action).—إِسْتَطَاعَ and إِسْطَاعَ X.,—though some have considered the latter to be a variation of the IV. f., D. S. Gr. T. 1, p. 224,—To be able, have power, be capable of (with acc. or acc. and عَلَى), as مَا لَمْ تَسْطِعْ عَلَيْهِ صَبْرًا 18 v. 81, "That which thou wast not able to bear patiently;" It is also used with أَنْ or with acc. and لِ; instances of both occur at 18 v. 96; or with acc. and إِلَى as at 3 v. 91; At several places in the 18th chapter it is found with مَعَ of pers. and acc. of thing; thus in the 66th verse لَنْ تَسْتَطِيعَ مَعِىَ صَبْرًا "Thou wilt not be able to have patience with me;" In translating such sentences as the above it is frequently necessary to supply a verb according to the context, thus فَلَا يَسْتَطِيعُونَ سَبِيلًا 17 v. 51, "But they were not able (to find) a ground of reproach (against thee)." A note explanatory of some of the above modes of construction will be found in De Sacy's Grammar, T. 2, p. 170.

طَارَ aor. i. To fly. طَيْرٌ generic nonn, Birds. *Note.* Verbs having for subject a noun of this description may be put in the fem. D. S. Gr. T. 2, p. 233; According to some there are two words of this form, one in the sing. meaning a bird, as at 3 v. 43, and the other an irregular plur. of طَآئِرٌ, meaning Birds. طَآئِرٌ part. act. A flying thing, an omen, and especially an evil one.—تَطَيَّرَ or إِطَّيَّرَ V. D. S. Gr. T. 1, p. 220, To angur evil, draw an evil angury from (with بِ).—مُسْتَطِيرٌ part. act. X. f. That which spreads itself far and wide.

طَافَ aor. i. *To appear (a spectre).* طَآئِفٌ part. act. *A spectral appearance of the Devil,* an instigation of the Devil; see طَافَ for طَوَفَ.

طَانَ aor. i. *To plaster with clay.* طِينٌ Clay.

ظ

ظَعَنَ *To migrate.* ظَعْنٌ n.a. Migration.

ظَفَرَ aor. i. *To claw with the nails.* ظُفُرٌ A nail or claw; ذِى ظُفُرٍ 6 v. 147 is translated by Sale "having an undivided hoof," but it may be doubted whether the words will bear this interpretation; a better translation would seem to be "having claws or nails," as wild beasts or camels.—أَظْفَرَ IV. To give the victory to (with acc. of pers. and عَلَى).

ظَلَّ aor. a.; 2nd pers. sing. pret. ظَلْتَ or ظِلْتَ for ظَلِلْتَ D. S. Gr. T. 1, p. 228, To continue all day, become (with aor. of verb following). ظِلٌّ Shade. ظُلَّةٌ Plur. ظُلَلٌ A covering, roof. ظِلَالٌ sing. and plur. Shadows, shady groves. ظَلِيلٌ Shady.—ظَلَّلَ II. To overshadow—with clouds—(with acc. of thing and عَلَى of pers.).

ظَلَمَ aor. i. To wrong, injure; to be unjust, oppressive, or tyrannical towards any one (with acc. also with بِ, or with acc. of pers. and بِ); to be guilty of injustice, to act wickedly; to be wanting in, or fail, as وَلَمْ تَظْلِمْ مِنْهُ شَيْئًا 18 v. 31, "Nor did they fail in any of it." ظُلْمٌ Injustice, tyranny, obscurity. ظُلْمَةٌ Plur. ظُلُمَاتٌ Darkness. ظَلُومٌ Unjust. ظَلَّامٌ Very unjust. ظَالِمٌ part. act. One who treats unjustly (with لِ). أَظْلَمُ (2nd declension) comp. form, More unjust. مَظْلُومٌ part. pass. Unjustly treated.—أَظْلَمَ IV. To injure; to be dark (with عَلَى). مُظْلِمٌ part. act. One who is in the dark.

ظَمِئَ aor. a. To thirst. ظَمَأٌ n.a. Thirst. ظَمْآنُ (2nd declension) D. S. Gr. T. 1, p. 403, Very thirsty.

ظَنَّ aor. o. To think, be of opinion, imagine (with acc. or بِ, or with أَنَّ); for the construction ظَنُّوا مَا لَهُمْ مِنْ مَحِيصٍ 41 v. 48, "They shall perceive that there is no way of escape for them," see D. S. Gr. T. 2, p. 297. ظَنٌّ Plur. ظُنُونٌ Opinion. ظَانٌّ part. act. One who forms an opinion.

ظَهَرَ aor. a. and i. To appear, be manifest (with فِى); to help, mount, ascend (with acc. or عَلَى); to get the better of, know, distinguish (with عَلَى). ظَهْرٌ Plur. ظُهُورٌ The back. ظَاهِرٌ part. act. One who is manifest, that which is apparent, outward (speech), as at 13 v. 33; clear, conspicuous, victorious; قُرًى ظَاهِرَةً 34 v. 17, "Conspicuous cities," or "cities connected one with another by a track called ظَهْرٌ; ظَاهِرَةً Outwardly. ظَهِيرٌ A helper. ظَهِيرَةٌ Mid-day heat. ظِهْرِيًّا Thrown behind the back, with neglect.—ظَاهَرَ III. To assist (with acc. and عَلَى); to divorce a wife, with the words أَنْتِ عَلَيَّ كَظَهْرِ أُمِّي, see 58 v. 2.—أَظْهَرَ IV. To make one acquainted with (with acc. of pers. and عَلَى of thing); to cause to appear (with فِى), as at 40 v. 27; to enter on the period of noon, as at 30 v. 17; to render superior (with acc. and عَلَى).—تَظَاهَرَ VI. To assist one another against (with عَلَى and بِ).

ع

عَبَأَ aor. a. *To mix scents;* to be solicitous about (with بِ).

عَبِثَ aor. a. To amuse one's-self. عَبَثٌ n.a. Sport, jest.

عَبَدَ aor. o. To adore, worship. عَبْدٌ Plur. عَبِيدٌ A servant; and Plur. عِبَادٌ Servants, especially of God. عَابِدٌ part. act. A worshipper. عِبَادَةٌ Service, worship.—عَبَّدَ II. To enslave.

عَبَرَ aor. o. *To pass over;* to interpret (with لِ). عِبْرَةٌ An instructive warning. عَابِرِى for عَابِرِينَ oblique plur. of عَابِرٌ part. act. One who passes over.—إِعْتَبَرَ VIII. To take warning.

عَبَسَ aor. i. *To be austere,* to frown. عَبُوسٌ Austere, dismal.

عَبْقَرَ *To glitter like the mirage.* عَبْقَرِيٌّ sing. and plur. A kind of rich carpet.

عَتَبَ aor. o. and i. *To be angry.*—مُعْتَبٌ part. pass. IV. f. Received into favour.—إِسْتَعْتَبَ X. To beg for favour, receive into favour, invite any one to make himself acceptable.

عَتَدَ *To be prepared.* عَتِيدٌ Ready.—أَعْتَدَ IV. To prepare (with acc. of pers. and لِ).

عَتَقَ aor. o. *To be old.* عَتِيقٌ Ancient.

عَتَلَ aor. i. and o. To drag violently (with acc. and إِلَى). عُتُلٌّ Violent, cruel.

عَتَا aor. o. To be proud, insolent, to offer an insolent opposition, to exceed all bounds—in impiety—(with عَنْ). عُتُوٌّ n.a. Insolence, pride. عَاتٍ for عَاتِىٌ, Fem. عَاتِيَةٌ part. act. Exceeding, violent. عِتِيٌّ A decrepit old man, an obstinate rebel.

عَثَرَ aor. o. *To stumble;* to perceive (with عَلَى).—أَعْثَرَ IV. To make one acquainted with a thing, or cause one to understand (with عَلَى of pers.).

عَثَا aor. a. i. and o. To do evil (with فِى).

عَجِبَ aor. a. To wonder (with مِنْ, or with أَنْ of following verb). عَجِيبٌ, عُجَابٌ, عَجَبٌ, and Wonderful.—أَعْجَبَ IV. To delight, please.

عَجَزَ aor. i. *To be weak.* عَجُوزٌ An old woman. أَعْجَازٌ Roots of palm-trees.—مُعَاجِزٌ part. act. III. f. One who baffles, or makes of none effect.—أَعْجَزَ IV. To weaken, to be unable, to frustrate, find one to be weak; إِنَّهُمْ لَا يُعْجِزُونَ 8 v. 61, "Verily they shall not find (God) to be weak," or "frustrate (his decree);" for the ellipse of the complement see D. S. Gr. T. 2, pp. 121 and 454; it is also found with the acc. and فِى. مُعْجِزِى for مُعْجِزِينَ oblique plur. of مُعْجِزٌ part. act. One who weakens or frustrates.

عَجَفَ aor. i. and o. *To emaciate.* عِجَافٌ plur. of عَجْفَآءُ fem. of أَعْجَفُ (2nd declension) Lean; at 12 v. 43 the word agrees with بَقَرَاتٌ understood.

عَجِلَ aor. a. To hasten, accelerate (with acc., or with إِلَى); to be hasty or act hastily (with عَلَى); to hurry over (with بِ), as لِتَعْجَلَ بِهِ 75 v. 16, "That thou mayest hurry over it," viz. the receiving of the Korân from the Angel Gabriel. عَجَلٌ Precipitation. عِجْلٌ A calf. عَاجِلٌ part. act. That which hastens away, transitory. عَجُولٌ Hasty.—عَجَّلَ II. To cause to hasten, give beforehand (with acc. and لِ).—أَعْجَلَ IV. To cause to hasten (with acc. of pers. and عَنْ).—تَعَجَّلَ V. To be in a hurry.—إِسْتَعْجَلَ X. To seek or desire to hasten (with لِ of pers. and بِ of thing), as وَلَا تَسْتَعْجِلْ لَهُمْ 46 v. 34, "Neither desire to hasten (their punishment) for them;" the first complement بِالْعَذَابِ being understood; D. S. Gr. T. 2, p. 454; to urge one to make haste in doing anything (with acc. of pers. and بِ of thing). إِسْتِعْجَالٌ n.a. The desire of hastening; إِسْتِعْجَالَهُمْ 10 v. 12, "According to their desire of hastening;" D. S. Gr. T. 1, p. 503.

عَجَمَ aor. o. *To try by biting.* أَعْجَمُ (2nd declension) A barbarian, a foreigner, one who speaks Arabic imperfectly. أَعْجَمِيٌّ Barbarous, foreign.

عَدَّ aor. o. To number, reckon, reckon up (with acc. and لِ of pers.). عَدٌّ n.a. A number, computation, determined number. عَدَدٌ A number. عِدَّةٌ A number, prescribed term. عُدَّةٌ A provision. عَادٌّ part. act. One who keeps an account. مَعْدُودٌ part. pass. Determined, computed.—عَدَّدَ II. To prepare, or lay up anything against the future.—أَعَدَّ IV. To prepare, arrange (with acc. and لِ); أَعِدُّوا 8 v. 62, "Prepare ye!" for أَعْدِدُوا imperat. see D. S. Gr. T. 1, p. 230.—إِعْتَدَّ VIII. To reckon or fulfil a term.

عَدَسَ aor. i. *To minister.* عَدَسٌ generic noun, Lentils.

عَدَلَ aor. i. To deal justly (with بِ or بَيْنَ); to establish justice (with بَيْنَ), as at 42 v. 14; to swerve from justice, as at 4 v. 134; to hold as equal (with acc. and بِ), as at 6 v. 1, where the first complement "other Deities" is understood; to pay as an equivalent, as at 6 v. 69; to dispose aright, as at 82 v. 7. عَدْلٌ n.a. Justice, recompense, ransom, equivalent, compensation; عَدْلُ ذَلِكَ 5 v. 96, "Instead thereof."

عَدَنَ aor. i. and o. *To abide constantly.* عَدْنٌ n.a. A perpetual abode, Eden, Paradise.

عَدَا aor. o. *To pass by;* to transgress (with فِي); to turn aside (with acc. and عَنْ). عَدْوٌ n.a. Malice, wickedness. عَادٍ for عَادِوٌ part. act. A transgressor. عَادِيَاتٌ Swift mares. عَدَاوَةٌ Enmity. عُدْوَةٌ The side of a valley. عُدْوَانٌ Injustice, hostility. عَدُوٌّ Plur. أَعْدَآءٌ An enemy; The sing. عَدُوٌّ is sometimes put for the plur., thus at 18 v. 48 وَهُمْ لَكُمْ عَدُوٌّ "And they are your enemies."—عَادَى III. To be at enmity with.—تَعَدَّى V. To transgress.—إِعْتَدَى VIII. To be wicked, to transgress (with acc. or فِي or with عَلَى of pers.). مُعْتَدٍ part. act. Wicked, a transgressor.

عَذَبَ aor. i. *To hinder.* عَذْبٌ n.a. Fresh, sweet. عَذَابٌ Punishment, torment.—عَذَّبَ II. To punish (with acc. of pers. and بِ of instrument, as also of crime, or with فِي); it is sometimes found with the double acc. thus أُعَذِّبُهُ عَذَابًا لَا أُعَذِّبُهُ أَحَدًا 5 v. 115, "I will punish him with a punishment, with which I will punish no one (else);" to afflict, as at 20 v. 49. مُعَذِّبٌ part. act. One who punishes. مُعَذَّبٌ part. pass. Doomed to punishment.

عَذَرَ aor. i. *To excuse.* عُذْرٌ n.a. An excuse. مَعْذِرَةٌ An excuse. مَعَاذِيرُ (2nd declension) plur. of مِعْذَارٌ Excuses.—مُعَذِّرٌ part. act. II. f. Uttering excuses.—إِعْتَذَرَ VIII. To excuse one's-self (with إِلَى of pers.).

عَرَّ aor. i. *To be scabby.* مَعَرَّةٌ A crime.—مُعْتَرٌّ part. act. VIII. f. One who does not beg, though poor.

عَرَبَ aor. i. *To eat;* and عَرُبَ *To be pure Arabic and free from faults (a speech).* عُرُبٌ Beloved wives, plur. of عَرُوبٌ. عَرَبِيٌّ Arabic, an Arabian. أَعْرَابٌ plur. no sing. The Arabs of the desert.

عَرَجَ aor. o. To mount, ascend (with إِلَى or فِي). أَعْرَجُ (2nd declension) Lame from birth. مَعَارِجُ (2nd declension) plur. of مَعْرَجٌ A ladder, place of ascending, stairs.

عَرْجَنَ *To stamp cloth with the figure of date-stalks.* عُرْجُونٌ A dry date-stalk.

عَرَشَ aor. i. and o. To construct, build houses. عَرْشٌ n.a. A throne; Plur. عُرُوشٌ Foundations, props, supports. مَعْرُوشٌ part. pass. Supported on trellis-work.

عَرَضَ aor. i. *To happen, come against;* to propose, set before (with acc. and لِ or عَلَى). عَرْضٌ n.a. Breadth, extent; عَرْضًا In an extended manner. عَرَضٌ Temporal goods or advantage, this world's gear. عُرْضَةٌ 2 v. 224, Object, butt, or impediment, according to different renderings. عَرِيضٌ Much, many. عَارِضٌ A cloud traversing the sky.—عَرَّضَ II. To make an offer (with بِ).—أَعْرَضَ IV. To turn aside, decline to do a thing, leave it undone (with عَنْ). إِعْرَاضٌ n.a. A turning away, aversion. مُعْرِضٌ part. act. One who turns away from, averse.

عَرَفَ aor. i. To know, discern (with acc. and بِ or فِي); The difference between عَرَفَ and عَلِمَ is that the former refers to distinct and specific knowledge, while the latter is more general; hence the opposite to عَرَفَ is أَنْكَرَ To deny, and to عَلِمَ, جَهِلَ To be ignorant. عُرْفٌ *Known,* just, a benefit; عُرْفًا 77 v. 1, "In a continual series," or according to another reading, "Conferring benefits;" Plur. with the article اَلْأَعْرَافُ The walls which divide Paradise from Hell. عَرَفَاتٌ Name of a mountain near Mecca, said to be so named because of the recognition which there took place between Adam and Eve, after a separation of 200 years. مَعْرُوفٌ part. pass. Known, recognized, honourable, good, befitting, a kindness; the opposite to مُنْكَرٌ.—عَرَّفَ II. To acquaint, make known (with acc. of thing and لِ of pers.).—تَعَارَفَ VI. To know one another (with بَيْنَ).—إِعْتَرَفَ VIII. To confess, acknowledge (with بِ).

عَرَمَ aor. o. *To strip meat from off a bone.* عَرِمٌ plur. no sing. *Mounds or dams for banking in a body of water;* اَلْعَرِمُ Name of an inundation which destroyed the city of Sabâ'.

عَرَا aor. o. *To come upon.* عُرْوَةٌ A handle.—إِعْتَرَى VIII. To come down upon, afflict (with acc. of pers. and بِ).

عَرَى aor. i. *To come upon;* and عَرِيَ aor. a. To be naked. عَرَآءٌ A bare place.

عَزَّ aor. i. *To be rare, precious;* to get the better of (with acc. of pers. and فِى). عِزٌّ n.a. Power, glory. عِزَّةٌ Power, honour, pride. عَزِيزٌ Plur. أَعِزَّةٌ Mighty, excellent, troublesome; grievous, as at 9 v. 129 (with عَلَى). أَعَزُّ (2nd declension) More excellent, mightier, worthier, most powerful; Fem. عُزَّى (2nd declension); اَلْعُزَّى El 'Uzza, name of an idol of the Pagan Arabs.—عَزَّزَ II. To give additional power, to corroborate (with بِ).—أَعَزَّ IV. To render powerful.

عَزَبَ aor. o. and i. To be away from, be hidden (with عَنْ).

عَزَرَ aor. i. *To reprehend.* عُزَيْرٌ Ezra.—عَزَّرَ II. To assist, honour.

عَزَلَ aor. i. To remove from a place or office, set aside. مَعْزِلٌ A place separate from the rest. مَعْزُولٌ part. pass. Removed.—إِعْتَزَلَ VIII. To separate one's-self from, remove one's-self from (with acc. of pers.).

عَزَمَ aor. i. To determine, resolve, purpose; to be determined on or decreed, as at 47 v. 23. عَزْمٌ n.a. Fixed determination; عَزْمُ ٱلْأُمُورِ "God's fixed resolve concerning human affairs."

عَزَا aor. o. *To bring one back.* عِزِينَ oblique plur. of عِزَةٌ A crowd, company, D. S. Gr. T. 1, p. 358.

عَسَرَ aor. i. and o. *To demand with harshness the repayment of a loan, to be difficult.* عُسْرٌ n.a. Difficulty. عَسِرٌ Difficult, unlucky, grievous. عُسْرَةٌ Difficulty, distress; ذُو عُسْرَةٍ 2 v. 280, "One who finds a difficulty in paying a debt." عَسِيرٌ Difficult, dire, grievous. عُسْرَى (2nd declension) Wretchedness.—تَعَاسَرَ VI. *To be difficult;* to be in a difficulty; إِنْ تَعَاسَرْتُمْ 65 v. 6, "If ye find yourselves in a difficulty;" the particle إِنْ gives the preterite a future signification; D. S. Gr. T. 1, p. 181.

عَسْعَسَ To come on by night (as a wolf); quadriliteral verb derived from عَسَّ *To go round by night to keep watch.*

عسق preceded by حم Initial letters at the commencement of the 42nd chapter, see آلم.

عَسَلَ aor. i. and o. *To mix food with honey.* عَسَلٌ comm. gend. Honey.

عَسَى It may be, perhaps (with أَنْ), a verb of proximity used only in the preterite; D. S. Gr. T. 2, p. 213; هَلْ عَسَيْتُمْ 2 v. 247, "Will it come to pass that ye?" "Would it have happened that ye?" 47 v. 24.

عَشَرَ aor. o. *To take away a tenth part;* aor. i. *To make ten by adding one to nine.* عَشْرٌ n.a. and عَشْرٌ fem.; عَشَرَةٌ and عَشْرَةٌ masc., Ten, a decade. *Note.* From three to ten inclusive the termination ة, which is generally the sign of the feminine, marks the masculine; These numerals usually agree in gender with the noun of which they express the number, but instances occur where this does not appear to be the case; thus at 6 v. 161 مَنْ جَآءَ بِٱلْحَسَنَةِ فَلَهُ عَشْرُ أَمْثَالِهَا "Whoever shall bring a good action shall have ten (good actions) equivalents of that which he has wrought;" Here, although the noun أَمْثَالٌ is masc. عَشْرٌ is fem. because it really refers to حَسَنَاتٌ understood; D. S. Gr. T. 2, p. 329; so also at 2 v. 234, where عَشْرًا agrees in gender with لَيَالِى understood. عِشْرُونَ Twenty. عِشَارٌ plur. of عُشَرَآءُ (2nd declension) Camels ten months gone with young. عَشِيرٌ A companion. عَشِيرَةٌ Kindred on the father's side. مَعْشَرٌ A company. مِعْشَارٌ The tenth part.—عَاشَرَ III. To live with, associate with (with acc. of pers. and بِ).

عَشَا aor. o. *To be purblind;* to withdraw from (with عَنْ). عِشَآءٌ Commencement of darkness, evening. عَشِيٌّ Evening. عَشِيَّةٌ An evening.

عَصَبَ aor. i. *To surround.* عُصْبَةٌ A body of men from ten to forty. عَصِيبٌ Grievous, heavy.

عَصَرَ aor. i. To press (grapes). عَصْرٌ n.a. Age, time, afternoon.—إِعْصَارٌ n.a. IV. f. A whirlwind. مُعْصِرَاتٌ part. act. fem. plur. (Clouds) emitting or pressing out rain.

عَصَفَ aor. i. *To blow violently.* عَصْفٌ n.a. Leaves and stalks of corn, of which the grain has been eaten by cattle; عَصْفًا In violent gusts. عَاصِفٌ part. act. Stormy, a tempestuous wind. عَاصِفَةٌ A violent wind.

عَصَمَ aor. i. *To make a profit;* to preserve, save harmless (with acc. and مِنْ). عِصَمٌ plur. of عِصْمَةٌ Defence, guardianship. عَاصِمٌ part. act. Defender.—إِعْتَصَمَ VIII. To take hold on, cleave firmly to (with بِ).—إِسْتَعْصَمَ X. To preserve one's-self from sin.

عَصَا aor. o. *To strike one with a stick.* عَصًا fem. for عَصَوٌ, عَصَوٌ and عَصَوًا A staff, rod. *Note.* و at the end of a word, when preceded immediately by fatḥa, does not take a vowel, but becomes quiescent, and is changed into ا in words of three letters, and into ي in words of four; where there is a tanween it is given to the preceding fatḥa, D. S. Gr. T. 1, p. 105; عِصِيٌّ plur. of عَصًا.

عَصَى aor. i. To rebel, disobey (with acc. and لِ or acc. and فِي). عَصِيٌّ Rebellious. عِصْيَانٌ Rebellion. مَعْصِيَةٌ Disobedience.

عَضَّ aor. a. To bite (with عَلَى 25 v. 29, or acc. and عَلَى 3 v. 115).

عَضَدَ aor. o. To strike any one on the arm. عَضُدٌ An arm, a helper.

عَضَلَ aor. a. o. and i. To hinder a woman from marrying (with أَنْ).

عَضَا aor. o. *To divide limb from limb.* عِضِينَ oblique plur. of عِضَةٌ A separate part. *Note.* Nouns from a defective root occasionally lose their last radical letter, which is then replaced by ة; thus عِضَوٌ becomes عِضَةٌ; on passing into the plur. they regain the masc. form, thus عِضُونَ is the plural of عِضَةٌ; D. S. Gr. T. 1, pp. 317 and 359.

عَطَفَ aor. i. *To incline towards, be well disposed towards.* عِطْفٌ A side.

عَطِلَ *To be bare of ornaments (a woman).*—عَطَّلَ II. *To deprive of ornament,* leave without care. مُعَطَّلٌ part. pass. Neglected.

عَطَا aor. o. *To take anything in the hand.* عَطَآءٌ A gift.—أَعْطَى IV. To give (with double acc.); to be docile, as at 92 v. 5.—تَعَاطَى VI. To undertake, or take (a sword) in the hand, 54 v. 29.

عَظَمَ *To give a dog a bone;* and عَظُمَ *To be great.* عَظْمٌ n.a. A bone; Plur. عِظَامٌ. عَظِيمٌ Great, heavy. أَعْظَمُ (2nd declension) Greater, superior, highest in rank.—عَظَّمَ II. To make great, honour.—أَعْظَمَ IV. To increase (with acc. and لِ of pers.).

عَفَّ aor. i. *To abstain from that which is unlawful or improper.*—تَعَفُّفٌ n.a. V. f. Modesty.—إِسْتَعَفَّ X. same as عَفَّ.

عَفَرَ aor. i. *To roll (one) in the dust.* عِفْرِيتٌ A dæmon, an 'Efreet.

عَفَا aor. o. *To obliterate all traces (as the wind);* to pardon (with عَنْ or لِ); to abound, as at 7 v. 93; to pass over, pass by (with عَنْ), as at 5 v. 18; to remit, as at 2 v. 238. *Note.* يَعْفُوا is found in some copies for يَعْفُو 3rd pers.

sing. aor.; this ا is called أَلِفُ ٱلْوِقَايَةِ or alif of precaution, D. S. Gr. T. 1, p. 109. عَفْوٌ n.a. Overplus, superfluity, 2 v. 217; pardon. عَافِينَ oblique plur. of عَافٍ for عَافِوٌ part. act. Forgiving. عَفُوٌّ Very forgiving.

عَقَبَ *To strike on the heel;* aor. o. *To succeed.* عُقْبٌ Success; خَيْرٌ عُقْبًا 18 v. 42, *Lit.* "The best as to success." عَقِبٌ comm. gend. *A heel,* posterity; Plur. أَعْقَابٌ Heels; عَقِبَيْهِ His two heels. عِقَابٌ Punishment; عِقَابِ for عِقَابِي 13 v. 32, etc. "My punishment." عَقَبَةٌ A place hard of ascent. عُقْبَى (2nd declension) End, success, reward, as عُقْبَى ٱلدَّارِ The reward of Paradise. عَاقِبَةٌ End, issue, (fortunate) result; عَاقِبَةُ ٱلدَّارِ same as عُقْبَى ٱلدَّارِ.—عَقَّبَ II. To retrace one's steps. مُعَقِّبٌ part. act. One who puts off or reverses; مُعَقِّبَاتٌ Angels (of the night and day) who succeed each other.—عَاقَبَ III. To punish (with بِ); to succeed in turn, as at 60 v. 11; Pass. عُوقِبَ To be punished or injured, as at 16 v. 127.—أَعْقَبَ IV. To cause to succeed or follow (with acc. and فِي).

عَقَدَ *To tie in a knot,* strike a bargain, make a compact, enter into an obligation. عَقْدٌ Plur. عُقُودٌ A compact. عُقْدَةٌ Plur. عُقَدٌ A knot, tie, obligation; ٱلنَّفَّاثَاتُ فِي ٱلْعُقَدِ 113 v. 4, "The women who blow on knots," witches.

عَقَرَ aor. i. To wound, hamstring. عَاقِرٌ Barren (woman).

عَقَلَ aor. i. *To keep back* (*a camel, by tying up the foreleg*); aor. i. and o. To understand, to be ingenious, prudent, sagacious; لَهُمْ قُلُوبٌ يَعْقِلُونَ بِهَا 22 v. 45, "They have hearts to understand with."

عَقَمَ aor. o. *To be barren* (*a woman*). عَقِيمٌ Barren, childless (man or woman); grievous (day), as at 22 v. 54; destroying, blasting (wind), as at 51 v. 41.

عَكَفَ aor. i. and o. To keep back, detain (with عَنْ); to give one's-self up to (with عَلَى). عَاكِفٌ part. act. One who remains constantly in any place, an inhabitant, as at 22 v. 25; assiduously devoting one's-self to, as at 20 v. 97. مَعْكُوفٌ part. pass. Detained.

عَلَقَ aor. o. *To cut off the top leaves of a tree, adhere to, hang from.* عَلَقٌ Clotted blood. عَلَقَةٌ A lump of clotted blood.—مُعَلَّقَةٌ part. pass. II. f. One in suspense.

عَلَمَ aor. i. and o. *To mark, sign;* and عَلِمَ aor. a. To know (with acc. and فِي, also with أَنْ); to distinguish (with acc. and مِنْ); to be learned or knowing; For the difference between عَلِمَ and عَرَفَ see عَرَفَ. عِلْمٌ n.a. Science, knowledge, learning, art; عِلْمٌ لِلسَّاعَةِ 43 v. 61, "A sign or means of knowing the last hour." عَلَمٌ A sign; Plur. أَعْلَامٌ Long mountains. عَالِمٌ part. act. One who knows, or is wise. عَلَامَةٌ A sign, mark. عَالَمِينَ oblique plur. of عَالَمٌ A world; The worlds spoken of in the Korân are taken to mean the three species of rational creatures, viz. men, genii, and angels. عَلِيمٌ Learned, knowing, wise; Plur. عُلَمَآءُ (2nd declension). عَلَّامٌ Very learned, wise or knowing. أَعْلَمُ (2nd declension) comp. form, More or most wise or knowing (with بِ). مَعْلُومٌ part. pass. Known, predetermined.—عَلَّمَ II. To teach (with بِ, or with double acc., or with acc. and مِنْ or بِ). مُعَلَّمٌ part. pass. Taught, instructed.—أَعْلَمَ IV. To make known.—تَعَلَّمَ V. To learn (with acc. or with مِنْ).

عَلَنَ aor. i. and o. *To be manifest.* عَلَانِيَةً In public, openly.—أَعْلَنَ IV. To make manifest, publish (with أَنَّ or with acc. and لِ).

عَلَا aor. a. and o. To be high, lofty, exalted, elated, proud (with فِي or عَلَى); to be upon, to be over, as مَا عَلَوْا 17 v. 7, "That over which they had gained the upper hand;" وَلَتَعْلُنَّ عُلُوًّا كَبِيرًا 17 v. 4, "And ye will verily be elated with great insolence;" تَعْلُنَّ is here put for تَعْلُونَ, the radical و being suppressed because of the quiescent ن contained in the teshdeed; it being contrary to the rule to have two quiescent letters together after the same vowel; D. S. Gr. T. 1, pp. 94 and 252. عُلُوٌّ n.a. Exaltation, insolence, pride; عُلُوًّا كَبِيرًا 17 v. 45; عُلُوًّا is said by Beiḍâwee to stand in this place for تَعَالِيًا; the literal meaning will therefore be "May he be exalted far above that which they utter by a great exaltation." عَالِينَ oblique plur. of عَالٍ for عَالِوٌ part. act. That which is high or haughty; Fem. عَالِيَةٌ Lofty, see D. S. Gr. T. 1, p. 330; عَالِيَهَا سَافِلَهَا 11 v. 84, "Upside down;" عَالِيَهُمْ ثِيَابُ سُنْدُسٍ 76 v. 21, "Having garments of silk as a covering;" The accus. of the part. or verbal adjective is here put for the verb, and the words have the same meaning as if they had been يَعْلُوهُمْ ثِيَابُ etc. "There were upon them garments," etc.; for the grammatical construction see D. S. Gr. T. 2, pp. 270 and 271; there are various readings of this passage.—تَعَالَى VI. *properly*, "He was exalted" (with عَلَى); also "He came" (with إِلَى or with aor. conditional); In an optative sense this word is frequently put after the name of God, and it then signifies "Be He exalted," or with عَنْ "Be He raised far above," as تَعَالَى عَمَّا يُشْرِكُونَ 16 v. 3, "Be He exalted far above that which they associate (with him)," see تَبَارَكَ. تَعَالَيْنَ "Come then!" fem. plur. imperat. اَلْمُتَعَالِ 13 v. 10 for اَلْمُتَعَالِي on account of the pause, D. S. Gr. T. 2, p. 496, part. act. The exalted, the High.—إِسْتَعْلَى X. *To mount*, get the upper hand.

عَلِيَ aor. i. *To mount up.* عَلَى preposition, Above, upon, over, in addition to, before, towards, against, opposite, alongside, to, according to, of, for, on account of, in, from, by; عَلَيْهِ He owes, it behoves him; عَلَى أَنْ In order that, on condition that, seeing that, although; عَلَى مَكَانَتِكُمْ 6 v. 135, "According to your power;" عَلَى أَدْبَارِهَا 4 v. 50, "As—or like—the hinder parts thereof;" عَلَى حَرْفٍ 22 v. 11, "After a way," or "upon the verge—as it were—(of religion);" The various meanings of عَلَى seem all to be more or less connected with the primary idea of something upon or over another. أَعْلَى (2nd declension) comp. form, Higher, highest, more or most exalted; Fem. عُلْيَا (2nd declension) for عُلْيَى in accordance with the rule that final ي when preceded by يَ is changed into short ا; D. S. Gr. T. 1, p. 111; Plur. masc. أَعْلَوْنَ for أَعْلَيُونَ according to the rule of permutation, D. S. Gr. T. 1, p. 354; Fem. Plur. عُلًى for عُلَيٌ and with the article اَلْعُلَى. عَلِيٌّ High, sublime, eminent; name of Mohammad's son-in-law. عِلِّيُّونَ *properly*, High places, a name of the upper part of the Heavens, where the register of men's good actions is preserved, or according to some, the register itself; Learned Moslims differ greatly abont this word and its meaning; it is found in Hebrew.

عَمَّ aor. o. *To be common.* عَمٌّ Plur. أَعْمَامٌ An nncle on the father's side. عَمَّةٌ An aunt on the father's side.

عَمَدَ aor. i. *To afflict.* عُمُدٌ plur. of عِمَادٌ comm. gend. A colnmn, a lofty structnre, a tent pole.—تَعَمَّدَ V. To propose. مُتَعَمِّدًا On purpose.

عَمَرَ aor. o. To cnltivate, make habitable, perform the sacred visitation—to Mecca—(with acc.). عَمْرٌ Life; لَعَمْرُكَ a form of oath, "Verily by thy life." *Note.* When not used in this manner the word is written and pronounced عُمْرٌ. عُمُرٌ Life, age, and especially long life, old age. عُمْرَةٌ The sacred visitation to Mecca. عِمَارَةٌ n.a. Religions cult, cnltnre. عِمْرَانُ (2nd declension); Two persons are called by this name in the Korân, viz. the father of the Virgin Mary, and the father of Moses and Aaron. مَعْمُورٌ part. pass. Visited, etc.—عَمَّرَ II. To cause to live, grant a long life to. مُعَمَّرٌ part. pass. One whose life is prolonged.—إِعْتَمَرَ VIII. To visit, pass one's time in visiting.—إِسْتَعْمَرَ X. To settle any one as an inhahitant (with acc. and فِى).

عَمُقَ aor. o. *To be deep.* عَمِيقٌ Deep, distant, far off.

عَمِلَ aor. a. *To be active (a camel)*; to do, make, act, work, operate; كُلٌّ يَعْمَلُ عَلَى شَاكِلَتِهِ 17 v. 86, see شَاكِلَةٌ, see also 6 v. 135; at 34 v. 12 hefore إِعْمَلُوا we must nnderstand the words وَقِيلَ لَهُمْ "It was said to them," viz. the honse of David; so also at the 10th verse the word أَمَرْنَاهُ "We commanded him," is to be nnderstood hefore أَنِ ٱعْمَلْ, see أَنْ. عَامِلٌ part. act. One who does, etc., an operator, worker, toiler. عَمَلٌ Plnr. أَعْمَالٌ Work, act, deed, labour, toil, action.

عَمَهَ aor. a. To wander distractedly to and fro (with فِى); to he struck with amazement.

عَمَى aor. i. *To flow*; and عَمِيَ aor. a. To be blind, dark, obscure; فَعَمِيَتْ عَلَيْهِمُ ٱلْأَنْبَآءُ 28 v. 66, "And the acconnt shall he (*was*) ohscure unto them." عَمًى n.a. Blindness (of heart). عَمٍ Plur. عَمُونَ Acc. عَمِينَ Blind, D. S. Gr. T. 1, p. 354. أَعْمَى (2nd declension); Plur. عُمْىٌ and عُمْيَانٌ Blind, dark.—عَمَّى II. To hlind, hide, conceal from (with عَلَى of pers.), as فَعُمِّيَتْ عَلَيْكُمْ 11 v. 30, "And it is hidden from yon."—أَعْمَى IV. To make hlind.

عَنْ Off, from, from off, away from, out of, in spite of, concerning; The primary signification of عَنْ conveys the idea of removal from off or away from a thing, and from this the other significations may be derived, see D. S. Gr. T. 1, p. 483; لَا تَجْزِى نَفْسٌ عَنْ نَفْسٍ شَيْئًا 2 v. 45, "One soul shall not at all make satisfaction for another," *i.e.* so that the punishment shonld be transferred from one to another; ٱللّٰهُ غَنِىٌّ عَنِ ٱلْعَالَمِينَ 3 v. 92, *Lit.* "God is rich away from his creatnres," *i.e.* rich enough to dispense with them.

عِنَبٌ generic noun, Plnr. أَعْنَابٌ A grape, grapes, a vine; no verbal root.

عَنِتَ aor. a. *To be corrupt*, fall into misfortnne, perish, to commit a crime; وَدُّوا مَا عَنِتُّمْ 3 v. 114, "They desire your ruin;" مَا with the verh following is here considered as equivalent to the nonn of action عَنَتُكُمْ, and is hence called مَا مَصْدَرِيَّةٌ D. S. Gr. T. 1, p. 541; لَعَنِتُّمْ 49 v. 7, "Ye wonld certainly be guilty of a crime."

عَنَتٌ n.a. Sin.—أَعْنَتَ IV. To destroy; لَأَعْنَتَكُمْ 2 v. 219, "He will surely distress or destroy you;" The preterite being put for the aorist to give greater energy to the expression, D. S. Gr. T. 1, p. 158.

عَنَدَ aor. o. *To go out of the right way.* عِنْدَ At, with, near, about, in; This particle is properly a noun in the accusative case, meaning a side, part or quarter; after the preposition مِنْ it is written عِنْدِ, as مِنْ عِنْدِ ٱللّٰهِ "From God;" also when followed by ي, as عِنْدِى (It is) in my power; (there is) with me, or I have, Lat. *mihi est;* فَلَا كَيْلَ لَكُمْ عِنْدِى 12 v. 60, "There will be no measuring (of corn) for you on my part;" D. S. Gr. T. 1, p. 496. عَنِيدٌ Contumacious, stubborn, refractory.

عَنَقَ *To hide the head and neck in its form (a hare).* عُنُقٌ comm. gend. Plur. أَعْنَاقٌ A neck.

عَنْكَبُوتٌ comm. gend. A spider; verbal root doubtful.

عَنَا aor. o. *To distress,* to be humble (with لِ); وَعَنَتِ ٱلْوُجُوهُ 20 v. 110, "And their faces shall be humbled."

عَهِدَ aor. a. To enjoin, command, stipulate, covenant (with إِلَى of pers. and أَنْ, or with عِنْدَ of pers.). عَهْدٌ A covenant, promise; also time, as at 20 v. 89.—عَاهَدَ III. To make a covenant with (with acc. of pers. and عَلَى of matter).

عَهَنَ aor. o. *To wither.* عِهْنٌ Particoloured wool.

عَاجَ aor. o. *To stand still, recede;* and عَوِجَ *To be bent, distorted.* عِوَجٌ Crookedness, curvature, distortion, obliquity; لَا عِوَجَ لَهُ 20 v. 107, "There is no obliquity in him," or "no receding." *Note.* لَا when used to deny the existence of a thing generally governs the accus. without tanween; D. S. Gr. T. 2, p. 63.

عَادَ aor. o. To return, turn (with لِ or فِى), frequently used with an ellipse of the complement; ثُمَّ يَعُودُونَ لِمَا قَالُوا 58 v. 4, "Then they would revert to or repair what they have said;" this passage admits of a variety of explanations. عَادٌ 'Àd, an ancient and powerful tribe of Arabs of prodigious stature, descended from 'Àd, the great-grandson of Shem. عَآئِدٌ part. act. One who returns. مَعَادٌ A place whither one returns, a name of Mecca.—أَعَادَ IV. To cause to return, restore (with acc. of pers. and فِى, or with double acc.).

عَاذَ aor. o. *To be next the bone (flesh);* to take or seek refuge, especially with God (with بِ of pers. and مِنْ); also used with أَنْ meaning lest, as at 2 v. 63, and again at 44 v. 19. مَعَاذٌ A refuge; مَعَاذَ ٱللّٰهِ 12 v. 23, "God forbid!" *Lit.* "(I seek) refuge with God," for أَعُوذُ بِٱللّٰهِ مَعَاذًا.—أَعَاذَ IV. To recommend to the protection—of God—(with acc. of pers. and بِ).—إِسْتَعَاذَ X. To take refuge (with بِ of pers. and مِنْ); فَٱسْتَعِذْ imperat. 7 v. 199, "Then fly for protection."

عَارَ aor. a. and o. *To be or to make one-eyed.* عَوْرَةٌ Pudendum, nakedness, a place lying naked and exposed to the enemy, as at 33 v. 13; ثَلٰثُ عَوْرَاتٍ لَكُمْ 24 v. 57, *Lit.* "There are three (times) of nakedness for you."

عَاقَ aor. o. *To keep back.*—ٱلْمُعَوِّقِينَ oblique plur. part. act. II. f. Those who hinder.

عَالَ aor. o. To swerve, turn aside (from the right way).

عَامَ aor. o. *To swim.* عَامٌ A year; عَامَيْنِ 31 v. 13 oblique dual, Two years.

عَانَ aor. o. *To be middle-aged (a woman).* عَوَانٌ

Middle-aged.—أَعَانَ IV. To assist (with acc. and عَلَى or بِ); فَأَعِينُونِي 18 v. 94, "Then assist me."—تَعَاوَنَ VI. To help one another (with عَلَى).—إِسْتَعَانَ X. To ask assistance (with acc. of pers. or with بِ). مُسْتَعَانٌ part. pass. One whose aid is to be implored.

عَيَّ aor. i. *To hesitate;* and عَيِيَ aor. a. To be hindered so as to be unable to complete a thing (with بِ); لَمْ يَعْىَ 46 v. 32 aor. cond. "He was not unable to complete;" أَفَعَيِينَا 50 v. 14, "Were we then unable to finish?" The verb عَيَّ being at the same time surd, concave, and defective, presents several apparent anomalies; these may, however, all be explained by the rules which affect such verbs.

عَابَ aor. i. *To be faulty;* to render faulty or unserviceable.

عَادَ aor. i. *To visit.* عِيدٌ A feast, festival.

عَارَ aor. i. *To go backwards and forwards.* عِيرٌ fem. A caravan.

عِيسَى (2nd declension) Jesus, Our Saviour.

عَاشَ aor. i. *To pass one's life, live.* عِيشَةٌ n.a. Life. مَعَاشٌ Whatever is necessary to support life. مَعِيشَةٌ Plur. مَعَايِشُ (2nd declension) Existence, manner of living, victuals, necessaries of life.

عَالَ aor. i. *To twist the body about in a conceited manner when walking, to be poor.* عَائِلٌ part. act. Poor. عَيْلَةٌ Poverty.

عَانَ aor. i. *To flow.* عَيْنٌ fem. Plur. عُيُونٌ A fountain, spring of water; Plur. أَعْيُنٌ An eye. عِينٌ for عُيْنٌ D. S. Gr. T. 1, p. 112, § 227, fem. plur. of أَعْيَنُ (2nd declension) Having large eyes. مَعِينٌ Clear-flowing, a fountain.

غ

غَوَى see غَاوِينَ.

غَبَرَ aor. o. *To delay.* غَبَرَةٌ Dust. غَابِرٌ part. act. One who stays behind, lags behind.

غَبَنَ aor. i. *To deceive.*—تَغَابُنٌ n.a. VI. f. Mutual deceit.

غَثَا aor. o. *To be covered with foam and dead leaves, etc. (a river).* غُثَآءٌ Scum and refuse, light straw, stubble.

غَدَرَ aor. i. and o. *To remain behind.*—غَادَرَ III. To leave out.

غَدِقَ aor. a. *To be full of water (a spring).* غَدَقٌ Copious, abundant.

غَدَا aor. o. To come or go early in the morning (with مِنْ or عَلَى). غَدٌ for غَدْوٌ The morrow; غَدًا To-morrow. غَدَآءٌ An early meal, dinner. غُدُوٌّ The morning, early morning. غَدَاةٌ same as غُدُوٌّ.

غَرَّ aor. o. To deceive with vain hopes (with acc. and فِي); when used with acc. and بِ it means to seduce from, as at 82 v. 6, and 57 v. 13. غَرُورٌ A deceiver, the Devil. غُرُورٌ A vain hope; غُرُورًا Deceitfully.

غَرَبَ aor. o. *To go away,* set, as the sun (with فِي). غُرَابٌ A raven. غُرُوبٌ Sunset. غَرْبِيٌّ Fem. غَرْبِيَّةٌ The West. غَرَابِيبُ (2nd declension) plur. of غِرْبِيبٌ A kind of black grapes. مَغْرِبٌ The West, setting of the sun; Plur. مَغَارِبُ (2nd declension) The western parts of the earth; Dual مَغْرِبَانِ 55 v. 17, The two points in the Heaveus, where the sun sets in summer and winter.

غَرَفَ aor. i. and o. *To draw water for drinking.* غُرْفَةٌ A draught of water taken up in the hand; the seveuth Heaveu, 25 v. 75. غُرَفٌ and غُرُفَاتٌ plurals of غُرْفَةٌ Lofty apartments.—إِغْتَرَفَ VIII. To drink out of the hand (with acc. and بِ).

غَرِقَ *To be submerged.* غَرْقٌ n.a. A dranght. غَرْقًا At a single draught; and hence, suddenly, violently. غَرَقٌ The act of drowning.—أَغْرَقَ IV. To drown (with acc. and فِى or بِ). مُغْرَقٌ part. pass. Drowned.

غَرِمَ aor. a. *To be in debt.* غَارِمٌ part. act. One in deht. غَرَامٌ A continuous torment. مَغْرَمٌ A deht that must be paid, a forced loan, 9 v. 99.—مُغْرَمٌ part. pass. IV. f. One who is involved in deht, or laid under an ohligatiou.

غَرَا aor. o. *To glue.*—أَغْرَى IV. To excite, incite against (with acc. and بِ); to cause enmity (with بَيْنَ).

غَزَلَ aor. i. *To spin.* غَزْلٌ n.a. A spiuniug, that which is spun.

غَزَا aor. o. *To will, seek, make an hostile excursion against.* غُزًّى for غُزَّى plur. of غَازٍ for غَازِيٌ A combatant.

غَسَقَ aor. i. *To be very dark (the night).* غَسَقٌ n.a. The commencement of night. غَاسِقٌ The moon, also the commencement of darkness. غَسَّاقٌ Corruption which flows from the bodies of the damned.

غَسَلَ aor. i. To wash. غِسْلِينٌ Same as غَسَّاقٌ q.v. —إِغْتَسَلَ VIII. To wash one's-self. مُغْتَسَلٌ A place for washing.

غَشِىَ aor. a. To cover over, come upon, as at 29 v. 55, يَوْمَ يَغْشَاهُمُ ٱلْعَذَابُ "On a certain day their punishmeut shall come upon them;" يَغْشَاهُمْ is here put for يَغْشِيهِمْ D. S. Gr. T. 1, p. 118; يُغْشَى عَلَيْهِ pass. *Lit.* "It is covered over upon him," a phrase meaning "he faints," 33 v. 19. غَاشِيَةٌ The day of judgment. غَوَاشٍ plur. of غَاشِيَةٌ A covering. غِشَاوَةٌ A covering, veil. مَغْشِىٌّ part. pass. One in a swoou.—غَشَّى II. To cover, to cause to cover (with donble acc.). —أَغْشَى IV. To cover, cause to cover or he covered (with donble acc.).—تَغَشَّى V. To have carnal connexion with.—إِسْتَغْشَى X. To cover one's-self with—a garment—(with acc. of garment).

غَصَّ aor. a. *To be annoyed by something sticking in the throat.* غُصَّةٌ Something which sticks in the throat, so as to cause pain.

غَصَبَ aor. i. *To carry off violently.* غَصْبًا By force.

غَضَّ aor. o. To cast down—the eyes, to lower—the voice (with مِنْ).

غَضِبَ aor. a. To he angry (with عَلَى of pers. against whom). غَضَبٌ n.a. Anger, indignation. غَضْبَانُ adj. (2nd declension) Angry. مَغْضُوبٌ part. pass. Incensed.—مُغَاضِبٌ part. act. III. f. Being angry.

غَطَشَ aor. i. *To be dark.*—أَغْطَشَ IV. To make dark.

غَطَا aor. o. *To be dark.* غِطَآءٌ A veil, covering.

غَفَرَ aor. i. *To cover*, pardon (with لِ of pers. and acc. of thing); to forgive (with أَنْ). غَافِرٌ part. act. One who forgives. غَفَّارٌ and غَفُورٌ Very forgiving. غُفْرَانٌ Pardon; غُفْرَانَكَ رَبَّنَا 2 v. 285, "(We implore) thy pardon, O our Lord;" There is here an ellipse of نَطْلُبُ or some similar word; see D. S. Gr. T. 2, p. 82. مَغْفِرَةٌ Pardon.—إِسْتَغْفَرَ X. To ask pardon for (with لِ); to ask pardon of (with acc. of pers. and لِ). إِسْتِغْفَارٌ n.a. The act of asking forgiveness. مُسْتَغْفِرٌ part. act. One who asks forgiveness.

غَفَلَ aor. o. To neglect, be negligent (with عَنْ). غَافِلٌ part. act. One who is negligent or careless. غَفْلَةٌ Negligence, carelessness.—أَغْفَلَ IV. To cause to be negligent (with acc. and عَنْ).

غَلَّ aor. o. *To insert*, defraud, bind—as the hand to the neck. غِلٌّ Hidden enmity, grudge. غُلٌّ Plur. أَغْلَالٌ A collar, yoke. مَغْلُولٌ part. pass. Bound, tied up; وَلَا تَجْعَلْ يَدَكَ مَغْلُولَةً إِلَى عُنُقِكَ 17 v. 31, "Nor let thy hand be tied up to thy neck," *i.e.* Be not niggardly.

غَلَبَ aor. i. To prevail (with عَلَى); overcome, conquer. غَلَبٌ n.a. Victory, conquest; مِنْ بَعْدِ غَلَبِهِمْ 30 v. 2, "After their conquest, or defeat;" the word is here used in a passive sense. غَالِبٌ part. act. One who overcomes, victorious, all powerful. غُلْبٌ plur. of أَغْلَبُ *Thick necked, lofty;* حَدَآئِقَ غُلْبًا 80 v. 30, "Gardens (planted) thick (with trees)." مَغْلُوبٌ part. pass. Overcome.

غَلَظَ aor. i. and غَلُظَ aor. o. *To be thick, rough,* severe (with عَلَى of pers.). غَلِيظٌ Plur. غِلَاظٌ Rough, severe, strong, firm; غَلِيظُ ٱلْقَلْبِ Hard-hearted. غِلْظَةٌ Severity.—إِسْتَغْلَظَ X. To be thick, strong.

غَلَفَ *To put a bottle into its case;* and غَلِفَ *To be uncircumcised.* أَغْلَفُ Plur. غُلْفٌ Uncircumcised.

غَلَقَ aor. i. *To shut (a door).*—غَلَّقَ II. Same as غَلَقَ.

غَلِمَ aor. a. *To be lustful.* غُلَامٌ Plur. غِلْمَانٌ A boy, a youth, frequently used in the Ḳorân for a son.

غَلَا aor. o. *To be dear, excessive;* to exceed what is just and proper (with فِى).

غَلَى aor. i. To boil. غَلْىٌ n.a. The act of boiling.

غَمَّ aor. o. *To cover.* غَمٌّ n.a. Anguish, affliction. غُمَّةٌ In the dark. غَمَامٌ plur. of غَمَامَةٌ Clouds covering the heavens.

غَمَرَ aor. a. *To abound (in water).* غَمْرَةٌ Plur. غَمَرَاتٌ A flood of water, a confused mass of anything; sometimes used metaphorically, as غَمَرَاتُ ٱلْمَوْتِ The pangs of death.

غَمَزَ aor. i. *To point, or wink at any one.*—تَغَامَزَ VI. To wink at one another.

غَمَضَ aor. o. *To be low and level (the ground).*—أَغْمَضَ IV. To connive at the payment of less than the full value (with فِى).

غَنِمَ To get as booty, acquire, gain without trouble. غَنَمٌ n.a. Sheep. مَغَانِمُ (2nd declension) plur. of مَغْنَمٌ Plunder, spoils.

غَنِىَ aor. a. To be rich; to dwell (with فِى). غَنِيٌّ Plur. أَغْنِيَآءُ (2nd declension) Rich, self-sufficient, able to do without others (with عَنْ).—أَغْنَى IV. To enrich (with acc. and مِنْ); to avail or be profitable to, satisfy, suffice for, fill the place of another for or against; used with عَنْ of pers. for whom, and مِنْ of pers. against whom, as at 12 v. 67; or with عَنْ of pers. and acc. as at 19 v. 43, see عَنْ; another construction is found at 53 v. 29, لَا يُغْنِى مِنَ ٱلْحَقِّ شَيْئًا "It profiteth nothing against the truth;" لَا يُغْنِى مِنَ ٱللَّهَبِ 77 v. 31, "It shall not avail against the flame;" It is also employed with the acc. alone, as at 80 v. 37. مُغْنٍ part. act. One who suffices or stands in the place of another.—إِسْتَغْنَى X. To become rich, desire riches, to be able to do without, to be self-sufficient.

غَاثَ aor. o. To assist, relieve (with بِ).—إِسْتَغَاثَ X. To implore assistance (with acc. and عَلَى).

غَارَ aor. o. *To come into a hollow place.* غَارٌ A cavern. غَوْرٌ n.a. (Water) running away under ground. مَغَارَةٌ A cave.—مُغِيرَاتٌ fem. plur. part. act. IV. f. Horses making an hostile excursion.

غَاصَ aor. o. To dive (with لِ at 21 v. 82). غَوَّاصٌ A diver.

غَاطَ aor. o. *To plunge into.* غَآئِطٌ *A hollow place,* a privy, easing one's-self.

غَالَ aor. o. *To seize.* غَوْلٌ Inebriation.

غَوَى aor. i. To wander, go astray. غَيٌّ n.a. Error, destruction. غَوِيٌّ One who is in the wrong. غَاوٍ part. act. Plur. غَاوُونَ, Oblique Plur. غَاوِينَ One who goes astray; expressions denoting Devils, or those who listen to them.—أَغْوَى IV. To lead astray.

غَابَ aor. i. *To be absent.* غَيْبٌ n.a. Plur. غُيُوبٌ A secret, mystery, whatever is absent or hidden. غَيَابَتٌ for غَيَابَةٌ, D. S. Gr. T. 1, p. 276, *note,* The bottom (of a well, etc.). غَآئِبٌ part. act. He or that which is absent or hidden.—إِغْتَابَ VIII. To traduce the absent, as وَلَا يَغْتَبْ 49 v. 12, "Neither traduce one another;" aor. conditional.

غَاثَ aor. i. To water by means of rain. غَيْثٌ Rain.

غَارَ aor. i. *To provide for.* غَيْرٌ A difference, an other; This word, which sometimes does duty as an adverb, is then indeclinable, as غَيْرُ Not, besides, unless; when used as a preposition, and meaning Without or Except, it becomes declinable, see بَعْدُ. *Note.* Much controversy exists as to the grammatical construction of this and similar words, D. S. Gr. T. 2, p. 153, *note.*—غَيَّرَ II. To alter, change. مُغَيِّرٌ part. act. One who changes.—مُغِيرَةٌ see غَارَ for غَوَرَ.—تَغَيَّرَ V. To be changed.

غَاضَ aor. i. To diminish, abate, be wanting, as مَا تَغِيضُ ٱلْأَرْحَامُ 13 v. 9, "What the wombs want (of their due time)."

غَاظَ aor. i. To incense, irritate (with acc. and بِ). غَيْظٌ n.a. Anger, fury. غَآئِظٌ part. act. One who is angry.—تَغَيُّظٌ n.a. V. f. A raging furiously.

ف

فَ A prefixed conjunction having less conjunctive power than وَ, and hence principally employed in connecting sentences; the following is from Johnson's Pers. Arab. and English Dictionary; فَ is a prefixed particle of inference and sequence, signifying And, then, for, therefore, so that, in order that, in that case, in consequence, afterwards, at least, lest, for fear that, truly; all or most of these significations may be found in the Korân, but this particle occurs so frequently in almost every page that the choice must be left to the reader's judgment, see D. S. Gr. T. 1, p. 549 *et seq.*, also T. 2, p. 396; It is constantly to be found prefixed to other particles, as فَإِنَّى, فَإِنَّ, فَأَمَّا, فَأَيْنَ etc. etc.

فَاتِحَةٌ An opening or commencement, rt. فَتَحَ q.v.

فَأَجِرْهُ "Then protect him;" imperat. iv. f. of جَارَ q.v.

فَأَدَ aor. a. *To hurt any one in the heart.* فُؤَادٌ Plur. أَفْئِدَةٌ The heart.

فَرِهَ see فَارِهِينَ.

فَأَرُونِى "Then show me;" imperat. iv. f. of رَأَى q.v. with فَ prefixed.

فَأَّ for فَأَوَ or فَأَى aor. o. and i. *To split (the head) with a sword.* فِئَةٌ A band or party of men, army.

فَيَأَ see فَآءَ for فَأَوْا.

وَجَسَ see فَأَوْجَسَ.

فَتَأَ aor. a. *To break,* cease, desist, as تَٱللّٰهِ تَفْتَؤُ تَذْكُرُ يُوسُفَ 12 v. 85, "By God! thou wilt (not) cease to remember Joseph;" for this ellipse of the negative see D. S. Gr. T. 2, p. 473; تَفْتَؤُ is here put for تَفْتَأُ, D. S. Gr. T. 1, p. 97.

فَتَحَ aor. a. To open (with acc. or with acc. of thing and عَلَى of pers.); to explain or reveal (with بِ of thing and عَلَى of pers.); To grant—a mercy or a victory—(with acc. and لِ of pers.), as at 48 v. 1; to adjudicate in a cause (with بَيْنَ); حَتَّى إِذَا فُتِحَتْ يَاجُوجُ وَمَاجُوجُ 21 v. 96, "Until Gog and Magog shall have had a way opened for them," alluding to the rampart mentioned at 18 v. 93, which being broken down, an irruption of those barbarous tribes is to take place shortly before the last day; the verb is here put in the feminine as having for subject the collective nouns يَاجُوجُ and مَاجُوجُ, D. S. Gr. T. 2, p. 233. فَتْحٌ Victory, a decision or judgment, the taking of a town, and especially of Mecca, which is sometimes called ٱلْفَتْحُ *par excellence,* as for example in the 48th chapter, which takes its name from that victory; N.B. The victory foretold at the close of the 27th verse is believed to be the taking of Khaibar. فَاتِحٌ part. act. *One who opens,* one who gives judgment; ٱلْفَاتِحَةُ Name of the opening chapter of the Korân. ٱلْفَتَّاحُ The Judge, an epithet of God. مَفَاتِحُ (2nd declension) plur. of مِفْتَحٌ or مِفْتَاحٌ A key.—فَتَّحَ II. To open (with لِ of pers.). مُفَتَّحٌ part. pass. Opened.—إِسْتَفْتَحَ X. To ask assistance—of God,—against (with عَلَى); to ask for a judgment or decision—in a suit,—as at 8 v. 19.

فَتَرَ aor. o. and i. *To be quiet;* to feel weak or faint, to desist. فَتْرَةٌ A cessation, or interval of time between two prophets.—فَتَّرَ II. To weaken, diminish—a punishment—(with عَنْ).

فَتَقَ To split, cleave asunder.

فَتَلَ aor. i. *To twist (a rope).* فَتِيلٌ A small skin in the cleft of a date-stone, hence a thing of no value.

فَتَنَ aor. i. To try, or prove—as gold in the fire—(with acc. and بِ or فِى); to afflict, persecute (by burning), which seems to be the meaning at 85 v. 10; to lead into temptation; to make an attempt upon, as at 4 v. 102; to seduce (with عَنْ); عَلَى ٱلنَّارِ يُفْتَنُونَ 51 v. 13, "They shall be proved, punished, or burnt in the fire." فُتُونٌ n.a. A trial. فَاتِنٌ part. act. One who leads into temptation. فِتْنَةٌ A temptation, trial, punishment, misfortune, discord, sedition or civil war, as at 8 v. 40; At 2 v. 187 it may be rendered "seduction from the truth," so also at 3 v. 5; فِتْنَةَ ٱلنَّاسِ 29 v. 9, "A trial or calamity proceeding from men;" At 8 v. 25 it is explained as meaning any crime common to the people at large; it has been translated "sedition," but the commentators are at a loss to fix the exact meaning; لَا تَجْعَلْنَا فِتْنَةً 10 v.

85 and 60 v. 5, "Do not make us (the subject of) punishment;" Beiḍâwëe says مَوْضِعُ فِتْنَةٍ; a similar ellipse occurs at 17 v. 62, also at 37 v. 61 and at 74 v. 31, where it means "a *cause* of contention;" At 33 v. 14 it may be rendered "desertion," and at 6 v. 23 it is said to mean "an excuse or answer," and only to be called فِتْنَةٌ because that excuse is a lie forged by the Idolators. مَفْتُونٌ part. pass. Distracted, demented.

فَتَا aor. o. *To be superior to another in generosity.* فَتًى A young man, man-servant; Dual فَتَيَانِ; Plur. فِتْيَةٌ of few, and فِتْيَانٌ of many. فَتَاةٌ Plur. فَتَيَاتٌ Young women, maid-servants.—أَفْتَى IV. To advise, give an opinion or instruction in a matter of law or judgment (with acc. of pers. and فِى).—إِسْتَفْتَى X. To consult, ask opinion or advice, chiefly in legal matters (with acc. of pers. and فِى, also with أَ interrogative); وَلَا تَسْتَفْتِ فِيهِمْ مِنْهُمْ أَحَدًا 18 v. 22, "Neither ask the opinion of any of them (the Jews or Christians) concerning them;" some of their views on the important matter in question are given in the preceding verse.

فَجَّ aor. o. *To straddle.* فَجٌّ n.a. Plur. فِجَاجٌ A broad way, especially between two mountains.

فَجَرَ aor. o. To cause water to pour forth (with acc. and مِنْ); to go aside from the right way, to act wickedly. فَجْرٌ n.a. The dawn, day-break. فَاجِرٌ part. act. Wicked; Plur. فَجَرَةٌ and فُجَّارٌ. فُجُورٌ n.a. Wickedness.—فَجَّرَ II. To cause to flow (with acc. and فِى, or with double acc.); وَإِذَا ٱلْبِحَارُ فُجِّرَتْ 82 v. 3, "And when the seas shall be made to flow (together)," so as to form but one sea. تَفْجِيرٌ n.a. The act of causing (water) to flow.—تَفَجَّرَ V. To flow (with مِنْ).—إِنْفَجَرَ VII. To flow (with مِنْ); at 2 v. 57 the verb is put in the fem., being (as *we* should say) governed by the nominative ٱثْنَتَا عَشْرَةَ عَيْنًا, "Twelve fountains," and the word عَيْنٌ being of the fem. gender; for the construction of the numerals see D. S. Gr. T. 1, p. 420, and T. 2, p. 318.

فَجَا aor. o. *To open (a door).* فَجْوَةٌ A clear open space, as between the sides of a cave.

فَحُشَ *To be shameful or infamous.* فَحْشَآءُ (2nd declension) Filthy, shameful, or dishonourable conduct, especially stinginess in the payment of tithes or other religious dues. فَاحِشَةٌ Filthiness, uncleanness, a filthy report, a crime, fornication or adultery; Plur. فَوَاحِشُ (2nd declension) Abominable crimes.

فَخَرَ aor. a. *To boast.* فَخُورٌ Vain-glorious, a boaster. فَخَّارٌ Earthenware.—تَفَاخُرٌ n.a. VI. f. Mutual boasting.

فَدَى aor. i. To ransom (with acc. and بِ). فِدَآءٌ n.a. A ransom. فِدْيَةٌ A ransom, that which is paid as ransom or to redeem a fault.—فَادَى III. To ransom, redeem.—إِفْتَدَى VIII. To ransom or redeem one's-self with (with بِ), or from (with مِنْ); thus at 5 v. 40, لِيَفْتَدُوا بِهِ مِنْ عَذَابِ "To redeem themselves with it from the punishment," etc.

فَدِيَةٌ see وَدَى.

فَذَرُوهُ see وَذَرَ.

فَرَّ aor. i. To flee, flee to (with إِلَى); fly from (with مِنْ). فِرَارٌ n.a. Flight, the act of fleeing away. مَفَرٌّ A place of refuge.

فَرُتَ aor. o. *To be wicked.* فُرَاتٌ Sweet (water).

فَرَثَ aor. i. and o. *To let out the contents—of a basket.* فَرْثٌ Fœces.

فَرَجَ aor. i. To split, cleave asunder. فَرْجٌ, Plur. فُرُوجٌ An interstice, break, flaw, private parts; وَٱلَّتِي أَحْصَنَتْ فَرْجَهَا 21 v. 91, "And she who preserved her chastity," viz. The Virgin Mary.

فَرِحَ aor. a. To be glad, rejoice (with بِ). فَرِحٌ Joyful; at 28 v. 76 it means one who exults (in riches).

فَرَدَ aor. o. *To be separated, alone.* فَرْدٌ, Plur. فُرَادَى (2nd declension) Alone, without companions, or as at 21 v. 89, without offspring.

فَرْدَسَ *To spread on the ground.* فِرْدَوْسٌ comm. gend. Paradise; the original meaning of the word is a park or garden planted with fruit-trees; it is from the Plur. فَرَادِيسُ that we have the Greek word Παράδεισος.

فَرَشَ aor. o. To spread as a carpet on the ground. فَرْشٌ n.a. Animals fit for slaughter. فَرَاشٌ generic noun, Moths. فِرَاشٌ n.a. Plur. فُرُشٌ A carpet used as a bed, a mattress, and metaphorically a wife; thus at 56 v. 33, وَفُرُشٍ مَرْفُوعَةٍ "And damsels raised on lofty couches."

فَرَضَ aor. i. *To notch*, ratify, appoint, fix (a time); to ordain, command an observance of, or obedience to (with acc. of thing and عَلَى of pers.); to sanction; to assign (with لِ of pers.); *To be aged (a cow)*, whence comes فَارِضٌ An old cow. فَرِيضَةٌ An ordinance (especially of God), a settled portion, dower or jointure; فَرِيضَةً see وَصِيَّةً. مَفْرُوضٌ part. pass. Appointed, determinate.

فَرَطَ aor. o. *To precede*, to be extravagantly reproachful or insolent (with عَلَى). فُرُطًا In advance of; وَكَانَ أَمْرُهُ فُرُطًا 18 v. 27, "And his affair is in advance of (the truth)," *i.e.* "He casts the truth behind his back;" the word in its most ordinary acceptation is applied to a horse who outstrips his competitors; it likewise means insolent or extravagant, an iniquity, that which goes beyond all bounds.—فَرَّطَ II. To be negligent, omit, act negligently (with فِي).—مُفْرَطٌ part. pass. IV. f. Made to hasten.

فَرَعَ aor. a. *To mount up.* فَرْعٌ A branch or top of a tree.

فِرْعَوْنُ (2nd declension) Pharaoh.

فَرَغَ aor. a. and o. *To empty*, finish; فَإِذَا فَرَغْتَ 94 v. 7, "And when thou hast finished (thy preaching);" to bring a matter to an end, settle an account with any one (with لِ of pers.). فَارِغٌ part. act. Empty, void.—أَفْرَغَ IV. To pour out (with acc. and عَلَى).

فَرَقَ aor. o. *To split*, divide, make a distinction (with بَيْنَ); to send down from Heaven (as the Ḳorân); thus at 44 v. 3, where it may also be rendered "is distinctly decreed;" as on the night there alluded to are settled all the affairs of this world for the ensuing year; فَرِقَ aor. a. To be afraid. فَرْقٌ n.a. The act of distinguishing or separating; فَٱلْفَارِقَاتِ فَرْقًا 77 v. 4, "And by the Angels who separate (truth from falsehood) by a discrimination;" there are also other interpretations of the passage. فِرْقٌ A separate part, heap, hillock. فِرْقَةٌ A band of men. فَرِيقٌ A part, portion, some, a party or band of men. فُرْقَانٌ A distinction; The Law of Moses and the Ḳorân are so called as distinguishing between truth and falsehood, see 2nd Epistle to Timothy ch. ii. v. 15; يَوْمَ ٱلْفُرْقَانِ 8 v. 42, "On the day of distinction (of the true believers from the infidels)," viz.

The Battle of Bedr; so also at 8 v. 29, where it is interpreted by some to mean a victory over the unbelievers.—فَرَّقَ II. To make a division or distinction (with بَيْنَ); to make a schism in (with acc.). تَفْرِيقٌ n.a. Division, dissension.—فَارَقَ III. To quit, part from (with acc.). فِرَاقٌ n.a. The act of quitting, a separation; at 18 v. 77 فِرَاقُ is antecedent to بَيْنِي; it must be borne in mind that بَيْنٌ although generally rendered "between" is in reality a substantive meaning interval, or, as in this passage, a connexion; at 75 v. 28 فِرَاقٌ means a departure from this life.—تَفَرَّقَ V. To be divided among themselves (with فِي); فَتَفَرَّقَ بِكُمْ 6 v. 154, "For fear lest ye be scattered away from" (with عَنْ), D. S. Gr. T. 2, p. 245; to be separated one from another. مُتَفَرِّقٌ part. act. Divers, different.

فَرِهَ *To be brisk.* فَارِهٌ part. act. One who is clever, insolent or petulant.

فَرَى aor. i. *To cut.* فَرِيٌّ New, strange, wonderful.—إِفْتَرَى VIII. To feign, forge, invent a lie (with acc. and عَلَى of pers.); بُهْتَانٍ يَفْتَرِينَهُ بَيْنَ أَيْدِيهِنَّ وَأَرْجُلِهِنَّ 60 v. 12, *Literally,* "A calumny which they have forged between their hands and their feet;" this passage has by some been interpreted as referring to the illegitimate children which the women attempted to father upon their husbands. مُفْتَرٍ for مُفْتَرِيٌ part. act. A forger. مُفْتَرًى for مُفْتَرَيٌ part. pass. Feigned, pretended, forged.

فَزَّ aor. i. *To flow as blood from a wound.*—إِسْتَفَزَّ X. To remove, expel (with acc. and مِنْ); to deceive, lead to destruction (with acc. of pers. and بِ).

فَزِعَ aor. a. To be terrified, smitten with fear (with مِنْ). فَزَعٌ n.a. Terror.—فَزَّعَ II. when used with عَنْ means To free from fear, as إِذَا فُزِّعَ عَنْ قُلُوبِهِمْ 34 v. 22, "(Until) their hearts shall have been freed from fear."

فَسَحَ aor. a. *To be spacious,* to make room for a person (with لِ of pers.).—تَفَسَّحَ V. To make room (with فِي of place).

فَسَحَقًا see سَحَقَ.

فَسَدَ aor. o. To be corrupt. فَسَادٌ n.a. The acting corruptly, corruption, violence; بِغَيْرِ نَفْسٍ أَوْ فَسَادٍ 5 v. 35, "Without (that soul having slain another) soul or (committed) violence."—أَفْسَدَ IV. To act corruptly, do violence (with فِي); to corrupt, despoil (with acc.). مُفْسِدٌ part. act. One who acts corruptly or commits violence, a spoiler.

فَسَرَ aor. i. and o. *To discover.*—تَفْسِيرٌ n.a. II. f. An explanation or interpretation.

فَسَقَ aor. i. and o. *To emerge from its husk (a date)*; to withdraw from the right way, disobey the commandment of God (with عَنْ); to be impious, act wickedly. فِسْقٌ and فُسُوقٌ ns.a. Transgression, impiety, wickedness. فَاسِقٌ part. act. A transgressor, one who is wicked.

فَشِلَ aor. a. *To be weak,* faint-hearted.

فَصَحَ aor. o. *To show itself (the dawn)*; and فَصُحَ *To be eloquent, speak with fluency and correctness.* أَفْصَحُ (2nd declension) comp. form, More eloquent.

فَصُرْهُنَّ "Then draw them (towards thee)," imperat. of صَارَ for صَوَرَ q.v.

فَصَلَ aor. i. *To dissect,* depart; to make a distinction or division, or judge between (with بَيْنَ of pers. and فِي of thing). فَصْلٌ n.a. A distinction, separation, a means of distinguishing good from evil, as at 86 v. 13; فَصْلَ ٱلْخِطَابِ 38 v. 19, see خِطَابٌ. فَاصِلٌ part. act. One who judges between truth and falsehood. فِصَالٌ Weaning. فَصِيلَةٌ A family, relations.—فَصَّلَ II. To explain distinctly (with acc. and لِ of pers.). تَفْصِيلٌ n.a. A clear explanation, exposition. مُفَصَّلٌ part. pass. Clearly explained, distinct.

فَصَمَ aor. i. *To break.*—إِنْفِصَامٌ n.a. VII. f. The act of being broken; لَا ٱنْفِصَامَ لَهَا 2 v. 257, "It has no flaw or break in it."

فَضَّ aor. o. *To break asunder.* فِضَّةٌ Silver.—إِنْفَضَّ VII. To be broken up, dispersed, separated (with مِنْ).

فَضَحَ aor. a. To expose to shame; لَا تَفْضَحُونِ 15 v. 68, "And do not expose me to disgrace (by ill-treating my guests)."

فَضَلَ aor. o. *To remain over and above.* فَضْلٌ Excellence, merit, favour, a free gift, bounty, grace, munificence, indulgence.—فَضَّلَ II. To prefer, favour, cause to excel, grant favours to one person in preference to another (with acc. and عَلَى, and with بِ of thing). تَفْضِيلٌ n.a. Excellence, preference.—تَفَضَّلَ V. To make one's-self superior (with عَلَى).

فَضَا aor. o. *To be roomy.*—أَفْضَى IV. To go in unto, as a husband to a wife (with إِلَى).

فَطَرَ aor. o. and i. *To split*, create. فَاطِرٌ part. act. A Creator. فِطْرَتْ for فِطْرَةٌ D. S. Gr. T. 1, p. 276, *note*, A creation; the word is found at 30 v. 29, and may there be taken to mean Religion, or a religious frame of mind inspired by God; it is put in the acc. after أَعْنِى (I mean) understood; D. S. Gr. T. 2, p. 94. فُطُورٌ A rent, flaw, or fissure.—تَفَطَّرَ V. To be rent asunder.—إِنْفَطَرَ VII. To be cloven asunder. إِنْفِطَارٌ n.a. The being cloven asunder. مُنْفَطِرٌ part. act. Cloven or rent asunder.

فَظَّ *To force water out of an animal's stomach.* فَظٌّ Harsh, severe.

فَعَلَ aor. a. To do, make, act, perform, accomplish. فِعْلٌ An action, a doing. فَعْلَةٌ A deed. فَاعِلٌ part. act. One who does, etc. فَعَّالٌ adjective of intensity, D. S. Gr. T. 1, p. 322, Doing or effecting much; used substantively it means a great or able worker. مَفْعُولٌ part. pass. Done, made, effected, performed, fulfilled; at 8 vv. 43 and 46 the past part. كَانَ مَفْعُولًا is put in prophetic language for the future أَنْ يُفْعَلَ; a similar instance occurs at 73 v. 18.

فَقَدَ aor. i. *To seek for that which is lost*, to lose.—تَفَقَّدَ V. *To make an inquisition into;* at 27 v. 20 it may be rendered "He reviewed."

فَقَرَ aor. o. and i. *To dig, break the vertebræ;* and فَقُرَ *To be poor.* فَقْرٌ n.a. Poverty. فَاقِرَةٌ A calamity, *properly* that which breaks the vertebræ. فَقِيرٌ Plur. فُقَرَآءُ (2nd declension) Poor, needy; when used with لِ as at 28 v. 24 لِمَا أَنْزَلْتَ إِلَيَّ . . . . فَقِيرٌ it may be rendered "In want of . . . . whatever thou mayest send down unto me;" a similar use of the word when employed with إِلَى may be observed at 35 v. 16.

فَقَعَ aor. a. and o. *To be of a pure yellow colour.* فَاقِعٌ part. act. comm. gend. Very yellow or red; according to some this word is applied to any pure colour.

فَقِنَا "Then deliver us," see وَقَى.

فَقُهَ *To be superior in wisdom;* and فَقِهَ aor. a. To be wise, understand, to be skilled or have understanding in matters pertaining to Law and Divinity.—تَفَقَّهَ V. To be assiduous in instructing one's-self (with فِى).

فَكَّ aor. o. *To break.* فَكٌّ n.a. The act of freeing (captives).—مُنفَكٌّ part. VII. f. *Dislocated,* one who vacillates (in his faith), as at 98 v. 1.

فَكَرَ *To think.*—فَكَّرَ II. To meditate; at 74 v. 18 it means to meditate blasphemies against the Korân.—تَفَكَّرَ V. To consider, meditate (with فِى).

فَكِهَ *To be very merry.* فَكِهٌ A jester, one who makes game of others. فَاكِهٌ part. act. One who is very joyful, rejoices greatly (with بِ or فِى). فَاكِهَةٌ Plur. فَوَاكِهُ (2nd declension) Fruit.—تَفَكَّهَ V. To wonder.

فُلّ *A certain person.* فُلَانٌ Such an one, a certain person.

فَلَحَ *To split.*—أَفْلَحَ IV. To prosper, be happy, attain one's desires. مُفْلِحٌ part. act. One who is prosperous or happy.

فَلَقَ aor. i. *To split, cause to come forth.* فَلَقٌ *A fissure,* Day-break, breaking forth (of the dawn); it is held by some to mean Creation in general, and especially of those things which are produced from others, as Fountains, plants, children, etc. فَالِقٌ part. act. One who causes to put forth or break forth.—إِنْفَلَقَ VII. To be split open, divided.

فَلَكَ *To be round (a breast).* فُلْكٌ comm. gend. and number, Ships, a ship, shipping, The Ark. فَلَكٌ The orbit of a celestial body.

فَلَنِعْمَ see نِعْمَ.

فَلْيَصُمْهُ see صَامَ for صَوَمَ.

فِيمَ for فِى مَا, see مَا.

فَنَّ *To drive camels.* أَفْنَانٌ plur. of فَنَنٌ A branch, or of فَنٌّ A species; if the latter meaning be adopted we must understand the words مِنَ ٱلْأَشْجَارِ "*Of trees,*" at 55 v. 48, where it occurs.

فَنِدَ *To dote.*—فَنَّدَ II. To make a dotard of, regard as a dotard.

فَنَى aor. i. *To vanish.* فَانٍ for فَانِىٌ part. act. Perishable, liable to decay.

فَهِمَ *To understand.*—فَهَّمَ II. To cause to understand (with double acc.).

فَاتَ aor. o. To pass away from, slip (an opportunity); escape (with acc.). فَوْتٌ n.a. Escape.—تَفَاوُتٌ n.a. VI. f. A disparity, or want of proportion.

فَاجَ aor. o. *To diffuse a fragrant odour.* فَوْجٌ A troop or company; Plur. أَفْوَاجٌ.

فَارَ aor. o. To boil, boil up or boil over; فَارَ ٱلتَّنُّورُ 11 v. 42, "The oven boiled over;" this oven is said to have originally belonged to Eve, and poured forth boiling water as a sign of the Deluge, the waters of which, according to Jewish fable, were boiling hot; see also 23 v. 27. فَوْرٌ n.a. Haste; مِنْ فَوْرِهِمْ 3 v. 121, "Immediately on their arrival, or before they had rested," see D. S. Gr. T. 1, p. 526.

فَازَ aor. o. To get possession of, gain, receive salvation, obtain one's desires. فَوْزٌ n.a. Victory, felicity, safety, salvation. فَائِزٌ part. act. One who enjoys felicity or receives salvation. مَفَازٌ A place of safety or felicity. مَفَازَةٌ An escape, place of refuge.

فَوَّضَ Not used in the primitive form, To submit a thing to the judgment of another (with acc. and إِلَى of pers.).

فَاقَ aor. o. *To be superior in rank or excellence.* فَوْقٌ n.a. is properly a noun expressive of superiority, which when used as an adverb is indeclinable; in tbe Korân it always appears as a preposition meaning over or above, and is then used in the accus. فَوْقَ as فَوْقَكُمْ "Over you," or in the genitive after a preposition, as مِنْ فَوْقِ ٱلْأَرْضِ 14 v. 31, "From above (or from tbe surface of) the earth;" D. S. Gr. T. 1, pp. 494 and 510; see also بَعْدُ. فَوَاقٌ A delay, properly the space of time between two milkings, or of the opening and closing of the hand in milking.—أَفَاقَ IV. To come to one's-self, recover (after a swoon or illness).

فُومٌ generic nonn, Garlic; no verbal root.

فَاهَ aor. o. *To pronounce a word.* فَمٌ or فُمٌ or with a complement فُو, Gen. فِي, Acc. فَا; Plur. أَفْوَاهٌ A mouth; The word فَمٌ is formed from the regular nonn فَوْهٌ by cutting off the two last radical letters, and substituting م; see D. S. Gr. T. 1, pp. 378 and 417; it is found in the Korân only in the acc. sing. and in the plnral.

فِي a preposition meaning In, into, among, in company with, as ٱدْخُلُوا فِي أُمَمٍ قَدْ خَلَتْ 7 v. 36, "Enter ye in company witb the nations which have already passed away;" It may sometimes be rendered On, of, to, witb, 51 v. 29; for, 2 v. 173; by, against, concerning, according to, or in comparison with; an instance of the last meaning occurs at 13 v. 26; D. S. Gr. T. 1, p. 487.

فَآءَ aor. i. To return, go back (with إِلَى); to go from a vow, as at 2 v. 226.—أَفَآءَ IV. To bring nnder the power or authority of any one (with acc. and عَلَى of pers.).—تَفَيَّأَ V. To tnrn itself about (as a shadow cast by the snn).

فَاضَ aor. i. *To be copious;* to overflow (with مِنْ).—أَفَاضَ IV. To ponr water over any one (with acc. and عَلَى); to rush impetuonsly (with مِنْ), as the pilgrims down Monnt 'Arafat; to be diffuse; to dilate or amplify in speaking (with فِي); to be immersed in any business (with فِي).

فَالَ aor. i. *To be weak-minded.* فِيلٌ An elephant.

ق

ق Name and initial letter of the 50tb cbapter, see آلم.

قَبَحَ *To abhor;* and قَبُحَ *To be ugly, loathsome.* مَقْبُوحٌ part. pass. Abhorred or rendered loathsome; at 28 v. 42 it may be taken in either sense.

قَبَرَ aor. o. and i. *To bury.* قَبْرٌ n.a. Plur. قُبُورٌ A grave. مَقَابِرُ (2nd declension) plnr. of مَقْبَرَةٌ A cemetery.—أَقْبَرَ IV. To cause to be buried.

قَبَسَ aor. i. *To get a light from another.* قَبَسٌ Lighted fuel.—إِقْتَبَسَ VIII. To take a light from another (with مِنْ).

قَبَضَ aor. i. To contract, take, seize, draw in (its wings in flying), as a bird; thns at 67 v. 19, where we may understand the word أَجْنِحَتَهُنَّ. قَبْضٌ n.a. A contraction. قَبْضَةٌ A handful. مَقْبُوضٌ part. pass. Taken.

قَبِلَ aor. a. To accept (with acc. and عَنْ or مِنْ); to admit (with acc. and لِ of pers.) قَابِلٌ part. act. One who accepts. قَبْلٌ *properly,* a noun meaning *the forepart;* bnt in tbe Korân used either as an adverb, and withont a complement, in whicb case it is indeclinable, as مِنْ قَبْلُ Before, formerly, or as a preposition in the acc. as قَبْلَ هٰذَا Before this; when preceded by the preposition مِنْ it is put in the genitive, as مِنْ قَبْلِ أَنْ Before that; it corresponds in its construction with بَعْدَ q.v.; see also D. S. Gr. T. 2, p. 152. قُبُلٌ The fore-part; قُبُلًا 6 v. 111, "Before their eyes," or "In hosts," with which meaning قُبُلٌ may be regarded as the plur. of قَبِيلٌ q.v. قِبَلٌ Power, a side or part; قِبَلَ Towards, in the direction of, as قِبَلَ ٱلْمَشْرِقِ 2 v. 172, "Towards the East;" لَا قِبَلَ لَهُمْ بِهَا 27 v. 37, "Against whom they will have no power;" مِنْ قِبَلِهِ 57 v. 13, "Alongside it." قِبْلَةٌ properly, *Anything opposite;* a Ḳibla, or the point in the direction of which, prayer must be made to be efficacious; see Daniel chap. vi. v. 10; Thus the Ḳibla of the Moḥammedans is the Ka'ba at Mecca; at 10 v. 87 the word has been interpreted "A place of worship;" The Jews in the days of Moses are supposed by the Commentators to have prayed towards the Ka'ba, it having been rebuilt by Abraham and Ishmael in place of the original house destroyed by the Flood. قَبُولٌ A favourable reception. قَبِيلٌ A surety, bail, sponsor; at 7 v. 26 it means a host (the ministers of Satan). قَبَائِلُ (2nd declension) plur. of قَبِيلَةٌ An Arab tribe.—أَقْبَلَ IV. To come, draw near, approach (with فِي in the sense of with), thus at 12 v. 82 and 51 v. 29; to turn towards (with عَلَى of pers.); to rush upon (with إِلَى).—تَقَبَّلَ V. To accept (with acc. and مِنْ or عَنْ of pers.); This verb is sometimes used with an ellipse of the immediate complement, or as we should call it, the accusative; thus at 3 v. 31 فَتَقَبَّلْ مِنِّي "Then accept from me (that which I have vowed"—مَا نَذَرْتُهُ); a similar passage is found at 2 v. 121, D. S. Gr. T. 2, p. 454.—مُتَقَابِلٌ part. act. VI. f. Opposite to, or facing one another.—مُسْتَقْبِلٌ part. act. X. f. Proceeding towards (with acc.).

قتر aor. o. and i. To be niggardly. قَتَرٌ and قَتَرَةٌ Black dust, blackness. قَتُورٌ Niggardly.—مُقْتِرٌ part. act. IV. f. To be in reduced circumstances.

قتل aor. o. To kill, slay; فَٱقْتُلُوا أَنْفُسَكُمْ 2 v. 51, "Then slay yourselves;" either figuratively, by mortifying your corrupt desires, or "one another;" the latter interpretation is in accordance with the account given in Exodus chap. xxxii. v. 27; In the Passive قُتِلَ is sometimes used as an imprecation, thus at 74 vv. 19 and 20, "May he be accursed;" the preterite being used for the optative; D. S. Gr. T. 1, p. 169; similar instances occur at 51 v. 10, 80 v. 16, and 85 v. 4. قَتْلٌ n.a. The act of putting to death, slaughter. قَتْلَى (2nd declension) for قَتْلَى D. S. Gr. T. 1, pp. 110 and 402, plur. of قَتِيلٌ One who is slain.—قَتَّلَ II. To slay, or cause to be slain. تَقْتِيلٌ n.a. The act of slaughtering.—قَاتَلَ III. To fight against (with acc. of pers.); قَاتَلَهُمُ ٱللّٰهُ 9 v. 30, "May God curse them," see قُتِلَ; At 3 v. 140 there seems to be an ellipse after قَاتَلَ of the objective or immediate complement, إِنْسَانًا or some similar word being understood, D. S. Gr. T. 2, p. 454. قِتَالٌ n.a. The act of fighting, war.—إِقْتَتَلَ VIII. To contend among themselves.

قِثَّآءٌ generic noun, Cucumbers; no verbal root.

قحم aor. o. *To rush headlong.*—إِقْتَحَمَ VIII. To undertake an enterprise in a headlong or impetuous manner. مُقْتَحِمٌ part. act. One who rushes or leaps headlong, found at 38 v. 59, where it means "Rushing headlong (into Hell)."

قَدْ A particle frequently prefixed to the preterite to give it a past signification; where among several verbs in the preterite one has the particle قَدْ prefixed, such verb is to be taken in the Pluperfect tense; so also among several Pluperfects the one which follows قَدْ will have a signification anterior to the others; in all the above cases it may generally be rendered already, and may frequently be understood to imply that the matter in question, although past, is of recent date, or that it was not unexpected; thus, وَقَدْ فَصَّلَ لَكُمْ مَا حَرَّمَ عَلَيْكُمْ 6 v. 119, "For he hath even now explained to you what he hath forbidden you;" another use of قَدْ is to add energy to an affirmation, and it may then be rendered truly, of a certainty, or verily; thus, قَدْ يَعْلَمُ مَا أَنْتُمْ عَلَيْهِ 24 v. 64, "He knows of a surety what ye are about;" so also at 91 v. 9, قَدْ أَفْلَحَ مَنْ زَكَّاهَا "Verily he who hath purified it is happy;" Lastly, قَدْ may sometimes be rendered frequently, as at 2 v. 139, قَدْ نَرَى تَقَلُّبَ وَجْهِكَ "We have frequently observed the turning of thy face;" It is found in combination with other particles as فَقَدْ ,لَقَدْ ,وَقَدْ etc. D. S. Gr. T. 1, p. 533.

قَدَّ aor. o. To rend. قِدَدٌ plur. of قِدَّةٌ A party of men at variance among themselves; كُنَّا طَرَآئِقَ قِدَدًا 72 v. 11, "We are (followers of) different ways."

قَدَحَ aor. a. *To strike fire.* قَدْحٌ n.a. The act of striking fire.

قَدَرَ aor. o. and i. To be able, to be able to do, have power over, prevail against (with عَلَى); to measure to an exact nicety (with acc. of thing and عَلَى of pers.), as at 89 v. 16; so also in the Pass. at 65 v. 7; to estimate the value of (with double acc.), thus مَا قَدَرُوا ٱللّٰهَ حَقَّ قَدْرِهِ 6 v. 91, "They have not made a just estimate of God;" to be sparing (with لِ); to determine, with which meaning it is found in the Pass. at 54 v. 12. قَدْرٌ n.a. That which is determined or predestined of God, measure, value, power; لَيْلَةُ ٱلْقَدْرِ 97 v. 1, The night of El Kadr, on which the Korân was sent down from Heaven; it may be rendered either "the night of Power," or "the night of the predetermined decree," from a Mohammedan fable, that on this night are issued the Divine decrees on all the affairs of the ensuing year; it is generally supposed to fall on the night preceding the 24th of Ramaḍân. قَدَرٌ n.a. The Divine decree, that which is predestined, a definite quantity, a determined measure; عَلَى ٱلْمُوسِعِ قَدَرُهُ 2 v. 237, "Upon him who is in easy circumstances (shall be set) an amount according to his ability;" it is also read قَدْرُهُ. قُدُورٌ plur. of قِدْرٌ comm. gend. A cauldron. قَادِرٌ part. act. One who is able or has power over, one who determines beforehand. قَدِيرٌ Able, potent. مَقْدُورٌ part. pass. Determined. مِقْدَارٌ A definite quantity, or determined measure, a space.—قَدَّرَ II. To make possible, dispose, prepare, to plan, devise, decree, determine, define; at 74 vv. 18, 19, and 20, it means to lay plans or plots against the Korân; at 34 v. 17 it may be translated "We have facilitated;" قَدَّرُوهَا تَقْدِيرًا 76 v. 16, "They shall determine the measure thereof (according to their desire)." تَقْدِيرٌ n.a. The act of measuring or determining, a Divine decree.—مُقْتَدِرٌ part. act. VIII. f. Powerful, able to prevail (with عَلَى).

قَدَسَ *To be pure.* قُدُسٌ Purity, sanctity; رُوحُ ٱلْقُدُسِ The Holy Spirit, by which name the Moḥammedans designate the Angel Gabriel. ٱلْقُدُّوسُ The Holy One, an epithet of God.—قَدَّسَ II. To sanctify, bless (with لِ). مُقَدَّسٌ part. pass. Sacred, holy.

قَدَمَ aor. o. To precede; and قَدِمَ aor. a. To betake one's-self, come to (with إِلَى). قَدَمٌ Merit; when of the fem. gend. it means A foot; Plur. أَقْدَامٌ. قَدِيمٌ Old, ancient. أَقْدَمُونَ Forefathers.—قَدَّمَ II. To bring upon (with acc. and لِ of pers.); to do a thing before, prepare beforehand, send before (with لِ and with or without acc.), as good works, which a man is said to send before to bear witness for him at the last day; see 1st Epistle of S. Paul to Timothy chap. v. v. 24; to put forward (a threat), threaten beforehand, as وَقَدْ قَدَّمْتُ إِلَيْكُمْ بِٱلْوَعِيدِ 50 v. 27, "Since we have already threatened you beforehand;" at 49 v. 1 there is an ellipse of the accus., the words لَا تُقَدِّمُوا may probably mean "Do not put yourselves forward," or "do not obtrude your opinions;" there are other readings, but this seems best to accord with the context, which contains several hints on good breeding and etiquette.—تَقَدَّمَ V. To go before; at 74 v. 40 it means to go forward in the right way.—إِسْتَقْدَمَ X. To desire to advance, wish to anticipate. مُسْتَقْدِمٌ part. act. One who goes forward, or desires to advance.

قَدَا aor. o. *To be agreeable in taste and smell* (*food*).—إِقْتَدَى VIII. To imitate, copy (with بِ). ٱقْتَدِهْ imperat. for ٱقْتَدِ with the addition of هْ called هَاءُ ٱلْوَقْفِ D. S. Gr. T. 1, p. 252. مُقْتَدٍ for مُقْتَدِيٌ part. act. One who imitates (with عَلَى).

قَذَفَ aor. i. *To pelt*, cast (with acc. and فِى or بِ); يَقْذِفُ بِٱلْحَقِّ 34 v. 47, "He casts his truth (over his servants);" at 20 v. 90 we must understand the words فِى ٱلنَّارِ; to asperse, pelt with abuse (with acc. and بِ).

قَرَّ aor. i. and a. *To stand fast;* remain quiet (with فِى), as at 33 v. 33, where قَرْنَ is for إِقْرَرْنَ 2nd pers. fem. plur. of the imperative, D. S. Gr. T. 1, p. 229. *Note.* This word is frequently spelt قِرْنَ, and is then to be derived in the usual way from the assimilated verb وَقَرَ q.v.; to be cool, applied to the eyes, thus at 20 v. 41 كَيْ تَقَرَّ عَيْنُهَا *literally*, "So that her eye might be cool," *i.e.* "That she might rejoice;" so also at 19 v. 26 وَقَرِّى عَيْنًا "And cool (or refresh) thyself," *literally*, "Be cool as to *thine* eye." قَرَارٌ n.a. Stability, a fixed or secure place, repository, place of abode. قُرَّةٌ Coolness; قُرَّةُ عَيْنٍ "Delight,—*literally*, coolness—of the eye." قَوَارِيرُ (2nd declension) plur. of قَارُورَةٌ A glass bottle;" at 27 v. 44 it must be translated "Slabs of glass;" قَوَارِيرَ مِنْ فِضَّةٍ 76 v. 16, "Glass bottles resembling silver," or it may be "Silver bottles resembling glass."—أَقَرَّ IV. To confirm, to cause to rest or remain (with فِى).—إِسْتَقَرَّ X. To remain firm (with acc. of place). مُسْتَقِرٌّ part. act. That which remains firmly fixed or confirmed, abiding, lasting. مُسْتَقَرٌّ part. pass. Firmly fixed or established; as a noun of place it means a fixed abode; and at 6 v. 66 "a fixed time;" at 6 v. 98 there is an ellipse, to complete the sense we must read

فَلَكُمْ مُسْتَقَرٌّ; the words may refer either to the loins of the Father, or a mansion upon earth.

قَرَأَ aor. a. and o. To read, rehearse to (with acc. and عَلَى of pers.). قُرُوءٌ Period of a woman's monthly courses. قُرْآنٌ The Ḳorân, properly pronounced Ḳor-ân.—أَقْرَأَ IV. To cause to read or rehearse.

قَرَبَ *To make a night journey;* and قَرِبَ aor. a. To approach, draw near to; لَا تَقْرَبُوهَا 2 v. 183, "And do not go near (to transgress) them." قُرْبَةٌ Proximity; at 9 v. 100 it may be rendered "A means of drawing nigh." قُرْبَةٌ Plur. قُرُبَاتٌ Pious works which draw men nigh unto God. قَرِيبٌ comm. gend. Nigh, near, near at hand, either in place or time; مِنْ قَرِيبٍ Shortly after; قَرِيبًا as an adverb, Lately. قُرْبَى for قُرْبَى (2nd declension) D. S. Gr. T. 1, pp. 110 and 402, Affinity, relationship; ذُو ٱلْقُرْبَى A relation. قُرْبَانٌ n.a. A sacrifice, or gift offered to God; see S. Mark chap. vii. v. 11; a familiar acquaintance, the *Entourage* of a prince; at 46 v. 27 it may perhaps be best translated "as a means of access to God;" the false Deities there mentioned being supposed to be on familiar terms with God, and therefore likely to act as intercessors with him. أَقْرَبُ (2nd declension) comp. form, Closer, closest, nearer, nearest, more probable; at 16 v. 79 it means "In a shorter time," or "quicker." ٱلْأَقْرَبُونَ Kinsfolk, kindred, those most nearly related. مَقْرَبَةٌ Relationship.—قَرَّبَ II. To set before (with acc. and إِلَى); to cause to draw nigh (with acc. and عِنْدَ or إِلَى); to offer (a sacrifice); مُقَرَّبٌ part. pass. One who is made or permitted to approach, honoured.—إِقْتَرَبَ VIII. To draw near.

قَرَحَ aor. a. *To wound.* قَرْحٌ n.a. A wound.

قَرَدَ aor. i. *To collect.* قِرَدَةٌ plur. of قِرْدٌ An ape.

قَرَشَ aor. i. and o. *To cut off.* قُرَيْشٌ Name of a noble Arab tribe descended from Ishmael, of which Moḥammad's grandfather was Prince.

قَرَضَ aor. i. *To cut;* to turn away from (with acc. of pers. or thing). قَرْضٌ n.a. A loan, especially one which is payable at the option of the borrower, and hence called قَرْضٌ حَسَنٌ; according to some, however, the meaning of this expression is "a loan at good interest."—أَقْرَضَ IV. To lend (with double acc.).

قَرْطَسَ quadriliteral, *To hit the mark.* قِرْطَاسٌ Plur. قَرَاطِيسُ (2nd declension) Paper.

قَرَعَ aor. o. *To get the better of another in drawing lots, to strike.* قَارِعَةٌ Adversity, that which strikes; a name of the Day of Judgment.

قَرَفَ aor. i. *To peel.*—إِقْتَرَفَ VIII. To acquire, gain. مُقْتَرِفٌ part. act. One who gains.

قَرْنَ for إِقْرِرْنَ fem. plur. imperat. of قَرَّ q.v.

قَرَنَ aor. i. *To join one thing to another.* قَرْنٌ n.a. A horn, a generation; Dual قَرْنَانِ, oblique قَرْنَيْنِ, as ذُو ٱلْقَرْنَيْنِ He of the two horns, Alexander the Great, see ذُو; Plur. قُرُونٌ. قَرِينٌ Plur. قُرَنَاءُ (2nd declension) An intimate companion. قَارُونُ Ḳorah, a proper name of foreign origin, and therefore of the 2nd declension, D. S. Gr. T. 1, p. 404.—مُقَرَّنٌ part. pass. II. f. Bound together.—مُقْرِنٌ part. act. IV. f. One who is able to do a thing (with لِ of thing).—مُقْتَرِنٌ part. act. VIII. f. One who is associated with another, or follows in procession.

قَرَى aor. i. *To entertain a guest.* قَرْيَةٌ A city, town, village; Dual ٱلْقَرْيَتَانِ The two cities Mecca and Eṭ-Ṭâ-if; Plur. قُرًى.

قَسَّ *To think evil.* قِسِّيسٌ A Christian Priest.

قَسَرَ *To compel any one to do a thing against his will.* قَسْوَرَةٌ *Powerful*, a lion.

قَسَطَ aor. i. *To swerve from justice;* also aor. i. and o. *To be just.* قِسْطٌ n.a. Justice, equity; at 21 v. 48 we have an instance of the noun of action used as an adjective, and remaining in the singular, although qualifying a noun in the plural; D. S. Gr. T. 2, p. 280. قَاسِطٌ part. act. One who acts unjustly or unrighteously. أَقْسَطُ (2nd declension) comp. form, More just.—أَقْسَطَ IV. To be just (with فِى or إِلَى). مُقْسِطٌ part. act. One who observes justice.

قُسْطَاسٌ A balance; this word is said to be of Greek origin.

قَسَمَ aor. i. *To divide into parts;* to portion out (with acc. and بَيْنَ). قَسَمٌ An oath. قِسْمَةٌ A partition, a dividing, an apportionment. مَقْسُومٌ part. pass. *Divided,* distinct.—مُقَسِّمٌ part. act. II. f. One who apportions.—قَاسَمَ III. To swear unto (with acc. of pers.).—أَقْسَمَ IV. To swear (with acc. of oath and بِ, or with a verb preceded by لَ); at 7 v. 47 and elsewhere the substance of the oath immediately follows the verb, without the intervention of any particle, thus يُقْسِمُ ٱلْمُجْرِمُونَ مَا لَبِثُوا 30 v. 54, "The wicked will swear (that) they have not tarried;" at 75 v. 1 the words لَا أُقْسِمُ are generally rendered "Verily I swear," لَا being held to be intensive; so also at 56 v. 74 and other passages; according to some however the words may mean "I will not swear;" the matter being too palpable to require the confirmation of an oath, see لَا.—تَقَاسَمَ VI. To swear one to another (with بِ).—مُقْتَسِمٌ part. act. VIII. f. One who divides.—إِسْتَقْسَمَ X. To draw lots or divine by means of headless arrows.

قَسَا aor. o. To be hard. قَسْوَةٌ n.a. Hardness. قَاسٍ for قَاسِوٌ D. S. Gr. T. 1, p. 330, part. act. Hard; for the construction of the phrase لِلْقَاسِيَةِ قُلُوبُهُمْ 39 v. 23 see D. S. Gr. T. 2, pp. 197 and 278; at the commencement of this verse there is a remarkable hiatus; Beiḍâwëe contents himself by saying خَبَرُ مَنْ مَحْذُوفٌ "The predicate of مَنْ is suppressed," but the sense may be gathered from the concluding portion; it may be supplied somewhat as follows: "Shall he then whose breast God hath opened, etc. (be like unto one whose heart is hardened?); Woe then unto those who are hard of heart;" D. S. Gr. T. 2, p. 475.

قِشْعَرٌ *A cucumber.* إِقْشَعَرَّ IV. f. quadriliteral, To become rough or creep with terror—the skin—(with مِنْ).

قَصَّ aor. o. *To cut, lop,* to follow, declare; to narrate or relate, to make mention of (with acc. and عَلَى of pers.). قَصَصٌ n.a. A narrative, story, history, the act of following; قَصَصًا 18 v. 63, "Following their footsteps." قِصَاصٌ Retaliation.

قَصَدَ aor. i. *To intend,* to be moderate, steer a middle course. قَصْدٌ The right way, the middle path, "Le juste milieu." قَاصِدٌ part. act. Easy or moderate (journey).—مُقْتَصِدٌ part. act. VIII. f. One who keeps to the right path, a man of good intentions; also one who halts between two opinions.

قَصُرَ *To be short;* aor. o. To diminish, cut short, as prayers (with مِنْ). قَصْرٌ n.a. Plur. قُصُورٌ A palace, castle. قَاصِرٌ part. act. One who keeps in restraint. مَقْصُورٌ part. pass. Confined, kept at home (a woman).—مُقَصِّرٌ part. act. II. f. One who cuts short (his hair).—أَقْصَرَ IV. To desist.

قَصَفَ aor. i. *To dash in pieces (a ship).* قَاصِفٌ A heavy gale of wind.

قَصَمَ aor. i. To break in pieces, demolish utterly.

قَصَا aor. o. *To be distant.* قَصِيٌّ Distant. أَقْصَى for أَقْصَوُ D. S. Gr. T. 1, p. 105, Fem. قُصْوَى (2nd declension) comp. form, More remote, further; ٱلْمَسْجِدُ ٱلْأَقْصَى 17 v. 1, "The further mosque," the Holy House at Jerusalem, on the site of which now stands the mosque of El Akṣa.

قَضَّ aor. o. *To bore.*—إِنْقَضَّ VII. To threaten to fall down.

قَضَبَ aor. i. *To cut off.* قَضْبٌ n.a. Trefoil or clover.

قَضَى aor. i. To decree, create, accomplish, bring to an end, complete; to fulfil (as a term or vow); to determine (with acc. and مِنْ of pers.); to pass a sentence (with acc. and عَلَى of pers.); قَضَى عَلَيْهِ 28 v. 14, "He slew him," or "made an end of him;" to command (with أَنْ); to make known or reveal (with acc. and إِلَى of pers.); to judge (with بِ); to judge between (with بَيْنَ of persons and بِ or فِي). قَاضٍ part. act. One who decrees, determines, judges, etc.; يَا لَيْتَهَا كَانَتِ ٱلْقَاضِيَةَ 69 v. 27, "Oh! would to God that it (death) had made an end of me." مَقْضِيٌّ part. pass. Decreed, D. S. Gr. T. 1, p. 330.

قَطَّ aor. o. *To cut.* قِطٌّ A judge's sentence.

قَطَرَ aor. o. *To drop.* قِطْرٌ Molten brass. أَقْطَارٌ plur. of قُطْرٌ A side, a tract of earth or heaven. قَطِرَانٌ Liquid pitch.

قَطَعَ aor. a. To cut asunder, cut down (a tree), cut off; to pass or traverse as at 9 v. 122; تَقْطَعُونَ ٱلسَّبِيلَ 29 v. 28, "Ye infest the highway," or "commit highway robbery;" at 22 v. 15 it is understood by some to mean "Let him hang himself," or "let him hang himself, and then cut (the rope);" the passage is rather obscure, but the idea seems to be, Let him resort to any means however extravagant. قِطْعٌ A part; according to some the first watch of the night. قِطَعٌ A part of the night, the darkness of the night towards morning; also plur. of قِطْعَةٌ A part or portion. قَاطِعٌ part. act. One who decides, as at 27 v. 32. مَقْطُوعٌ part. pass. Cut off.—قَطَّعَ II. To cut off, cut in pieces, divide, disperse separately; وَتُقَطِّعُوا أَرْحَامَكُمْ 47 v. 24, "And would ye sever the ties of relationship?" to cut out (clothes), as at 22 v. 20.—تَقَطَّعَ V. To be cut up into pieces, divided asunder; تَقَطَّعَ بَيْنَكُمْ 6 v. 94, "A schism has been made between you," or "ye have been cut off from one another;" For the impersonal use of verbs see D. S. Gr. T. 2, p. 245.

قَطَفَ aor. i. *To gather the vintage.* قُطُوفٌ plur. of قِطْفٌ A bunch of grapes.

قِطْمِيرٌ The thin skin which envelops a date-stone.

قَعَدَ aor. o. *To sit,* sit upon, sit still, remain quiet at home; it is sometimes used in a manner similar to those verbs which are styled by grammarians أَخَوَاتُ كَانَ and may then be rendered to become; instances occur at 17 vv. 23 and 31; D. S. Gr. T. 1, p. 121, *note;* to beset (with بِ), as at 7 v. 84; to set snares for (with لِ); thus at 7 v. 15, لَأَقْعُدَنَّ لَهُمْ صِرَاطَكَ ٱلْمُسْتَقِيمَ "Verily I will set snares—or lie in ambush—for them (in) thy straight way;" the word صِرَاطَكَ is here put in the accus. as being a ظَرْف or adverbial expression embodying the idea of place; it stands for عَلَى صِرَاطِكَ or فِى D. S. Gr. T. 2, p. 393, *note;* a similar passage is found at 9 v. 5. قُعُودٌ n.a. The act of sitting still, see قَاعِدٌ. قَعِيدٌ comm. gend. and number, Sitting. قَاعِدٌ Plur. قُعُودٌ part. act. One who sits still or remains at home; Fem. Plur. قَوَاعِدُ (2nd declension) Foundations, women who are past child-bearing. مَقْعَدٌ n.a. Plur. مَقَاعِدُ (2nd declension) The act of sitting still or remaining at home, a seat or place of sitting down, a station, encampment, as at 3 v. 117.

قَعَرَ aor. a. *To descend.*—مُنْقَعِرٌ part. act. VII. f. That which is torn up by the roots.

قَفَلَ aor. i. and o. *To return from a journey.* أَقْفَالٌ plur. of قُفْلٌ A lock.

قَفَا aor. o. To follow.—قَفَّى II. To cause to follow or succeed (with بِ of pers. and عَلَى).

قَلَّ aor. i. *To be few,* to be little. قَلِيلٌ Few, little, small. أَقَلُّ (2nd declension) comp. form, Fewer, poorer.—قَلَّلَ II. To make few, cause to appear few, as at 8 v. 46.—أَقَلَّ IV. To bear, carry.

قَلَبَ aor. i. To turn, return (with إِلَى). قَلْبٌ n.a. Plur. قُلُوبٌ A heart.—قَلَّبَ II. To cause to turn, turn upside down, upset; يُقَلِّبُ كَفَّيْهِ 18 v. 40, "He turned his hands upside down," or with the backs to his belly, a sign of grief; to turn about; يُقَلِّبُ ٱللّٰهُ ٱللَّيْلَ وَٱلنَّهَارَ 24 v. 44, "God maketh the night and the day to take turns, or succeed each other in turns."—تَقَلَّبَ V. To be turned about, changed. تَقَلُّبٌ n.a. The act of turning about, a vicissitude of fortune, whether good or bad; at 16 v. 48 it means employment in business, and at 26 v. 219 it may either be translated behaviour or going to and fro, or it may refer to the various postures assumed by the Moslems when at prayers. مُتَقَلَّبٌ Time or place where any one is busily employed, as in journeying to and fro, etc.—إِنْقَلَبَ VII. To be turned about, troubled, to turn one's-self or return back (with or without إِلَى); to be overthrown or turned back, as at 3 v. 122; to be turned from the true faith, in which sense it may be taken at 2 v. 138, as well as in other places, where the words يَنْقَلِبُ عَلَى عَقِبَيْهِ occur; أَىَّ مُنْقَلَبٍ يَنْقَلِبُونَ 26 v. 228, "What turn their affairs shall take," meaning "what shall be their future state;" *Literally,* "By what kind of a return they shall return (to God)." مُنْقَلِبٌ part. act. One who returns. مُنْقَلَبٌ part. pass. That which is exchanged; at 26 v. 228 it must be considered as a noun of time and place, D. S. Gr. T. 1, p. 305.

قَلَدَ aor. i. *To collect (water, etc.).* قَلَائِدُ (2nd declension) plur. of قِلَادَةٌ An ornament of the neck, wreath or garland. مَقَالِيدُ (2nd declension) plur. of مِقْلَادٌ A key.

قَلَعَ aor. a. *To remove, extract.*—أَقْلَعَ IV. To desist.

قَلَمَ aor. i. *To pare (the nails, etc.).* قَلَمٌ Plur. أَقْلَامٌ A pen; a headless arrow used in casting lots.

قَلَى aor. i. *To fry;* to hate. قَالٍ part. act. One who abhors (with لِ).

قَمَحَ *To raise the head and refuse to drink (a camel).*—مُقْمَحٌ part. pass. IV. f. One whose head is forced up so that he cannot see.

قَمَرَ aor. o. and i. *To game with dice;* and قَمِرَ aor. a. *To be white.* قَمَرٌ n.a. The moon (especially from the 3rd to the 26th day).

تَمَصَ aor. i. and o. *To canter or bound.* قَمِيصٌ A shirt; Fr. *Chemise.*

قَمْطَرَ quadriliteral, *To tie up the neck of a leather bottle.* قَمْطَرِيرٌ Calamitous (day).

قَمَعَ aor. a. *To goad (an elephant) on the head.* مَقَامِعُ (2nd declension) plur. of مِقْمَعَةٌ A mace.

قَمِلَ *To be lousy.* قُمَّلٌ generic noun, Lice.

قَنَتَ aor. o. To be devout, obedient to God (with لِ). قَانِتٌ part. act. One who is obedient to God, devout, constant in prayer.

قَنَطَ *To hinder;* and قَنِطَ aor. a. To despair (with مِنْ). قُنُوطٌ n.a. Despair. قَانِطٌ part. act. One who despairs.

قَنْطَرَ quadriliteral, *To leave the country and inhabit a town.* قِنْطَارٌ Plur. قَنَاطِيرُ (2nd declension) A talent, 1200 ounces of gold. مُقَنْطَرٌ part. pass. Counted by talents; the expression وَٱلْقَنَاطِيرِ ٱلْمُقَنْطَرَةِ 3 v. 12 is equivalent to "Heaps of talents."

قَنَعَ aor. a. *To beg;* and قَنِعَ aor. a. *To be content.* قَانِعٌ part. act. One who asks humbly, also one who is content.—مُقْنِعٌ part. act. IV. f. One who lifts up the head.

قَنَا aor. o. *To get, acquire.* قِنْوَانٌ plur. of قِنًا A cluster of dates.

قَنَى aor. i. *To acquire.*—أَقْنَى IV. To cause to acquire, to make contented.

قَهَرَ aor. a. *To overcome,* oppress. ٱلْقَهَّارُ The Omnipotent, the Victorious God. قَاهِرٌ part. act. One who subdues (used with فَوْقَ); ٱلْقَاهِرُ The Conqueror, a name of God.

قُوا plur. imperat. of وَقَى q.v.

قَابَ aor. o. *To dig.* قَابٌ A space, distance.

قَاتَ aor. o. *To nourish.* أَقْوَاتٌ plur. of قُوتٌ Nourishment.—مُقِيتٌ part. act. IV. f. Watchful, a guardian.

قَاسَ aor. o. *To compare by measurement.* قَوْسَيْنِ oblique dual of قَوْسٌ comm. gend. A bow.

قَاعَ aor. o. *To cover (a female).* قَاعٌ Plur. قِيعَةٌ A level plain.

قَالَ aor. o. To say, speak (with لِ); instances not unfrequently occur where this word is altogether omitted; for example at 39 v. 4, where قَالُوا is understood before the words مَا نَعْبُدُهُمْ; and again at the commencement of the 15th verse of the 25th chapter, where we must understand يُقَالُ لَهُمْ; this ellipse is generally indicated by the conjunction أَنْ, D. S. Gr. T. 1, p. 568, and T. 2, p. 468; see also أَنْ. قَوْلٌ n.a. A saying, speech, that which is pronounced, a sentence, a word; Plur. أَقْوَالٌ, Plur. of Plur. أَقَاوِيلُ (2nd declension). قِيلٌ A word, saying, pronouncing, speech, discourse, conversation; at 43 v. 88 if we read وَقِيلِهِ "And the saying (of the prophet)," it must be considered as the complement to the antecedent عِلْمُ in the 85th verse. قَآئِلٌ part. act. A speaker, see also قَالَ for قِيلَ.—تَقَوَّلَ V. To fabricate falsely, counterfeit (with acc. and عَلَى of pers.).

قَامَ aor. o. To stand, stand fast or firm, stand still, stand up—to prayer (with إِلَى and فِى, or عَلَى of place); to come (with مِنْ of place); يَوْمَ يَقُومُ ٱلْحِسَابُ 14 v. 42, "On the day when their account shall stand good, or when the reckoning shall come;" to stand before (with لِ); لِيَقُومَ ٱلنَّاسُ بِٱلْقِسْطِ 57 v. 25, "That men should be righteous in their dealings," used also with لِ of pers., as at 4 v. 126. قَوْمٌ n.a. A people. قَيِّمٌ or قِيَمٌ Right, true; at 98 v. 4 we may understand the word ٱلْمِلَّةِ Religion, before ٱلْقَيِّمَةِ. قَآئِمٌ part. act. Standing, firm, upright, certain to come, as at 18 v. 34. قَوَّامٌ Right, eqnity. قِيَامٌ plnr. of قَوِيمٌ Standing npright, erect; قِيَامٌ is also a noun of action, at 4 v. 4 it may be rendered a means of support, and at 5 v. 98 an asylum. قَوَّامٌ One who has a high standing, superior to, firm, upright, as كُونُوا قَوَّامِينَ بِٱلْقِسْطِ شُهَدَآءَ لِلّٰهِ 4 v.134, "Observe strict integrity when bearing witness before God." ٱلْقَيُّومُ The Self-subsisting (God). ٱلْقِيَامَةُ The Resurrection. أَقْوَمُ (2nd declension) comp. form, More or most right; at 17 v. 9 there is an ellipse, the sentence if completed would stand thus يَهْدِى لِلطَّرِيقَةِ ٱلَّتِى هِىَ أَقْوَمُ ٱلطُّرُقِ; for the syntax of adjectives of this form see D. S. Gr. T. 2, p. 301 *et seq.*; أَقْوَمُ قِيلًا *Lit.* "More correct in pronnnciation," or "more suitable for distinct pronunciation." مَقَامٌ Time or place of standing, stationary abode; state or dignity, in which sense it may be applied at 55 v. 46, and elsewhere; it may also mean God's trihnnal; مَقَامَهُمَا 5 v. 106, "In their place."—تَقْوِيمٌ n.a. II. f. Symmetry. —أَقَامَ IV. To cause to stand upright; to observe or continue in (with acc.), as أَقَامَ ٱلصَّلَوٰةَ 2 v. 172, "He is constant at prayer;" To set straight, institute or appoint (with acc. and لِ); فَلَا نُقِيمُ لَهُمْ يَوْمَ ٱلْقِيَامَةِ وَزْنًا 18 v. 105, "And we will allow them (their works) no weight on the day of resurrection." وَأَقِيمُوا ٱلشَّهَادَةَ لِلّٰهِ 65 v. 2, "And offer straightforward evidence before God." إِقَامٌ for إِقَامَةٌ D. S. Gr. T. 1, p. 294, n.a. The act of being constant (in prayer); يَوْمَ إِقَامَتِكُمْ 16 v. 82, "On the day of your halting, or pitching your tents." مُقَامٌ and مُقَامَةٌ Time or place of abode, station; دَارُ ٱلْمُقَامَةِ 35 v. 32, "The mansion of eternal abode." مُقِيمٌ part. act. One who observes religious rites, constant, lasting, permanent; وَإِنَّهَا لَبِسَبِيلٍ مُقِيمٍ 15 v. 76, "And verily they serve to confirm men in the right way;" the construction of the passage is rather involved, but the meaning seems pretty clear; ٱلْمُقِيمِى ٱلصَّلَوٰةِ "Those who are constant in prayer;" for the constrnction see D. S. Gr. T. 2, p. 183. —إِسْتَقَامَ X. To act nprightly (with إِلَى of pers.); walk uprightly in the paths of religion (with عَلَى). مُسْتَقِيمٌ part. act. Right, righteons, upright, well constituted.

قَوِىَ *To excel in strength*; and قَوِىَ aor. a. *To be strong.* قُوَّةٌ Plnr. قُوًى Power, strength, vigonr, resolution, firmness, force, determination to observe a law. قَوِىٌّ Strong, powerful.—مُقْوٍ for مُقْوِىٌ part. act. IV. f. One who inhabits a desert.

قَاضَ aor. i. *To break the shell (a chicken).*—قَيَّضَ II. To prepare or destine for any one (with acc. and لِ of pers.).

قَالَ aor. i. *To take a siesta at noon.* قَائِلٌ part. act. One who sleeps at mid-day. مَقِيلٌ Place of repose at noon.

ك

كَ Fem. كِ affixed pronoun of the second person singular, meaning thee when affixed to verbs and prepositions, and thy when affixed to nonns.—كَ is also a particle prefixed to nouns, and to other particles, and meaning as, like; it is considered as a preposition, and governs nouns in the genitive; when prefixed to the noun مَثَلٌ the latter is redundant; Example, كَمَثَلِ حَبَّةٍ 2 v. 263, "Like the resemblance of a grain," D. S. Gr. T. 1, p. 473.

كَأْسٌ fem. A cup; no verbal root.

كَأَيِّنْ How many (with مِنْ); this word is regarded by grammarians as an indeclinable noun; D. S. Gr. T. 1, p. 454.

كَبَّ aor. o. *To invert*, throw face downwards (with فِي).—مُكِبٌّ part. act. IV. f. Grovelling (with عَلَى of face).

كَبَتَ aor. i. To throw prostrate, expose to ignominy.

كَبَدَ aor. i. and o. *To injure any one in the liver.* كَبَدٌ Trouble, misery.

كَبَرَ aor. o. *To be older than another;* كَبِرَ aor. a. *To be aged;* and كَبُرَ aor. o. To be great; to be a weighty or grievous matter (with عَلَى or عِنْدَ of pers.); كَبُرَ مَقْتًا 40 v. 37, "It is grievously odious;" the subject of the verb is here said to be كَذٰلِكَ meaning مِثْلُ ذٰلِكَ ٱلْجِدَالِ; كَبُرَتْ كَلِمَةً 18 v. 4, "How odious a word;" كَبُرَتْ is here used as a verb of blame, D. S. Gr. T. 2, p. 225, *note;* خَلْقًا مِمَّا يَكْبُرُ فِي صُدُورِكُمْ 17 v. 53, "Created matter of that kind which in your opinions it is most hard (to raise to life);" To attain majority. كِبْرٌ Greatness, pride; وَٱلَّذِي تَوَلَّى كِبْرَهُ 24 v. 11, "He who hath taken in hand to magnify it." كِبَرٌ n.a. of كَبِرَ Old age. كَبِيرٌ Plur. كُبَرَآءُ (2nd declension) Great, grand, large, aged, grievous; إِنَّهُ لَكَبِيرُكُمْ 20 v. 74, "Verily he is your chief, or your master;" كَبِيرُهُمْ "The biggest or the eldest of them." كَبَآئِرُ (2nd declension) plur. of كَبِيرَةٌ A grievous sin. كُبَّارٌ Of great magnitude. أَكْبَرُ Plur. أَكَابِرُ (2nd declension) comp. form, Greater, more grievous, etc., greatest; Fem. كُبْرَى (2nd declension), Fem. Plur. كُبَرٌ; إِنَّهَا لَإِحْدَى ٱلْكُبَرِ 74 v. 38, "Verily it is one of the greatest (calamities);" ٱلْبَلَايَا plur. of بَلِيَّةٌ being understood. كِبْرِيَآءُ (2nd declension) Greatness, glory.—كَبَّرَ II. To magnify (God) by saying ٱللّٰهُ أَكْبَرُ. تَكْبِيرٌ n.a. The act of magnifying God by saying ٱللّٰهُ أَكْبَرُ.—أَكْبَرَ IV. To extol.—تَكَبَّرَ V. To act insolently (with فِي of place). مُتَكَبِّرٌ part. act. One who is haughty and arrogant. ٱلْمُتَكَبِّرُ The Self-exalting, a name of God.—إِسْتَكْبَرَ X. To be puffed up with pride, to behave with insolence (with فِي of place); at 38 v. 76 أَسْتَكْبَرْتَ is for أَأَسْتَكْبَرْتَ D. S. Gr. T. 1, p. 71; to reject with insolence (with عَنْ). إِسْتِكْبَارٌ n.a. Arrogance. مُسْتَكْبِرٌ part. act. One who is proud and haughty.

كَبْكَبَ To throw down headlong (with فِي), rt. كَبَّ q.v.

كَتَبَ aor. o. To write, write down, transcribe; to prescribe, command, ordain or decree in writing (with acc. and لِ or عَلَى of pers. and also with أَنْ); Ex. وَكَتَبْنَا عَلَيْهِمْ فِيهَا أَنَّ 5 v. 49, "And we wrote for them therein a command that, etc.;" to inscribe (with acc. and فِي); at 52 v. 41, and 68 v. 47 the sense requires that we understand the words "from the preserved table of God's decrees." كَاتِبٌ part. act. A writer or scribe. كِتَابٌ n.a. Plur. كُتُبٌ A book, writing, Scripture, written revelation, decree, letter; at 2 v. 236 it may be translated "the prescribed period;" كِتَابٌ مُبِينٌ is a name given to the preserved tablet of God's decrees, from which the Ḳorân is said to have been copied; these words are generally found without the definite article, in order to enhance by a certain vagueness our ideas of its magnificence—"Omne ignotum pro magnifico!" أَلْكِتَابُ The Holy Scriptures, the Ḳorân, also the book in which a record is kept of all men's actions, and an extract from which, each one shall have placed in his hand at the last day, 17 v. 14; أَهْلُ ٱلْكِتَابِ The Jews and Christians. كِتَابِيَةٌ for كِتَابِى, see حِسَابِيَةٌ. مَكْتُوبٌ part. pass. Written down.—كَاتَبَ III. To give a slave a contract of freedom on payment of a certain sum (with acc.).—إِكْتَتَبَ VIII. To cause to be written.

كَتَمَ aor. o. To conceal, hide (with double acc.); to keep back (evidence).

كَثَبَ aor. o. and i. *To collect into one place.* كَثِيبٌ A heap of sand.

كَثَرَ *To be superior to in point of numbers;* and كَثُرَ aor. o. To be much, many, numerous. كَثْرَةٌ Multitude, abundance. كَوْثَرٌ Abundance, and especially of good things; name of a river in Paradise; this word is variously expounded. كَثِيرٌ Much, many, numerous. أَكْثَرُ (2nd declension) comp. form, More, most, more abundant, the greater number.—كَثَّرَ II. To multiply.—أَكْثَرَ IV. To multiply, as فَأَكْثَرْتَ جِدَالَنَا 11 v. 34, "And thou hast multiplied disputes with us."—تَكَاثُرٌ n.a. VI. f. The act of multiplying.—إِسْتَكْثَرَ X. To wish for much, make great use of (with مِنْ of thing).

كَدَحَ aor. a. *To study or labour after anything.* كَدْحٌ n.a. The act of labouring after anything. كَادِحٌ part. act. One who labours after (with إِلَى).

كَدَرَ aor. o. *To be muddy.*—إِنْكَدَرَ VII. To shoot downwards (the stars).

كَدَا aor. a. (apparently for كَدَأَ) *To be hard;* and كَدَى aor. i. *To be niggardly.*—أَكْدَى IV. To be niggardly.

كَذَبَ aor. i. To lie, lie to, falsely invent (with acc.); to tell lies about or against (with عَلَى). كُذِبُوا pass. "They were the victims of falsehood." كَذِبٌ n.a. A lie; used also as an adjective, lying, false, as بِدَمٍ كَذِبٍ 12 v. 18, "With false blood," D. S. Gr. T. 2, p. 280. كَاذِبٌ part. act. Lying, a liar; at 56 v. 2 كَاذِبَةٌ agrees with نَفْسٌ understood. كَذَّابٌ One given to lying, a great liar. كِذَّابٌ n.a. A falsehood. مَكْذُوبٌ part. pass. *Belied;* غَيْرُ مَكْذُوبٍ Infallible.—كَذَّبَ II. To accuse of falsehood or imposture, falsely deny (with acc. or with بِ); frequently used without any object being expressed; thus at 6 v. 149 where we may understand ٱلرُّسُلَ as the complement of the verb, D. S. Gr. T. 2, p. 454; بِمَا كَذَّبُونِ for كَذَّبُونِى 23 v. 26, "In respect of their having accused me of falsehood," D. S. Gr. T. 2, p. 497; At chapter 55 the word تُكَذِّبَانِ "Do ye both falsely deny," which occurs so frequently, is addressed to men and genii, the two species of rational beings who are mentioned in the 13th and 14th verses. تَكْذِيبٌ n.a. The act of imputing falsehood. مُكَذِّبٌ part. act. One who falsely denies, or accuses of falsehood or imposture.

كَرَّ aor. a. *To return.* كَرَّةٌ A return, a turn of luck; كَرَّتَيْنِ 67 v. 4, Two other times, twice again.

كَرَبَ *To twist a rope, grieve.* كَرْبٌ n.a. Grief, distress.

كَرْسٌ *A shed or stable for goats;* no verbal root. كُرْسِيٌّ A throne.

كَرُمَ aor. o. *To be superior to another in generosity.* كَرِيمٌ Plur. كِرَامٌ Honourahle, noble, generous, kind, heneficent, gracious, munificent, agreeable, as at 56 v. 43; كِرَامًا 25 v. 72, "Courteonsly." أَكْرَمُ (2nd declension) comp. form, Most beneficent, most honourable.—كَرَّمَ II. To honour. مُكَرَّمٌ part. pass. Honoured.—أَكْرَمَ IV. To honour, make honourable. إِكْرَامٌ n.a. Honour. مُكْرِمٌ part. act. One who honours. مُكْرَمٌ part. pass. Honoured.

كَرِهَ aor. a. To detest, dislike, be averse from (with acc.). كَرْهٌ and كُرْهٌ ns.a. Repngnance, a tronhle, something disagreeable; كَرْهًا Against one's will; كُرْهًا 46 v. 14, "With pain and grief." كَارِهٌ part. act. One who dislikes or is averse from anything. مَكْرُوهٌ part. pass. Abominated, hateful.—كَرَّهَ II. To render hateful (with acc. and إِلَى of pers.).—أَكْرَهَ IV. To compel one to do a thing against his will (with acc. of pers. and عَلَى of thing, also with acc. of pers. and حَتَّى). إِكْرَاهٌ n.a. Compulsion.

كَسَبَ aor. i. To gain, acquire, seek after, gather (riches); in the Ḳorân it is frequently used in reference to the provision which a man has laid np against a futnre life, be it good or bad; in this sense it may often be translated to do or commit; مَا كَسَبَتْ قُلُوبُكُمْ 2 v. 225, *Lit.* "What yonr hearts have gained," meaning "what yonr hearts have assented to."—إِكْتَسَبَ VIII. To seek after, seek to gain; there seems to he bnt little difference in the Ḳorân between the 1st and the 8th forms; the latter like كَسَبَ may occasionally require to be rendered to deserve; بِغَيْرِ مَا ٱكْتَسَبُوا 33 v. 58, "Without their having been guilty of anything to deserve such treatment."

كَسَدَ aor. o. *To fail in finding customers.* كَسَادٌ n.a. A want of pnrchasers; the act of remaining nnsold.

كَسَفَ aor. i. *To cut up (cloth).* كِسْفٌ A segment, a piece cnt off. كِسَفٌ plnr. of كِسْفَةٌ A piece or segment; كِسَفًا adverhially, In pieces.

كَسِلَ aor. a. *To be lazy.* كُسَالَى plur. of كَسْلَانٌ Lazy, sluggish.

كَسَا aor. o. To clothe (with double acc.). كِسْوَةٌ Clothing.

كَشَطَ To remove, take off—a cover.

كَشَفَ aor. i. To nncover, lay bare, remove, take off (with acc. and عَنْ); يَوْمَ يُكْشَفُ عَنْ سَاقٍ 68 v. 42, "On a certain day a leg shall be made bare;" a phrase expressive of very great calamity; it is left vague and indeterminate to increase the feeling of awe; the idea is taken from a woman who tncks up her garments in flight. كَشْفٌ n.a. The act of removing, etc. كَاشِفٌ part. act. One who removes, takes off, or reveals; at 58 v. 58 كَاشِفَةٌ agrees with نَفْسٌ, and كَاشِفَاتُ at 39 v. 39 with آلِهَتُكُمْ understood.

كَظَمَ aor. i. *To abstain from chewing the cud (a camel).* كَاظِمٌ part. act. One who restrains, obstrncts or chokes. كَظِيمٌ Grieving inwardly and in silence. مَكْظُومٌ part. pass. Oppressed with silent sorrow.

كَعَبَ aor. o. and i. *To have swelling breasts (a girl).* ٱلْكَعْبَانِ dual of كَعْبٌ The ankle-joint. كَعْبَةٌ A die, a bnilding in form of a Cube, and hence the Ka'ba or sqnare temple at Mecca. كَوَاعِبُ (2nd declension) plnr. of كَاعِبٌ part. act. A damsel with swelling hreasts; D. S. Gr. T. I, p. 343, *note.*

كَفَّ aor. o. *To hem a garment*, to withhold, restrain, keep back (with acc. and عَنْ). كَفٌّ n.a. fem. A hand. كَافَّةً The whole; كَافَّةً Altogether, wholly, entirely, universally; قَاتِلُوا ٱلْمُشْرِكِينَ كَافَّةً 9 v. 36, "War with the idolaters throughout the whole of them."

كَفَأَ aor. a. *To turn back* (transitive). كُفُوٌ Like, equal.

كَفَتَ aor. i. *To gather together*. كِفَاتٌ A place where things are gathered together.

كَفَرَ aor. i. *To cover*; aor. o. To deny—the Grace or the existence of God,—to be ungrateful, impious or an unbeliever, to disbelieve (with بِ). كُفْرٌ and كُفُورٌ ns.a. Infidelity, disbelief, ingratitude. كُفْرَانٌ n.a. Denial. كَافِرٌ part. act. One who denies or is ungrateful for benefits received, an unbeliever, infidel; Plurals كُفَّارٌ كَافِرُونَ and كَفَرَةٌ; at 57 v. 19 ٱلْكُفَّارُ may be translated "Husbandmen," as those who cover over the seed; Fem. Plur. كَوَافِرُ (2nd declension). كَفُورٌ An ungrateful, disbelieving person. كَفَّارٌ Very ungrateful or unbelieving. كَفَّارَةٌ An atonement, an expiation, or that which is given as an expiation. كَافُورٌ Camphor.—كَفَّرَ II. To cover over, expiate (with acc. of crime, and عَنْ of pers.).—أَكْفَرَ IV. To make one an unbeliever.

كَفَلَ aor. o. To nourish, take care of, bring up for another (with acc. and لِ). كِفْلٌ A portion, a like part; ذُو ٱلْكِفْلِ Dhúl-kefl, a name assigned by commentators to a variety of individuals, as Elijah, Joshua, Zachariah, etc. According to some the name was given to Elijah on account of his long-continued fasting, that being one of the meanings of the verb كَفَلَ; or because he is said to have maintained a number of his countrymen who fled to him for protection; a tradition probably founded upon the story of Obadiah in the Old Testament. كَفِيلٌ A sponsor, surety, bail.—كَفَّلَ II. same as كَفَلَ.—أَكْفَلَ IV. To make one answerable, as أَكْفِلْنِيهَا 38 v. 22, "Make me responsible for her, or commit her into my care."

كَفَى aor. i. To be enough, to suffice; as كَفَى بِٱللّٰهِ شَهِيدًا 13 v. 43, "God is sufficient as a witness," see بِ; for the substitution of the preposition and genitive for the nominative case, see D. S. Gr. T. 2, p. 55; كَفَى is also used with a double accusative, as وَكَفَى ٱللّٰهُ ٱلْمُؤْمِنِينَ ٱلْقِتَالَ 33 v. 25, "And God was a sufficient (protector) to the true believers in battle;" similar instances are found at 2 v. 131 and 15 v. 95; another usage is with بِ and أَنَّ, thus أَوَلَمْ يَكْفِ بِرَبِّكَ أَنَّهُ 41 v. 53, "Is it not enough that thy Lord is, etc.;" or with acc. and أَنْ, as أَلَنْ يَكْفِيَكُمْ أَنْ 3 v. 120, "Is it not enough for you that, etc." كَافٍ for كَافِيٌ part. act. One who is sufficient for; أَلَيْسَ ٱللّٰهُ بِكَافٍ عَبْدَهُ 39 v. 37, "Is not God a sufficient (protector of) his servant?" for the construction see D. S. Gr. T. 2, p. 182.

كَلَّ aor. i. *To be weary*. كَلٌّ n.a. A heavy burthen, also a domestic servant who is maintained by his master. كَلَّا By no means; known by grammarians as a particle of reprimand or repulsion, in the latter sense it may be rendered "Out upon him or them," and although by some it has been interpreted occasionally to mean certainly or assuredly, others have in these instances supposed an ellipse; D. S. Gr. T. 1, p. 534, *note*. كُلٌّ a noun substantive meaning totality or universality; it is always used with a complement either expressed or understood, D. S. Gr. T. 2, p. 145, and is then to be translated All, the whole, each, every one; when the complement is understood it takes the tanween and governs alike the sing. and plur., thus كُلٌّ يَجْرِى لِأَجَلٍ مُسَمًّى 13 v. 2, "Each (one) runs to an appointed goal;" again وَكُلٌّ كَانُوا ظَالِمِينَ for كُلُّهُمْ 8 v. 56, "And they were all (of them) unrighteous." كُلَّمَا As often as, how often soever; for its employment with the Preterite see D. S. Gr. T. 1, p. 185, and with the Aorist T. 2, p. 33. كِلَا masc. and كِلْتَا fem. Both, each of the two; these words are never used without a determinate complement, as كِلَاهُمَا 17 v. 24, "Both of them;" and كِلْتَا ٱلْجَنَّتَيْنِ 18 v. 31, "Each of the two gardens," D. S. Gr. T. 2, pp. 155 and 243. كَلَالَةٌ Kindred, a distant relative.

كَلَأَ aor. a. To keep safe.

كَلَبَ aor. o. *To sew a leathern thong into a bag;* and aor. i. *To imitate the barking of dogs.* كَلْبٌ A dog.—مُكَلِّبٌ One who trains dogs or other animals to hunt. N.B. The verb is not found in the ii. f.

كَلَحَ aor. a. *To put on a sour or austere look.* كَالِحٌ part. act. One who grins and shows his teeth.

كَلِفَ aor. a. *To be engrossed by an object.*—كَلَّفَ II. To compel a person to do anything difficult, or above his strength (with double acc.); In the Korân we invariably find this verb used with لَا and إِلَّا; at 4 v. 86, if we read لَا تُكَلِّفُ we must understand نَفْسٌ as the nominative, "No soul shall be compelled (to fight) except thine own soul," but there are other readings. —مُتَكَلِّفٌ part. act. V. f. A troublesome meddler, or a specious pretender.

كَلَمَ aor. i. *To wound.* كَلَامٌ A word; بِكَلَامِى 7 v. 141, "By my speaking to thee." كَلِمَةٌ Plur. كَلِمَاتٌ and كَلِمٌ A word, a decree; كَلِمَةُ ٱلْعَذَابِ 39 v. 20, "The sentence of punishment;" at 3 v. 57 the words إِلَى كَلِمَةٍ سَوَآءٍ may be translated "To a like or equal determination;" The Word of God, Jesus Christ, who is said by the Moslems to be so named, because he was conceived from the word of God alone without Father; at 35 v. 11 and elsewhere كَلِمٌ is used in the sing. as though it were a collective noun, thus إِلَيْهِ يَصْعَدُ ٱلْكَلِمُ ٱلطَّيِّبُ "To him ascends the good word."—كَلَّمَ II. To speak to or with (with acc.). تَكْلِيمٌ n.a. The act of speaking to.—تَكَلَّمَ V. To utter a word, speak of (with بِ).

كُلِى imperat. fem. of أَكَلَ q.v.

كَمْ interrogative conjunctive particle, *How much,* how many, followed by مِنْ with the genitive; How long a time, followed by the verb, or the verb and the acc. as كَمْ لَبِثْتُمْ . . . عَدَدَ سِنِينَ 23 v. 114, "What number of years have ye remained?"

كُمْ affixed masc. pronoun of the 2nd pers. plur. You, your; Dual كُمَا. *Note.* Each of the Arab pronouns is considered an indeclinable noun; D. S. Gr. T. 1, p. 455.

كَمَّ aor. o. *To cover.* أَكْمَامٌ plur. of كِمٌّ The sheath or spathe in which the flowers of the Date-Palm are enveloped, a bud.

كَمَلَ aor. o. *To be whole, perfect.* كَامِلٌ part. act. Whole, complete.—أَكْمَلَ IV. To perfect (with acc. of thing and لِ of pers.); to fulfil, complete.

كَمِهَ aor. a. *To be blind from birth.* أَكْمَهُ (2nd declension) D. S. Gr. T. 1, p. 403, Blind from birth.

كَنَّ *To cover.* أَكْنَانٌ and أَكِنَّةٌ plurs. of كِنٌّ A covering of any kind, as a veil, shelter, etc. أَكِنَّةٌ is also the plur. of كِنَانٌ Idem. مَكْنُونٌ part. pass. Covered over, hidden, close kept.—أَكَنَّ IV. To hide (with acc. and فِي).

كَنَدَ *To cut, to be ungrateful.* كَنُودٌ n.a. comm. gender, Ungrateful.

كَنَزَ aor. i. *To bury (a treasure) beneath the earth;* to treasure up (with acc. and لِ). كَنْزٌ n.a. Plur. كُنُوزٌ A treasure.

كَنَسَ aor. i. *To lie in a covert (a deer).* كَانِسٌ part. act. *That which hides itself;* Plur. كُنَّسٌ A name applied to the stars, and especially to those planets which, from their proximity to the sun, occasionally hide themselves in his rays.

كَهْفٌ A cave, cavern; no verbal root.

كَهَلَ *To be of mature age, from* 30 *to* 50. كَهْلٌ One of full age, from 30 to 50 years old.

كَهَنَ aor. a. and o. *To prophesy, to be a soothsayer.* كَاهِنٌ part. act. A soothsayer.

كَهَيْئَةِ see هَآءٌ for هَيْأَ.

كهيعص Initial letters of the 19th chapter, see آلم.

كَوَاعِبُ plur. of كَاعِبٌ, see كَعَبَ.

كَابَ aor. o. *To drink out of a* كُوبٌ. كُوبٌ Plur. أَكْوَابٌ A goblet without spout or handle, a cup.

كَادَ for كَوِدَ aor. a; كِدْتُ or كِدْتَ 2nd pers. sing. pret. for كَوِدْتَ; D. S. Gr. T. 1, p. 242, *To impede;* to be just on the point of, to want but little of, as يَكَادُ ٱلْبَرْقُ يَخْطَفُ أَبْصَارَهُمْ 2 v. 19, "The lightning all but took away their sight;" when used with a negative, the negation applies to the verb which follows كَادَ, thus وَمَا كَادُوا يَفْعَلُونَ 2 v. 66, "And they wanted but little of not doing it;" وَلَا يَكَادُ يُبِينُ 43 v. 52, *Lit.* "And he wants but little of not articulating," or "he can hardly articulate clearly;" D. S. Gr. T. 2, p. 213.

كَارَ aor. o. *To twist up a turban.*—كَوَّرَ II. To cause to intertwine, or make one thing lap over another (with acc. and عَلَى); this seems to be the literal meaning of the word at 39 v. 7; at 81 v. 1 it may be translated "It is folded up," as a garment that is laid away; a parallel passage is found in St. Paul's Epistle to the Hebrews ch. 1 v. 12, where the Apostle in translating the 102nd Psalm uses the word ἑλίξεις, "Thou shalt roll or fold them up." تَكْوِيرٌ n.a. The act of folding up.

كَوْكَبَ *To shine brilliantly (iron).* كَوْكَبٌ Plur. كَوَاكِبُ (2nd declension) A star.

كَانَ aor. o. To be, become, happen, exist; for its influence on the formation of various tenses see D. S. Gr. T. 1, p. 160 *et seq.* كَانَ governs its attribute in the acc., Ex. كَانَ ٱلنَّاسُ أُمَّةً وَاحِدَةً 2 v. 209, "Mankind were one people or sect;" with the preposition لِ it signifies to have, *mihi est,* possess; قَدْ كَانَ لَكُمْ آيَةٌ 3 v. 11, "Ye have already had a miracle;" to have in one's power, as مَا كَانَ لَهُمْ أَنْ يَدْخُلُوهَا 2 v. 108, "They cannot enter them;" also to be fit and proper, as مَا كَانَ لِبَشَرٍ أَنْ 3 v. 73, "It is not fitting for a man that;" كُنَّ 3rd pers. plur. fem. pret. for كُنَّ; يَكُ, تَكُ, أَكُ, and نَكُ, for يَكُنْ etc. aorist conditional; وَلَيَكُونًا 12 v. 32 for وَلَيَكُونَنْ energetic form of aorist, "And verily he shall be." مَكَانٌ A place; مَكَانَكُمْ 10 v. 29, "(Remain in) your places;" Beidâwee explains the acc. in this place by an ellipse of the verb إِلْزَمُوا "Remain in," which governs the acc.; another explanation is given by De Sacy, Gr. T. I, p. 502. مَكَانَةٌ A place, purpose, intention; عَلَى مَكَانَتِكُمْ 6 v. 135, "According to your ability."—إِسْتَكَانَ X. To humiliate one's-self; اَسْتَكَانُوا 3 v. 140 is thought by some to be the viii. f. of سَكَنَ q.v. and with the above meaning, the ا being due to a poetic license known as إِشْبَاعٌ or Saturation; D. S. Gr. T. 2, p. 497.

كَوَى aor. i. To cauterize.

كَيْ So that. كَيْلَا Lest. لِكَيْلَا So that not; particles governing the subjunctive, D. S. Gr. T. 1, p. 202.

كَادَ aor. i. To contrive a stratagem for (with لِ of pers.); to plot against (with acc. of pers. or with لِ); كِيدُونِ for كِيدُونِي 7 v. 194, "Devise a plot against me," D. S. Gr. T. 2, p. 497. For كِدتُّ 17 v. 76 and 37 v. 54 see كَادَ for كَوِدَ. كَيْدٌ n.a. A plot, stratagem, fraud, trick, cunning, contrivance. مَكِيدٌ part. pass. Plotted against.

كَافَ aor. i. *To cut.* كَيْفَ How? in what way? D. S. Gr. T. 1, pp. 185 and 205, and T. 2, p. 33.

كَالَ aor. i. To measure, measure out to any one (with acc. of pers.). كَيْلٌ n.a. A measuring out, a measure or quantity; كَيْلَ بَعِيرٍ 12 v. 65, "A camel's load." مِكْيَالٌ The vessel in which things are measured.—إِكْتَالَ VIII. To receive by measure from (with عَلَى of pers.).

ل

لَ a prefixed affirmative particle, Verily, surely, certainly; when prefixed to the article اَلْ the latter loses its اَ, thus وَإِنَّهُ لَلْحَقُّ for لَاَلْحَقُّ 2 v. 144, "Verily it is the truth." For the divers applications of لَ and the names it bears in consequence see D. S. Gr. T. 1, p. 504, see also لِ.

لِ a prefixed preposition which denotes both the genitive and dative cases, meaning To, for, unto, on account of, in order to, belonging to, see كَانَ; As عَلَى expresses the condition of a debtor, so does لِ that of a creditor, thus لِي عَلَيْهِ He owes me; thus also فَلَهُ مَا سَلَفَ 2 v. 276, "What is past shall be credited to him," *i.e.* he shall be pardoned; يُغْفَرْ لَهُ, see 8. v. 39; when prefixed to the aorist conditional it gives it the force of an Imperative, as وَعَلَيْهِ فَلْيَتَوَكَّلِ الْمُتَوَكِّلُونَ 12 v. 67, "And on him let those who trust repose their confidence." *Note.* When immediately following وَ and فَ لِ is generally written with a jezm لْ, and with a fatha لَ when preceding any of the affixed pronouns, as لَكَ, لَنَا, لَهُ, etc., the affix of the first person singular is an exception to this rule, لِي being written with a kesra; Like لَ when preceding the article اَلْ it causes the latter to drop its اَ, as لِلرَّبِّ for لِاَلرَّبِّ "To the Lord;" It is frequently used as a conjunction with an ellipse of أَنْ and then means so that, in order that; D. S. Gr. T. 1, p. 477.

لَا Not, no; when followed by the aorist conditional it serves as a negative Imperative, thus لَا تُؤَاخِذْنَا 2 v. 286, "Do not punish us;" When used to deny the existence of a thing (equivalent to لَيْسَ) it generally governs the accus. which then loses its tanween, as in the words لَا إِلَهَ إِلَّا ٱللَّهُ "There is no Deity but God;" for the exceptions to this rule see D. S. Gr. T. 2, p. 63 *et seq.*; لَا is sometimes redundant or pleonastic; see 35 v. 20; so also when commencing a form of oath; Examples of this occur at 56 v. 74 and at 75 vv. 1 and 2, where the words لَا أُقْسِمُ must be translated "I swear;" on the other hand an ellipse of the negative is to be observed at 12 v. 85, see فَتَأَ and أَلَّا for أَلُو; D. S. Gr. T. 1, pp. 167 and 516, also T. 2, pp. 413, 482, 490, and 563. وَلَا, Neither, nor.

لَأَحْتَنِكَنَّ see حَنَكَ.

لَأَعْنَتَكُمْ see عَنِتَ.

لَأَكَ *To send;* this verb is not found in the primitive form. مَلْأَكٌ spelt also مَلَكٌ, Plur. مَلَائِكَةٌ An angel, see also مَلَكٌ.

لَأْلَأَ *To glitter, shine.* لُؤْلُؤٌ generic noun, Pearls, large pearls.

لَبَّ aor. o. *To remain in a place.* أَلْبَابٌ plur. of لُبٌّ The heart, understanding, intellect.

لَبِثَ aor. a. To delay, tarry, sojourn (with فِي or with أَنْ of following verb). لَابِثٌ part. act. One who tarries.—تَلَبَّثَ V. To tarry, remain in a place (with بِ).

لَبَدَ aor. o. *To remain in a place.* لُبَدٌ Much (wealth). لِبَدٌ plur. of لِبْدَةٌ *That which is close packed like a lion's mane,* and hence A dense crowd.

لَبَسَ aor. i. To cover, cloak, obscure (with acc. and بِ); to mystify (with double acc.); to render a thing obscure and confused to another (with acc. of thing and عَلَى of pers.); this appears to be the true meaning of the word at 6 v. 9, وَلَلَبَسْنَا عَلَيْهِمْ مَا يَلْبِسُونَ "And we would certainly have obscured for them that which they themselves rendered obscure or confused," viz. The Angelic Glory, or the Heavenly Mission. لَبْسٌ n.a. Confusion. لَبِسَ aor. a. To wear, put on, be clothed in. لِبَاسٌ A garment, clothing; لِبَاسُ ٱلْجُوعِ 16 v. 113, "The extreme of hunger;" a hunger which closes them in on every side like a vesture. لَبُوسٌ A coat of mail.

لَبَنَ aor. i. and o. *To eat much;* and لَبِنَ *To abound in milk.* لَبَنٌ n.a. Milk.

لَجَّ aor. a. and i. *To be obstinately litigious,* to persist obstinately (with فِي). لُجَّةٌ A great body of water. لُجِّيٌّ Vast and deep (sea).

لَجَأَ aor. a. *To flee to.* مَلْجَأٌ n.a. A place of refuge.

لَحَدَ aor. a. *To make a receptacle for a corpse in the side of a tomb.*—أَلْحَدَ IV. To deviate from that which is lawful and right, to put to a perverted use, act profanely towards (with فِي); at 16 v. 105 it may be rendered "They wickedly incline towards" (with إِلَى). إِلْحَادٌ n.a. Profanity.—مُلْتَحَدٌ noun of place VIII. f. A place of refuge; D. S. Gr. T. 1, p. 305.

لَحَفَ aor. a. *To cover with a cloak.*—إِلْحَافٌ n.a. IV. f. Importunity.

لَحِقَ aor. a. To overtake, reach, attain unto (with بِ).—أَلْحَقَ IV. To join to or unite with another (with acc. and بِ of pers.).

لَحَمَ aor. o. *To establish firmly;* and aor. a. *To feed with flesh.* لَحْمٌ n.a. Plur. لُحُومٌ Flesh.

لَحَنَ aor. a. *To incline towards any one.* لَحْنٌ n.a. A vicious pronunciation.

لَحَى aor. a. D. S. Gr. T. 1, p. 250, *To bark a tree.* لِحْيَةٌ The beard.

لَدَّ aor. o. *To hold an altercation with any one.* لُدٌّ plur. of أَلَدُّ for أَلْدَدُ (2nd declension) Very contentious, fond of quarrelling.

لَدُنَ *To be soft and tender.* لَدُنْ although properly a noun, is always employed as a preposition, At, near, with; مِنْ لَدُنْ From before, from the presence of, from; D. S. Gr. T. 2, p. 154.

لَدَى and لَدَا Prepositions said by De Sacy to be only different forms of لَدُنْ q.v.; their meaning is the same, but whereas لَدُنْ in the Korân is always found preceded by مِنْ, with لَدَا and لَدَى this is not the case.

لَذَّ aor. a. To find agreeable, take pleasure in. لَذَّةٌ Pleasure, delight.

لَزَبَ aor. o. *To stick closely.* لَازِبٌ part. act. Adhesive.

لَزِمَ aor. a. *To be assiduous, stick close to.*—لِزَامٌ n.a. III. f. Death, the day of Judgment, as ensuing of necessity; at 20 v. 129, and at 25 v. 77, we have instances of the noun of action used adjectively لِزَامًا for لَازِمًا, D. S. Gr. T. 2, p. 280; It may also be translated an abiding punishment.—أَلْزَمَ IV. To affix firmly (with double acc.); to compel one to do a thing, as أَنُلْزِمُكُمُوهَا 11 v. 30, "Do we compel you to (accept) it?"

لَسَنَ aor. o. *To seize one by the tongue.* لِسَانٌ comm. gend. Plur. أَلْسِنَةٌ A tongue, language, speech; لِسَانَ صِدْقٍ عَلِيًّا 19 v. 51, *Lit.* "A lofty tongue of truth," *i.e.* "High and truthful praise;" a similar expression is found at 26 v. 84.

لَطَفَ aor. o. *To draw near;* and لَطُفَ aor. o. *To be thin, fine.* لَطِيفٌ Gracious, kind, sharp-sighted, acute, one who understands mysteries; اَللَّطِيفُ A name of God.—تَلَطَّفَ V. To act with courtesy and gentleness; at 18 v. 18 it would seem to mean With cleverness, see لَطِيفٌ.

لَظِيَ aor. a. *To blaze.* لَظَى fem. (2nd declension) Hell-fire; This word appears to be of the second declension as being a proper name and of the feminine gender, otherwise the ى being radical it would have been written لَظًى, indeed the noun of action of the verb is so written, see D. S. Gr. T. 1, p. 404; or it may be, that coming at the end of a verse at 70 v. 15 it is put by poetic license for لَظًى.—تَلَظَّى V. To blaze fiercely.

لَعَبَ aor. a. *To slaver, as an infant;* and لَعِبَ aor. a. To play, sport, trifle (with فِي). لَعِبٌ n.a. Playing, play, sport. لَاعِبٌ part. act. Sporting, one who jests.

لَعَلَّ Perhaps, one of those particles which are said by grammarians to resemble verbs; like أَنَّ it governs the noun following in the accus.; it is frequently used with the affixed pronouns, as لَعَلِّي, لَعَلَّكَ Perhaps I, perhaps thou, etc.

لَا see لَا.

لَعَنَ aor. a. *To drive away,* curse. لَعْنٌ n.a. and لَعْنَةٌ A curse. لَاعِنٌ part. act. One who curses. مَلْعُونٌ part. pass. Accursed.

لَعَنِتُّمْ see عَنِتَ.

لَغَبَ aor. a. and o. *To be greatly fatigued.* لُغُوبٌ n.a. Weariness.

لَغَا aor. o. *To speak;* and لَغِيَ aor. a. To use vain words. لَغْوٌ n.a. Vain discourse, a trifling word or inconsiderate language. لَاغِيَةٌ Vain or obscene (discourse).

لَفَّ aor. o. *To be thick and entangled (trees).* أَلْفَافٌ Trees thickly planted and with interlacing boughs. لَفِيفٌ A mingled crowd.—إِلْتَفَّ VIII. To be joined—one thing to another (with بِ).

لَفَتَ aor. i. *To bend,* turn aside (with acc. and عَنْ).—إِلْتَفَتَ VIII. To turn or look (back).

لَفَحَ aor. a. To burn, scorch.

لَفَظَ aor. i. *To cast forth*, utter.

لَفَا *To diminish.*—أَلْفَى IV. To find.

لَقَبٌ Plur. أَلْقَابٌ A nickname; no verbal root in the primitive form.

لَقَحَ *To impregnate* (*the female Palm-tree*). لَوَاقِحُ (2nd declension) plur. of لَاقِحٌ part. act. That which renders pregnant or fecundates; an epithet applied to the winds, as by their instrumentality the clouds are said to be rendered pregnant with rain, and the female Palm-tree is impregnated with pollen from the male. Shakspeare puts the idea in a somewhat different form.

> "When we have laughed to see the sails conceive,
> And grow big-bellied with the wanton wind."
>
> *Midsummer Night's Dream.*

لَقَطَ *To gather.*—إِلْتَقَطَ VIII. To happen on, light upon, also to pick up.

لَقِفَ aor. a. *To catch up hurriedly;* in the Ḳorân it may be translated to swallow up quickly.

لَقَمَ aor. o. *To obstruct* (*a path*). لُقْمَانُ (2nd declension) Lokmân, an Arab sage, to whom the origin of Æsop's fables is ascribed.—إِلْتَقَمَ VIII. To swallow a mouthful.

لَقِيَ aor. a. To meet, meet with, see; to suffer from, experience (with acc. and مِنْ). لِقَآءٌ n.a. see iii. f. لَاقٍ for لَاقِيٌ part. act. One who meets with. تِلْقَآءٌ n.a. A meeting; تِلْقَآءَ Towards; مِنْ تِلْقَآءِ نَفْسِي 10 v. 16, "Of my own accord."—لَقَّى II. To cast upon, shed over (with double acc.); لَتُلَقَّى ٱلْقُرْآنَ 27 v. 6, "Verily thou art gifted with the Ḳorân," or "it is shed upon thee from above;" D. S. Gr. T. 2, p. 124; a somewhat similar rendering is required at 25 v. 75 and in other places; وَمَا يُلَقَّاهَا 41 v. 35, "And no one shall be granted it," viz. such a disposition; Beiḍâwee supplies the ellipse by the words هَذِهِ ٱلسَّجِيَّةَ.—لَاقَى III. To meet with. لِقَآءٌ n.a. of both 1st and 3rd forms, A meeting, an occurring; the words مِنْ لِقَآئِهِ 32 v. 23 are variously understood; they may refer to the giving of the Law to Moses, the giving the Ḳorân to Moḥammad, or to the meeting between Moses and Moḥammad, fabled to have taken place on the occasion of the famous night journey to the 6th Heaven. مُلَاقٍ for مُلَاقِيٌ part. act. One who meets; أَنَّهُمْ مُلَاقُوا رَبِّهِمْ 2 v. 43, "That they are about to meet their Lord;" مُلَاقُوا is here put for مُلَاقُونَ as being the antecedent to رَبِّهِمْ D. S. Gr. T. 1, p. 416.—أَلْقَى IV. To throw, cast, throw down, send down, shed (with acc. and بِ, بَيْنَ, عَلَى, or فِي, or with acc. and إِلَى of pers.); to cast forth, utter, throw out a suggestion, as at 22 v. 51; to offer, make an offer, as لِمَنْ أَلْقَى إِلَيْكُمُ ٱلسَّلَامَ 4 v. 96, "To him who offers you the salutation;" used also with إِلَى of pers. and بِ of thing, as at 60 v. 1; أَوْ أَلْقَى ٱلسَّمْعَ 50 v. 36, "Or who gives ear;" فَأَلْقِهْ 27 v. 28, "And throw it," for فَأَلْقِهِ D. S. Gr. T. 1, p. 460; The dual أَلْقِيَا at 50 v. 23 is probably addressed to "the driver and the witness" spoken of at v. 20; وَلَا تُلْقُوا بِأَيْدِيكُمْ إِلَى ٱلتَّهْلُكَةِ 2 v. 191, "Neither make your own hands accessory to your destruction;" بِأَيْدِيكُمْ in the passage has the meaning of أَنْفُسَكُمْ, the بِ is superfluous; D. S. Gr. T. 2, p. 55. مُلْقٍ for مُلْقِيٌ part. act. One who throws or sends down.—تَلَقَّى V. To meet; to receive or learn (with acc. and مِنْ); إِذْ تَلَقَّوْنَهُ بِأَلْسِنَتِكُمْ

for تَتَلَقَّوْنَهُ 24 v. 14, "When ye receive it with your tongues (one from another)" by asking questions about it; there are a variety of different readings; إِذْ يَتَلَقَّى ٱلْمُتَلَقِّيَانِ 50 v. 16, *Lit.* "When the two learners learn;" the meaning is said to be, When the two guardian angels note down a man's words or thoughts, I (God) am aware of them beforehand. مُتَلَقِّيَانِ dual part. act. v. *suprà.*—تَلَاقٍ for تَلَاقِيٌ n.a. VI. f. D. S. Gr. T. 1, p. 111, A meeting one with another; at 40 v. 15 يَوْمَ ٱلتَّلَاقِ "The day of Judgment," is for يَوْمَ ٱلتَّلَاقِي, the final ي, not being pronounced before the وَقْف, at the end of the verse, is omitted; D. S. Gr. T. 2, p. 496.—إِلْتَقَى VIII. To meet, meet one another.

لَكِنَ aor. a. *To speak bad Arabic.* لَكِنَّ and لَكِنْ But, still, nevertheless. لَكِنَّ in the same way as إِنَّ and أَنَّ takes the affixed pronouns after it, as لَكِنِّي لَكِنَّهُ But I, but he, etc.; in like manner also it governs the accus. of the noun following; for the exceptions to this rule see D. S. Gr. T. 2, p. 62.

لِلْأَوَّابِينَ see أَوَّابٌ, rt. آبَ for أَوَبَ.

لَمْ Not, and لَمَّا Not yet, when prefixed to the aorist, govern it in the conditional, and generally give it a past signification; De Sacy says they give to the aorist the same value in point of time, as the preterite would have had if the proposition had been affirmative; لَمَّا Not yet seems to be frequently used indifferently for لَمْ; it is evidently composed of لَمْ and مَا, the latter being redundant; For أَوَلَمَّا, أَفَلَمْ, أَلَمْ, etc. see أ; for لَمَّا When v. لَمَّ.

لَمَّ aor. o. *To assemble, collect, to be near.* لَمَّا an adverb meaning When or after that, would appear to be the noun of action لَمٌّ in an adverbial form, it is used when speaking of past events; according to some commentators it is occasionally found in the sense of إِلَّا Except, unless, thus إِنْ كُلُّ نَفْسٍ لَمَّا عَلَيْهَا حَافِظٌ 86 v. 4, where if إِنْ is held to be for إِنَّ and the مَا of لَمَّا to be redundant, the sense will be "Verily every soul has of a surety a Guardian over it;" with this reading لَمَّا would appear to stand for لَ مَا or rather لَمِنْ مَا; according to others, as above mentioned, the construction is the same as if the words were إِنْ كُلُّ نَفْسٍ إِلَّا عَلَيْهَا حَافِظٌ, the particle إِنْ having here a negative meaning, see إِنْ; in the above and in several other instances, such as 11 v. 113, 36 v. 32, and 43 v. 34, it is undecided whether لَمَّا should be spelt with or without the teshdeed, see مَا; it is frequently followed by أَنْ. لَمًّا Altogether, entirely. لَمَمٌ n.a. That which is near; hence Small faults, as being those which are near being sins, without being quite so; the word in this sense may be regarded as a generic noun.

لَمَحَ aor. a. *To give a glance with the eye.* لَمْحٌ n.a. The twinkling of an eye.

لَمَزَ aor. o. and i. *To wink,* defame. لُمَزَةٌ A slanderer.

لَمَسَ aor. o. and i. To feel with the hand, pry into the secrets of.—لَامَسَ III. To touch, have intercourse with, as at 4 v. 46.—إِلْتَمَسَ VIII. To seek for.

لَنْ Not, by no means, governs the aorist in the subjunctive and with a future signification.

لَهِبَ aor. a. *To blaze.* لَهَبٌ Flaming fire. أَبُو لَهَبٍ Aboo Lahab, an uncle of Moḥammad.

لَهَثَ aor. a. To hang out the tongue (a dog).

لَهِمَ aor. a. *To gulp down food.*—أَلْهَمَ IV. To inspire one with (with double acc.).

لَهَا aor. o. *To play.* لَهْوٌ n.a. A plaything, toy, sport, amusement; لَهْوَ ٱلْحَدِيثِ 31 v. 5, "The amusing story," *i.e.* a *certain* amusing story, or the amusing story (with which thou art acquainted). لَاهٍ for لَاهِيٌ D. S. Gr. T. 1, p. 330, part. act. One who sports or jests; لَاهِيَةً قُلُوبُهُمْ 21 v. 3, "Jesting in their hearts;" for the construction see D. S. Gr. T. 2, pp. 79, 197, and 270.— أَلْهَى IV. To occupy, amuse; to divert from (with acc. and عَنْ).— تَلَهَّى V. To be unmindful of, or careless of (with عَنْ).

لَوْ If; for the difference between لَوْ and إِنْ see إِنْ; when immediately followed by a noun the particle أَنْ is interposed as at 7 v. 94, D. S. Gr. T. 1, pp. 161 and 561; With لَوْ at the head of a sentence we have sometimes an ellipse of the correlative proposition called by grammarians جَوَابُ ٱلشَّرْطِ, an instance occurs at 21 v. 40, where the sense may be well rendered in English by a similar ellipse, "If they did *but* know the time," etc. وَلَوْ Although. لَوْلَا Unless, as لَوْلَا رَهْطُكَ لَرَجَمْنَاكَ 11 v. 93, "Had it not (been for) thy family surely we had stoned thee;" in this as in numerous other instances the predicate is understood, indeed this ellipse is customary in all cases where no confusion is likely to arise in consequence; sometimes also there is an ellipse of the correlative proposition, as for example at 24 v. 10, where we may understand the word لَفَضَحَكُمْ "Verily he would have exposed your wickedness;" another instance may be found at 48 v. 25, see وَطِئَ.

لَوْلَا is also used as a particle of instigation or reprimand, being followed in the former case by a verb in the aorist, and in the latter by the preterite; in this sense it is usually translated Will ye not? or have they not? etc. Ex.: لَوْلَا تَسْتَغْفِرُونَ ٱللّٰهَ لَعَلَّكُمْ تُرْحَمُونَ 27 v. 47, "Will ye not ask pardon of God, perhaps ye might be graciously accepted." This and many similar passages could be easily explained by an ellipse, still retaining for لَوْلَا its original meaning of unless; but the grammarians and commentators prefer the analysis above given, D. S. Gr. T. 1, p. 529.

لَاتَ aor. o. *To give a reply which was not called for.* لَاتَ It is not; grammarians are not agreed on the subject of this word, according to some it is an indeclinable verb, whilst others consider it as a kind of feminine form of the adverb لَا; D. S. Gr. T. 1, p. 262.— ٱللَّاتُ (2nd declension) Allât, a female Idol of the Pagan Arabs.

لَاحَ aor. o. *To appear (a star); to cause one to change colour.* لَوْحٌ Plur. أَلْوَاحٌ n.a. A broad table or plank. لَوَّاحٌ verbal adjective of intensity, D. S. Gr. T. 1, p. 322, Darkening the colour (with لِ of pers.).

لَاذَ aor. o. *To seek the protection of.* لِوَاذٌ n.a. The act of flying for shelter.

لَاطَ aor. o. and i. *To be fixed in the affections.* لُوطٌ Lot; proper name.

لُؤْلُؤٌ A pearl, see لَأْلَأَ.

لَامَ aor. o. To blame a person for anything (with acc. of pers. and فِي of thing). لَوْمَةٌ Blame, reproof. لَائِمٌ part. act. One who finds fault. لَوَّامٌ adjective of intensity, D. S. Gr. T. 1, p. 322, One who is constantly blaming others, or accusing himself; the words ٱلنَّفْسِ ٱللَّوَّامَةِ at 75 v. 2 are among other interpretations referred to the soul of Adam. مَلُومٌ D. S. Gr.

T. 1, p. 329, part. pass. Blamed, reprehensible. —مُلِيمٌ part. act. IV. f. Deserving of blame.— تَلَاوَمَ VI. To blame one another.

لَوْنٌ Plur. أَلْوَانٌ Colour, external form, species; no verbal root; مُخْتَلِفًا أَلْوَانُهُ 16 v. 13, "Of different colours;" D. S. Gr. T. 2, pp. 79, 197, and 270.

لَوَى aor. i. To twist, pervert, turn back (with acc. and بِ or عَلَى); يَلْوُونَ أَلْسِنَتَهُمْ بِٱلْكِتَابِ 3 v. 72, "They pervert the Scripture with their tongues;" this word is by some spelt يَلُونَ or يَلْوُونَ. لَيٌّ n.a. The act of twisting or perverting.—لَوَّى II. To turn aside.

لَاتَ aor. i. *To hinder.*—لَيْتَ or يَا لَيْتَ is called by grammarians a particle of desire, and may be rendered I wish, would that, or would to God! it is one of those particles which, like أَنَّ, require the noun following to be in the accus.; it takes the affixed pronouns as لَيْتَنِي etc.; it seems probable that this word is of Hebrew origin; D. S. Gr. T. 1, p. 536, *note.*

لَيْسَ for لَيِسَ It was not, is not; a negative verb used only in the preterite, D. S. Gr. T. 1, p. 262; لَيْسَ is one of those verbs known as أَخَوَاتُ كَانَ or sisters of كَانَ, which govern the attribute in the accusative; D. S. Gr. T. 2, p. 60.

لَيْلٌ comm. gend. generic noun, Night, also the civil day from sunset to sunset; Plur. nom. and gen. لَيَالٍ for لَيَالِيُ and لَيَالِي, acc. لَيَالِيَ By night; D. S. Gr. T. 1, pp. 402 and 410; see also مَثَانٍ, rt. ثَنَى. لَيْلَةٌ noun of unity, A night.

لِئَلَّا Lest, for لِ أَنْ لَا; at 57 v. 29 the لَا of لِئَلَّا is said to be redundant, لِئَلَّا يَعْلَمَ must therefore be translated "That they may know;" D. S. Gr. T. 2, p. 490, *note.*

لَانَ aor. i. To be or become soft; to be mild towards (with لِ). لِينَةٌ A kind of Palm-tree. لَيِّنٌ Soft, gentle.—أَلَانَ IV. To soften (with لِ); أَلَنَّا for أَلْيَنَّا 34 v. 10, "We rendered soft."

م

مَ for مَا q.v.

مَا conjunctive pronoun, That which, which, that, what, whatsoever, as, in such a manner as, as much as, as far as; مَا دُمْتُ 5 v. 117, "As long as I remained;" مَثَلًا مَا 2 v. 24, "A parable of any kind whatsoever;" مَا does not as a rule refer to reasonable beings, but instances to the contrary sometimes occur, thus فَٱنْكِحُوا مَا طَابَ لَكُمْ 4 v. 3, "Then marry such (women) as may be agreeable to you;" it is used in the formula of admiration, فَمَا أَصْبَرَهُمْ 2 v. 170, "How great will be their sufferings;" it is one of those particles which in conditional propositions govern the verb in the conditional mood; when affixed to إِنَّ, أَنَّ, and such like particles, it destroys the effect which they have of putting the noun following them in the accusative; it is frequently a mere expletive, see لَمَّا, when placed between a preposition and its complement it is invariably so, Ex. فَبِمَا رَحْمَةٍ مِنَ ٱللّٰهِ 3 v. 153, "For by the mercy of God;" When used interrogatively after a prefixed preposition the ا is generally omitted, thus بِمَ for بِمَا, عَمَّ for عَنْ مَا, مِمَّ or مِمَّا for مِنْ مَا etc.; For an instance of what is known as مَا مَصْدَرِيَّة see عَنِتَ; For its influence on the temporal value of verbs see D. S. Gr. T. 1, p. 180 *et seq.*, see also p. 537 *et seq.*

مَا is also a negative adverb, Not; in general it denies a circumstance either present, or if past, but little remote from the present; like لَا it governs the attribute in the accus. thus مَا هٰذَا بَشَرًا 12 v. 31, "This is not a man;" for the exceptions to the above rule see D. S. Gr. T. 2, p. 413.

مَآءٌ see مَاءٌ for مَوَهٌ.

مَآبٌ see آبَ for أَوَبَ.

مَاجُوجُ (2nd declension) Magog, a tribe of barbarians from the borders of the Caspian Sea; see Rev. ch. xx. v. 8.

مَآرِبُ see أَرِبَ.

مَارُوتُ (2nd declension) Maroot, name of a rebellious angel, who for his disobedience is said to be suspended by the heels at Babel.

مَاعُونٌ see مَعَنَ.

مَأْوًى see أَوَى.

مَأَى aor. a. *To extend.* مِائَةٌ or مِأَيَةٌ for مِئْيٌ A hundred.

مُتَحَيِّزًا see حَازَ for حَوَزَ.

مُتْرَفٌ see تَرِفَ.

مُتَشَابِهٌ part. act. vi. f. of شَبَّهَ q.v.

مَتَعَ aor. a. *To be advanced* (*the day*). مَتَاعٌ Household stuff, utensils, goods, chattels, provision, convenience; Plur. أَمْتِعَةٌ.—مَتَّعَ II. To suffer to live; to permit one to enjoy (with acc. of pers. and بِ); to bestow freely (with double acc.).—تَمَتَّعَ V. To enjoy, delight one's-self, pass one's time agreeably (with بِ or فِى); فَمَنْ تَمَتَّعَ بِٱلْعُمْرَةِ 2 v. 192, "And he who passes his time in the delights of visiting the temple of Mecca."—إِسْتَمْتَعَ X. To enjoy, derive pleasure or advantage from (with بِ).

مُتَّكَأً see وَكَأَ.

مُتِمٌّ see تَمَّ.

مَتُنَ *To be strong, robust.* مَتِينٌ Strong, powerful.

مَتَا aor. o. *To move quickly.* مَتَى interrogative particle, When?

مُتَوَسِّمٌ see وَسَمَ.

مَثَانِى see ثَنَى.

مَثَلَ aor. o. *To be like.* مِثْلٌ Similitude, likeness, like, similar, equal, as much as, the same as; مِثْلَ ذٰلِكَ In like manner; مِثْلَيْهِمْ 3 v. 11, *Lit.* "Two equivalents of them;" the meaning is that the Idolaters thought the number of their enemies to be twofold that of their own men; so also at v. 159, where مِثْلَيْهَا refers to the advantage obtained by the true believers at Bedr being equal to double their loss at Ohod. مَثَلٌ Plur. أَمْثَالٌ Like, a likeness, equivalent, similitude, comparison, parable, figure of speech; an example as at 43 v. 56; وَلَهُ ٱلْمَثَلُ ٱلْأَعْلَى 30 v. 26, "And His is the most exalted similitude," *i.e.* He is above all comparison; مَثَلًا مَا 2 v. 24, "Any kind of parable;" D. S. Gr. T. 1, p. 539. أَمْثَلُ Fem. مُثْلَى (2nd declension) Most distinguished, thus طَرِيقَتِكُمُ ٱلْمُثْلَى 20 v. 66, "Your most distinguished nobility," see طَرِيقَةٌ. مَثُلَةٌ A punishment to be taken as an example. تَمَاثِيلُ (2nd declension) plur. of تِمْثَالٌ An image, statue.—تَمَثَّلَ V. To seem like to any one (with acc. and لِ of pers.).

مَثْوَاهُ for مَثْوِيَهُ D. S. Gr. T. 1, p. 118, see ثَوَى.

مَجَدَ aor. o. *To excel in glory.* مَجِيدٌ Glorious, glorified.

مَجُوسُ (2nd declension) collective noun of Persian origin, Magi or fire-worshippers.

مَحَصَ aor. a. *To run swiftly (a deer).*—مَحَّصَ II. To prove, try.

مَحَقَ aor. a. To destroy utterly, deprive of blessing, as at 2 v. 277.

مَحَلَ *To inform against any one before the King.* مِحَالٌ n.a. *Fraud*, power.

مُحِلِّى for مُحِلِّينَ see حَلَّ.

مَحَنَ aor. a. *To strike.*—إِمْتَحَنَ VIII. To try; to dispose (with acc. and لِ). مُمْتَحَنٌ part. pass. One who is tried or examined.

مَحَا aor. o. and a. To obliterate, blot out, totally abolish.

مَحْيَا see حَيَّ.

مَحِيصٌ see حَاصَ for حَيَصَ.

مُخْتَالٌ see خَالَ for خَيَلَ.

مَخَرَ aor. a. *To plough the waves.* مَوَاخِرُ (2nd declension) plur. of مَاخِرَةٌ fem. part. act. That which ploughs the waves with a dashing noise.

مَخَضَ aor. a. i. and o. *To churn.* مَخَاضٌ collective noun, The pains of child-birth.

مَدَّ aor. o. To stretch forth, extend, stretch, draw out (with acc. or بِ and لِ of pers. or إِلَى of place); to cause to increase or abound (with acc. of pers. and فِى), as at 2 v. 14. مَدٌّ n.a. The act of extending, etc.; فَلْيَمْدُدْ لَهُ ٱلرَّحْمٰنُ مَدًّا 19 v. 76, "To him let the Merciful grant an extension (of days)." مَدَدٌ An additional help, auxiliary. مِدَادٌ Ink. مُدَّةٌ A space of time, an allotted period. مَمْدُودٌ part. pass. Extended, extensive.—مُمَدَّدٌ part. pass. II. f. Widely extended.—أَمَدَّ IV. To bestow, assist, cause to abound (with acc. of pers. and بِ or مِنْ). مُمِدٌّ part. act. One who assists.

مُدَّثِّرٌ see دَثَرَ.

مَدَنَ *To remain in a place.* مَدِينَةٌ Plur. مَدَآئِنُ (2nd declension) A city, Medina. مَدَنِىٌّ Fem. مَدَنِيَّةٌ Of or belonging to Medina, revealed at Medina. مَدْيَنُ (2nd declension) Midian, name of a city and tribe of Ḥejâz.

مُدْهَامٌّ part. xi. f. of دَهَمَ q.v.

مَدِينٌ see دَانَ for دَيَنَ.

مَرَّ aor. o. To pass by (with عَلَى or بِ); pass on, go (with بِ). مَرٌّ n.a. The act of passing away. مَرَّةٌ One time, turn; أَوَّلَ مَرَّةٍ At first, the first time; فِى كُلِّ مَرَّةٍ 8 v. 58, "On every occasion;" مَرَّةً adverbially, Once; مَرَّتَانِ or مَرَّتَيْنِ Twice, as ٱلطَّلَاقُ مَرَّتَانِ 2 v. 229, "Divorce (is permitted you) twice." مِرَّةٌ *Gall*, understanding, as at 53 v. 6. أَمَرُّ (2nd declension) comp. form, More bitter.—مُسْتَمِرٌّ part. act. X. f. That which is transient, also powerful; either interpretation may be employed at 54 v. 2; at v. 19 it is by some rendered bitter, by others grave or heavy (misfortune).

مَرَأَ aor. a. *To be wholesome (food).* مَرْءٌ n.a. A man. مَرِىءٌ Easy of digestion, wholesome, salutary; مَرِيًّا, مَرِيئًا, مَرِئًا, or With easy digestion. إِمْرُؤٌ Gen. إِمْرِئٍ, Acc. إِمْرَءًا, D. S. Gr. T. 1, p. 398, A man. إِمْرَأَةٌ A woman, a wife; both this and the preceding word are written with Weṣla when not commencing a sentence.

مُرْتَابٌ see رَابَ for رَيَبَ.

مَرَجَ aor. o. *To send (cattle) to pasture*, to let loose.

مَارِجٌ Fire free from smoke. مَرِيجٌ Confused.
مَرْجَانٌ Small pearls; or it may be coral.

مَرِحَ aor. a. To be joyful, elated. مَرَحٌ Insolence; مَرَحًا In a saucy, insolent manner.

مَرَدَ aor. o. *To moisten* (*bread*) *in order to soften it;* to be obstinate (with عَلَى). مَارِدٌ part. act. One who is obstinately rebellious. مَرِيدٌ Obstinate in rebellion.—مُمَرَّدٌ part. pass. II. f. Rendered smooth.

مَرِضَ To be ill. مَرَضٌ n.a. Illness, sickness, disease, infirmity. مَرِيضٌ Plur. مَرْضَى Sick, ill.

مَرْوٌ generic noun, *Flint-stones.* اَلْمَرْوَةُ El Marwa, name of a mountain near Mecca.

مَرَى aor. i. *To press the teats in milking.* مِرْيَةٌ A doubt.—مَارَى III. To dispute with one concerning a thing (with acc. of pers. and عَلَى or فِي of thing). مِرَآءٌ n.a. The act of disputing, a disputation.—تَمَارَى VI. To doubt concerning a thing (with بِ).—إِمْتَرَى VIII. To doubt of (with فِي or بِ of thing). مُمْتَرٍ for مُمْتَرِي part. act. One who doubts.

مَرْيَمُ (2nd declension) Mary.

مَزَجَ aor. a. *To mix.* مِزَاجٌ That which is mixed with wine.

مُزْجَاةٌ see زَجَا.

مُزَخْرِجٌ part. act. of زَخْرَجَ q.v.

مُزْدَجَرٌ part. pass. viii. f. of زَجَرَ q.v.

مَزَقَ aor. i. *To tear.*—مَزَّقَ II. To scatter, disperse, tear in pieces. مُمَزَّقٌ Time or place of scattering, etc.

مُزَّمِّلٌ see زَمَلَ.

مَزَنَ *To go in the same direction as another.* مُزْنٌ Cloud.

مَسَّ aor. a. and o. To touch, befall. مَسٌّ n.a. A touch.—مِسَاسٌ n.a. III. f. Mutual contact; لَا مِسَاسَ 20 v. 97, "Touch me not," D. S. Gr. T. 2, p. 63.—تَمَاسَّ VI. To touch one another.

مُسْتَطِيرٌ part. act. x. f. of طَارَ for طَيَرَ.

مُسْتَوْدَعٌ part. pass. x. f. of وَدَعَ q.v.

مَسَحَ aor. a. To wipe, pass the hand over anything in order to wipe it (with بِ of thing); *to smite with a sword.* مَسْحٌ n.a. The act of smiting with a sword. اَلْمَسِيحُ The Messiah, *Lit.* The Anointed.

مَسَخَ aor. a. To change, transform; لَمَسَخْنَاهُمْ عَلَى مَكَانَتِهِمْ 36 v. 67, "Verily we could have transformed them in their places;" so that they should have remained without power of motion.

مَسَدَ aor. o. *To twist* (*a rope*) *strongly.* مَسَدٌ Twisted fibres of the Palm-tree, coir.

مَسَكَ *To take hold of.* مِسْكٌ comm. gend. Musk.—مَسَّكَ II. To hold fast (with بِ).—أَمْسَكَ IV. To hold, take, catch hold of, hold fast, withhold, keep back, hold up, retain. إِمْسَاكٌ n.a. The act of retaining, etc. مُمْسِكٌ part. act. One who withholds, etc.—إِسْتَمْسَكَ X. To take hold on, hold fast (with بِ). مُسْتَمْسِكٌ part. act. One who holds fast.

مَسَا aor. o. *To wipe out the uterus of a camel, to come in the evening.*—أَمْسَى IV. To be or do anything in the evening, as حِينَ تُمْسُونَ 30 v. 16, "At eventide." *Note.* مَسَا or مَسَى is one of those verbs known as أَخَوَاتُ كَانَ, D. S. Gr. T. 2, p. 60.

مُسَيْطِرٌ see سَطَرَ.

مَشَجَ *To mingle.* أَمْشَاجٌ plur. of مَشِيجٌ Mingled.

مِشْكَاةٌ see شَكَا.

مَشَى aor. i. To walk, go, proceed (with عَلَى or فِي

of place). مَشْىٌ n.a. The act of walking, walk. مَشَّآءٌ One who goes about with lying slanders.

مَصَرَ aor. o. *To milk with the tips of the fingers.* مِصْرُ (1st and 2nd declension) comm. gend. A large city, Egypt, D. S. Gr. T. 1, p. 405.

مُصَيْطِرٌ for مُسَيْطِرٌ see سَطَرَ.

مُضَارٌّ plur. of مُضَارَّةٌ, rt. ضَرَّ q.v.

مَضَغَ aor. a. and o. *To chew.* مُضْغَةٌ A morsel of flesh.

مَضَى aor. i. To pass by, pass away, go away. مُضِيٌّ n.a. The act of going away.

مَطَرَ aor. o. *To rain upon.* مَطَرٌ n.a. Rain.—أَمْطَرَ IV. To cause to rain; وَأَمْطَرْنَا عَلَيْهِمْ مَطَرًا 7 v. 82, "And we rained down upon them a shower (of stones);" see also 11 v. 84. مُمْطِرٌ part. act. That which causes or brings rain.

مُطْمَئِنٌّ see طَمْأَنَ, rt. طَمَنَ.

مَطَا aor. o. *To travel at a quick pace.*—تَمَطَّى V. To walk in a haughty, conceited manner.

مُطَّوِّعٌ see طَاعَ for طَوَعَ.

مَعَ properly an indeclinable noun used as a preposition, With, together or in company with.

مَعَاذَ see عَاذَ for عَوَذَ.

مُعْتَدٍ see عَدَا.

مُعْتَرٌّ and مَعَرَّةٌ, see عَرَّ.

مَعَزَ aor. o. *To separate the goats from the sheep.* مَعْزٌ generic noun, Goats.

مَعَنَ aor. a. *To travel fast and far.* مَاعُونٌ Household stuff, whatever is of common and necessary use, also alms.

مَعًى comm. gend. Plur. أَمْعَآءٌ Intestines; no verbal root.

مَعِينٌ see عَانَ for عَيَنَ.

مُغِيرَاتٌ see غَارَ for غَوَرَ.

مُغْنُونَ plur. of مُغْنٍ see غَنِىَ.

مَفْتُونٌ see فَتَنَ.

مَقَتَ *To hate.* مَقْتٌ n.a. Hatred, anger; at 4 v. 26 it means an odious and abominable thing.

مُقْوٍ for مُقْوِىٌ, see قَوِىَ.

مُقِيتٌ see قَاتَ for قَوَتَ.

مَكَّ *To suck dry.* مَكَّةُ (2nd declension) Mecca. مَكِّىٌّ Fem. مَكِّيَّةٌ Of or belonging to Mecca, revealed at Mecca.

مَكَثَ aor. o. To delay, tarry, abide, remain (with فِى). مُكْثٌ n.a. The act of tarrying, etc.; عَلَى مُكْثٍ 17 v. 107, "Slowly and deliberately." مَاكِثٌ part. act. One who tarries or remains.

مَكَرَ aor. o. To contrive a plot; to plot against (with بِ); to act deceitfully. مَكْرٌ A plot, a deceitful trick, contrivance. مَاكِرٌ part. act. One who lays plots.

مَكُنَ *To hold high rank or authority.* مَكَانٌ see كَانَ. مَكِينٌ Firmly fixed, one whose rank is firmly established.—مَكَّنَ II. To establish firmly, strengthen, give authority to any one (with acc. or لِ of pers. and فِى of place, or with acc. of thing and لِ of pers.); at 18 v. 94 مَكَّنِّى is for مَكَّنَنِى, D. S. Gr. T. 1, p. 458, *note*.—أَمْكَنَ IV. To give power, as فَأَمْكَنَ مِنْهُمْ 8 v. 72, "And he hath given thee power over them;" D. S. Gr. T. 2, p. 454.

مَكَا aor. o. *To whistle.* مُكَآءٌ n.a. Whistling.

مَلَّ *To baste a garment, convert.* مِلَّةٌ A religion, form of worship.—أَمَلَّ IV. To dictate.

مَلَأَ aor. a. To fill, as لَأَمْلَأَنَّ 7 v. 17, "Verily I will fill" (with acc. and مِنْ). مِلْءٌ for مِلْأٌ, D. S. Gr. T. 1, p. 62, A quantity that fills anything, as مِلْءُ الْأَرْضِ 3 v. 85, "The Earth full." مَلَأٌ A band, company, assembly; also chief men, princes, the nobility; اَلْمَلَأُ ٱلْأَعْلَى 38 v. 69, "The exalted Chiefs," *i.e.* the Angels; for the changes which this word undergoes when followed by an affixed pronoun see D. S. Gr. T. 1, pp. 95 and 117. مَالِئُ for مَالِأُ D. S. Gr. T. 1, p. 97, part. act. One who fills.—إِمْتَلَأَ VIII. to be full.

مُلَاقٍ part. act. iii. f. of لَقِيَ q.v.

مَلَائِكَة see أَلَكَ for لَأَكَ.

مَلَحَ aor. a. and i. *To salt.* مِلْحٌ fem. Salt.

مَلَقَ *To wipe out.*—إِمْلَاقٌ n.a. IV. f. Poverty, want.

مَلَكَ aor. i. To possess, have power or dominion over; to be capable of, able to obtain (with acc. of thing and لِ of pers.), as فَمَنْ يَمْلِكُ لَكُمْ مِنَ ٱللّٰهِ شَيْئًا 48 v. 11, "For who hath any power to prevail for you with God?" مَلْكٌ n.a. That which is in any one's power; بِمَلْكِنَا 20 v. 90, "As far as lay in our power." مُلْكٌ Dominion, power, kingdom. مَلَكٌ sing. and plur. An angel, angels; see also أَلَكَ for لَأَكَ. مَلِكٌ One who possesses, a king; Plur. مُلُوكٌ. مَالِكٌ part. act. One who is lord over, a possessor; Mâlec, name of the angel who has charge over Hell. مَلَكُوتٌ Dominion, kingdom. مَلِيكٌ A monarch. مَمْلُوكٌ part. pass. Possessed, owned.

مَلَا aor. o. *To run violently.* مَلِيًّا For a considerable time.—أَمْلَى IV. To prolong one's life, grant a respite (with لِ of pers.); at 47 v. 27 the word may be rendered "he has continued to buoy them up with false hopes;" to dictate (with acc. of thing and عَلَى of pers.).

مِمَّ and مِمَّا for مِنْ مَا.

مَمَات see مَاتَ.

مُمْتَحَنَة see مَحَنَ.

مُمْتَرِين Oblique plur. part. act. viii. f. of مَرَى q.v.

مَمَدّ see مَدَّ.

مِمَّنْ for مِنْ مَنْ.

مَنْ an indeclinable conjunctive pronoun meaning He she or they who, one who, some who, whosoever; also interrogatively Who? In conditional propositions it governs the aorist in the conditional mood, D. S. Gr. T. 2, p. 32; for its influence on the temporal value of verbs see D. S. Gr. T. 1, p. 185, *et seq.*; although generally used to designate reasonable beings, instances may occasionally be noted to the contrary, as for example at 24 v. 44, but in these cases the irrational creatures are to some extent, by a figure of speech, assimilated to reasonable beings; D. S. Gr. T. 2, p. 356. أَمَّنْ and مِمَّنْ for أَمْ مَنْ and مِنْ مَنْ.

مِنْ a preposition signifying origin, composition, explanation, commencement, or separation; in its ordinary acceptation it is equivalent to of, from, or out of; or, when following a comparative, than; but it may occasionally be rendered on, by, by reason of, some or a portion of, of the same kind as, after the manner of, etc. It is frequently employed in negative propositions with the sense of any, as وَمَا مِنْ إِلٰهٍ إِلَّا ٱللّٰهُ 3 v. 55, "Nor is there any Deity but God," or it may be regarded as an expletive, "There is no Deity," D. S. Gr. T. 1, p. 490; مِنْهُمْ 28 v. 5, "At their hands," *i.e.* "At the hands of the Children of Israel;" مِنْ فَوْرِهِمْ 3 v. 121, "Of a sudden," or "on their arrival," see فَوْرٌ; مِنْ خِلَافٍ 5 v. 37, "On opposite sides;" مِنْ وُجْدِكُمْ 65 v. 6, "According to your means;" It is found occasionally with the meaning of عَنْ, thus at 9 v. 38, أَرَضِيتُمْ بِٱلْحَيَوٰةِ ٱلدُّنْيَا مِنَ ٱلْآخِرَةِ "Are ye content with this present life in preference to that which is to come?" فَلَيْسَ مِنَ ٱللّٰهِ فِى شَىْءٍ 3 v. 27, "He has nothing to look to from (the friendship of) God," D. S. Gr. T. 1, p. 492, *note*.

مَنَّ aor. o. *To fatigue;* to be gracious towards (with عَلَى of pers.); to reproach (with عَلَى of pers.), as at 49 v. 17; to be liberal, as وَلَا تَمْنُنْ تَسْتَكْثِرُ 74 v. 6, "And be not liberal in the hope of receiving more;" at 26 v. 21 it is used transitively, to bestow—a favour—on any one (with acc. of thing and عَلَى of pers.). مَنٌّ n.a. The act of reproaching, and especially by reminding any one of benefits conferred; also liberality, as at 47 v. 5, فَإِمَّا مَنًّا بَعْدُ وَإِمَّا فِدَآءً "And either (show) liberality afterwards, or (exact) a ransom." ٱلْمَنُّ Manna. مَنُونٌ Time; رَيْبَ ٱلْمَنُونِ 52 v. 30, "Adverse fortune," by some interpreted to mean Death. مَمْنُونٌ part. pass. Diminished, broken off; أَجْرٌ غَيْرُ مَمْنُونٍ 41 v. 7, "An uninterrupted reward."

مَنَاصٌ see نَاصَ for نَوَصَ.

مُنْتَهَى see نَهَى.

مِنْسَأَةٌ see نَسَأَ.

مُنْشَآتٌ see نَشَأَ.

مَنَعَ aor. a. To refuse; to prohibit, hinder, forbid, prevent (with acc. and أَنْ or أَنْ لَا followed by a verb); to defend as at 21 v. 44 and at 4 v. 140 (with مِنْ); مُنِعَ مِنَّا ٱلْكَيْلُ 12 v. 63, "The measurement (of any corn) is forbidden us." مَانِعٌ part. act. That which defends. مَنُوعٌ One who holds back (his hand), niggardly. مَنَّاعٌ One who hinders or obstructs; مَنَّاعٌ لِلْخَيْرِ 50 v. 24, "One who hinders men from following the right path." مَمْنُوعٌ part. pass. Forbidden.

مُنْفَكِّينَ see فَكَّ.

مِنْهَاجٌ see نَهَجَ.

مَنَى aor. i. *To try.* مَنَاةُ (2nd declension) Manât, an idol worshipped by the Pagan Arabs. مَنِىٌّ Sperma genitale. أُمْنِيَّةٌ Plur. أَمَانِىُّ (2nd declension) A wish, desire; لَا يَعْلَمُونَ ٱلْكِتَابَ إِلَّا أَمَانِىَّ 2 v. 73, "They know not the Scripture, but according to their own vain imaginations or desires;" see next verse, also verse 105.—مَنَّى II. To create desires in any one (with acc. of pers.), thus at 4 v. 118, وَلَأُمَنِّيَنَّهُمْ "And verily I will excite in them vain desires."—أَمْنَى IV. To emit (seed).—تَمَنَّى V. To desire, read; at 22 v. 51 a passage occurs where this word is by some rendered according to the former of these meanings, while others have followed the latter; see Sale's Korân, vol. 2, p. 168, *note;* to long for, covet; at 3 v. 137 تَمَنَّوْنَ is for تَتَمَنَّوْنَ D. S. Gr. T. 1, p. 221.

مَهَدَ aor. a. To spread open a bed; فَلِأَنْفُسِهِمْ يَمْهَدُونَ 30 v. 43, "Verily they shall spread for themselves a couch (in Paradise)." مَهْدٌ n.a. A bed, cradle. مَاهِدٌ part. act. One who spreads a couch. مِهَادٌ A couch, a place of wide extent.—مَهَّدَ II. To make (things) smooth and agreeable. تَمْهِيدٌ n.a. The act of making smooth.

مَهَلَ *To do a thing quietly and gently.* مُهْلٌ Fused brass, the dregs of oil.—مَهَّلَ II. To grant a delay, bear with for a time.—أَمْهَلَ IV. To act quietly and gently towards.

مَهْلِكٌ see هَلَكَ.

مَارَ aor. o. To be moved to and fro. مَوْرٌ n.a. Agitation, fluctuation.

مُورِيَاتُ see وَرَى.

مُوسَى (2nd declension) Moses.

مُوصَدَةٌ see أَصَدَ.

مَوْقُوتٌ see وَقَتَ.

مَوْقُوذَةٌ see وَقَذَ.

مَالَ aor. o. *To be rich, especially in cattle.* مَالٌ Plur. أَمْوَالٌ Riches, wealth, substance, possessions, and especially flocks and herds; مَالِيَهْ 69 v. 28, for مَالِى "My wealth;" the هْ is affixed because followed by a pause, and is hence named هَآءُ ٱلْوَقْفِ D. S. Gr. T. 1, p. 459.

مَوْلًى see وَلِىَ.

مُؤْمِنٌ see أَمِنَ.

مَاهَ aor. a. o. and i. *To be full of water (a well).* مَآءٌ for مَوَهٌ Water, liquor. *Note.* The hamza when followed by an affixed pronoun and moveable by Damma is changed into ؤ, as مَآؤُكُمْ for مَآءُكُمْ D. S. Gr. T. 1, p. 118.

مَوْءُودَةٌ see وَأَدَ.

مَوْئِلٌ see وَأَلَ.

مِيثَاقٌ see وَثِقَ.

مَادَ aor. i. To be moved; أَنْ تَمِيدَ بِكُمْ 16 v. 15, "Lest it should move with you;" for the ellipse of the negative see أَنْ. مَائِدَةٌ A table, *properly*, when set out with food.

مَارَ aor. i. To provide food for.

مَازَ aor. i. To separate, discriminate, distinguish (with acc. and مِنْ).—تَمَيَّزَ V. To burst, as تَكَادُ تَمَيَّزُ مِنَ ٱلْغَيْظِ 67 v. 8, "It will almost burst with fury" (for تَتَمَيَّزُ).—إِمْتَازَ VIII. To be separated; وَٱمْتَازُوا 36 v. 59, "And be ye separated" (from the righteous).

مَهْمَا Whatsoever or whensoever, see D. S. Gr. T. 1, p. 194.

مَهَنَ aor. a. and o. *To serve;* and مَهُنَ *To be despicable.* مَهِينٌ Despicable, contemptible; it may also be derived from هَانَ for هَوَنَ q.v.

مُهَيْمِنٌ see هَيْمَنَ, rt. هَمَّنَ.

مَوَاخِرُ plur. of مَاخِرَةٌ, rt. مَخَرَ q.v.

مَوَاطِنُ see وَطَنَ.

مَوَاقِيتُ plur. of مِيقَاتٌ, see وَقَتَ.

مَوَالِىَ acc. plur. of مَوْلًى, rt. وَلِىَ q.v.

مَوْثِقٌ see وَثِقَ.

مَاتَ for مَوَتَ aor. o. To die; this is the usual form, but others are mentioned by lexicographers, as مَوِتَ or مَيِتَ aor. a. and مَيَتَ aor. i.; instances of the preterite with the first letter kesrated are found in most copies of the Korân, as مِتُّمْ 23 v. 37, and مِتْنَا 23 v. 84; so also we have مِتُّ in the 19th and مِتَّ in the 21st chapter; see D. S. Gr. T. 1, pp. 114 and 242. مَوْتٌ and مَمَاتٌ Death. مَيْتٌ Plur. مَوْتَى أَمْوَاتٌ Dead. مَيِّتٌ Plurs. مَيِّتُونَ and مَيِّتَاتٌ Dead, mortal, about to die. مَوْتَةٌ noun of unity, One single death. مَيْتَةٌ A dead body, that which is dead or dies of itself.—أَمَاتَ IV. To cause to die; أَمَتَّنَا ٱثْنَتَيْنِ 40 v. 11, "Thou hast caused us to die twice," in allusion to the second death which the body is said to undergo after its examination in the sepulchre by the two angels Munkar and Nakeer.

مُؤْتَفِكٌ see أَفَكَ.

مَاجَ aor. o. *To be agitated with waves (the sea);* to press tumultuously like waves (with فِى). مَوْجٌ n.a. A wave, the surge; used also as a collective noun, فِى مَوْجٍ كَٱلْجِبَالِ 11 v. 44, "On waves like mountains."

يَسَرَ see مَيْسَرَةٌ.
وَعَدَ see مِيعَادٌ.
وَقَتَ see مِيقَاتٌ.
مِيكَالُ (2nd declension) Michael the Archangel.
مَالَ aor. i. *To incline*, turn away from, turn aside from the right way (with n.a. in acc.); to turn against (with عَلَى). مَيْلٌ n.a. The act of turning aside. مَيْلَةٌ noun of unity, A single act of turning, as مَيْلَةً وَاحِدَةً 4 v. 103, "At once," *und vice*.

ن

نٓ Initial letter of the 68th chapter, see آلٓمٓ.
نَا an indeclinable affixed pronoun meaning Our when following nouns, and Us when following verbs or prepositions; when affixed to the particles إِنَّ or أَنَّ and written إِنَّنَا or أَنَّا, إِنَّا or أَنَّنَا, although representing an accusative, it must be rendered We, as وَٱشْهَدْ بِأَنَّنَا مُسْلِمُونَ 5 v. 111, "And bear thou witness that we are Moslems," or "resigned unto thee."
نَادَتْ 3rd pers. sing. fem. of نَادَى iii. f. of نَدَا q.v.
نَأَى aor. a. To retire, as وَنَأَى بِجَانِبِهِ 17 v. 85, "And he goes aside;" to go far away (with عَنْ).
نَبَأَ aor. a. *To be exalted, to announce.* نَبَأٌ Plur. أَنْبَآءٌ News, an announcement, message, account or story, a prophecy, as at 6 v. 66. نَبِيٌّ A prophet, Plurs. نَبِيُّونَ and أَنْبِيَآءُ (2nd declension). نُبُوَّةٌ Prophecy.—نَبَّأَ II. To announce, to make acquainted with, declare or relate a circumstance to another (with بِ of thing, or with acc. of pers. and بِ, مِنْ, or عَنْ, also with acc. of pers. and أَنْ).—أَنْبَأَ IV. To make one acquainted with, to inform (with double acc. or with acc. and بِ).—إِسْتَنْبَأَ X. To seek information from (with acc. of pers. and أَ).
نَبَتَ aor. o. *To germinate*, to produce—as a tree—(with بِ). نَبَاتٌ n.a. The germinating or springing up of plants; when used collectively, Plants, that which is produced from the ground; at 3 v. 32 it is figuratively applied to the "fruit of the womb."—أَنْبَتَ IV. To produce, put forth, to cause to grow or spring up (with acc. and فِى, بِ, مِنْ or عَلَى).
نَبَذَ aor. i. To throw (with acc. and بِ or فِى of place); to reject; فَنَبَذْتُهَا 20 v. 96, "And I threw it (into the mouth of the calf)," which thereupon became alive; The handful of dust to which this miraculous power is attributed was supposed to have been taken from the footsteps of the horse ridden by the angel Gabriel; at 8 v. 60 after فَٱنْبِذْ إِلَيْهِمْ we must understand the accus. عَهْدَهُمْ, "Then throw back to them their covenant;" for the ellipse of the accusative or immediate objective complement see D. S. Gr. T. 2, p. 454.—إِنْتَبَذَ VIII. To go aside (with مِنْ).
نَبَزَ aor. i. *To defame.*—تَنَابَزَ VI. To call one another names (with بِ).
نَبَطَ aor. i. and o. *To gush out.*—إِسْتَنْبَطَ X. To elicit or discover (the truth) in matters of difficulty.
نَبَعَ aor. a. i. and o. *To gush forth.* يَنْبُوعٌ Plur. يَنَابِيعُ (2nd declension) A fountain, spring of water.

نَتَقَ aor. o. To shake.

نَثَرَ aor. o. and i. *To disperse.* مَنْثُورٌ part. pass. Scattered.—إِنْتَثَرَ VIII. To be scattered.

نَجَدَ aor. o. *To overcome.* نَجْدٌ n.a. An open highway; at 90 v. 10 it is to be understood of the two highways of good and evil.

نَجِسَ aor. a. *To be dirty and impure.* نَجَسٌ n.a. Filth, uncleanness.

نَجَلَ aor. i. *To throw.* اَلْإِنْجِيلُ (common gender) The Gospel, from the Greek *εὐαγγέλιον*.

نَجَمَ aor. o. *To appear.* نَجْمٌ Plur. نُجُومٌ A star, or collectively, Stars, as at 16 v. 16 and 53 v. 1; a plant growing close to the earth with little or no stalk, as grass.

نَجَا aor. o. To escape, go free (with مِنْ). نَاجٍ part. act. One who escapes. نَجَاةٌ n.a. Salvation. نَجِيٌّ A secret; نَجِيًّا Privately. نَجْوَى n.a. (2nd declension) for نَجْوٌ D. S. Gr. T. 1, pp. 105 and 402, A private conference, clandestine discourse; at 17 v. 50 it appears to be used adverbially وَإِذْ هُمْ نَجْوَى "And when they confer in private;" but Beiḍâwëe inclines to the opinion that this word both here and at 58 v. 8 is a plural of نَجِيٌّ with the sense of مُتَنَاجُونَ, viz. "Those who confer privately together."—نَجَّى II. To deliver, set free (with acc. and مِنْ, إِلَى, or بِ); to raise up, as at 10 v. 92. مُنَجٍّ for مُنَجِّيٌ Plur. مُنَجُّونَ for مُنَجِّيُونَ, D. S. Gr. T. 1, p. 113, part. act. One who delivers.—نَاجَى III. To hold a discourse with any one in private (with acc. of pers.).—أَنْجَى IV. To deliver (with acc. and مِنْ); ثُمَّ يُنْجِيهِ 70 v. 14, "Then (he wishes that this) might deliver him;" the nominative اَلْإِفْتِدَاءُ "This ransom" being understood.—تَنَاجَى VI. To hold a private discourse one with another (with بِ of matter).

نَحَبَ aor. o. *To vow.* نَحْبٌ n.a. A vow, as قَضَى نَحْبَهُ 33 v. 23, "He has fulfilled his vow" by offering up his life for the Faith.

نَحَتَ aor. i. and o. To scrape, carve, prepare by scraping (with double acc. or with acc. and مِنْ).

نَحَرَ aor. a. *To injure the jugular vein,* to sacrifice by cutting the jugular vein.

نَحَسَ aor. a. *To vex;* and نَحِسَ *To be unlucky.* نَحْسٌ Bad luck. نَحِسٌ Unlucky. نُحَاسٌ Smoke without flame, also molten brass, both of which meanings have been assigned at 55 v. 35.

نَحَلَ aor. a. *To make one a present;* and نَحِلَ aor. a. *To be thin.* نَحْلٌ comm. gend. generic noun, Bees. نِحْلَةٌ A free gift, especially one given as dowry.

نَحْنُ personal pronoun of comm. gender used both in the dual and plur. We.

نَخِرَ aor. a. *To be worn full of holes.* نَخِرٌ *Worn,* rotten (a bone).

نَخَلَ *To sift.* نَخْلٌ comm. gend. Plur. نَخِيلٌ generic noun, A date-palm; or collectively, Palm-trees. نَخْلَةٌ noun of unity, A (single) Palm-tree.

نَدَّ aor. i. *To flee, run away.* نِدٌّ Plur. أَنْدَادٌ Like, equal, a match, an image or idol.

نَدِمَ aor. a. *To be repentant, repent.* نَادِمٌ part. act. One who repents, a penitent. نَدَامَةٌ n.a. Repentance.

نَدَا aor. o. *To call.* نَادٍ for نَادِيٌ A council. نَدِيٌّ A council.—نَادَى III. To call to, call upon, invoke, cry aloud; to make a proclamation (with فِى); to call, or invite (with إِلَى or لِ),

as وَإِذَا نَادَيْتُمْ إِلَى ٱلصَّلَوٰةِ 5 v. 63, "And when ye call to prayer;" (also with مِنْ), as يُنَادِى ٱلْمُنَادِى مِنْ مَكَانٍ قَرِيبٍ 50 v. 40, "The crier shall call from a near place;" said to be from Mount Moriah at Jerusalem, whence the angel Gabriel is to make a proclamation to all flesh to come to judgment; the meaning is that it shall be a proclamation to be heard by all; see also 41 v. 44, where the words يُنَادَوْنَ مِنْ مَكَانٍ بَعِيدٍ are interpreted "They shall be (like) those who are called to from afar," *i.e.* They shall not hear. نِدَآءٌ for نِدَاىٌ n.a. A cry, act of calling. مُنَادٍ for مُنَادِىٌ part. act. One who makes a proclamation, a crier, a preacher.—تَنَادَى VI. To call one to another. تَنَادٍ for تَنَادِىٌ for تَنَادُىٌ, D. S. Gr. T. 1, p. 111, n.a. The act of calling one to another; ٱلتَّنَادِ 40 v. 34 is for ٱلتَّنَادِى the ي being omitted by poetic license at the end of the verse to preserve the rhyme.

نَذَرَ aor. o. and i. To vow, devote (with acc. and لِ). نَذْرٌ Plur. نُذُورٌ n.a. A vow. نُذْرٌ or نُذُرٌ A menacing, or warning; نُذُرٌ is also plur. of نَذِيرٌ A warner or preacher.—أَنْذَرَ IV. To warn, admonish, preach to (with acc. of pers. and بِ, or with أَنْ لَا); to threaten with, give warning of (with double acc.). مُنْذِرٌ part. act. A preacher, One who warns, admonishes, or threatens. مُنْذَرٌ part. pass. Warned.

نَزْدَادُ 1st pers. plur. aor. viii. f. of زَادَ for زَيَدَ q.v.

نَزَعَ aor. i. To pluck out, bring out, snatch away, extract, withdraw, or draw out somewhat sharply (with acc. and مِنْ); to strip off (with acc. and عَنْ). نَازِعٌ part. act. One who plucks out, as وَٱلنَّازِعَاتِ غَرْقًا 79 v. 1, "By (the angels) who tear out (the souls of the wicked) with violence." نَزَّاعٌ adjective of intensity, Plucking forcibly or continuously, D. S. Gr. T. 1, p. 322.—نَازَعَ III. To dispute with any one (with acc.).—تَنَازَعَ VI. To dispute one with another (with فِى of matter, or with acc. and بَيْنَ); at 52 v. 23 it is used with acc. of thing and فِى of place, and is there to be interpreted "They shall present to one another."

نَزَغَ aor. a. *To slander*, sow dissensions (with بَيْنَ); to incite to evil, as at 7 v. 199. نَزْغٌ n.a. An evil suggestion, incitement to evil.

نَزَفَ aor. i. *To exhaust* (*a well*); in the Pass. it means to be exhausted or inebriated from drink (with عَنْ).

نَزَلَ aor. i. To descend (with بِ into, or مِنْ from, a place). نُزُلٌ That which is prepared for a guest, entertainment, an abode, a gift. نَزْلَةٌ noun of unity, *Literally*, One descent; نَزْلَةً Once, as رَآهُ نَزْلَةً أُخْرَى 53 v. 13, "He saw him once again." مَنَازِلُ (2nd declension) plur. of مَنْزِلٌ A mansion, station, as of the moon at 10 v. 5 and 36 v. 39.—نَزَّلَ II. To cause to descend, send down, especially from Heaven (with acc. and عَلَى, إِلَى, مِنْ, and بِ). تَنْزِيلٌ n.a. A sending down (from Heaven), a divine revelation, a name given to the Ḳorân as having been sent down from Heaven. مُنَزِّلٌ part. act. One who sends down. مُنَزَّلٌ part. pass. Sent down.—أَنْزَلَ IV. To cause to descend, send down, make to come down (with acc. and مِنْ, عَلَى, إِلَى, لِ, and فِى). مُنْزِلٌ part. act. One who causes to descend, a receiver of guests, one who provides hospitality. مُنْزَلٌ part. pass. Sent down; At 23 v. 30 مُنْزَلًا may be considered as the nonn of time or place of coming down; it is also written مُنْزَلًا v. *suprà;* in the former case it may be rendered "Cause my descent to be blessed;" in the latter, "Make me to inhabit a blessed abode."—تَنَزَّلَ V. To descend gently and gradually (with عَلَى).

نَسَأَ aor. a. *To chide (camels).* نَسِيءٌ The putting off a sacred month till a later month. مِنْسَأَةٌ A staff.

نَسَبَ aor. o. and i. *To make mention of any one's lineage.* نَسَبٌ Plur. أَنْسَابٌ n.a. Consanguinity; at 25 v. 56 the words نَسَبًا وَصِهْرًا must be taken adverbially as though the phrase were ذَا نَسَبٍ وَصِهْرٍ "Capable of consanguinity and affinity;" meaning perhaps male and female.

نَسَخَ aor. a. To abolish, destroy, abrogate, nullify; *to transcribe or copy.* نُسْخَةٌ A copy or exemplar (of a book).—إِسْتَنْسَخَ X. To transcribe or copy out.

نَسَرَ aor. o. and i. *To remove, tear with the beak.* نَسْرٌ n.a. *An eagle or vulture;* Nasr, name of an idol worshipped by the Pagans both before and after the Flood.

نَسَفَ aor. i. To destroy from the foundations, uproot, reduce to powder and scatter abroad, to winnow as chaff. نَسْفٌ n.a. The act of reducing to powder and winnowing, etc.

نَسَكَ aor. o. *To lead a religious life, to sacrifice.* نُسُكٌ n.a. Religious service, a victim for sacrifice. نَاسِكٌ part. act. One who is devoted to religious observances. مَنْسَكٌ A ceremonial. مَنَاسِكُ (2nd declension) plur. of مَنْسِكٌ Places for sacrifice, rites and ceremonies.

نَسَلَ aor. o. *To beget or bring forth (an animal);* aor. i. and o. To hasten (with مِنْ). نَسْلٌ n.a. Progeny, stock; at 2 v. 201 it would seem to be understood of the young of flocks and other domestic animals.

نَسِيَ aor. a. To forget, neglect. نَسْيٌ A forgotten thing. نَسِيٌّ Forgetful. نِسْوَةٌ and نِسَآءٌ Women; The sing. of these words is wanting, but instead of it the word إِمْرَأَةٌ is employed, see مَرَأَ. مَنْسِيٌّ part. pass. Forgotten, neglected, D. S. Gr. T. 1, p. 108.—أَنْسَى IV. To cause to forget (with double acc.); at 2 v. 100 نُنْسِهَا may be taken to signify "We cause it to be forgotten;" there are also other readings.

نَشَأَ aor. a. *To grow, increase, to be raised up.* نَاشِئَةٌ The first hour or early portion of the day or night; various interpretations are given of 73 v. 6 where this word occurs; according to one it is the part. act. and agrees with نَفْسًا understood, "The person who rises by night (to prayer);" others hold it to be a form of the noun of action, and translate it "To rise by night." نَشْأَةٌ Production.—نَشَّأَ II. To bring up, educate (with acc. and فِي).—أَنْشَأَ IV. To produce, raise, create (with acc. and فِي or مِنْ). إِنْشَآءٌ n.a. Production, creation; إِنَّا أَنْشَأْنَاهُنَّ إِنْشَآءً 56 v. 34, "Verily we have created them by a (novel or peculiar) creation." مُنْشِئٌ part. act. One who produces. مُنْشَأَةٌ Plur. مُنْشَآتٌ for مُنْشَأَاتٌ Having lofty sails, or it may be the part. pass. Raised on high (by the waves).

نَشَرَ aor. o. To unfold, spread abroad (with acc. and لِ). نَشْرٌ n.a. A spreading abroad. نُشُورٌ n.a. A bringing to life, resurrection, resuscitation (from sleep), as at 25 v. 49. نَاشِرٌ part. act. One who spreads abroad; the words وَٱلنَّاشِرَاتِ

نَشْرًا 77 v. 3 may refer either to the Angels who spread abroad God's decrees, or to the winds which spread rain over the earth; some again have understood the passage to refer to the verses of the Korân, etc. مَنْشُورٌ part. pass. Spread open.—مُنَشَّرٌ part. pass. II. f. Unfolded, expanded.—أَنْشَرَ IV. To resuscitate (with acc. and بِ); to raise the dead. مُنْشَرٌ part. pass. Raised from the dead.—إِنْتَشَرَ VIII. To be spread abroad, disperse themselves (with فِى). مُنْتَشِرٌ part. act. That which spreads itself abroad.

نَشَزَ aor. o. and i. To rise up, *to behave ill—a woman towards her husband, or a husband towards his wife.* نُشُوزٌ n.a. Ill-conduct or perverseness on the part of a husband or wife towards one another.—أَنْشَزَ IV. To raise.

نَشَطَ aor. i. To go out from a place, *draw up a bucket at one pull.* نَشْطٌ n.a. The act of drawing up quickly and easily. نَاشِطٌ part. act. One who draws up easily; the words وَٱلنَّاشِطَاتِ نَشْطًا which occur at 79 v. 2 are by some referred to the Angels who draw forth the souls of the blessed in a smooth and gentle manner; but as with the commencement of the 77th chapter, the explanations of the whole passage vary greatly, see نَاشِرٌ.

نَصَبَ aor. o. To place, fix, erect, *afflict;* and نَصِبَ aor. a. To use diligence, as at 94 v. 7, فَإِذَا فَرَغْتَ فَٱنْصَبْ "And when thou hast finished (thy relaxation) be instant (in prayer, or in thanks to God)." نُصْبٌ n.a. Calamity. نَصَبٌ n.a. Labour, fatigue. نُصُبٌ Plur. أَنْصَابٌ A standard, as at 70 v. 43; a stone used by the Pagan Arabs on which they made sacrifices, as at 5 v. 4; an idol, image, or statue, as at 5 v. 92. نَصِيبٌ A part, portion. نَاصِبٌ part. act. Labouring, weary.

نَصَتَ aor. i. *To be silent.*—أَنْصَتَ IV. Idem.

نَصَحَ aor. a. To admonish, counsel, give good advice, be sincere and faithful (with لِ of pers.). نُصْحٌ n.a. Counsel, advice. نَاصِحٌ part. act. One who counsels or advises, one who acts as a sincere friend to (with لِ). نَصُوحٌ True and sincere (repentance).

نَصَرَ aor. o. To aid, assist, succour, protect; to deliver (with acc. and مِنْ); وَلَيَنْصُرَنَّ ٱللّٰهُ مَنْ يَنْصُرُهُ 22 v. 41, "And verily God will succour those who aid him," *i.e.* his religion; to grant a victory to (with acc. and عَلَى), thus at 9 v. 14, وَيَنْصُرْكُمْ عَلَيْهِمْ "And he will give you the victory over them." نَصْرٌ n.a. Aid, assistance, victory. نَاصِرٌ part. act. Plurs. نَاصِرُونَ and أَنْصَارٌ One who aids, etc., a protector. نَصِيرٌ Plur. أَنْصَارٌ A helper, defender, protector; the name ٱلْأَنْصَارُ "The helpers or allies," was given as an honorary distinction to those of the inhabitants of Medina who were the first to take part with Moḥammad. نَصَارَى (2nd declension) plur. of نَصْرَانٌ A Christian, so called from نَصْرَانُ Nazareth. نَصْرَانِيٌّ Christian. مَنْصُورٌ part. pass. Aided, assisted.—تَنَاصَرَ VI. To aid one another; at 37 v. 25 تَنَاصَرُونَ is for تَتَنَاصَرُونَ D. S. Gr. T. 1, p. 221.—إِنْتَصَرَ VIII. To avenge one's-self, take vengeance (with مِنْ of pers.); to defend one's-self, deliver one's-self. مُنْتَصِرٌ part. act. One who is able to defend himself.—إِسْتَنْصَرَ X. To ask assistance of any one (with acc. of pers.).

نَصَفَ aor. o. *To reach the middle, or take half of anything.* نِصْفٌ The half.

نَصَا aor. o. *To seize by the forelock.* نَاصِيَةٌ Plnr. نَوَاصِى (2nd declension) A forelock.

نَضِجَ aor. a. *To be ripe,* done enough in cooking.

نَضَخَ aor. a. *To sprinkle with water.* نَضَّاخٌ Pouring forth copiously and continuously.

نَضَدَ aor. i. *To spread (carpets) one over another.* نَضِيدٌ Piled one over another. مَنْضُودٌ part. pass. Spread over one another, piled up in order; وَطَلْحٍ مَنْضُودٍ 56 v. 28, "And the acacia overspread with piles of flowers."

نَضَرَ aor. o. *To endow with brilliancy and beauty, to shine.* نَضْرَةٌ Brightness, refulgence. نَاضِرٌ part. act. Shining.

نَطَحَ aor. a. *To butt at with the horns.* نَطِيحَةٌ That which is gored to death. *Note.* The ة is commonly added to adjectives when changed into nouns substantive by what is called آلنَّقْلُ D. S. Gr. T. 2, p. 279, *note.*

نَطَفَ aor. o. and i. *To drop.* نُطْفَةٌ Sperma genitale.

نَطَقَ aor. i. To speak articulately and clearly, to speak (with عَلَى and بِ), as يَنْطِقُ عَلَيْكُمْ بِٱلْحَقِّ 45 v. 28, "It speaks concerning you with truth;" وَمَا يَنْطِقُ عَنِ ٱلْهَوَى 53 v. 3, "Neither doth he speak of his own will." مَنْطِقٌ n.a. Speech, language, as عُلِّمْنَا مَنْطِقَ ٱلطَّيْرِ 27 v. 16, "We have been taught the language of birds."—أَنْطَقَ IV. To cause to utter articulate sounds.

نَظَرَ aor. o. To look, behold (with إِلَى or فِى); to look on, look at (with acc.); to look for, expect (with acc. or with أَنْ), as at 2 v. 206, 38 v. 14, etc.; to see, consider (sometimes with إِلَى, also with هَل, أَنَّى, or كَيْفَ); عَلَى ٱلْأَرَآئِكِ يَنْظُرُونَ 83 v. 23, "Seated upon couches they shall contemplate (objects of delight);" to wait for (with acc.), as at 57 v. 13; to regard, as وَلَاهُمْ يُنْظَرُونَ 2 v. 157, "They shall not be regarded," or it may be "Neither shall they be waited for," *i.e.* time shall not be given them for repentance. نَظَرٌ n.a. A look. نَاظِرٌ part. act. One who looks at, beholds, observes, or waits for, a spectator. نَظْرَةٌ A single glance. نَظِرَةٌ A respite.—أَنْظَرَ IV. To grant one a respite; to put off, as فَلَا تُنْظِرُونِ Poeticé for تُنْظِرُونِى 7 v. 194, "And do not put me off (by any delay)." مُنْظَرٌ part. pass. Respited.—إِنْتَظَرَ VIII. To expect, wait, await. مُنْتَظِرٌ part. act. One who waits or expects.

نَعَجَ aor. a. and o. *To go quickly (a camel)*; aor. o. *To be very white.* نَعْجَةٌ Plnr. نِعَاجٌ An ewe sheep.

نَعَسَ aor. a. *To be weak, somnolent.* نُعَاسٌ n.a. Drowsiness, sleepiness.

نَعَقَ aor. a. and i. To call aloud to (with بِ); *properly, To call sheep, croak as a raven.*

نَعَلَ aor. a. *To give shoes to any one.* نَعْلٌ fem. A shoe.

نَعِمَ aor. a. o. and i. *To enjoy the comforts and conveniences of life, to be joyful.* نَعَمْ Yea; For the difference between نَعَمْ and بَلَى see بَلَى. نِعْمَ an irregular verb found in the Korân only in the masc. 3rd pers. sing., it is called by grammarians فِعْلُ ٱلْمَدْحِ or verb of praise, its meaning is To be excellent, thus نِعْمَ ٱلْمَوْلَى 8 v. 41, "He is an excellent master;" it may generally be rendered How excellent! as نِعْمَ ٱلثَّوَابُ 18 v. 30, "How excellent a reward!" It is used alike with both sing. and plnr., thus فَنِعْمَ ٱلْمَاهِدُونَ 51 v. 48, *Lit.* "How excellent (are we) who spread it out;" فَلَنِعْمَ ٱلْمُجِيبُونَ 37 v. 73, "Verily how excellent—

or gracions,—were those who answered," *i.e.* "We retnrned a gracious answer." نِعِمًّا for نِعْمَ مَا or نِعِمَ مَا, as نِعِمَّا يَعِظُكُمْ بِهِ 4 v. 61, "How excellent is the admonition which he gives you;" it is also written نِعْمَّا. نَعَمٌ Plnr. أَنْعَامٌ Cattle. نَاعِمٌ part. act. Rejoicing, joyful. نَعْمَةٌ Comfort and convenience of life. نِعْمَةٌ Plur. أَنْعُمٌ Grace, kindness, favonr, heneficence; this word is sometimes spelt نِعْمَتٌ, see D. S. Gr. T. 1, p. 276, *note.* نَعِيمٌ Happiness, delight, pleasure. نَعْمَآءُ (2nd declension) Grace, favour.—نَعَّمَ II. To provide good things for any one (with acc. of pers.).—أَنْعَمَ IV. To be gracious towards (with عَلَى of pers.); to confer (benefits) upon (with acc. and عَلَى of pers.).

نَغَضَ aor. o. and i. *To shake—the head.*—أَنْغَضَ IV. To wag the head at any one (with aco. of رَأْسٌ and إِلَى of pers.).

نَفَثَ aor. i. and o. *To blow.* نَفَّاثٌ One who hlows, as ٱلنَّفَّاثَاتُ فِى ٱلْعُقَدِ 113 v. 4, "The women who hlow on knots," a kind of incantation.

نَفَحَ aor. a. *To diffuse an odour, to blow (the wind).* نَفْحَةٌ One single breath.

نَفَخَ aor. o. To blow with the mouth, hreathe (with فِى). نَفْخَةٌ A single blast.

نَفِدَ aor. a. To vanish, fail, to he exhausted. نَفَادٌ n.a. A failure, failing.

نَفَذَ aor. o. *To penetrate (as an arrow),* to pass beyond or out of (with مِنْ).

نَفَرَ aor. o. and i. *To run away through fright,* to go forth to any hnsiness, as to war, at 9 v. 123 (with فِى). نَفَرٌ People, a company of men not exceeding ten nor less than three. نُفُورٌ n.a. The act of running away, or being a fngitive; in the Ḳorân it means the act of flying from the truth. نَفِيرٌ A company or nnmber of men taking part with any one, as in war.—مُسْتَنْفِرٌ part. act. X. f. One who takes to flight, fugitive.

نَفَسَ *To injure by casting an evil eye upon any one.* نَفْسٌ fem. Plur. أَنْفُسٌ and نُفُوسٌ A soul, a living soul or person; as in Arahic there are no reflective personal pronouns, their place is partly supplied by the words عَيْنٌ, نَفْسٌ, etc., see D. S. Gr. T. 2, p. 286, *et seq.;* in this sense أَنْفُسُهُمْ, نَفْسُهُ and the rest must he translated himself, itself, themselves, etc.; بِغَيْرِ نَفْسٍ 5 v. 35, "Without (his having slain) a soul,"—nnless in case of retaliation or as a pnnishment for mnrder; نَفْسًا when used adverbially, as at 4 v. 3, means willingly, see طِبْنَ, rt. طَابَ for طَيَبَ; مِنْ تِلْقَآءِ نَفْسِى 10 v. 16, "Of my own accord, at my own pleasnre."—تَنَفَّسَ V. To shine (the dawn); وَٱلصُّبْحِ إِذَا تَنَفَّسَ 81 v. 18, "By the dawn when it clears away the darkness hy its hreath."—تَنَافَسَ VI. To long for, aspire after. مُتَنَافِسٌ part. act. One who longs or aspires after.

نَفَشَ aor. o. *To pick or tease wool;* to stray for food hy night (with فِى). مَنْفُوشٌ part. pass. Teased, carded.

نَفَعَ aor. a. To be useful to, to profit; to avail (with عِنْدَ). نَفْعٌ n.a. Use, utility, nsefulness, profit. مَنَافِعُ (2nd declension) plnr. of مَنْفَعَةٌ An advantage, that which is nseful or profitahle.

نَفَقَ *To be saleable;* aor. a. and o. *To come out of its hole (a jerboa).* نَفَقٌ n.a. A hole, *properly,* in a place from whence there is another exit; the word occurs at 6 v. 35, and the meaning of the passage is as follows, "If thou art ahle to seek out for thyself a hole, so that thou mayest enter into the bowels of the earth, etc., and bring them a sign (*then do so*);" the correlative proposition known as the جَوَابُ ٱلشَّرْطِ or answer to the condition being understood; D. S. Gr. T. 2, p. 611. نَفَقَةٌ Expenditure, that which any one expends.—نَافَقَ III. *To enter into its hole, to which there are generally ten or a dozen entrances* (*a jerboa*), and hence, as it is said, to be a hypocrite in religion, professing to believe first one thing and then another. نِفَاقٌ n.a. Hypocrisy. مُنَافِقٌ part. act. One who is a hypocrite in religion.—أَنْفَقَ IV. To spend, expend one's substance (with acc. and فِى or مِنْ, also with عَلَى of pers.); this word is frequently used in the Korân to signify to expend one's substance in alms or other good works, and in this sense the accus. is occasionally understood, as at 2 v. 2. مُنْفِقٌ part. act. One who expends his substance in almsgiving and other good works. إِنْفَاقٌ n.a. The act of spending.

نَفَلَ *To give booty.* نَفَلٌ Plur. أَنْفَالٌ Booty, spoils. نَافِلَةٌ A gift, a work of supererogation, as prayers over and above what are commanded, or a gift over and above what is asked.

نَفَا aor. o. To remove, expel (with مِنْ).

نَقَبَ aor. o. *To dig through* (*a wall*). نَقْبٌ n.a. The act of digging through. نَقِيبٌ A captain or leader.—نَقَّبَ II. To pass or wander through, to search out (with فِى).

نَقَذَ *To liberate.*—أَنْقَذَ IV. To set free, deliver (with acc. and مِنْ), إِسْتَنْقَذَ X. To seek to deliver (with acc. and مِنْ).

نَقَرَ aor. o. *To strike;* Pass. نُقِرَ To be blown (a trumpet). نَقِيرٌ The groove in a date-stone; نَقِيرًا In the smallest matter. نَاقُورٌ A trumpet.

نَقَصَ aor. o. *To be deficient,* to diminish, lessen; to cause a loss or deficiency as at 50 v. 4, مَا تَنْقُصُ ٱلْأَرْضُ مِنْهُمْ "What part of them the earth consumes," viz. their bodies; to fall short, fail or be wanting in anything (with double acc.), as at 9 v. 4. نَقْصٌ n.a. Loss, diminution. مَنْقُوصٌ part. pass. Diminished.

نَقَضَ aor. o. and i. *To make a crashing noise,* to break or violate (a treaty), to untwist, as at 16 v. 94. نَقْضٌ n.a. The act of violating (a covenant).—أَنْقَضَ IV. To wring, as a load from getting loose on the back.

نَقَعَ aor. a. *To soak, raise a sound.* نَقْعٌ n.a. Dust rising and floating in the air.

نَقَمَ *To devour;* aor. i. To dislike, disapprove; وَمَا نَقَمُوا إِلَّا أَنْ أَغْنَاهُمُ ٱللّٰهُ 9 v. 75, "And their only reason for disliking (the plot to destroy Mohammad) was that God had enriched them, etc.;" to reject, take vengeance on (with مِنْ of pers.).—إِنْتَقَمَ VIII. To take vengeance on (with مِنْ of pers.). إِنْتِقَامٌ n.a. Vengeance. مُنْتَقِمٌ part. act. One who takes vengeance, an avenger.

نَكَبَ aor. o. To turn aside (with عَنْ). نَاكِبٌ part. act. One who turns aside. مَنَاكِبُ (2nd declension) plur. of مَنْكِبٌ *A shoulder,* a tract of country.

نَكْتَلْ 1st pers. plur. aor. cond. viii. f. of كَالَ for كَيْل q.v.

نَكَثَ aor. o. and i. *To untwist* (*a rope*), break (a covenant), violate an oath; used both with and without an accusative. نِكْثٌ Plur. أَنْكَاثٌ The untwisted strands of a rope.

نَكَحَ aor. a. and i. *To perforate;* to marry a husband or wife. نِكَاحٌ n.a. Marriage.—أَنْكَحَ IV. To give in marriage (with acc. of pers. given, as at 24 v. 32, also of pers. to whom given, as at 2 v. 220).—إِسْتَنْكَحَ X. To wish to marry.

نَكَدَ aor. o. *To croak with all his might (a raven)*; and نَكِدَ aor. a. *To be wretched and miserable (life)*. نَكِدٌ Niggardly.

نَكِرَ aor. a. *To be ignorant of, to ignore, disavow*, to feel a repugnance towards. نُكْرٌ and نُكُرٌ Iniquitous, horrible, unknown, unheard of, as at 18 v. 86. نَكِيرٌ Denial, reprobation, change; كَيْفَ كَانَ نَكِيرِ 22 v. 43, "How great was the change which I made in their condition;" نَكِيرِ is here put Poeticè for نَكِيرِي D. S. Gr. T. 2, p. 497. أَنْكَرُ (2nd declension) comp. form, Most disagreeable.—نَكَّرَ II. To transform (a thing) so that it cannot be recognized (with acc. and لِ of pers.).—أَنْكَرَ IV. *To be ignorant of*, deny. مُنْكِرٌ part. act. One who knows not, disavows, or denies. مُنْكَرٌ part. pass. Unknown, disallowed, unwarrantable, unlawful, the opposite to مَعْرُوفٌ, see 3 v. 100; denial, as at 22 v. 71.

نَكَسَ aor. o. To turn down or upside down, as نُكِسُوا عَلَى رُؤُوسِهِمْ 21 v. 66, *Lit.* "They were turned upside down upon their heads," meaning that they relapsed into idolatry. نَاكِسٌ part. act. One who bends down.—نَكَّسَ II. To cause one to bend or bow down.

نَكَصَ aor. i. To fall back, retreat, as نَكَصَ عَلَى عَقِبَيْهِ 8 v. 50, *Lit.* "He retreated upon his two heels."

نَكَفَ aor. o. *To endure a shower of rain to the end, to wipe tears from off the face.*—إِسْتَنْكَفَ X. To disdain (with أَنْ or عَنْ).

نَكَلَ aor. o. and i. *To retire*; and نَكِلَ *To take example.* نِكْلٌ Plur. أَنْكَالٌ A fetter. نَكَالٌ An example, a punishment.—تَنْكِيلٌ n.a. II. f. The act of punishing or making an example.

نَمَّ aor. o. and i. *To spread calumnies.* نَمِيمٌ Calumny, slander.

نَمَارِقُ (2nd declension) plur. of نُمْرُقٌ A cushion, *prop.* a pad placed upon a saddle; no verbal root.

نَمَلَ aor. o. *To malign.* نَمْلٌ generic noun, Ants. نَمْلَةٌ noun of unity, A single ant. أَنَامِلُ (2nd declension) plur. of أَنْمُلَةٌ The tips of the fingers.

نَهَجَ aor. a. *To point out the way.* مِنْهَاجٌ A clear and open way.

نَهَرَ aor. a. *To cause (a stream) to flow*, to repulse, reproach. أَنْهَارٌ plur. of نَهْرٌ A river. نَهَرٌ A river. نَهَارٌ A day from dawn or from sunrise till sunset as opposed to night.

نَهَى aor. a. D. S. Gr. T. 1, p. 250, To forbid, interdict, prohibit, hinder (with acc. or with acc. and عَنْ); also نَهُوَ aor. o. *To be intelligent;* نَهَى ٱلنَّفْسَ 79 v. 40, "He restrained his soul;" نَهَى is also used with أَنْ, as إِنِّي نُهِيتُ أَنْ أَعْبُدَ 6 v. 56, "I am forbidden to worship," (see أَنْ). نُهَى Understanding. نَاهٍ for نَاهِيٌ part. act. One who forbids.—تَنَاهَى VI. To forbid one another (with عَنْ).—إِنْتَهَى VIII. To refrain one's-self, to abstain, desist (used occasionally with عَنْ). مُنْتَهَى noun of time or place, A fixed term, a terminus or limit; سِدْرَةُ ٱلْمُنْتَهَى 53 v. 14, "The Lote-tree beyond which there is no passing," see سِدْرَةٌ. مُنْتَهٍ for مُنْتَهِيٌ part. act. One who desists; Plur. مُنْتَهُونَ for مُنْتَهِيُونَ D. S. Gr. T. 1, p. 113.

نَآءَ aor. o. *To rise with difficulty;* to weigh down—a load (with بِ of pers.).

نَوَاصِي plur. of نَاصِيَةٌ, rt. نَصَا q.v.

نَابَ aor. o. *To supply the place of another.*—أَنَابَ IV. To repent and turn to God (with إِلَى). مُنِيبٌ part. act. One who turns with repentance to God.

نَاحَ aor. o. *To lament.* نُوحٌ proper name, Noah.

نُودُوا 3rd pers. plur. pret. pass. of نَادَى iii. f. of نَدَا q.v.

نَارَ aor. o. *To shine.* نَارٌ fem. Fire. نُورٌ Light.—مُنِيرٌ part. act. IV. f. He or that which gives light, enlightening.

نَاسَ aor. o. *To be shaken to and fro (anything hanging).* نَاسٌ for أُنَاسٌ Men, people; a collective noun regarded as the plur. of إِنْسَانٌ A man, human being, rt. أَنِسَ q.v. It is said to embrace also the Genii and evil spirits, but I can recall no passage in the Ḳorân where it is so employed.

نَاشَ aor. o. *To take, seize.*—تَنَاوُشٌ n.a. VI. f. The act of taking or receiving, reception; وَأَنَّى لَهُمُ ٱلتَّنَاوُشُ مِنْ مَكَانٍ بَعِيدٍ 34 v. 51, "And how should they receive (the faith) from a far distant place?" *i.e.* beyond the grave.

نَاصَ aor. o. *To retreat, remain behind, fly.* مَنَاصٌ Time or place of retreat.

نَاقَ aor. o. *To clean the flesh from fat.* نَاقَةٌ A she-camel.

نَالَ aor. o. *To bestow;* and aor. a. for نَوِلَ D. S. Gr. T. 1, p. 242, to grant (with acc. of pers. and بِ of thing), see نَالَ for نَيِلَ.

نَامَ aor. o. *To win a sleeping match.* نَوْمٌ n.a. Sleep. نَائِمٌ part. act. One who sleeps. مَنَامٌ Time or place of sleeping, a dream.

نُونٌ *The letter* ن, a fish; ذُو ٱلنُّونِ The Lord of the Fish, name of the Prophet Jonah.

نَوَى aor. i. *To intend.* نَوًى *Intention,* a date-stone.

نَالَ aor. i. and a. D. S. Gr. T. 1, p. 243, To obtain, get (with مِنْ); to attain, reach, be acceptable to (with acc. of pers.), as at 22 v. 38; it may occasionally be rendered by the Passive It is given, as يَنَالُهُمْ نَصِيبُهُمْ مِنَ ٱلْكِتَابِ 7 v. 35, "Their portion (of the good things of this life) shall be given them from (that which is written in) the Book of God's decrees." نَيْلٌ n.a. That which any one gets or receives; at 9 v. 121, the only place where it occurs, it must be taken in a bad sense, meaning death, imprisonment, or other injury.

ه

هُ and when preceded by kesra or by ي either quiescent after kesra or jazmated after fatha, هِ, an indeclinable affixed personal or possessive pronoun of 3rd pers. sing. masc.; when affixed to a verb or preposition as a personal pronoun it means him or it, and when to a noun as a possessive, his or its; This particle must not be confounded with هْ, which is occasionally found at the end of words in case of pause, and hence called هَاءُ ٱلسُّكُوتِ or هَاءُ ٱلْوَقْفِ; see instances in the 69th chapter, at the 19th and some following verses.

هَا indeclinable affixed personal or possessive pronoun of 3rd pers. sing. fem. Her, it, its, see هُ.

هَا is likewise an interjection, Lo! behold!; it is occasionally prefixed to other words, as هَاهُنَا written also هٰهُنَا Here, هَاذَا or more commonly هٰذَا This, and other words, without apparently adding much to their signification; D. S. Gr. T. 1, pp. 441 and 536. هَآؤُمْ Take ye! for هَاكُمْ, the ك being changed into hamza; هَا when thus followed by the affixed pronoun كَ has the sense of خُذْ Take! the word occurs at 69 v. 19; see D. S. Gr. T. 1, p. 579.

هَاتُوا Bring! produce! Some doubt exists as to the derivation of this word; according to De Sacy it stands for the Plur. Imperat. of the iii. f. of أَتَى To come, but it bears a meaning more in conformity with the iv. f. of that verb q.v. See also D. S. Gr. T. 1, p. 256.

هَاتَيْنِ oblique fem. dual of هَذَا q.v.

هَارُوتُ (2nd declension) Hároot, name of a rebellious angel, see مَارُوتُ.

هَآؤُمْ see هَا.

هَبَطَ aor. i. and o. To fall down, descend, come down (with مِنْ); to go down into (with acc.), as at 2 v. 58.

هَبَا aor. o. *To be raised so as to float in the air* (*dust*). هَبَآءٌ Dust floating in the air.

هَجَدَ *To sleep, watch.*—تَهَجَّدَ V. To watch (with بِ).

هَجَرَ aor. o. To separate one's-self from, break off an acquaintance with, leave off, abstain from, quit, leave alone; to rave deliriously, to talk nonsense. هَجْرٌ n.a. The act of separating one's-self from another. مَهْجُورٌ part. pass. Spoken in a wild and delirious manner.—هَاجَرَ III. To migrate (with إِلَى, also with فِى); to fly one's country, emigrate, become a refugee (with فِى), as آلَّذِينَ هَاجَرُوا فِى آللّٰهِ 16 v. 43, *i.e.* فِى حَقِّ آللّٰهِ "Those who have fled their country in pursuance of their duty to God, or for his sake," so also مَنْ يُهَاجِرْ فِى سَبِيلِ آللّٰهِ 4 v. 101, "He who flies his country (walking) in the path of God's religion." مُهَاجِرٌ part. act. One who flies from his country, a refugee; آلْمُهَاجِرُونَ Those who fled from Mecca to avoid persecution on account of their religion.

هَجَعَ aor. a. To sleep.

هَدَّ aor. o. *To break, demolish.* هَدٌّ n.a. Demolition; هَدًّا In utter ruin.

هَدَمَ aor. i. *To overturn.*—هَدَّمَ II. To demolish.

هَدْهَدَ *To coo* (*as a dove*). هُدْهُدٌ A Hoopoe.

هَدَى aor. i. To lead in the right way, direct aright (with double acc. or with acc. and لِ or إِلَى); *to follow a right course;* هَدَانِ 6 v. 80, "He has directed me," for هَدَانِى D. S. Gr. T. 1, p. 118, and T. 2, p. 497. هَدْىٌ n.a. A victim for sacrifice, an offering. هُدًى n.a. comm. gend. A direction, that which indicates the right way. هَدِيَّةٌ A gift, offering. هَادٍ part. act. One who directs, a director, guide. أَهْدَى (2nd declension) comp. form, One who is a better guide, or who follows a better direction.—إِهْتَدَى VIII. To be directed aright (with لِ or إِلَى). مُهْتَدٍ part. act. having like the verb a pass. signification, Guided aright, led into the right way.

هَذَا or هٰذَا Fem. هَذِهِ; Dual هَذَانِ Fem. هَتَانِ and oblique Fem. هَاتَيْنِ or هَتَيْنِ; Plur. هٰؤُلَآءِ This, these; a compound word consisting of the particle هَا Lo! behold! and the demonstrative pronoun ذَا. *Note.* According to the system of the Arab grammarians all the above words are considered indeclinable nouns, and totally independent of each other, see ذَا.

هَرَبَ aor. o. *To fly, run away.* هَرَبٌ n.a. Flight.

هَرَعَ *To walk with quick and trembling gait.*—

أَهْرَعَ IV. To make to go hastily (with إِلَى or عَلَى).

هَٰرُونُ (2nd declension) Aaron.

هَزَّ aor. o. *To move*, shake (with إِلَى of pers. and بِ, as at 19 v. 25).—إِهْتَزَّ VIII. To stir one's-self, to be stirred or set in motion.

هَزَأَ aor. a. *To break;* and هَزِئَ aor. a. *To mock, ridicule.* هُزُوٌ n.a. A mockery, derision, ridicule, jest, laughing-stock.—إِسْتَهْزَأَ X. To mock, scoff, ridicule, laugh any one to scorn (with بِ). مُسْتَهْزِئٌ part. act. One who scoffs.

هَزَلَ aor. o. *To be thin;* and هَزِلَ aor. a. *To joke.* هَزْلٌ n.a. A joke.

هَزَمَ aor. i. *To squeeze with the hand*, to put to flight. مَهْزُومٌ part. pass. Routed, put to flight.

هَشَّ aor. o. and i. To beat down leaves from a tree, as أَهُشُّ بِهَا عَلَى غَنَمِي 20 v. 19, "By means of it I beat down the leaves (as food) for my cattle."

هَشَمَ aor. i. *To break, especially anything dry or hollow.* هَشِيمٌ Dry sticks or stubble.

هَضَمَ aor. i. *To break, injure, withhold that which is due;* and هَضِمَ aor. a. *To be thin and graceful.* هَضْمٌ n.a. The withholding of that which is due. هَضِيمٌ Thin and smooth, as the spathe of the Palm when distended with flowers.

هَطَعَ aor. a. *To run forward with the eyes fixed in horror.*—مُهْطِعٌ part. act. IV. f. One who hastens with fixed gaze or extended neck.

هٰكَذَا Thus, a word compounded of the particles هَا Behold, كَ As, and ذَا This.

هَلْ particle of interrogation, Whether? Is there? Does he? etc.

هَلَّ *To appear.* أَهِلَّةٌ plur. of هِلَالٌ A new moon, or according to some the moon during the first and last two or three nights; at other times the moon is called قَمَرٌ.—أَهَلَّ IV. To invoke the name of God upon an animal in slaughtering it, as وَمَا أُهِلَّ بِهِ لِغَيْرِ ٱللّٰهِ 2 v. 168, *Lit.* "That on which invocation has been made to any other than God;" since the only flesh that can be lawfully used for food is that on which at the time of slaughter the words بِٱسْمِ ٱللّٰهِ have been pronounced.

هَلِعَ *To be very impatient.* هَلُوعٌ Very impatient.

هَلَكَ aor. a. and i. To perish, die, fall; it is sometimes found with عَنْ, as لِيَهْلِكَ مَنْ هَلَكَ عَنْ بَيِّنَةٍ 8 v. 44, "That he who perishes may perish in spite of clear evidence;" هَلَكَ عَنِّي سُلْطَانِيَهْ 69 v. 29, "My power has fallen away from me." هَالِكٌ part. act. One who perishes. تَهْلُكَةٌ Perdition. مَهْلِكٌ Time or place of destruction.—أَهْلَكَ IV. To destroy, waste, cause to perish (with acc. and بِ). مُهْلِكٌ part. act. One who destroys. مُهْلَكٌ part. pass. Destroyed.

هَلُمَّ Come! bring! an anomalous verb, D. S. Gr. T. 1, p. 546; it is found in the Ḳorân only in the above form, as هَلُمَّ إِلَيْنَا 33 v. 18, "Come to us;" هَلُمَّ شُهَدَآءَكُمْ 6 v. 151, "Bring forward your witnesses."

هُمْ or after kesra, etc. هِمْ, see هُ, an indeclinable pronoun of 3rd pers. masc. plur.; Fem. هُنَّ or هِنَّ They; Dual هُمَا or هِمَا They two; when used as an affix after a verb or preposition هُمْ etc. must be rendered Them, and when after a noun, Their. All the above words are properly speaking distinct and indeclinable; D. S. Gr. T. 1, p. 455.

هَمَّ aor. o. To ponder anything in the mind, to meditate, think about, design, to be anxious about (with أَنْ, also with بِ); to plot against, as وَهَمَّتْ كُلُّ أُمَّةٍ بِرَسُولِهِمْ 40 v. 5, "And every nation has laid plots against their prophet."— أَهَمَّ IV. To make anxious.

هُمَا or هِمَا, see هُمْ.

هَمَدَ aor. o. *To be extinguished, lifeless.* هَامِدٌ part. act. Barren and lifeless.

هَمَرَ aor. i. and o. *To impel, pour forth.*—مُنْهَمِرٌ part. act. VII. f. Pouring forth.

هَمَزَ aor. i. and o. *To squeeze in the hand, to bite.* هُمَزَةٌ comm. gend. A back-biter. هَمَّازٌ A slanderer. هَمَزَاتٌ Evil suggestions of the Devil.

هَمَسَ *To break, march all night without halting.* هَمْسٌ n.a. A shuffling sound, *properly*, of camels' feet.

هَمَنَ no primitive form, *To put anything in the girdle called* هِيمَانٌ. هَامَانُ (2nd declension) proper name, Haman.

هُنَّ or هِنَّ They, them, their; an indeclinable pronoun of the 3rd pers. fem. plur., see هُمْ.

هَنَأَ aor. a. o. and i. *To anoint a camel with pitch, to be wholesome.* هَنِيئًا May it be wholesome or profitable, much good may it do you; the accusative or adverbial form of هَنِيءٌ Wholesome, digestible, as فَكُلُوهُ هَنِيئًا مَرِيئًا 4 v. 3, *Literally*, "Then eat it with easy digestion and wholesomeness," a figurative expression meaning "Take it and make use of it to your profit and advantage."

هُنَالِكَ There, in that place, composed of هُنَا Here, with the affix لِكَ, in the same way as from the pronoun ذَا is formed the word ذٰلِكَ or ذَالِكَ, D. S. Gr. T. 1, p. 513.

هَهُنَا for هَاهُنَا Here, composed of هَا Behold! and هُنَا Here, in this place.

هُوَ He, it, an indeclinable personal pronoun of the third pers. sing. masc.

هَادَ aor. o. To return to one's duty (with إِلَى); to become a Jew. هُودٌ Hood, name of a prophet said to have been sent to the tribe of 'Àd; the Jews, generic noun, same as يَهُودٌ q.v.

هَارَ aor. o. *To fall to ruin.* هَارٌ Weak, infirm, tottering.—إِنْهَارَ VII. To fall in ruin, tumble to pieces (with بِ).

هٰؤُلَاءِ These; an indeclinable pronoun used as the plural of هٰذَا, and composed of هَا and أُولَاءِ q.v.

هَانَ aor. o. *To be light, vile, despicable, quiet.* هَوْنٌ n.a. Meekness, quietness, modesty. هُونٌ n.a. Contempt, ignominy. هَيِّنٌ Light, easy. أَهْوَنُ (2nd declension) comp. form, More or most easy.—أَهَانَ IV. To despise, render contemptible. مُهِينٌ part. act. That which renders contemptible, ignominious, shameful. مُهَانٌ part. pass. Despised, rendered contemptible.

هَوَى aor. i. To fall, to stoop as a bird to its prey, also to rise; هَوِىَ aor. a. To love, desire; وَٱلنَّجْمِ إِذَا هَوَى 53 v. 1, by some interpreted "By the stars when they set," and by others "when they rise;" فَٱجْعَلْ أَفْئِدَةً مِنَ ٱلنَّاسِ تَهْوِي إِلَيْهِمْ 14 v. 40, "Make the hearts of some men to be well inclined towards them;" to blow away as the wind (with بِ), see 22 v. 32. هَوًى Plur. أَهْوَآءٌ Desire, will, lust, inclination. هَوَآءٌ Void. هَاوِيَةٌ The lowest pit of Hell.—أَهْوَى IV. To overthrow.—إِسْتَهْوَى X. To infatuate.

هِيَ She, it, an indeclinable personal pronoun of the 3rd pers. fem. sing.

هَاءَ aor. a. and i. *To be prepared.* هَيْئَةٌ Form, figure.—هَيَّأَ II. To dispose aright (with acc. and لِ of pers.).

هَيْتَ an anomalous verb used with the preposition لِ, as هَيْتَ لَكَ 12 v. 23, "Come!" It is spelt in a variety of ways, as هِيتَ, هَيْتُ, هَيْتِ, etc., D. S. Gr. T. 1, p. 546.

هَاجَ aor. i. *To be raised or excited, as dust, anger, etc.*, to wither.

هَالَ aor. i. *To pour out.* مَهِيلٌ Poured out.

هَامَ aor. i. *To be captivated by love*, to wander abroad like one distracted (with فِى). هِيمٌ plur. of هَيْمَآءُ A female camel raging with thirst from disease.

هَيْمَنَ quadriliteral verb, *To say Amen! to keep anything safe.* مُهَيْمِنٌ part. act. That which preserves anything safe (with عَلَى), as مُهَيْمِنًا عَلَيْهِ 5 v. 52, "Preserving it (the Scripture) safe from change or corruption;" اَلْمُهَيْمِنُ The Guardian, a name of God.

هَيْهَاتَ an anomalous verb used like هَيْتَ with the preposition لِ, as هَيْهَاتَ لِمَا تُوعَدُونَ 23 v. 38, "Away with that which ye are threatened with;" it is equivalent to بَعُدَ, the Preterite being used for the Optative, D. S. Gr. T. 1, p. 545, but there are sundry ways of spelling it.

و

وَ an inseparable prefixed conjunction, And, also, but, whilst; when meaning together with it is said to govern the accus., thus it is that some at 2 v. 33 read اَسْكُنْ أَنْتَ وَزَوْجَكَ ٱلْجَنَّةَ "Do thou inhabit the garden together with thy wife;" however the nominative وَزَوْجُكَ both here and in similar passages would seem to be preferred; وَ is also used in forms of oaths, and then governs the genitive, as فَوَرَبِّ ٱلسَّمَآءِ وَٱلْأَرْضِ 51 v. 23, "Then by the Lord of heaven and earth." For the difference between وَ and فَ see D. S. Gr. T. 1, p. 555.

وَأْتَمِرُوا see أَمَرَ.

وَأَدَ aor. يَئِدُ *To bury alive.* مَوْؤُدَةٌ fem. part. pass. (A damsel) buried alive.

وَأَلَ aor. i. *To fly for refuge.* مَوْئِلٌ A refuge.

وَبَرَ aor. i. *To stand still;* and وَبِرَ *To have much hair or wool.* أَوْبَارٌ plur. of وَبَرٌ Soft camel's-hair or felt.

وَبَقَ aor. يَبِقُ; and وَبِقَ aor. يَوْبَقُ *To perish.* مَوْبِقٌ A place of destruction.—أَوْبَقَ IV. To destroy, cause to perish.

وَبَلَ aor. يَبِلُ *To pursue eagerly, pour forth rain in large drops;* and وَبُلَ aor. o. *To be heavy and unwholesome, as air, food, etc.* وَابِلٌ A heavy shower of rain. وَبَالٌ Gravity, grievousness, heinousness. وَبِيلٌ A heavy blow, chastisement.

وَتَدَ aor. يَتِدُ *To drive in a stake.* أَوْتَادٌ plur. of وَتِدٌ A stake; فِرْعَوْنُ ذُو ٱلْأَوْتَادِ 38 v. 11, "Pharaoh lord of the stakes," either because his kingdom was firmly established, as a tent when secured by stakes and pegs, or because he was in the habit of fastening the hands and feet of his victims to pickets driven into the ground.

وَتَرَ aor. يَتِرُ *To hate*, defraud any one of a thing (with double acc.). وَتْرٌ n.a. Single; for the meaning of the words وَٱلشَّفْعِ وَٱلْوَتْرِ 89 v. 2, see شَفَعَ.

وَتَنَ aor. يَتِنُ *To injure any one in the* وَتِينٌ or aorta, the large artery which rises from the upper part of the beart.

وَثِقَ aor. يَثِقُ *To confide or trust in any one.* وَثَاقٌ A bond, tbat with which anything is tied or bound. وُثْقَى fem. of أَوْثَقُ comp. form, Very firm. مَوْثِقٌ A compact, bond. مِيثَاقٌ A covenant, treaty.—وَاثَقَ III. To enter into a compact or treaty with any one (with acc. of pers. and بِ).—أَوْثَقَ IV. To bind, draw tigbt.

وَثَنٌ Plur. أَوْثَانٌ An idol; the verbal root is not fonnd in the primitive form.

وَجَبَ aor. يَجِبُ *To be necessary,* to fall down dead, as فَإِذَا وَجَبَتْ جُنُوبُهَا 22 v. 37, "And when they—*Lit.* their sides—have fallen dead."

وَجَدَ aor. يَجِدُ To find, perceive. وُجْدٌ n.a. Competence, means, as مِنْ وُجْدِكُمْ 65 v. 6, "According to your means."

وَجَسَ *To entertain fear.*—أَوْجَسَ IV. To conceive in the mind (with acc. and مِنْ), as وَأَوْجَسَ مِنْهُمْ خِيفَةً 11 v. 73, "And he conceived a fear of tbem."

وَجَفَ aor. يَجِفُ *To be agitated.* وَاجِفٌ part. act. Palpitating.—أَوْجَفَ IV. To make a horse or camel move briskly with a bounding pace.

وَجِلَ aor. يَوْجَلُ To fear. وَجِلٌ Afraid, smitten witb fear.

وَجَهَ aor. يَجِهُ *To strike in the face.* وَجْهٌ Plur. وُجُوهٌ A face, countenance, favour, honour, sake, as لِوَجْهِ ٱللّٰهِ 76 v. 9, "For the sake of God;" a beginning, as وَجْهَ ٱلنَّهَارِ 3 v. 65, "In the early part of the day;" intention, as أَنْ يَأْتُوا بِٱلشَّهَادَةِ عَلَى وَجْهِهَا 5 v. 107, "That they should bear testimony in accordance with its true meaning or intention;" essence, being, substance, as كُلُّ شَيْءٍ هَالِكٌ إِلَّا وَجْهَهُ 28 v. 88, "Everything shall perish except bimself," *Lit.* his essence; see D. S. Gr. T. 2, p. 404; so also at 2 v. 106, مَنْ أَسْلَمَ وَجْهَهُ لِلّٰهِ "He who submits bimself to God;" إِنْقَلَبَ عَلَى وَجْهِهِ 22 v. 11, "He becomes a pervert," *Lit.* "He is turned upon himself;" عَلَى وَجْهِهِ may also be rendered "according to his manner or way." وِجْهَةٌ A tract. وَجِيهٌ Honourable, held in high repute.—وَجَّهَ II. To turn, direct (with acc. and لِ).—تَوَجَّهَ V. To proceed (witb تِلْقَآء and name of place).

وَحِدَ aor. يَحِدُ *To be one, alone, unique.* وَحْدٌ n.a. *Alone;* وَحْدَهُ He or bim alone, by himself; This word وَحْدَ when followed by an affixed pronoun is to be regarded as an adverbial expression and indeclinable, D. S. Gr. T. 1, p. 512, and T. 2, p. 291, *note.* وَاحِدٌ One, single. وَحِيدٌ Alone.—تَوْحِيدٌ n.a. II. f. The worship of one God, belief in tbe Unity of tbe Godhead.

وَحَشَ aor. يَحِشُ *To throw away (arms, etc.) in flight.* وُحُوشٌ plur. of وَحْشٌ Wild beasts.

وَحَى aor. يَحِي *To indicate, reveal.* وَحْيٌ n.a. A revelation, بِأَعْيُنِنَا وَوَحْيِنَا 11 v. 39, "Under our inspection, and according to onr revelation."—أَوْحَى IV. To reveal (with acc. and إِلَى, لِ, or فِي, also with فِي and أَنْ); to make signs (with إِلَى of pers. and أَنْ), thus at 19 v. 12, فَأَوْحَى إِلَيْهِمْ أَنْ سَبِّحُوا "And be made signs to them (as though he wonld say) praise God;" see أَنْ; to inspire, speak by inspiration or revelation (with إِلَى and أَنْ); to suggest (with acc. and إِلَى), as at 6 v. 112; also with إِلَى of pers. and لِ with subjunctive, as at 6 v. 121.

وَدَّ aor. a. *To love*, desire, wish (with acc. or with لَوْ, or أَنْ, or لَوْ أَنَّ). وَدٌّ n.a. Wadd, name of an Idol worshipped originally by the antediluvians, and subsequently by the Pagan Arabs. وُدٌّ n.a. Love. وَدُودٌ Loving. مَوَدَّةٌ n.a. Love, affection, friendship.—وَادَّ III. To love.

وَدَعَ aor. يَدَعُ *To place*, leave, used only in the aor. and imperat.; imperat. دَعْ Leave alone, permit, take no notice of.—وَدَّعَ II. To leave.—مُسْتَوْدَعٌ noun of time and place X. f. A place of deposit, as the womb or the grave.

وَدَقَ aor. يَدِقُ *To drop rain.* وَدْقٌ n.a. Rain.

وَدَى aor. يَدِى *To pay a fine as expiation for manslaughter.* وَادٍ for وَادِىٌ, and with the article ٱلْوَادِ Poetice for ٱلْوَادِى, see D. S. Gr. T. 2, p. 497; Plur. أَوْدِيَةٌ A valley, channel of a river, a river. دِيَةٌ A fine to be paid for manslaughter, as فَدِيَةٌ مُسَلَّمَةٌ 4 v. 94, "Then let a fine be given."

وَذَرَ aor. يَذِرُ *To fall upon, wound;* aor. يَذَرُ not used in the preterite; Imperat. ذَرْ To leave, let, forsake, let go (with acc. and عَلَى or فِي, or with acc. and لِ followed by the aorist subjunctive); it is also used with وَ as ذَرْنِى وَمَنْ خَلَقْتُ وَحِيدًا 74 v. 11, "Let me alone with him whom I have created;" فَذَرُوهُ 12 v. 47, "Leave it."

وَرِثَ aor. يَرِثُ To be heir to any one (with acc. of pers. or مِنْ); to inherit. وَارِثٌ Plur. وَرَثَةٌ part. act. One who inherits, an heir. تُرَاثٌ and مِيرَاثٌ Inheritance.—أَوْرَثَ IV. To constitute one heir of anything, to give for an inheritance (with double acc.).

وَرَدَ aor. يَرِدُ *To be present*, arrive at, *properly*, at water, to drink thereof; to go down into. وِرْدٌ A place of descent, an approach, especially to water for the purpose of drinking, thus وَنَسُوقُ ٱلْمُجْرِمِينَ إِلَى جَهَنَّمَ وِرْدًا 19 v. 89, "And we will drive the wicked into Hell, as cattle are driven to water." وَارِدٌ part. act. One who goes down (with لِ); one who goes before a caravan to draw water, one who is present at. وَرْدَةٌ fem. of وَرْدٌ *A rose*, rosy. وَرِيدٌ The jugular vein. مَوْرُودٌ part. pass. Descended into, arrived at.—أَوْرَدَ IV. To lead one into (with double acc.).

وَرَقَ aor. يَرِقُ *To put forth leaves.* وَرَقٌ collective noun, Leaves. وَرَقَةٌ A single leaf. وَرِقٌ Money.

وَرَى aor. يَرِى *To eat away the interior of the body (matter).* وَرَآءٌ *That which is behind.* وَرَآءَ Behind, before, beyond, beside or except is never found in the Korân without a complement either expressed or understood, see D. S. Gr. T. 2, p. 152; مَا وَرَآءَ ذَٰلِكُمْ 4 v. 28, "Whatever is beside this," or "all with this exception;" مِنْ وَرَآئِهِمْ 45 v. 9, may be rendered either "Before them," or "behind them."—وَارَى III. To hide (with acc. and عَنْ)—أَوْرَى IV. To strike fire. مُورِيَةٌ fem. part. act. One who strikes fire.—تَوَارَى VI. To be hidden, hide one's-self (with بِ or مِنْ); at 38 v. 31 the word تَوَارَتْ is used with an ellipse of the nominative, ٱلشَّمْسُ being understood; D. S. Gr. T. 2, p. 451.

وَزَرَ aor. يَزِرُ To bear, carry (a burthen). وِزْرٌ Plur. أَوْزَارٌ n.a. A burthen, heavy weight, load; at 47 v. 5 it means "Arms, or other burthens imposed by war." وَزَرٌ An inaccessible mountain, and hence a place of refuge. وَازِرٌ part.

act. One who bears a burthen. وَزِيرٌ A counsellor or minister who bears the burthen of state, commonly spelt and pronounced Vizier.

وَزَعَ aor. يَزَعُ To keep back, keep (men) in their ranks while marching.—أَوْزَعَ IV. To incite, put into the mind, instigate, inspire (with acc. and أَنْ).

وَزَنَ aor. يَزِنُ, Imperat. زِنْ To weigh (with بِ); to weigh out for any one (with acc. of pers.). وَزْنٌ n.a. A weighing, weight. مَوْزُونٌ part. pass. Evenly and equally balanced, that which has its weights evenly adjusted. مِيزَانٌ Plur. مَوَازِينُ (2nd declension) A balance; at 101 vv. 5 and 6 مَوَازِينُهُ may be rendered "The measure of his good works."

وَسَطَ aor. يَسِطُ To be in the midst, penetrate into the midst of. وَسَطٌ The middle, middle; أُمَّةً وَسَطًا 2 v. 137 must, according to the commentators, be rendered "A nation who have hit the golden mean or *juste milieu*." أَوْسَطُ Fem. وُسْطَى comp. form, The middle, the more worthy, as at 68 v. 28; مِنْ أَوْسَطِ مَا تُطْعِمُونَ أَهْلِيكُمْ 5 v. 91, "Of the middling or ordinary kind of food which ye provide for your families."

وَسِعَ aor. يَسَعُ *To be ample*, to take in, embrace, comprehend. وُسْعٌ Means, ability to perform a thing. وَاسِعٌ One who or that which is ample, extensive, one who comprehends; as an attribute of God it means the Omnipresent or Omniscient, He whose mercy is over all his works. سَعَةٌ n.a. Plenty, opulence.—مُوسِعٌ part. act. IV. f. One who enlarges, or makes of large extent, one who is in easy circumstances.

وَسَقَ aor. يَسِقُ To gather together (in one herd).—إِتَّسَقَ VIII. To be complete or in perfect order, as the moon at the full.

وَاسِلٌ *Devout, religious.* وَسِيلَةٌ Close proximity; no verbal root in the primitive form.

وَسَمَ aor. يَسِمُ To brand (with acc. and عَلَى).—مُتَوَسِّمٌ part. act. V. f. One who knows a thing by its outward signs, intelligent.

وَسِنَ aor. يَوْسَنُ *To be buried in sleep.* سِنَةٌ Sleep, slumber, drowsiness.

وَسْوَسَ quadriliteral; aor. يُوَسْوِسُ To whisper evil, make evil suggestions (with لِ, إِلَى, or بِ of pers. or with فِي). اَلْوَسْوَاسُ The Tempter, Satan.

وَشَى aor. يَشِي *To paint cloth.* شِيَةٌ An admixture of colour (in an animal); thus لَا شِيَةَ فِيهَا 2 v. 66 means "She is of a whole colour."

وَصَبَ aor. يَصِبُ *To be perpetual.* وَاصِبٌ part. act. Lasting; وَاصِبًا For ever.

وَصَدَ aor. يَصِدُ *To weave.* وَصِيدٌ A threshold.

وَصَفَ aor. يَصِفُ To describe, assert. وَصْفٌ n.a. *Description*, act of attributing or ascribing.

وَصَلَ aor. يَصِلُ To join; to come to, arrive at, reach, attain unto (with إِلَى). وَصِيلَةٌ Waṣeela, a she camel or ewe, concerning which the Pagan Arabs were wont to observe certain superstitions in honour of their idols; see Sale's Ḳorân, Preliminary Discourse, p. 172.—وَصَّلَ II. To cause to reach (with acc. and لِ of pers.).

وَصَى aor. يَصِي *To join together.* وَصِيَّةٌ A mandate, command, testament, legacy; the accusative وَصِيَّةً at 2 v. 241 and 4 v. 16 must be regarded as an elliptical expression equivalent to هٰذَا وَصِيَّةٌ "This is a Law;" D. S. Gr. T. 2, p. 83; مِنْ بَعْدِ وَصِيَّةٍ يُوصِي بِهَا 4 v. 12, "After (the payment of) any legacy which he may have bequeathed."—وَصَّى II. To enjoin, command (with acc. of pers. and بِ, or with acc. and

(أَنْ). تَوْصِيَةٌ n.a. A testamentary disposition—of property.—أَوْصَى IV. To order, command (with acc. of pers. and بِ or فِى); to bequeath (with بِ). مُوصٍ for مُوصِىٌ part. act. A testator.—تَوَاصَى VI. To give one another a command, to enjoin or recommend to one another (with بِ).

وَضَعَ aor. يَضَعُ To put, place, lay down, lay aside, fix, bring forth a child; to put off, remove (with acc. and عَنْ); to appoint (with لِ); وَوُضِعَ ٱلْكِتَابُ 18 v. 47, "And the Book (of the account of each man's actions) shall be put (into his hands);" at 39 v. 69 these words would seem rather to refer to the Book of God's decrees, which "shall be laid open" on the day of Judgment. مَوَاضِعُ (2nd declension) plur. of مَوْضِعٌ A place; at 4 v. 48 مَوَاضِع may be rendered "The true meanings (of words)." مَوْضُوعٌ part. pass. Placed.—أَوْضَعَ IV. To drive (a camel) quickly, as وَلَأَوْضَعُوا خِلَالَكُمْ 9 v. 47, "And they would have driven about your camels,"—worrying them by constantly passing in and out among them.

وَضَنَ aor. يَضِنُ *To plait or fold a thing with one part over another.* مَوْضُونٌ part. pass. Interwoven (with gold and precious stones).

وَطِئَ aor. يَطَأُ To tread, trample on, as at 48 v. 25; on referring to this passage the reader will observe a notable instance of the ellipse of the correlative proposition or جَوَابُ ٱلشَّرْطِ after لَوْلَا, D. S. Gr. T. 2, p. 420; the hiatus is supplied by Beiḍâwëe as follows, لَمَا كَفَّ أَيْدِيَكُمْ عَنْهُمْ, see v. 24. وَطْأً n.a. *properly*, The act of trampling on; at 73 v. 6 the words أَشَدُّ وَطْأً may perhaps be translated "More capable of, or fitted for earnest devotion," or "for keeping down all impure and unbecoming thoughts." مَوْطِئٌ A step.—وَاطَأَ III. To make to agree, or render equal—in number, etc.

وَطَرٌ A thing necessary to be done; no verbal root.

وَطَنَ aor. يَطِنُ *To remain in a place.* مَوَاطِنُ (2nd declension) plur. of مَوْطِنٌ A battle-field.

وَعَدَ aor. يَعِدُ *To predict*, promise, threaten (with double acc. or with acc. of pers. and لَ followed by energetic aorist, also with acc. of pers. and أَنْ); to make any one a promise (with acc. of pers.). وَعْدٌ n.a. A promise, threat, prediction; وَعْدَ ٱللّٰهِ حَقًّا 4 v. 121, The ellipse is thus explained by Beiḍâwëe, وَعَدَهُ وَعْدًا وَحَقَّ ذٰلِكَ حَقًّا, see D. S. Gr. T. 2, p. 85. وَعِيدٌ Threatening, a threat. مَوْعِدٌ, مَوْعِدَةٌ, or مِيعَادٌ A promise; time or place of the fulfilment of a prediction, promise, or threat; an appointment for a meeting. مَوْعُودٌ part. pass. Predicted, promised.—وَاعَدَ III. To appoint a fixed time or place for any one (with double acc.); to plight faith to any one (with acc. of pers.)—تَوَاعَدَ VI. To make a mutual appointment.

وَعَظَ aor. يَعِظُ, Imperat. عِظْ To warn, admonish (with acc. of pers. and بِ of thing, or with أَنْ meaning Lest or that not); to advise (with acc. of pers., بِ, of thing, and أَنْ that). وَاعِظٌ part. act. One who warns. مَوْعِظَةٌ A warning, an admonition.

وَعَى aor. يَعِى *To collect*, retain in the memory. وِعَآءٌ Plur. أَوْعِيَةٌ A locker, box, vessel or bag, where anything is stowed away. وَاعِيَةٌ fem. part. act. That which retains in the memory. —أَوْعَى IV. To be miserly, to secrete or hoard —*properly*, in a وِعَآءٌ; at 84 v. 23 it means to "secrete in the breast."

وَفَدَ aor. يَفِدُ *To come, as an ambassador into the presence of a king.* وَفْدٌ n.a. The act of coming into the presence of Royalty.

وَفَرَ aor. يَفِرُ *To be plentiful.* مَوْفُورٌ part. pass. Full, ample.

وَفَضَ aor. يَفِضُ *To run.*—أَوْفَضَ IV. To hasten (with إِلَى).

وَفِقَ aor. يَفِقُ *To find a thing to be fitting.*—وَفَّقَ II. To cause an agreement or reconciliation between two parties (with بَيْنَ). تَوْفِيقٌ n.a. Reconciliation, success, prosperity, accomplishment of one's wishes.—وِفَاقٌ n.a. III. f. The act of suiting, becoming; جَزَآءً وِفَاقًا 78 v. 26, for ذَا وِفَاقٍ "A fitting reward."

وَفَى aor. يَفِي *To perform a promise.* أَوْفَى for أَوْفَيُ comp. form, Most complete or perfect, more strict in the performance of a covenant.—وَفَّى II. To fulfil an engagement, pay or repay (a debt) in full (with double acc.); to recompense fully for anything (with إِلَى of pers. and acc. of thing, or with double acc.); thus, وَإِنَّ كُلًّا لَمَّا لَيُوَفِّيَنَّهُمْ رَبُّكَ أَعْمَالَهُمْ 11 v. 113, "And indeed unto every one thy Lord will surely give the full reward of his works;" there are several ways of explaining the pleonasms with which this sentence appears to be encumbered; according to one لَمَّا should be spelt لَمًّا meaning جَمِيعًا, see لَمَّا, see also D. S. Gr. T. 1, p. 540, *note.* مُوَفٍّ for مُوَفِّيٌ part. act. One who pays in full.—أَوْفَى IV. To fulfil or perform—a covenant—(with acc. or with بِ); to give full measure (with acc. and لِ of pers.). مُوفٍ for مُوفِيٌ part. act. One who fulfils (his covenant).—تَوَفَّى V. To receive or take to one's-self, as God receives the soul of one who dies; to take the life of any one (with acc.); In the Passive, To be received by God, an euphemism for to die. مُتَوَفٍّ for مُتَوَفِّيٌ part. act. He who receives the soul, or takes away the life.—إِسْتَوْفَى X. To take full measure, demand full payment.

وَقَبَ aor. يَقِبُ *To enter,* to overspread,—as darkness,—to be eclipsed (the moon).

وَقَتَ *To appoint a fixed time.* وَقْتٌ n.a. Time; لِوَقْتِهَا 7 v. 186, "To define its fixed time." مِيقَاتٌ Plur. مَوَاقِيتُ (2nd declension) A fixed or stated time or period, time or place of appointment. مَوْقُوتٌ part. pass. That of which the time is defined.

وَقَدَ aor. يَقِدُ *To burn.* وَقُودٌ Fuel.—أَوْقَدَ IV. To set fire to, kindle (with acc. and لِ or مِنْ); also with عَلَى, thus وَمِمَّا يُوقِدُونَ عَلَيْهِ فِي ٱلنَّارِ . . . زَبَدٌ مِثْلُهُ 13 v. 18, "And from that (ore) which they ignite in the fire . . . there comes a scum like unto it," *i.e.* like froth. مُوقَدٌ part. pass. Kindled.—إِسْتَوْقَدَ X. To light (a fire).

وَقَذَ aor. يَقِذُ *To strike violently, beat to death.* مَوْقُوذٌ part. pass. Killed by a blow from a club.

وَقَرَ aor. يَقِرُ *To weigh down, make deaf;* to sit quiet (with فِي); قِرْنَ Sit quiet! fem. plur. imperat.; see قَرَّ. وَقْرٌ n.a. Deafness. وِقْرٌ A heavy burthen. وَقَارٌ Kindness and long-suffering.—وَقَّرَ II. To revere.

وَقَعَ aor. يَقَعُ To fall, befall, fall upon (with عَلَى and مِنْ); to be incumbent upon (with عَلَى); to come to pass, to be confirmed, as at 7 v. 115; to fall down into (with لِ). وَاقِعٌ part. act. Falling upon (with بِ or لِ of pers.); that which comes to pass; ٱلْوَاقِعَةُ That which will surely come to pass, the inevitable Day of

وكد aor. يكد *To stand still.*—تَوْكِيدٌ n.a. II. f. Confirmation, ratification.

وكز aor. يكز To strike with the fist.

وكل aor. يكل *To commit anything into another's keeping.* وكيل One who takes care of anything for another, the guardian of one's interests, a patron, administrator, disposer of affairs, the witness to a bargain; وَكَفَى بِٱللّٰهِ وَكِيلًا 4 v. 83, "And God is all sufficient as a guardian," see ب—وكّل II. To appoint one keeper or guardian over, or entrust one with the care of anything (with acc. of pers. and ب of thing).—تَوَكَّلَ V. To put trust in any one, and especially in God (with عَلَى). مُتَوَكِّل part. act. One who puts his trust in another.

ولت aor. يلت To diminish, defraud one of anything (with acc. of pers. and thing).

ولج aor. يلج To enter (with فى). وَلِيجَةٌ An intimate friend.—أَوْلَجَ IV. To cause to enter (with acc. and فى).

ولد aor. يلد To bring forth, or beget offspring; Pass. وُلِدَ To be born. وَلَدٌ sing. and plur. Issue, offspring, a child, a son; Plur. أَوْلَادٌ Children. وَالِدٌ part. act. One who begets, a parent, a father, and وَالِدَةٌ A mother; Dual ٱلْوَالِدَانِ The parents, father and mother; وَلِوَالِدَىَّ 14 v. 42, "And to both my parents;" D. S. Gr. T. 1, p. 459. وَلِيدٌ Plur. وِلْدَانٌ A child, youth. مَوْلُودٌ part. pass. One who is born, a child; مَوْلُودٌ لَهُ One to whom a child is born, a father.

ولى aor. يلى To be very near to any one, either as kindred or neighbours (with acc.). وَالٍ for وَالِىٌ part. act. One who guards over the public safety. وَلِىٌّ Plur. أَوْلِيَآءُ (2nd declension)

Judgment. وَقْعَةٌ noun of unity, A coming to pass. مَوَاقِعُ (2nd declension) plur. of مَوْقِعٌ The time or place of falling.—مُوَاقِعٌ part. act. III. f. One who falls into (with acc.).—أَوْقَعَ IV. To bring about, excite—enmity—(with بَيْنَ).

وقف aor. يَقِفُ, Imperat. قِفْ *To stand,* make to stand, as وَقِفُوهُمْ 37 v. 24, "And make them to stand (before the Judgment seat of God);" so also with عَلَى at 6 v. 30. مَوْقُوفٌ part. pass. Made to stand (with عِنْدَ).

وقى aor. يَقِى, Imperat. قِ To keep, preserve; to defend, keep one safe from (with double acc.). وَاقٍ for وَاقِىٌ part. act. One who keeps safe, a defender, protector. تَقِىّ Devout, see تقى. تُقَاةٌ Fear, and تَقْوَى (2nd declension) Fear of God, reverence, piety, are irregular nouns of action (D. S. Gr. T. 1, p. 293) thought by some to be derived from the viii. f., see تقى; the words وَآتَاهُمْ تَقْوَاهُمْ 47 v. 19 are by some explained, "And he shall show them what to fear or avoid;" by others, "He will give them (the reward of) their piety."—إِتَّقَى VIII. To take heed to one's-self, to fear; also to fear God, to be devout. يَتَّقْهِ is found in some copies for يَتَّقِهِ at 24 v. 51, but this must be regarded as a license; some read يَتَّقِهْ, D. S. Gr. T. 1, p. 252; فَاتَّقُون 2 v. 38 before a pause, for فَاتَّقُونِى "Fear me!" D. S. Gr. T. 2, p. 497. مُتَّقٍ for مُتَّقِىٌ Plur. مُتَّقُونَ part. act. One who fears God, devout.

وكأ *To take up a burthen.*—تَوَكَّأَ V. To lean (with عَلَى).—إِتَّكَأَ VIII. To recline (with عَلَى). مُتَّكِئٌ part. act. Reclining (with فى and عَلَى). مُتَّكَأٌ A place where any one reclines, a day couch or "Triclinium," and hence a banquet.

Near, a friend, patron, benefactor, helper, protector; at 2 v. 282 وَلِيُّهُ would seem to have nearly the same meaning as وَكِيلُهُ q.v.; at 27 v. 50 it refers to the avenger of blood, who, as mentioned at 17 v. 35, is to be the heir or next of kin; at 19 v. 5 وَلِيًّا may be rendered "Heir apparent," or "next of kin," so also at 8 v. 73; the passage at 17 v. 111 is explained under the word ذُلّ q.v. وَلَايَةٌ n.a. Help, the act of taking as a friend, or appointing as heir, as مَا لَكُمْ مِنْ وَلَايَتِهِمْ مِنْ شَيْءٍ 8 v. 73, where the meaning would seem to be, "It is in no wise right for you to appoint them as your heirs." أَوْلَى for أَوْلَىٰ (2nd declension); Dual أَوْلَيَانِ comp. form, Nearer, more or most near of kin, more worthy, more proper, nearest (with بِ and لِ); أَوْلَى لَكَ, see iv. f. مَوْلَى Plur. مَوَالِي (2nd declension) A lord, companion, protector, a patron or client; a master or servant; at 44 v. 41 it is found with both these meanings, or it may in both instances be rendered partner; one nearly related by blood, as at 4 v. 37, or a nephew, as at 19 v. 5; هِيَ مَوْلَاكُمْ 57 v. 14, "It is the proper place for you," or "a place nigh unto you," مَوْلَى being here considered as a noun of place, D. S. Gr. T. 1, p. 302.—وَلَّى II. To retreat, turn the back (with إِلَى or مِنْ, or with the words عَلَى أَدْبَارِهِمْ or ٱلْأَدْبَارَ); it is sometimes found with a double acc., thus وَمَنْ يُوَلِّهِمْ يَوْمَئِذٍ دُبُرَهُ 8 v. 16, "And he who turns his back unto them on that day;" to cause to turn towards (with double acc.); to turn away (with acc. and عَنْ); to turn—one's face—towards (with double acc.); to set one over, or give one authority over (with double acc.); نُوَلِّهِ مَا تَوَلَّى 4 v. 115, "We will put it into his power to follow the bent of his inclination." مُوَلٍّ for مُوَلِّيٌ part. act. He who causes one to turn towards a thing; thus, هُوَ مُوَلِّيهَا 2 v. 143, "It is He—God—who turns (them) towards it;" the other acc. كُلُّ أُمَّةٍ "Every nation," being understood.—أَوْلَى IV. To cause to draw nigh; أَوْلَى لَكَ 75 v. 34, "Woe unto thee!" *Lit.* "May He—God—cause (evil) to draw nigh unto thee," or "May it—evil—draw nigh unto thee," the preterite being here used for the optative; D. S. Gr. T. 1, p. 169.—تَوَلَّى V. To turn back, turn one's back; to retire (with إِلَى); to turn away (with عَنْ); to adopt or choose any one—as a friend—(with acc. of pers.), as at 5 v. 61; to take upon one's-self, as وَٱلَّذِى تَوَلَّى كِبْرَهُ 24 v. 11, "And he who hath taken upon himself to aggravate it;" to be put in authority, as at 47 v. 24; Instances are not uncommon in which the تَ of the second person aorist is omitted, as تَوَلَّوْا for تَتَوَلَّوْا 11 v. 3, see D. S. Gr. T. 1, p. 221.

وَلَيَكُونًا And verily he shall be, see كَانَ.

وَنَى aor. يَنِى To be slack or negligent (with فِى).

وَهَبَ aor. يَهَبُ, Imperat. هَبْ To give, bestow; to restore, as at 38 v. 42 (with acc. and لِ). وَهَّابٌ A free and liberal giver; ٱلْوَهَّابُ An epithet of the Deity.

وَهَجَ aor. يَهِجُ *To burn.* وَهَّاجٌ Brightly burning.

وَهَنَ aor. يَهِنُ To be weak, faint, infirm, languid, remiss (with فِى). وَهْنٌ Weakness, faintness; وَهْنًا عَلَى وَهْنٍ 31 v. 13, "With weakness upon weakness." أَوْهَنُ (2nd declension) comp. form, Weakest.—مُوهِنٌ part. act. IV. f. One who makes weak.

وَهَى aor. يَهِى *To be torn.* وَاهٍ Fem. وَاهِيَةٌ part. act. Torn, rent.

وَىْ an interjection regarded by some as an abbreviation of وَيْلٌ q.v.; it takes the affix كَ of the second person, and may then be translated Woe unto thee! In some copies we find وَيْكَأَنَّ as one word, in which case it may be considered as composed of the interjection وَىْ Oh! or Ah! and كَأَنَّ As if; according to some وَيْكَ is equivalent to إِعْلَمْ Know, an interpretation which it may well bear at 28 v. 82, where it occurs; see D. S. Gr. T. 1, p. 580.

وَيْلٌ A great misfortune, woe; no verbal root; this word is commonly employed as an interjection with لِ, as فَوَيْلٌ لَهُمْ 2 v. 73, "Then woe to them," or with an affixed pronoun as وَيْلَكَ آمِنْ 46 v. 16, "(They say) Alas for thee! Believe." وَيْلَةٌ Shame, as يَا وَيْلَتِى (for وَيْلَتِى) 11 v. 75, "Alas my shame!" D. S. Gr. T. 2, p. 90, *note.*

ى

ى affix of the first person singular, Me, my, frequently spelt and pronounced ىَ; when affixed to a verb it is written نِى; it is not unfrequently omitted as رَبِّ for رَبِّى, إِتَّقُونِ for إِتَّقُونِى etc., D. S. Gr. T. 1, p. 457 *et seq.*

يَا O! a vocative particle governing the nominative and accus. cases, D. S. Gr. T. 2, p. 82.

يَأْتَلِ see إِئْتَلَى viii. f. of أَلَا.

يَاجُوجُ (2nd declension) Gog, name of a tribe of barbarians near the Caspian Sea, v. مَاجُوجُ.

يَئِسَ aor. يَيْأَسُ, D. S. Gr. T. 1, p. 240, To despair (with مِنْ); at 13 v. 30 it is used with أَنْ, and is there generally understood to mean to know. يَؤُسٌ Despairing, desperate.—إِسْتَيْأَسَ X. To reject all hope, despair (with مِنْ).

يَاقُوتٌ collective noun, Rubies; a word of Persian origin.

يَأْنِ aor. cond. of أَنَى q.v.

يَبِسَ aor. يَيْبَسُ *To be dry.* يَبَسٌ n.a. *Dryness*, dry. يَابِسٌ part. act. That which is dry or withered.

يَتَّخِذُ aor. viii. f. of أَخَذَ q.v.

يَتَعَدَّ aor. cond. v. f. of عَدَا q.v.

يَتَفَيَّؤُ aor. v. f. of فَآءَ for فَيَأَ q.v.

يَتِمَ and يَتَمَ aor. يَيْتَمُ *To be an orphan.* يَتِيمٌ Plur. يَتَامَى (2nd declension) An orphan.

يَتِيهُونَ see تَاهَ.

يَثْرِبُ (2nd declension) Yathreb, the original name of Medina.

يَحْمُومٌ Black smoke, said to be derived from حَمَّ q.v.

يَدٌ see يَدَى.

يَدَّبَّرُ aor. v. f. of دَبَرَ q.v.

يُدْنِينَ 3rd pers. fem. plur. aor. iv. f. of دَنَا q.v.

يَدَى *To touch or injure in the hand.* يَدٌ for يَدَىٌ n.a. feminine, A hand; Dual يَدَانِ, oblique يَدَيْنِ, and when in connexion with a complement يَدَا and يَدَىْ; Plur. أَيْدٍ for أَيْدِىٌ D. S. Gr. T. 1, p. 111; the phrase عَنْ يَدٍ 9 v. 29 admits of divers interpretations; according to one it means that payment should be made by the hand of the parties themselves without the intervention of a third person; or it may mean willingly, or by a ready money payment, or in token of subjection; بَيْنَ يَدَيْهِ Before him, in his presence; *Lit.* between his two hands; أُولِى ٱلْأَيْدِى وَٱلْأَبْصَارِ 38 v. 45, "Men of power and prudence," *Lit.* "Gifted with hands and eyes;" سُقِطَ فِى أَيْدِيهِمْ 7 v. 148, an idiomatic expression meaning "They repented bitterly;" the idea seems to be that they bit their fingers in grief and contrition, but it is rather hinted at than expressed; see سَقَطَ.

يَذَرُ aor. of وَذَرَ q.v.

يُرِدْ aor. cond. iv. f. of رَادَ q.v.

يٰسٓ Yà seen, initial letters of the 36th chapter, see آلٓمٓ.

يَسَرَ aor. يَيْسِرُ *To play at dice, to be easy.* يُسْرٌ n.a. Facility, ease, that which is easy. يَسِيرٌ Small, easy; يَسِيرًا 33 v. 14, A little while. يُسْرَى (2nd declension) Prosperity; it may also be the fem. of the comp. form, More or most easy; وَنُيَسِّرُكَ لِلْيُسْرَى 87 v. 8, "And we will facilitate for thee—or prepare thee for—the easiest (way in matters of faith)," or "the way of happiness." مَيْسِرٌ Drawing lots. مَيْسُورٌ part. pass. *Facilitated;* قَوْلًا مَيْسُورًا 17 v. 30, "A kind word." مَيْسَرَةٌ A time of ease or convenience.—يَسَّرَ II. To facilitate, make easy (with acc. and لِ or بِ, or with double acc.); to second any one or help one forward (with acc. of pers. and لِ).—تَيَسَّرَ V. To be easy.—إِسْتَيْسَرَ X. To be easy.

يَسَعُ (2nd declension) and with the article ٱلْيَسَعُ Elisha.

يَصِفُونَ 3rd pers. masc. plur. aor. of وَصَفَ q.v.

يَطْمِثْنَ see طَمَثَ.

يَعْقُوبُ (2nd declension) Jacob.

يَعُوقُ (2nd declension) Ya'ook, name of an Idol worshipped originally before the Flood, and afterwards by the Pagan Arabs.

يَعْتَبْ see غَابَ for غَيَبَ.

يَغُوثُ Yaghooth, name of an Idol of the Pagan Arabs, see يَعُوقُ.

يُغْوِى see غَوَى.

يَقْطِينٌ A gourd, probably derived from قَطَنَ To inhabit.

يَقِظَ aor. a.; also يَقُظَ *To be vigilant.* أَيْقَاظٌ plur. of يَقِظٌ *Watchful*, awake.

يَقِنَ aor. a. *To be certain.* يَقِينٌ Certain, a certainty, that which is certain, as death at 15 v. 99, and 74 v. 48; يَقِينًا Surely, of a certainty.—أَيْقَنَ IV. aor. يُوقِنُ To know for certain, firmly believe, feel a certainty about (with بِ); to form a right judgment. مُوقِنٌ part. act. One who believes firmly, or forms a right judgment.—إِسْتَيْقَنَ X. To believe firmly. مُسْتَيْقِنٌ part. act. One who is firmly assured.

يَكُ see كَانَ.

يَلْوُنَ or يَلُونَ see لَوَى.

يُمَّ pass. for يُمِمَ; no active voice, *To be thrown into the sea.* يَمٌّ A sea, flood; a river, as at 20 v. 39.—تَيَمَّمَ V. To aim at getting for one's-self, choose for one's-self.

يَمَنَ aor. يَيْمِنُ *To place (a corpse) on its right side in the grave.* يَمِينٌ Plur. أَيْمَانٌ fem. The right hand, an oath, power; عَنِ ٱلْيَمِينِ 37 v. 28, *Lit.* "From the right hand," meaning with a good omen, or with force, or with an oath, etc. أَيْمَنُ (2nd declension) The right (hand). مَيْمَنَةٌ The right hand.

يَنَابِيعُ plur. of يَنْبُوعٌ A fountain, rt. نَبَعَ q.v.

يَنَعَ aor. يَيْنَعُ *To be ripe.* يَنْعٌ n.a. Ripeness, the act of coming to maturity.

يَهُودٌ generic noun, Jews. يَهُودِىٌّ Of the Jewish nation.

يُؤْتِى aor. iv. f. of أَتَى q.v.

يَوُدُّ aor. of آدَ for أَوَدَ q.v.

يُؤَدِّ aor. conditional ii. f. of أَدَى q.v.

يُؤْذَيْنَ 3rd pers. fem. plur. aor. pass. iv. f. of أَذِىَ q.v.

يَئِسَ see يُوسَ.

يُوسُفُ (2nd declension) Joseph.

يُوعُونَ 3rd pers. plur. aor. iv. f. of وَعَى q.v.

يُوقِنُونَ 3rd pers. plur. aor. iv. f. of يَقِنَ q.v.

يَوِمَ aor. يَيْوَمُ *To be or exist for a day.* يَوْمٌ Plur. أَيَّامٌ A day, the civil day of 24 hours; a day of battle, thus at 45 v. 13, where the words أَيَّامَ ٱللّٰهِ mean those days when it might please God to bestow victory on the Moslems; يَوْمَ On that day, on a certain day; ٱلْيَوْمَ To-day, on this day. يَوْمَئِذٍ Then, on that day, a word composed of يَوْمَ and إِذٍ or إِذْ, D. S. Gr. T. 1, p. 521.

يُونُسُ (2nd declension) Jonah.

FINIS.

ERRATA.

PAGE	COL.	LINE
9	2	23 *for* آلْقَرى *read* آلْقَرَى.
13	1	24 *for* ذُو *read* ذُو.
23	2	19 *for* آلْفُ *read* آلِفُ.
25	1	6 lines from bottom *for* teschdeed *read* teshdeed.
28	2	12 *for* جَلْبَبٌ *read* جَلْبَبَ.
70	2	21 *for* Schechinah *read* Shechinah.
91	2	5 lines from bottom *for* Those who purify, etc., *read* One who purifies himself, or is clean, pure.
107	1	7 *for* o. and i. *read* a.
112	1	last line but one نِيمَ should come after نَالَ p. 113.
139	1	8 *for* plur. of مُقَارَةٌ, rt. *read* part. act. iii. f. of.